STUDY GUIDE

INTERMEDIATE FINANCIAL MANAGEMENT

FIFTH EDITION

EUGENE F. BRIGHAM
and
LOUIS C. GAPENSKI
University of Florida

The Dryden Press
Harcourt Brace College Publishers
Fort Worth Philadelphia San Diego New York Orlando Austin San Antonio
Toronto Montreal London Sydney Tokyo

Cover Image: Marco Ruiz

Address for Editorial Correspondence
The Dryden Press, 301 Commerce Street, Suite 3700, Fort Worth, TX 76102

Address for Orders
The Dryden Press, 6277 Sea Harbor Drive, Orlando, FL 32887
1-800-782-4479, or 1-800-433-0001 (in Florida)

ISBN: 0-03-015939-3

Printed in the United States of America

8 9 0 1 2 3 4 095 9 8 7 6 5 4

The Dryden Press
Harcourt Brace College Publishers

PREFACE

This *Study Guide* is designed primarily to help you develop a working knowledge of the concepts and principles of financial management. Additionally, it will familiarize you with the types of true/false and multiple choice test questions that are being used with increasing frequency in finance courses.

The *Study Guide* follows the outline of *Intermediate Financial Management*. You should read carefully the next section, *How To Use This Study Guide*, to familiarize yourself with its specific contents and to gain some insights into how it can be used most effectively.

We would like to thank Bob Karp and Susan Sternberg for their considerable assistance in the preparation of this *Study Guide*.

We have tried to make the *Study Guide* as clear and error-free as possible. However, some mistakes may have crept in, and there are almost certainly some sections that could be clarified. Any suggestions for improving the *Study Guide* would be greatly appreciated. Since instructors almost never read study guides, we address this call for help to students!

Eugene F. Brigham
Louis C. Gapenski
College of Business Administration
University of Florida
PO Box 117160
Gainesville, FL 32611-7160

June 1995

HOW TO USE THIS STUDY GUIDE

Different people will tend to use the *Study Guide* in somewhat different ways. This is natural, because both intermediate finance courses and individual student's needs vary widely. However, the tips contained in this section should help all students use the *Study Guide* more effectively, regardless of these differences.

Each chapter contains (1) an overview, (2) an outline, (3) some definitional questions, (4) some conceptual questions, and (5) answers to the questions. In addition, all but the first chapter (Chapter 1) contain a set of problems with solutions. You should begin your study by reading the overview; it will give you an idea of what is contained in the chapter and how this material fits into the overall scheme of things.

Next, read over the outline to get a better fix on the specific topics covered in the chapter. It is important to realize that the outline does not list every facet of every topic covered in the textbook--the *Study Guide* is intended to highlight and summarize the textbook, not to supplant it.

The definitional questions are intended to test your knowledge of, and also to reinforce your ability to work with, the terms and concepts introduced in the chapter. If you do not understand the definitions thoroughly, review the outline prior to going on to the conceptual questions and problems.

The conceptual questions focus on the same kinds of ideas that the text book end-of-chapter questions address, but in the *Study Guide* the questions are less complex and set out in a true/false or multiple choice format. Thus, these questions can be used to practice for the types of tests that are being used with increasing frequency. However, regardless of the types of tests you must take, working through the conceptual questions will help drive home the key concepts of financial management.

The numerical problems are also written in a multiple choice format. Generally, the problems are arranged in order of increasing difficulty. Also, note that some of the *Study Guide* problems are convoluted in the sense that information normally available to financial managers is withheld, and information normally unknown is given. Such problems are designed to test your knowledge of a subject, and you must work "backwards" to solve them. Furthermore, such problems are included in the *Study Guide* in part because they provide a good test of how well you understand the material, and in part because you may well be seeing similar problems on your exams.

Finally, each *Study Guide* chapter provides the answers and solutions to the questions and problems. The rationale behind a question's correct answer is explained where necessary, but the problem solutions are always complete. Note that the answers to numerical problems were obtained using a financial calculator. You should not be concerned if rounding differences cause your answer to differ from ours by a small amount.

Of course, each student must decide how to incorporate the *Study Guide* in his or her overall study program. Many students begin an assignment by reading the *Study Guide* overview and outline to get the "big picture," then read the chapter in the textbook. Naturally, the *Study Guide* overview and outline is also used extensively to review for exams. Most students work the textbook questions and problems prior to tackling the *Study Guide* questions and problems, using the latter as a self-test and review tool. However, if you are stumped by a text problem, try the *Study Guide* problems first, because their detailed solutions can get you over stumbling blocks.

CONTENTS OF THE STUDY GUIDE

CHAPTER 1
AN OVERVIEW OF FINANCIAL THEORY

OVERVIEW

Chapter 1 provides an overview of financial theory, including a discussion of the following topics: (1) the concept of perfect capital markets, (2) discounted cash flow (DCF) analysis, (3) Modigliani and Miller's capital structure theory, (4) Modigliani and Miller's dividend theory, (5) portfolio theory and the Capital Asset Pricing Model (CAPM), (6) option pricing theory, (7) market efficiency and the risk/return tradeoff, (8) agency theory, (9) MVA and EVA, and (10) asymmetric information theory. Many of the topics in this chapter will be covered in depth in later chapters -- portfolio theory in Chapter 2, the CAPM in Chapter 3, option pricing theory in Chapter 5, capital structure theory in Chapters 11 and 12, and dividend policy in Chapter 13. Other material is covered in depth in Chapter 1 and then drawn upon throughout the remaining chapters. In this chapter of the Study Guide, we focus on the material that is covered in depth in Chapter 1: DCF analysis, the efficient markets hypothesis, agency theory, MVA and EVA, and asymmetric information theory.

KEY CONCEPTS

> The process of valuing future cash flows is called *discounted cash flow (DCF) analysis.*

The rationale for discounted cash flow analysis is the *time value of money:* A dollar in hand today is worth more than a dollar due some time in the future.

Discounted cash flow analysis requires (1) future cash flow estimates and (2) a discount rate.

The *discount rate* must reflect the opportunity cost, the return foregone by choosing one investment over another. Thus, the discount rate is the expected rate of return on alternative investments of similar risk.

The discount rate must reflect the risk inherent in the cash flows to be discounted -- the higher the risk, the higher the discount rate. It also must reflect the prevailing level of returns in the economy and should consider the periodicity of the cash flows.

The *Efficient Markets Hypothesis (EMH)* states that stock prices reflect current information, and that it is impossible for an investor to consistently "beat the market."

The weak form of the EMH states that past trends in stock prices cannot be used to predict future prices. Empirical tests support weak-form efficiency.

The semistrong form of the EMH states that all publicly announced information is reflected in stock prices. This form is supported by empirical tests to a reasonable extent, especially for large companies that are followed by many analysts.

The strong form of the EMH states that all information, both public and private, is reflected in stock prices. This is not true, because insiders can and do make excess profits using private information, although such actions are illegal.

The EMH has implications for both investors and financial managers.

- Since security prices do appear to generally reflect all public information, most securities are fairly valued. Therefore, investors can only expect to receive a return that approximately compensates them for the risks involved.
- Since financial assets appear to be fairly valued, financial management decisions should, in general, not be made on the basis of the firm's securities being either under or over valued.

Financial markets are generally efficient, but product markets are not usually efficient, and hence excess returns can be earned in product markets. Thus, it makes sense for financial managers to seek real asset investment opportunities which provide excess returns (positive NPVs).

There are three key questions in every financial decision.

- What is the return involved?
- What is the risk involved?
- Is the return commensurate with the risk?

An *agency relationship* exists when one or more persons (the principals) hire another person (the agent) to act on their behalf, delegating decision-making authority to that agent. In the financial management framework, this relationship exists (1) between stockholders and managers and (2) between creditors and stockholders.

A potential agency problem exists whenever a manager owns less than 100 percent of the firm's common stock.

- Since the firm's earnings do not go solely to the manager, he or she may not concentrate exclusively on maximizing shareholder wealth. Also, because costs are borne by all stockholders, the manager may consume too many perquisites.
- Another potential conflict between management and stockholders arises in a management sponsored leveraged buyout, because management might attempt to minimize the stock price just prior to the buyout.

To insure that managers act in the best interest of shareholders, shareholders must incur agency costs, which include:

- Expenditures to monitor managerial actions.
- Expenditures to structure the organization to minimize undesirable managerial behavior.
- Opportunity costs associated with lost profits due to an organizational structure which does not allow managers to act on a timely basis.

Complete monitoring of managerial activity would solve the agency problem, but it would be costly and inefficient. Managerial compensation solely in the form of shares of the firm's stock would also solve the problem, but it would be difficult to hire managers on this basis. The optimal solution includes some monitoring as well as compensation that includes both a fixed salary and performance incentives.

Several mechanisms tend to force managers to act in the shareholders' best interest, thus minimizing the agency problem.

- Because stock ownership is becoming concentrated in the hands of large institutions, the firing of management by dissatisfied stockholders has become a reality. Shareholders can remove inefficient managers through a proxy fight in which proxy votes are obtained by a dissident group who install new management.
- Any managerial decision that results in the undervaluation of a firm's stock price makes the firm more likely to be the target of a hostile takeover. In a hostile takeover, management is either fired or else loses a great deal of autonomy.
- Tying managers' compensation to the company's performance motivates managers to operate in a manner consistent with stock price maximization. The main tool being

used now, which is based on factors over which managers have control, is performance shares (or bonuses). These are given to executives on the basis of performance as measured by such criteria as growth in earnings per share and return on assets.

An agency problem also exists between a firm's creditors (usually bondholders) and its stockholders (actually managers acting on behalf of stockholders). Conflict arises if (1) stockholders (management) take on projects that have greater risk than was anticipated by creditors or (2) the firm increases its level of debt without changing its assets. Both of these actions decrease the value of the debt outstanding. It is in the stockholders' best interest to deal fairly with the firm's creditors in order to assure future access to debt markets at reasonable interest costs.

The fair and ethical treatment of the firm's other *stakeholders*, including employees, suppliers, customers, and even the communities in which the firm operates, is also in the stockholders' best interest. Fair and ethical treatment of these parties promotes long-term profitability, and hence stock price maximization.

Two new analytical approaches have been developed that focus directly on management's success or failure in maximizing shareholders' wealth: Market Value Added (MVA) and Economic Value Added (EVA).

The primary goal of any firm should be shareholders' wealth maximization. Shareholders' wealth is maximized by maximizing the difference between the firm's total market value and the amount of capital that investors have supplied to the firm. This difference is called *Market Value Added (MVA).*

- There is a direct tie between MVA and the net present value (NPV) capital budgeting rule.
- Since NPV measures the amount that a project can be expected to add (or subtract) from MVA, by following the NPV rule managers should, at a minimum, be able to avoid creating negative MVA.
- The companies with the highest MVAs have done a spectacular job of ferreting out high-NPV projects, which produce high MVAs.

Whereas MVA measures the combined effect of managerial actions to enhance shareholders' wealth since the inception of the company, *Economic Value Added (EVA)* focuses on managerial effectiveness in a given year. The basic formula for EVA is this: EVA = Operating profit - (Total capital supplied × Cost of capital).

- EVA is an estimate of a business's true economic profit for the year, and it differs substantially from accounting profitability measures.
- EVA represents the residual income that remains after the opportunity cost of the employed capital has been deducted, whereas accounting profit is figured without imposing a charge for equity capital.
- EVA (but not MVA) can be applied to divisions as well as the entire company, but the charge for capital must reflect the risk of the business unit, be it the whole company or an operating division.
- EVA is a link in the chain that begins with the NPV of a individual project and ends with the firm's MVA. Each project's economic profitability, which is initially measured by its NPV, contributes to the firm's EVA for any given year, and MVA is the present value of the EVAs that the firm is expected to produce in the future.
- In the past few years, many highly successful firms have adopted incentive compensation systems based on EVA. The primary rationale is that EVA is linked both theoretically and empirically to shareholders' wealth. When executive compensation is tied to EVA, managers are given the proper incentive to take actions that contribute the most to shareholders' wealth.

> An *asymmetric information* situation exists when a firm's managers know significantly more about the future prospects of their firm than do informed analysts and investors.

Since one of management's important goals is to maximize stock price, managers are motivated to announce inside information, especially when the information is favorable.

To support the announcement, management can signal the information regarding favorable future prospects so investors will take the news more seriously and use it to revalue the firm's stock. One example of signaling is a dividend increase.

The presence of asymmetric information can influence many managerial actions, including capital structure, dividend policy, and financing decisions.

DEFINITIONAL QUESTIONS

1. An __________ relationship exists when one or more persons (the principals) hire another person (the agent) to act on their behalf, delegating decision-making authority to that agent.

2. Potential agency problems exist between a firm's shareholders and __________ and also between shareholders and __________.

3. __________ must incur agency costs to ensure managers act in their best interest.

4. According to the __________ __________ __________, stock prices reflect all public information, and hence investors without inside information cannot consistently beat the market.

5. Agency problems could be solved by complete monitoring of managerial activity, but this would be __________ and __________.

6. In order to perform discounted cash flow analysis, one needs to estimate __________ __________ __________ and a __________ __________.

7. The opportunity cost of any investment is the return that can be earned on alternative investments of __________ risk.

8. Although capital markets are generally acknowledged to be efficient, __________ markets are not efficient, especially in the short run.

9. MVA stands for __________ __________ __________ and EVA stands for __________ __________ __________.

CONCEPTUAL QUESTIONS

10. Managers always operate in the best interest of shareholders.

    a. True **b.** False

11. The existence of asymmetric information, where managers know more about their firms' prospects than the public, is inconsistent with the Efficient Markets Hypothesis (EMH).

    a. True **b.** False

12. In determining the best course of action, financial managers ultimately choose the alternative that has the highest return.

    a. True **b.** False

13. Which of the following statements about the Efficient Markets Hypothesis is true?

    a. The U.S. capital markets are generally acknowledged to be semi-strong form efficient.

b. Managers often have more information about their firm's prospects than do well-informed analysts and investors.
c. Past price, or interest rate, movements cannot be used to predict future price, or interest rate, movements.
d. Strong-form efficiency does not generally hold, because insiders can make excess profits.
e. All the above statements are true.

14. Which of the following factors tend to encourage management to pursue stock price maximization as a goal?

a. Shareholders link management's compensation to company performance.
b. Managers' reactions to the threat of tender offers and proxy fights.
c. Managers do not have goals other than stock price maximization.
d. Statements a and b are both correct.
e. Statements a, b, and c are all correct.

15. How might a manager best signal his or her beliefs about an optimistic earnings future to the public?

a. Declare a dividend decrease.
b. Hold a press conference to paint a rosy picture for the future.
c. Declare a dividend increase.
d. Declare a program to buy back debt, and hence decrease the firm's use of financial leverage.
e. Any of the above actions would provide the correct signal.

16. Why is EVA being used more and more in managerial incentive systems?

a. It is linked directly to shareholders' wealth.
b. It can be applied to divisions as well as entire firms.
c. It measures economic rather than accounting profitability.
d. It gives managers the incentive to take those actions that contribute most to shareholders' wealth maximization.
e. All of the above statements are true.

ANSWERS

1. agency
2. managers; debtholders
3. Shareholders
4. Efficient Markets Hypothesis
5. costly; inefficient
6. future cash flows; discount rate
7. similar
8. product
9. Market Value Added; Economic Value Added

10. b. Unfortunately, managers sometimes play it safe, or even purposely ignore stockholders' interests to pursue their own. However, in most circumstances, mechanisms exist which persuade managers to act in the shareholders' best interest.

11. b. The Efficient Markets Hypothesis applies only to public information, and hence managers can hold inside information about their own firms.

12. b. The correct choice must consider each alternative's risk as well as its expected return.

13. e.

14. d.

15. c. By declaring a dividend increase, the manager clearly signals his or her positive beliefs. A press conference alone would not be regarded as a legitimate signal, because the announcement is not verifiable. A program to reduce debt, or a dividend decrease, is a signal of a poor earnings future.

16. e.

CHAPTER 2
RISK AND RETURN: PART 1

OVERVIEW

As we discussed in Chapter 1, neither an individual acting on his or her own behalf nor a manager acting for a firm's shareholders should make an investment decision solely on the basis of expected return. Decision makers must assess the riskiness of the investment, and then ask whether the return is sufficient to compensate for the risk assumed.

Since risk analysis is critically important, it is essential that one understand how risk is defined and measured. We will see in Chapter 2 that risk can be defined in two ways: (1) as *stand-alone* risk, which focuses on a single asset and which involves the dispersion of outcomes around the expected return on that asset, and (2) as *market* risk, which focuses on a portfolio of assets and which measures each asset's contribution to the riskiness of the portfolio.

Measuring risk is only one part of the task. We must be able to relate risk to expected returns, and to answer this question: How much return is required to compensate for a given degree of risk? As we shall see in Chapter 3, the Capital Asset Pricing Model (CAPM) provides one neat, precise answer to this question. However, the CAPM has not been and indeed cannot be confirmed empirically--it may or may not represent the way investors actually behave, so a CAPM-based analysis may or may not lead to a decision that will maximize the firm's stock price. This fact does not by itself invalidate the CAPM, but it does force us to consider alternative ways of specifying both how risk should be measured and how the expected return required to compensate for a given degree of risk should be established.

KEY CONCEPTS

Risk refers to the possibility that some unfavorable event will occur. Investment risk is associated with the probability of low or negative returns.

The *probability distribution for an event* is the listing of all the possible outcomes for the event, with mathematical probabilities assigned to each.

Probability distributions may be either *discrete* or *continuous*.

Discrete distributions, which have a finite number of outcomes, are often used to specify risk. However, continuous distributions are also extensively used in financial analysis.

The expected rate of return, $\hat{k}$, is the sum of the products of each possible return times its associated probability -- it is a weighted average of the various possible returns, with the weights being their probabilities of occurrence:

$$\hat{k} = \sum_{i=1}^{n} P_i k_i .$$

Stand-alone risk is the riskiness of an asset held in isolation, whereas *market risk* is the asset's relevant risk if it is held as part of a well-diversified portfolio.

Stand-alone risk is measured by the dispersion of returns about the expected return. Market risk measures the stock's contribution to the overall riskiness of the portfolio.

In general, combining stocks into portfolios reduces risk, because returns on stocks that are less than expected will be offset to some degree by other stocks whose returns are greater than expected. Thus, a stock's market risk is generally less than its stand-alone risk.

Variance is a measure of the dispersion of a distribution around its expected value.

Variance is calculated using the following formula:

$$\sigma^2 = \sum_{i=1}^{n} (k_i - \hat{k})^2 P_i .$$

Variance is measured in the same units as the outcome--generally percent--but squared.

Standard deviation is another measure of the tightness of a distribution around its mean, and it is often used as an alternative to variance.

The standard deviation is found by taking the square root of the variance:

$$\sigma = \sqrt{\sum_{i=1}^{n} (k_i - \hat{k})^2 P_i} .$$

The smaller the standard deviation, the tighter the distribution and the lower the stand-alone risk associated with the investment.

Standard deviation is one measure of an asset's stand-alone risk.

When comparing investments with different expected returns, the *coefficient of variation (CV)* is a better measure of stand-alone risk than the standard deviation.

The CV, which measures the risk per unit of return, is calculated as follows:

$$CV = \frac{\sigma}{\hat{k}}.$$

The investment with the higher CV has more stand-alone risk per unit of expected return.

Subjective probability distributions are estimated using expected (ex ante) return data and objective probability distributions are obtained using historical (ex post) data.

Two sources of risk exist in financial analysis:

- Risk associated with uncertain outcomes, given a known probability distribution.
- The additional risk that results because the assumed distribution may itself be incorrect.

Most institutions and individual investors hold *portfolios*, or combinations of securities, rather than one stock. Thus, the risk and return of any one security is less important than the risk and return of the portfolio as a whole.

Diversification can lower a portfolio's risk without changing its overall expected rate of return.

- This may be accomplished by selecting stocks whose returns do not move together. Such stocks are less than perfectly positively correlated.

- As a rule, as the number of securities in the portfolio increases, the standard deviation of the portfolio's returns decreases, so portfolio risk decreases.
- The expected return on a portfolio, $\hat{k}_p$, is the weighted average of the expected returns on the individual stocks in the portfolio. The weight assigned to each stock (x_i) is its fraction of the total dollar value of the portfolio:

$$\hat{k}_p = \sum_{i=1}^{n} x_i \hat{k}_i .$$

The riskiness of a portfolio is not the weighted average of the standard deviations of the individual stocks in the portfolio. The riskiness (standard deviation) of a portfolio depends not only on the standard deviations of the individual stocks, but also on the correlations among the stocks.

Covariance and the *correlation coefficient* are important concepts in portfolio theory.

Covariance is a measure which combines the volatility of a stock's returns with the tendency of those returns to move up or down at the same time other stocks move up or down. The following equation defines the covariance (Cov) between two variables such as Stocks A and B:

$$\text{Covariance} = \text{Cov(AB)} = \sum_{i=1}^{n} (k_{Ai} - \hat{k}_A)(k_{Bi} - \hat{k}_B)P_i .$$

The correlation coefficient also measures the degree of co-movement between two stocks, but its values are limited to the range from -1.0 (perfect negative correlation) to +1.0 (perfect positive correlation). The relationship between covariance and the correlation coefficient can be expressed as

$$\text{Correlation coefficient (AB)} = r_{AB} = \frac{\text{Cov(AB)}}{\sigma_A \sigma_B} .$$

In a two-asset portfolio, risk can be completely eliminated if the returns on the two securities move exactly opposite to one another (correlation coefficient = -1.0). If they respond identically (correlation coefficient = +1.0), then portfolio diversification has no effect on risk.

The following equation can be used to determine the riskiness of a two-asset portfolio, assuming the distributions of returns on the individual securities are normal:

$$\text{Portfolio SD} = \sigma_p = \sqrt{x^2\sigma_A^2 + (1 - x)^2\sigma_B^2 + 2x(1 - x)r_{AB}\sigma_A\sigma_B}.$$

An *efficient portfolio* provides the highest expected return for any degree of risk, or the lowest degree of risk for any expected return.

While the riskiness of a multi-asset portfolio usually decreases as the number of stocks increase, the portfolio's risk depends on the degree of correlation among the stocks.

In general, the average correlation between two stocks is +0.5 to +0.7, and hence holding stocks in portfolios will reduce, but not eliminate, risk.

The attainable, or feasible, set of portfolios represents all portfolios that can be constructed from a given set of stocks.

Stand-alone risk can be separated into two parts, *market (or nondiversifiable) risk* and *company-specific (or diversifiable) risk.*

Market risk is the risk that remains present in a portfolio due to general economic conditions and stock market forces. It cannot be reduced or eliminated by further diversification. The riskiness, or standard deviation, of the market portfolio (a portfolio consisting of all stocks) is about 15 percent, while the average standard deviation of a single stock is about 28 percent.

Company-specific, or diversifiable risk, is risk due to events that are unique to a particular firm. It can be eliminated by holding a well-diversified portfolio of at least 40 randomly selected stocks.

The relevant riskiness of an individual stock is its contribution to the riskiness of a well-diversified portfolio.

The *optimal portfolio* is found by determining the efficient set of portfolios and then choosing the portfolio that is best for the individual investor.

An *indifference curve* (or *risk/return trade-off function*) reflects an individual investor's attitude towards risk. The optimal portfolio for each investor is found at the tangency point between the efficient set of portfolios and one of the investor's indifference curves.

The efficient set of portfolios is also called the *efficient frontier.*

DEFINITIONAL QUESTIONS

1. Investment risk is associated with the __________of low or negative returns; the greater the chance of loss, the __________ the investment.

2. A listing of all possible __________, with a probability assigned to each, is known as a __________ __________.

3. Weighting each possible return of a distribution by its __________ of occurrence and summing the results gives the __________ __________ of the distribution.

4. One measure of the tightness of a probability distribution is its __________ __________.

5. To evaluate risk per unit of return, the standard deviation must be converted to the __________ of __________.

6. __________probability distributions are estimated using historical returns, while__________ probability distributions are obtained using estimated future returns.

7. Owning a __________ of securities enables investors to benefit from the risk reduction inherent in __________.

8. Diversification of a portfolio can result in lower __________ for the same level of __________.

9. Diversification of a portfolio is achieved by selecting securities with returns that are not perfectly __________ correlated with each other.

10. That part of a stock's risk that can be reduced by __________ is known as __________ risk, while the portion of a stock's risk that cannot be eliminated is called __________ risk.

11. An ____________ ____________ is that portfolio which provides the highest expected return for any given degree of risk or the least risk for a given amount of return.

CONCEPTUAL QUESTIONS

12. The standard deviation of a portfolio is not the weighted average of the standard deviations of the individual stocks in the portfolio.

a. True **b.** False

13. If the correlation coefficient between two stocks is +1.0, risk can be completely diversified away.

a. True **b.** False

14. Stand-alone risk is relevant only for assets held in isolation.

a. True **b.** False

PROBLEMS

The following data apply to the next two problems.

Stock A has the following probability distribution of expected returns:

Probability	Rate of Return
0.1	-15%
0.2	0
0.4	5
0.2	10
0.1	25

15. What is Stock A's expected rate of return and standard deviation?

a. 8.0%; 9.5% **b.** 8.0%; 6.5% **c.** 5.0%; 3.5% **d.** 5.0%; 6.5% **e.** 5.0%; 9.5%

16. What is Stock A's coefficient of variation?

a. 1.2 **b.** 1.9 **c.** 1.3 **d.** 0.7 **e.** 1.0

17. You are evaluating two potential investment opportunities: Projects A and B. The expected rate of return on Project A is 15.8% and its standard deviation is 2.8%. Project B's expected rate of return is 20.5% with a standard deviation of 3.5%. What is the coefficient of variation (CV) for Projects A and B, respectively?

a. 0.12; 0.12 **b.** 0.18; 0.12 **c.** 0.18; 0.17 **d.** 0.25; 0.17 **e.** 0.25; 0.25

The following data apply to the next three problems.

Probability	Return
0.2	$60
0.6	50
0.2	-40

18. What is the expected dollar return?

a. $30.00 **b.** $45.00 **c.** $50.00 **d.** $34.00 **e.** $42.00

19. What is the variance of the expected dollar return?

a. $1,384.00 **b.** $989.00 **c.** $1,025.00 **d.** $1,250.00 **e.** $975.00

20. What is the coefficient of variation of the expected dollar return?

a. 1.00 **b.** 1.09 **c.** 1.15 **d.** 1.20 **e.** 1.25

The following data apply to the next three problems.

State of the Economy	Probability of Each State Occurring	Rates of Return If State Occurs		
		A	B	C
Recession	0.25	5.0%	4.5%	7.0%
Average	0.50	7.0	6.5	6.0
Boom	0.25	8.0	9.0	5.0

21. What are the expected rates of return for Stocks A, B, and C, respectively?

a. 6.75%; 6.0%; 6.625%
b. 6.0%; 6.625%; 6.75%
c. 6.75%; 6.625%; 6.0%
d. 6.75%; 6.625%; 5.75%
e. 6.625%; 6.0%; 6.75%

22. What is the covariance between Stocks A and B?

a. 1.2500 **b.** 1.3504 **c.** 1.4500 **d.** 1.5250 **e.** 1.6560

23. What is the correlation coefficient between Projects A and B?

a. 0.75 **b.** 0.95 **c.** 0.50 **d.** 1.0 **e.** 0.65

ANSWERS

1. probability; riskier
2. outcomes; probability distribution
3. probability; expected value
4. standard deviation
5. coefficient; variation
6. Objective; subjective
7. portfolio; diversification
8. risk; return
9. positively
10. diversification; company-specific (diversifiable or unsystematic); market (nondiversifiable or systematic)
11. efficient portfolio

12. a. The standard deviation of a portfolio depends on the correlations among the stocks as well as their individual standard deviations.

13. b. A correlation coefficient of -1.0 is required to combine two stocks into a riskless portfolio.

14. a. When assets are combined into portfolios, then the relevant risk is an asset's market risk, which is the contribution of the asset to the riskiness of the portfolio.

15. e. $\hat{k}_A = 0.1(-15\%) + 0.2(0\%) + 0.4(5\%) + 0.2(10\%) + 0.1(25\%) = 5.0\%$.

$$\text{Variance} = 0.1(-0.15 - 0.05)^2 + 0.2(0.0 - 0.05)^2 + 0.4(0.05 - 0.05)^2 + 0.2(0.10 - 0.05)^2 + 0.1(0.25 - 0.05)^2 = 0.009.$$

$$\text{Standard deviation} = (0.009)^{1/2} = 0.0949 \approx 9.5\%.$$

16. b. Coefficient of variation = CV = $\sigma/\hat{k}$ = 9.5%/5.0% = 1.9.

17. c. Project A: CV = 2.8%/15.8% = 0.18. Project B: CV = 3.5%/20.5% = 0.17.

Since the CV for Project A is higher than Project B's CV, Project A has more risk per unit of expected return than does Project B.

18. d. $\hat{k}$ = 0.2(\$60) + 0.6(\$50) + 0.2(-\$40) = \$12 + \$30 - \$8 = \$34.

19. a. $\sigma^2 = 0.2(\$60 - \$34)^2 + 0.6(\$50 - \$34)^2 + 0.2(-\$40 - \$34)^2$
$= \$135.20 + \$153.60 + \$1,095.20$
$= \$1,384.00.$

20. b. $\sigma = (1,384.00)^{½} = \$37.20.$

$CV = \sigma/\hat{k} = \$37.20/\$34.00 = 1.09.$

21. c. $\hat{k}_A = 0.25(5\%) + 0.5(7\%) + 0.25(8\%) = 1.25\% + 3.5\% + 2\% = 6.75\%.$

$\hat{k}_B = 0.25(4.5\%) + 0.5(6.5\%) + 0.25(9\%) = 1.125\% + 3.25\% + 2.25\% = 6.625\%.$

$\hat{k}_C = 0.25(7\%) + 0.5(6\%) + 0.25(5\%) = 1.75\% + 3.0\% + 1.25\% = 6.0\%.$

22. e.

$$\begin{aligned}Cov(AB) &= \sum_{i=1}^{n}(k_{Ai} - \hat{k}_A)(k_{Bi} - \hat{k}_B)P_i \\ &= (5\% - 6.75\%)(4.5\% - 6.625\%)(0.25) \\ &\quad + (8\% - 6.75\%)(9.0\% - 6.625\%)(0.25) \\ &= 1.656.\end{aligned}$$

23. b.

$$\text{Correlation coefficient (AB)} = r_{AB} = \frac{Cov(AB)}{\sigma_A \sigma_B}.$$

$$\begin{aligned}\sigma_A &= \sqrt{(5\% - 6.75\%)^2 0.25 + (7\% - 6.75\%)^2 0.5 + (8\% - 6.75\%)^2 0.25} \\ &= \sqrt{0.766 + 0.031 + 0.391} \\ &= \sqrt{1.188} \\ &= 1.09.\end{aligned}$$

$$\begin{aligned}\sigma_B &= \sqrt{(4.5\% - 6.625\%)^2 0.25 + (6.5\% - 6.625\%)^2 0.5 + (9\% - 6.625\%)^2 0.25} \\ &= \sqrt{1.129 + 0.008 + 1.410} \\ &= \sqrt{2.547} \\ &= 1.596.\end{aligned}$$

$$r_{AB} = \frac{1.656}{1.09(1.596)} = 0.952 \approx 0.95.$$

CHAPTER 3
RISK AND RETURN: PART 2

OVERVIEW

We began our discussion of risk and return in Chapter 2. There, we saw that some of the stand-alone risk inherent in an asset can be eliminated by diversification; thus, investors should hold diversified portfolios of assets. Further, each investor should choose between alternative efficient portfolios on the basis of his or her degree of risk aversion as reflected by indifference curves.

In this chapter, we continue the discussion of risk and return by adding a risk-free asset to the set of investment opportunities. As we will see, this leads all investors to hold the same well-diversified portfolio of risky assets, and then to account for differing degrees of risk aversion by combining the risky portfolio in different proportions with the risk-free asset. However, this basic question remains to be answered: How much return is required to compensate investors for a given amount of risk? The Capital Asset Pricing Model (CAPM) provides one neat, precise answer. However, the CAPM has not been, and indeed cannot be, confirmed empirically -- it may or may not represent the way investors actually behave. Thus, other risk/return models have been proposed, and we close this chapter with a discussion of the CAPM's most prominent competitor, the Arbitrage Pricing Theory (APT).

KEY CONCEPTS

The *Capital Asset Pricing Model (CAPM)* defines the risk/return relationship of assets in equilibrium. It uses a stock's beta coefficient, the risk-free rate, and a measure of investors' risk aversion to specify the required rate of return on a particular stock.

The CAPM is a useful tool for investment analysis because it specifies how market risk should be measured (by beta) and how risk affects required rates of return.

Since the CAPM deals with market risk, it is only useful for assets held in well-diversified portfolios.

The *Capital Market Line (CML)* specifies a linear relationship between expected return and risk for any efficient portfolio.

The equation of the CML may be expressed as follows:

$$\text{CML:}\quad \hat{k}_p = k_{RF} + \left(\frac{\hat{k}_M - k_{RF}}{\sigma_M}\right)\sigma_p.$$

Here $\hat{k}_p$ is the expected (and in equilibrium required) rate of return on an efficient portfolio, k_{RF} is the rate of interest on risk-free securities, $\hat{k}_M$ is the return on the market portfolio, σ_M is the standard deviation of the market portfolio, and σ_p is the standard deviation of the efficient portfolio in question. In other words, the expected rate of return on any efficient portfolio (that is, any portfolio on the CML) is equal to the riskless rate plus a risk premium, and the risk premium is equal to $(\hat{k}_M - k_{RF})/\sigma_M$ multiplied by the portfolio's standard deviation.

The relationship between a security's market risk (expressed by beta) and its return is known as the *Security Market Line (SML)*.

The SML equation is

$$k_i = k_{RF} + (k_M - k_{RF})b_i.$$

Here k_i is the required rate of return on Stock i, k_{RF} is the rate of interest on risk-free securities, b_i is the stock's beta, and k_M is the return on the market portfolio, or, alternatively, on an average stock.

- The term $(k_M - k_{RF})$ is the market risk premium, RP_M. This is a measure of the additional return over the risk-free rate that is required to compensate investors for assuming an average amount of risk. It is dependent on the degree of aversion that investors in the aggregate have to risk--the higher investors' risk aversion, the larger RP_M.
- In the SML, the market risk premium $(k_M - k_{RF})$ is multiplied by the stock's beta coefficient to determine the additional premium over the risk-free rate that is required to compensate investors for the risk inherent in a particular stock.
- An increase (decrease) in inflation will lead to an equal increase (decrease) in the rate of return on all risky assets, because the inflation premium is built into the required rate of return of both riskless and risky assets.
- The slope of the SML reflects the extent to which investors are averse to risk--the steeper the slope of the line, that is, the greater the value of $(k_M - k_{RF})$, the greater the average aversion to risk.
- Changes in a stock's beta coefficient will cause the stock's required rate of return to change. A firm can affect its market risk through changes in the composition of its

assets and its use of debt financing. In addition, a firm's beta can be changed as a result of external factors.

For a management whose goal is stock price maximization, the overriding consideration is the riskiness of the firm's stock, and the relevant risk of any physical asset must be measured in terms of its effect on the stock's risk.

The real issue each time a firm makes a major asset investment is this: How does this investment affect the risk of our stockholders? The stand-alone risk of an individual project might look quite high, but viewed in the context of the project's effect on stockholder's risk, the project might not be very risky.

The market riskiness of an individual stock is its contribution to the riskiness of a well-diversified portfolio. Different stocks will affect a portfolio differently; thus, they have different degrees of market risk. This risk can be measured by the relationship of the individual stock's movements to overall market movements. This measurement is called the stock's *beta coefficient.*

An "average stock" by definition has a beta coefficient of 1.0.

A stock that is twice as volatile as the market will have a beta of 2.0, while a stock that is half as volatile as the market will have a beta coefficient of 0.5.

Most stocks have betas in the range of 0.75 to 1.50.

The beta coefficient of a portfolio of securities is the weighted average of the betas of the individual stocks:

$$b_p = \sum_{i=1}^{n} x_i b_i .$$

The beta coefficient of an individual stock measures that stock's volatility relative to an average stock. It is estimated by plotting historical returns on a particular stock versus returns on a market index. The slope of the *regression line,* or *characteristic line,* is the stock's beta coefficient.

The statistical equation for beta is:

$$b_i = \frac{\text{Cov}(\bar{k}_i, \bar{k}_M)}{\sigma_M^2} = \frac{r_{iM}\sigma_i\sigma_M}{\sigma_M^2} = r_{iM}\frac{\sigma_i}{\sigma_M},$$

where,

b_i = the slope, or beta coefficient, for Stock i.
$\bar{k}_i$ = the historical (realized) rate of return on Stock i.
$\bar{k}_M$ = the historical (realized) rate of return on the market.
r_{iM} = the correlation between Stock i and the market.
σ_i = the standard deviation of Stock i.
σ_M = the standard deviation of the market.

Here are some observations about betas:

- We assume that the historical relationship between Stock i and the market as a whole will continue into the future.
- Besides general market movements, each firm also faces events that are both peculiar to it and independent of the general economic climate. This component of stand-alone risk is the stock's diversifiable, or company-specific, risk.
- An individual stock tends to move with the market as economic conditions change. This component of stand-alone risk is the stock's market, or nondiversifiable, risk.
- Stand-alone risk equals market risk plus diversifiable risk:

Stand-alone risk	=	Market risk	+	Diversifiable risk
σ_i^2	=	$b_i^2\sigma_M^2$	+	$\sigma_{e_i}^2$

- If the stock market never fluctuated, then stocks would have no market risk.
- Beta is the measure of relative market risk, but the stock's actual risk depends on both its beta (market risk), and on the volatility of the market.
- The diversifiable risk can and should be eliminated by diversification.
- A stock's risk premium, $(k_M - k_{RF})b_i$, depends only on its market risk, not its stand-alone risk.

> Since the CAPM depends on some unrealistic assumptions, it must be tested empirically to determine if it gives accurate estimates of k_i.

Betas are generally calculated for some past period, and the assumption is made that the relative volatility of a stock will remain constant in the future. However, conditions may change and alter a stock's future volatility, which is the item of real concern to investors.

The CAPM should use expected (future) data, yet only historical data are generally available.

Studies indicate that the CAPM is a better concept for structuring investment portfolios than it is for purposes of estimating the cost of capital for individual securities.

The CAPM assumes that required rates of return depend on only one risk factor, the stock's beta coefficient, but required returns may be a function of several risk factors. An approach called the *Arbitrage Pricing Theory (APT)* can include any number of risk factors.

Rather than specifying a stock's returns as a function of one factor, one could specify required and realized returns to be a function of various fundamental economic factors:

$$\bar{k}_i = \hat{k}_i + (\bar{F}_1 - \hat{F}_1)b_{i1} + \dots + (\bar{F}_j - \hat{F}_j)b_{ij} + e_i,$$

where,

$\bar{k}_i$ = the realized return on Stock i.
$\hat{k}_i$ = the expected rate of return on Stock i.
$\bar{F}_j$ = the realized value of economic Factor j.
$\hat{F}_j$ = the expected value of Factor j.
b_{ij} = the sensitivity of Stock i to economic Factor j.
e_i = the effect of unique events on the realized return of Stock i .

This equation shows that the realized return on any stock is equal to the stock's expected return plus increments or decrements which depend on (1) changes in fundamental economic factors, (2) the sensitivity of this stock to these changes, plus (3) a random term which reflects changes in those factors unique to the firm or industry.

Theoretically, one could construct such a portfolio such that (1) the portfolio was riskless and (2) the net investment was zero. Such a zero investment portfolio would have to have a zero expected return, or else prices of the underlying assets would change until the portfolio's expected return was zero.

The end result is the APT:

$$\hat{k}_i = k_i = k_{RF} + (\lambda_1 - k_{RF})b_{i1} + \dots + (\lambda_j - k_{RF})b_{ij},$$

where λ_j is the required rate of return on a portfolio with unit sensitivity to the jth economic factor (b_j = 1.0) and zero sensitivity to all other factors.

The primary advantage of the APT is that it assumes that several economic factors influence individual stock returns, whereas the CAPM assumes that the impact of all factors, except those unique to the firm, can be captured in one measure.

However, the APT does not identify the relevant factors beforehand, nor does it even tell us how many factors should appear in the model.

DEFINITIONAL QUESTIONS

1. The __________ __________ measures a stock's relative volatility as compared with a stock market index.

2. A stock that is twice as volatile as the market in general would have a beta coefficient of __________, while a stock with a beta of 0.5 would be only __________ as volatile as the market.

3. The beta coefficient of a portfolio is the __________ __________ of the betas of the individual stocks.

4. The risk-free rate is measured by the return available on ______ ______ __________ securities.

5. The __________ ________ ______ expresses the relationship between a security's risk (beta) and its return.

6. The difference between the required rate of return on a risky asset and the __________-__________ rate is referred to as a __________ __________.

7. The risk premium for an individual stock may be calculated by multiplying the stock's __________ __________ times the __________ risk premium.

8. A stock's required rate of return is equal to the __________-__________ rate plus the stock's __________ __________.

9. The __________ ________ ______ specifies a linear relationship between expected return and risk for any efficient portfolio.

10. Changes in investors' __________ __________ alter the __________ of the Security Market Line.

11. The __________ __________ __________ uses several risk factors for determining the required return on a stock, while the __________ __________ __________ __________ assumes that the impact of all factors, except those unique to the firm, can be captured in one measure.

Conceptual Questions

12. The Y-axis intercept of the Security Market Line indicates the required rate of return on an asset with a beta of 1.0.

    a. True **b.** False

13. If a stock has a beta of zero, it will be riskless when held in isolation.

    a. True **b.** False

14. The Arbitrage Pricing Theory identifies the relevant factors for determining the required return beforehand.

    a. True **b.** False

15. Which is the best measure of risk for an asset held in a well-diversified portfolio?

    a. Variance
    b. Standard deviation
    c. Beta coefficient
    d. Semi-variance
    e. Expected value

16. In a portfolio of three different stocks, which of the following could **not** be true?

    a. The riskiness of the portfolio is less than the riskiness of each stock held in isolation.
    b. The riskiness of the portfolio is greater than the riskiness of one or two of the stocks.
    c. The beta of the portfolio is less than the beta of each of the individual stocks.
    d. The beta of the portfolio is greater than the beta of one or two of the individual stocks.
    e. The beta of the portfolio is equal to the beta of one of the individual stocks.

PROBLEMS

17. If k_{RF} = 5%, k_M = 11% and b = 1.3 for Stock X, what is k_X, the required rate of return for Stock X?

a. 18.7% **b.** 16.7% **c.** 14.8% **d.** 12.8% **e.** 11.9%

18. Refer to Problem 17. What would k_X be if investors' risk aversion increased by 3 percentage points, but the risk-free rate did not change?

a. 18.7% **b.** 16.7% **c.** 14.8% **d.** 12.8% **e.** 11.9%

19. CrewSox Corporation's stock has a beta of 1.5. If the market risk premium is 5 percent and the required rate of return on the market is 15 percent, what is CrewSox's required rate of return?

a. 15.5% **b.** 16.0% **c.** 16.5% **d.** 17.0% **e.** 17.5%

20. The Apple Investment Fund has a total investment of $450 million in five stocks:

Stock	Investment (millions)	Beta
1	$130	0.4
2	110	1.5
3	70	3.0
4	90	2.0
5	50	1.0

What is the fund's overall, or weighted average, beta?

a. 1.14 **b.** 1.22 **c.** 1.35 **d.** 1.46 **e.** 1.53

21. Refer to Problem 20. If the risk-free rate is 12 percent, and the market risk premium is 6 percent, what is the required rate of return on the Apple Fund?

a. 20.8% **b.** 19.9% **c.** 18.8% **d.** 17.6% **e.** 15.8%

22. You are managing a portfolio of 10 stocks which are held in equal dollar amounts. The current beta of the portfolio is 1.8, and the beta of Stock A is 2.0. If Stock A is sold, and the proceeds are used to purchase a replacement stock, what does the beta of the replacement stock have to be to lower the portfolio beta to 1.7?

a. 1.4 **b.** 1.3 **c.** 1.2 **d.** 1.1 **e.** 1.0

The following data apply to the next five problems.

The Stern Company has developed the following data regarding the rates of return available on a potential project and the market:

State of the Economy	Probability of Each State Occurring	Rates of Return If State Occurs: Market	Project
Deep recession	0.05	(10.0%)	(15.0%)
Mild recession	0.25	5.0	2.5
Average	0.35	7.5	10.0
Mild boom	0.20	10.0	12.5
Strong boom	0.15	12.5	15.0

Further, Stern's financial analysts estimate the risk-free rate at 4.5 percent.

23. What are the expected rates of return on the market and the project, respectively?

a. 8.125%; 7.25%
b. 8.25%; 9.625%
c. 9.625%; 8.25%
d. 7.5%; 10.0%
e. 7.25%; 8.125%

24. What is the market's beta?

a. 0.75 **b.** 0.90 **c.** 1.0 **d.** 1.10 **e.** 1.25

25. What is the project's beta?

a. 0.75 **b.** 0.95 **c.** 1.25 **d.** 1.36 **e.** 1.45

26. What is the required rate of return on the project according to the CAPM?

a. 7.75% **b.** 8.24% **c.** 8.125% **d.** 7.5% **e.** 8.0%

27. Should the project be accepted?

a. Yes, because the project's expected return is greater than its required return.
b. Yes, because the project's required return is greater than its expected return.
c. No, because the project's expected return is less than its required return.
d. No, because the project's required return is less than its expected return.
e. There is not enough information to make a decision.

ANSWERS

1. beta coefficient
2. 2.0; half
3. weighted average
4. U. S. Treasury
5. Security Market Line
6. risk-free; risk premium
7. beta coefficient; market
8. risk-free; risk premium
9. Capital Market Line
10. risk aversion; slope

11. Arbitrage Pricing Theory; Capital Asset Pricing Model

12. b. The Y-axis intercept of the SML is k_{RF}, which is the required rate of return on an asset with a beta of zero; that is, a stock with zero market risk.

13. b. A zero beta stock is riskless from a market risk viewpoint, that is, when held as part of a well-diversified portfolio, but it probably has company-specific risk and will be risky when held in isolation.

14. b. The APT does not identify the relevant factors beforehand, nor does it even tell how many factors should appear in the model.

15. c. The other listed risk measures all measure stand-alone risk which is relevant to assets held in isolation but not to assets held in well-diversified portfolios.

16. c. Since the beta of a portfolio is the weighted average of the betas of the individual stocks, it cannot be less than the lowest beta in the portfolio.

17. d. $k_X = k_{RF} + (k_M - k_{RF})b_X = 5\% + (11\% - 5\%)1.3 = 12.8\%.$

18. b. $k_X = k_{RF} + (k_M - k_{RF})b_X = 5\% + (14\% - 5\%)1.3 = 16.7\%.$

19. e. $k_C = k_{RF} + (k_M - k_{RF})b_C = 10\% + (15\% - 10\%)1.5 = 17.5\%.$

20. d. $$b_p = \sum_{i=1}^{5} w_i b_i = (\$130/\$450)(0.4) + (\$110/\$450)(1.5) + (\$70/\$450)(3.0) + (\$90/\$450)(2.0) + (\$50/\$450)(1.0) = 1.46.$$

21. a. $k_p = k_{RF} + (k_M - k_{RF})b_p = 12\% + (6\%)1.46 = 20.76\% \approx 20.8\%.$

22. e. First find the beta of the remaining 9 stocks, b_R:

$$1.8 = 0.9(b_R) + 0.1(b_A)$$
$$1.8 = 0.9(b_R) + 0.1(2.0)$$
$$1.8 = 0.9(b_R) + 0.2$$
$$1.6 = 0.9(b_R)$$
$$b_R = 1.78.$$

Now find the beta of the new stock, b_N, that produces $b_p = 1.7$:

$$1.7 = 0.9(1.78) + 0.1(b_N)$$
$$1.7 = 1.6 + 0.1(b_N)$$
$$0.1 = 0.1(b_N)$$
$$b_N = 1.0.$$

23. e. $\hat{k}_M$ = 0.05(-10.0%) + 0.25(5.0%) + 0.35(7.5%) + 0.20(10.0%) + 0.15(12.5%)
= -0.5% + 1.25% + 2.625% + 2.0% + 1.875%
= 7.25%.

$\hat{k}_p$ = 0.05(-15.0%) + 0.25(2.5%) + 0.35(10.0%) + 0.20(12.5%) + 0.15(15.0%)
= -0.75% + 0.625% + 3.50% + 2.5% + 2.25%
= 8.125%.

24. c. By definition, the market's beta is equal to 1.0.

25. d. Use the regression feature of the calculator. Enter data for the market and the project, and then find the project's beta = 1.36.

26. b. $k = k_{RF} + (k_M - k_{RF})b_i$
= 4.5% + (7.25% - 4.5%)1.36
= 4.5% + 3.74%
= 8.24%.

27. c.

CHAPTER 4
BOND AND STOCK VALUATION

OVERVIEW

There are actually two separate and distinct approaches to security valuation, depending on the type of security being valued. First, some securities, such as stocks and bonds, have direct claims against a firm's cash flows. Securities of this type are valued using discounted cash flow (DCF) models. Second, other securities, such as options, have only an indirect claim against a firm's cash flows. Securities of the second type are called derivative securities, because their values are derived from the values of other securities which do have direct claims against a firm's cash flows. Derivative securities are valued using option pricing models, which are quite different from discounted cash flow models. The discounted cash flow models used to value stocks and bonds are discussed in this chapter, while the option pricing models used to value options are discussed in the next chapter.

Valuation concepts are critical in financial management, because managers must know how to value individual assets the firm might acquire. Further, managers must know how investors value a firm's securities, because managers must know how alternative courses of action will affect the values of the firm's stocks and bonds.

KEY CONCEPTS

Valuation is an important concept to financial managers because they must value their firm's real asset investment opportunities and the securities the firm issues.

The values of most assets stem from streams of expected cash flows, and hence can be found by:

- Estimating the cash flow stream.
- Estimating the required rate of return. This rate reflects the riskiness of the cash flow stream and the general level of interest rates.
- Discounting each cash flow by its required rate of return.
- Finding the sum of the present values to obtain the value of the asset.

The value of real (physical) assets, as well as securities, can be estimated by this method.

Bonds are the primary type of long-term debt. They provide a fixed stream of semiannual interest payments, plus a lump sum equal to the face value at maturity.

The value of a bond is the present value of the bond's payment stream:

$$V_B = \sum_{t=1}^{2n} \frac{I/2}{(1 + k_d/2)^t} + \frac{M}{(1 + k_d/2)^{2n}}.$$

Here I = annual coupon payment which is divided by 2 to obtain the semiannual interest payment, M = par value, which is the amount repaid at maturity, and n = number of years to maturity, which is multiplied by 2 to adjust for semiannual compounding.

The expected rate of return on a bond that will be held to maturity is known as the ***yield to maturity (YTM)***. The YTM is that discount rate which causes the present value of the promised payment stream to equal the current price of the bond.

The YTM for a bond that sells at par consists entirely of an interest yield, but if the bond sells at a price other than its par value, the YTM consists of an interest yield plus a positive or negative capital gains yield.

The YTM is obtained by solving the bond valuation equation for k_d and multiplying by 2. This YTM is the nominal, or stated, yield to maturity, and is the value generally used by bond traders and investors.

If there is some probability of default on the bond, then the expected rate of return is less than the YTM.

A bond is *callable* if the issuer can redeem the bond prior to maturity.

A callable bond is most likely to be called when interest rates are below the outstanding bond's coupon rate.

In this case, the expected rate of return on the bond should be the yield to call (YTC) rather than the yield to maturity (YTM):

$$V_B = \sum_{t=1}^{2m} \frac{I}{2} \frac{1}{(1 + k_d/2)^t} + \text{Call price} \frac{1}{(1 + k_d/2)^{2m}},$$

where m = number of years to call.

The YTC is obtained by solving the above equation for k_d and multiplying by 2.

Since various types of income are subject to different tax rates, investors must consider after-tax returns if they are to make sound decisions among alternative investment opportunities.

The relevant cash flows (to an investor) produced by a security are the after-personal-tax cash flows.

The relevant rate of return to investors is the after-tax return, which is the rate of return on the after-tax cash flows.

Semiannual, quarterly, and other compounding periods are often used in financial transactions. Compounding on a nonannual basis requires an adjustment in the way returns are calculated to put all returns on an equal basis.

The *effective annual rate (EAR)* is the rate that produces the final future value under annual compounding. The effective annual rate is determined by

$$EAR = (1 + k_{Nom}/m)^m - 1.0,$$

where k_{Nom} is the stated annual rate and m is the number of compounding periods per year.

For example, the EAR on a 10 percent nominal coupon rate bond with semiannual coupons is 10.25 percent:

$$EAR = (1 + 0.10/2)^2 - 1.0 = 10.25\%.$$

Equity capital is usually raised by selling common stock, but it also can be raised through the sale of preferred stock.

Preferred stocks generally offer the expectation of a fixed dividend, sometimes forever, but usually for a fixed term.

The value of *perpetual preferred stock* is found as follows:

$$P_0 = D/k_{ps}.$$

Here D is the dividend to be received in each year, and k_{ps} is the required rate of return on the preferred stock.

The expected rate of return on a share of preferred stock can be found as follows:

$$\hat{k}_{ps} = D/P_0.$$

Tax effects should be considered in evaluating the expected yield on a share of perpetual preferred stock.

- If the owner of the preferred stock is an individual investor, the dividend is taxed at the investor's marginal tax rate; $\hat{k}_{psAT} = \hat{k}_{ps}(1 - T)$.
- If the owner is a corporation, 70 percent of the dividend is exempt from income taxes; ; $\hat{k}_{psAT(Corp)} = \hat{k}_{ps}(1 - 0.30T)$.

Preferred stocks offer higher returns to corporations because of the dividend exemption. Consequently, most nonconvertible preferred stocks are owned by corporations.

Many preferred stocks issued in recent years contain sinking fund provisions which require that a percentage of the issue be retired each year. These stocks are valued in the same way as bonds since they have a finite maturity. Preferred stocks with mandatory redemption provisions are also valued like bonds.

The expected cash flows from common stock consist of (1) the dividend expected in each year and (2) the price an investor expects to receive from selling the stock.

However, the value of a stock today can be calculated as the present value of an infinite stream of dividends, because the future selling price is the present value of a future dividend stream:

$$\hat{P}_0 = \frac{D_1}{(1 + k_s)^1} + \frac{D_2}{(1 + k_s)^2} + \ldots + \frac{D_\infty}{(1 + k_s)^\infty}.$$

Here, $\hat{P}_0$ = stock's current value, D_t = dividend the stockholder expects to receive in Year t, and k_s = the required rate of return on the stock.

The equation for valuing a constant growth stock was developed by Myron J. Gordon and is often called the *Gordon model.*

For many companies, earnings and dividends are expected to grow at some "normal" or constant rate.

If dividend growth, g, is constant, and if k_s is greater than g, the Gordon model can be used:

$$\hat{P}_0 = \frac{D_0(1 + g)}{k_s - g} = \frac{D_1}{k_s - g}.$$

D_0 is last year's annual dividend, while D_1 is the dividend expected in the coming year.

For all stocks in any year, the total expected return is composed of an expected dividend yield plus an expected capital gains yield:

$$\hat{k}_s = \text{Dividend yield} + \text{Capital gains yield}.$$

For a constant growth stock, both dividend yield and capital gains yield remain constant over time:

$$\hat{k}_s = \frac{D_1}{P_0} + g = \begin{matrix}\text{Constant}\\ \text{dividend}\\ \text{yield}\end{matrix} + \begin{matrix}\text{Constant}\\ \text{capital gains}\\ \text{yield}\end{matrix}.$$

For a constant growth stock, investors expect earnings, dividends, and stock price to all grow at the same rate, g.

Firms typically go through periods of nonconstant growth, after which time their growth rate settles to a rate close to the overall growth rate in the economy. Like all stocks, the value of such a stock is equal to the present value of its expected future dividends.

To find the value of such a stock, we proceed in four steps:

- Partition the dividend stream into a beginning period of nonconstant growth followed by a period of permanent constant growth.
- Find the present value of the dividends during the period of nonconstant growth.
- Find the expected value of the stock at the end of the nonconstant growth period (the beginning of the constant growth phase), and then find the present value.
- Add these two components to determine the present value of the stock, $\hat{P}_0$.

Time lines are useful in setting up the calculations, especially to illustrate the change from nonconstant growth to constant growth.

Prior to 1987, capital gains were taxed at a significantly lower rate than dividends, making high-growth stocks more attractive than high-yields.

Although capital gains are no longer taxed at a significantly lower rate, the tax advantage of capital gains has not been eliminated.

Capital gains still have some tax advantage because taxes on dividends must be paid when the dividends are received, typically quarterly. However, taxes on capital gains are not paid until the security is sold and the gains are realized. Thus, capital gains taxes are deferred into the future, while taxes on dividends are not. Further, the capital gains tax rate is currently (1995) capped at 28 percent, while the top personal tax rate is 39.6 percent.

Stock and bond prices are generally in equilibrium, that is, prices reflect the intrinsic values estimated by investors.

Stock prices are not constant; they regularly fluctuate as random buy and sell orders arrive in the markets. Further, stock prices react to buy and sell orders that are generated as new public information becomes available.

However, as we discussed in Chapter 1, the capital markets are efficient in the sense that the prices of widely-traded stocks and bonds fully and instantaneously reflect all public information, and hence such securities are generally in equilibrium.

DEFINITIONAL QUESTIONS

1. The value of most assets comes from streams of __________ __________ __________.

2. A bond with semiannual coupon payments represents an annuity of I/2 dollars per semiannual period for 2n years, plus a lump sum of M dollars at the end of 2n years. The bond's value, V, is the __________ __________ of this payment stream.

3. The expected rate of return earned by purchasing a bond and holding it until maturity is known as the bond's __________ _______ __________.

4. A bond's yield to maturity (YTM) represents its nominal expected rate of return, not its __________ annual rate of return.

5. Like other financial assets, the value of common stock is the __________ value of a future cash flow stream.

6. The total return expected from a common stock consists of a __________ yield and a __________ __________ yield.

7. If interest rates fall below the bond's coupon rate, a __________ bond is likely to be redeemed by the issuer and the relevant rate of return is the __________ _______ __________.

8. When a bond is redeemed by the issuer prior to maturity, the price paid to the bondholder is called the __________ __________.

9. The __________ __________ __________ places different investments with different compounding periods on a common basis for comparative analysis.

10. Preferred stocks which contain _________ _________ provisions require that some quantity of outstanding shares be retired each year.

11. A _________ preferred stock can be valued by the formula $P_0 = D/k_{ps}$.

12. In valuing a constant growth stock, the Gordon model assumes _________ dividend growth and that the required ___________ ______ _________ is greater than the growth rate.

Conceptual Questions

13. A 20-year bond with 1 year left to maturity has the same interest rate risk as a 10-year bond with 1 year left to maturity. Both bonds have the same coupon rate.

    a. True **b.** False

14. According to the valuation model developed in this chapter, the value that an investor assigns to a share of stock is independent of the length of time the investor plans to hold the stock.

    a. True **b.** False

15. The YTM on a bond will consist entirely of an interest yield independent of its selling price.

    a. True **b.** False

16. The dividend yield and capital gains yield remain constant for constant growth stocks.

    a. True **b.** False

17. The 1986 Tax Reform Act eliminated the tax advantage of capital gains over dividends.

    a. True **b.** False

18. Which of the following assumptions would cause the constant growth stock valuation model to be invalid?

    a. The growth rate is negative.
    b. The growth rate is zero.
    c. The growth rate is less than the required rate of return.
    d. The required rate of return is above 30 percent.
    e. None of the above assumptions would invalidate the model.

PROBLEMS

19. The Murdock Corporation has a bond issue outstanding with a coupon rate of 7 percent per year and 4 years remaining until maturity. The par value of the bond is $1,000. Determine the current value of the bond if present market conditions justify a 14 percent required rate of return. The bond pays interest semiannually.

a. $1,126.42 **b.** $1,000.00 **c.** $903.05 **d.** $791.00 **e.** $533.39

20. Refer to Problem 19. Suppose the bond had a required rate of return of 10 percent. Now what would be the current value?

a. $1,126.42 **b.** $1,000.00 **c.** $903.05 **d.** $791.00 **e.** $533.39

21. Refer to Problem 19. Now assume 20 years remain to maturity. What is the current value under these conditions? (Remember that the required rate of return is 14 percent.)

a. $1,126.42 **b.** $1,000.00 **c.** $903.05 **d.** $791.00 **e.** $533.39

22. Wiley Products has a bond issue outstanding with 8 years remaining to maturity, a coupon rate of 10 percent with interest paid semiannually, and a par value of $1,000. If the current market price of the bond issue is $853.48, what is its yield to maturity?

a. 12% **b.** 13% **c.** 14% **d.** 15% **e.** 16%

23. Refer to Problem 22. Suppose the bond issue were callable in three years at a call price of $1,115. What is its yield to call?

a. 24.3% **b.** 22.2% **c.** 20.1% **d.** 19.7% **e.** 15.9%

24. Burrito Brothers has maintained a dividend payment of $4 per share for many years. The same rate is expected to be paid in future years. If investors require a 12 percent rate of return on similar investments, determine the present value of the company's stock.

a. $15.00 **b.** $30.00 **c.** $33.33 **d.** $35.00 **e.** $40.00

25. Your sister-in-law, a stockbroker at HiReturn, Inc., is trying to sell you a stock with a current market price of $25. The stock's last dividend (D_0) was $2.00, and earnings and dividends are expected to increase at a constant growth rate of 10 percent. Your required return on this stock is 20 percent. From a strict valuation standpoint, you should:

a. Buy the stock; it is fairly valued.

b. Buy the stock; it is undervalued by $3.00.
c. Buy the stock; it is undervalued by $2.00.
d. Not buy the stock; it is overvalued by $2.00.
e. Not buy the stock; it is overvalued by $3.00.

26. Lucas Laboratories' last dividend was $1.50. Its current equilibrium stock price is $15.75, and its expected growth rate is a constant 5 percent. If the stockholders' required rate of return is 15 percent, what is the expected dividend yield and expected capital gains yield for the coming year?

a. 0%; 15% b. 5%; 10% c. 10%; 5% d. 15%; 0% e. 15%; 15%

27. The Roadrunner Demolition Company has been hard hit by increased competition from Acme Products. Analysts predict that earnings (and dividends) will decline at a rate of 5 percent annually into the foreseeable future. If Roadrunner's last dividend (D_0) was $2.00, and investors' required rate of return is 15 percent, what will be Roadrunner's stock price in 3 years?

a. $8.15 b. $9.50 c. $10.00 d. $10.42 e. $10.96

The following data apply to the next three problems.

The Extra Parts Auto Company has just recently been organized. It is expected to experience no growth for the next 2 years as it identifies its market and acquires its inventory. However, Extra Parts will grow at an annual rate of 5 percent in the third year, and, beginning with the fourth year, should attain a 10 percent growth rate which it will sustain thereafter. The first dividend (D_1) to be paid at the end of the first year is expected to be $0.50 per share. Investors require a 15 percent rate of return on Extra Parts' stock.

28. What is the current equilibrium stock price?

a. $5.00 b. $8.75 c. $9.57 d. $12.43 e. $15.00

29. What will Extra Parts' stock price be at the end of the first year (P_1)?

a. $5.00 b. $8.76 c. $9.56 d. $12.43 e. $15.00

30. What dividend yield and capital gains yield should an investor in Extra Parts expect for the first year?

a. 0%; 15% b. 3%; 12% c. 6%; 9% d. 10%; 5% e. 12%; 3%

31. You have just been offered a bond for $863.731. The coupon rate is 8 percent, payable annually, and interest rates on new issues with the same degree of risk are 10 percent. You want to know how many more interest payments you will receive, but the party selling the bond cannot remember. If the par value is $1,000, how many interest payments remain?

a. 10 b. 11 c. 12 d. 13 e. 14

32. Johnson Corporation's stock is currently selling at $45.83 per share. The last dividend paid (D_0) was $2.50. Johnson is a constant growth firm. If investors require a return of 16 percent on Johnson's stock, what do they think Johnson's growth rate will be?

a. 6% b. 7% c. 8% d. 9% e. 10%

The following data apply to the next five problems.

The Henderson Company has a perpetual preferred stock issue outstanding that pays a 12 percent dividend. The par value of each share is $100 and the dividend is paid quarterly. The shares are currently trading for $90.

33. What is the expected nominal rate of return on the issue?

a. 10.00% b. 13.33% c. 12.50% d. 13.75% e. 11.63%

34. What is the expected effective annual rate of return on the issue?

a. 10.65% b. 12.00% c. 11.88% d. 14.01% e. 13.25%

35. What is the expected after-tax return to an individual in the 28 percent marginal tax bracket?

a. 9.60% b. 12.33% c. 10.75% d. 11.93% e. 13.42%

36. What is the expected after-tax return to a corporate investor in the 35 percent marginal tax bracket?

a. 9.60% b. 12.33% c. 10.75% d. 11.93% e. 13.42%

37. Now assume that the issue has a sinking fund provision whereby the firm redeems 10 percent of the issue in each year over the next 10 years at a share price equal to par value, or $100. What is the expected pretax rate of return with a sinking fund provision? (Hint: No investor knows when his or her shares will be redeemed, but the expected time to redemption is 5 years.)

a. 13.87% b. 14.98% c. 12.55% d. 11.15% e. 12.89%

ANSWERS

1. expected cash flows
2. present value
3. yield to maturity
4. effective
5. present
6. dividend; capital gains
7. callable; yield to call
8. call price
9. effective annual rate
10. sinking fund
11. perpetual
12. constant; rate of return

13. a. Both bonds are valued as 1-year bonds regardless of their original issue dates, and since they have the same coupon rate, their prices must be equal. Since at this point in time the bonds are identical, their interest rate risk is the same.

14. a. The model considers all future dividends. This produces a current value which is appropriate for all investors independent of their expected holding period.

15. b. If a bond sells at a price other than par value, the YTM consists of an interest yield plus a positive or negative capital gains yield.

16. a. These yields are constant over time for all constant growth stocks.

17. b. Capital gains are no longer taxed at a significantly lower rate; however, capital gains still have an advantage because taxes are deferred until the security is sold and capital gains are realized.

18. e. The model would be invalid, however, if the growth rate exceeded the required rate of return. Note that this would never happen because no stock would be expected to grow indefinitely at a rate above its required rate of return.

19. d.

$$V = \sum_{t=1}^{2n} \frac{I/2}{(1 + k_d/2)^t} + \frac{M}{(1 + k_d/2)^{2n}} = \sum_{t=1}^{8} \frac{\$35}{(1.07)^t} + \frac{\$1,000}{(1.07)^8}$$

$= \$791.00.$

Alternatively, using a financial calculator, input N = 8, I = 7, PMT = 35, FV = 1,000 to solve for PV = \$791.00.

20. c.

$$V = \sum_{t=1}^{2n} \frac{I/2}{(1 + k_d/2)^t} + \frac{M}{(1 + k_d/2)^{2n}} = \sum_{t=1}^{8} \frac{\$35}{(1.05)^t} + \frac{\$1,000}{(1.05)^8}$$

$$= \$903.05.$$

Alternatively, with the inputs from Problem 19 still in your calculator change I from 7 to 5, and then solve for PV = $903.05.

21. e.

$$V = \sum_{t=1}^{2n} \frac{I/2}{(1 + k_d/2)^t} + \frac{M}{(1 + k_d/2)^{2n}} = \sum_{t=1}^{40} \frac{\$35}{(1.07)^t} + \frac{\$1,000}{(1.07)^{40}}$$

$$= \$533.39.$$

Alternatively, using a financial calculator, input N = 40, I = 7, PMT = 35, FV = 1,000 to solve for PV = $533.39.

22. b.

$$V = \sum_{t=1}^{2n} \frac{I/2}{(1 + k_d/2)^t} + \frac{M}{(1 + k_d/2)^{2n}}$$

$$\$853.48 = \sum_{t=1}^{16} \frac{\$50}{(1 + k_d/2)^t} + \frac{\$1,000}{(1 + k_d/2)^{16}}$$

$$k_d/2 = 6.50\%$$

$$k_d = YTM = 13.00\%.$$

Alternatively, using a financial calculator, input N = 16, PV = -853.48, PMT = 50, FV = 1,000 and solve for I = 6.50%. However, this is a semiannual rate ($k_d/2$), so YTM = 2 × 6.50% = 13%.

23. d.

$$V = \sum_{t=1}^{2m} \frac{I/2}{(1 + k_d/2)^t} + \frac{\text{Call price}}{(1 + k_d/2)^{2m}}$$

$$\$853.48 = \sum_{t=1}^{6} \frac{\$50}{(1 + k_d/2)^t} + \frac{\$1,115}{(1 + k_d/2)^6}$$

$$k_d/2 = 9.85\%$$

$$k_d = \text{YTC} = 19.7\%.$$

Alternatively, using a financial calculator, input N = 6, PV = -853.48, PMT = 50, FV = 1115, and then solve for I = kd/2 = 9.85%. YTC = kd = 2 × 9.85% = 19.7%.

24. c. This is a zero-growth stock, or perpetuity:

$$\hat{P}_0 = D/k_{ps} = \$4.00/0.12 = \$33.33.$$

25. e.

$$\hat{P}_0 = \frac{D_0(1 + g)}{k_s - g} = \frac{\$2.00(1.10)}{0.20 - 0.10} = \$22.00.$$

Since the stock is currently selling for \$25.00, the stock is not in equilibrium and is overvalued by \$3.00.

26. c.

$$\text{Dividend yield} = \frac{D_1}{P_0} = \frac{D_0(1 + g)}{P_0} = \frac{\$1.50(1.05)}{\$15.75} = 10\%.$$

$$\text{Capital gains yield} = \frac{P_1 - P_0}{P_0} = \frac{P_0(1 + g) - P_0}{P_0}$$

$$= \frac{\$16.54 - \$15.75}{\$15.75} = g = 5\%.$$

For a constant growth stock the capital gains yield is equal to g.

Note that the dividend yield plus the capital gains yield = 10% + 5% = 15%, which is the required rate of return on the stock.

27. a.

$$\hat{P}_0 = \frac{D_0(1 + g)}{k_s - g} = \frac{\$2.00(0.95)}{0.15 - (-0.05)} = \frac{\$1.90}{0.20} = \$9.50.$$

$$\hat{P}_3 = \hat{P}_0(1 + g)^3 = \$9.50(0.95)^3 = \$9.50(0.8574) = \$8.15.$$

The Gordon model can also be applied directly to the dividend in Year 4:

$$\hat{P}_3 = \frac{D_4}{k_s - g} = \frac{D_0(1 + g)^4}{0.15 - (-0.05)} = \frac{\$2.00(0.95)^4}{0.20} = \frac{\$2.00(0.8145)}{0.20} = \$8.15.$$

28. b. To calculate the current value of a nonconstant growth stock, follow these steps:

(1) Determine the expected stream of dividends during the nonconstant growth period. Also calculate the expected dividend at the end of the first year of constant growth that will be used later to calculate stock price:

$$D_1 = \$0.50$$
$$D_2 = D_1(1 + g) = \$0.50(1 + 0.0) = \$0.50.$$
$$D_3 = D_2(1 + g) = \$0.50(1.05) = \$0.525.$$
$$D_4 = D_3(1 + g) = \$0.525(1.10) = \$0.5775.$$

(2) Discount the expected dividends during the nonconstant growth period at the investor's required rate of return to find their present value:

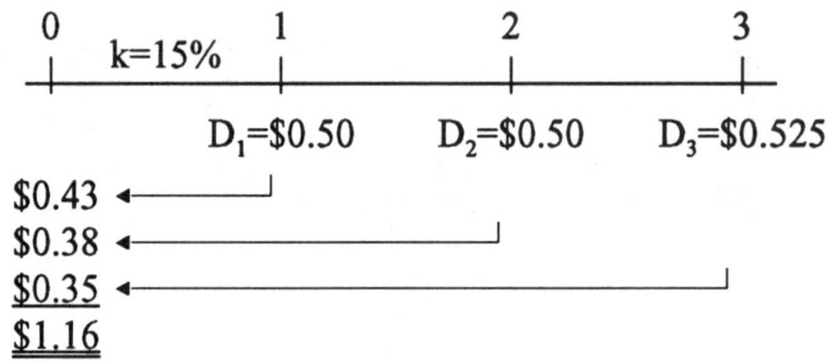

(3) Calculate the expected stock price at the end of the final year of nonconstant growth. This occurs at the end of Year 3. Use the Gordon model for this calculation:

$$\hat{P}_3 = D_4/(k_s - g) = \$0.5775/(0.15 - 0.10) = \$11.55.$$

Then discount this stock price 3 periods at the investor's required rate of return to find its present value:

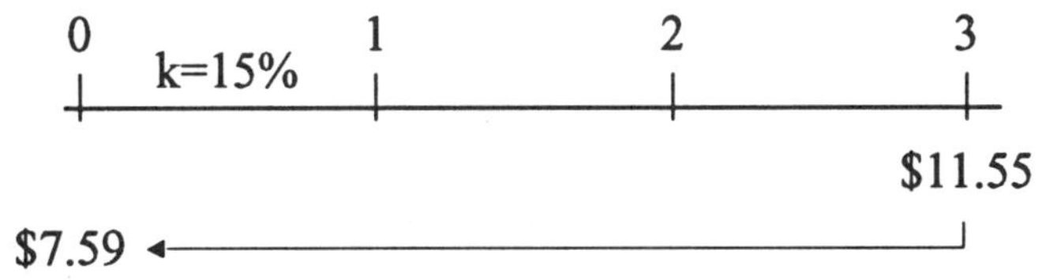

(4) Add the present value of the stock price expected at the end of Year 3 plus the present value of the dividends expected in Years 1, 2, and 3 to find the present value of the stock, $\hat{P}_0$ = \$7.59 + \$1.16 = \$8.75.

29. c. To calculate the expected stock price at the end of Year 1, $\hat{P}_1$, follow the same procedure you would to find the value at Year 0. However, discount values to Year 1 instead of Year 0. Also, remember the dividend in Year 1, D_1, is not included in the valuation because it has already been paid and therefore adds nothing to the wealth of the investor buying the stock at the end of Year 1.

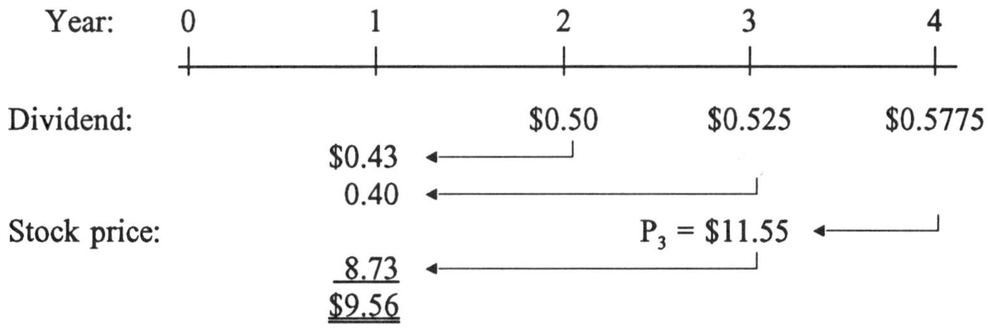

30. c. Dividend yield = D_1/P_0 = \$0.50/\$8.75 = 0.057 ≈ 6%.

Capital gains yield = $(P_1 - P_0)/P_0$ = (\$9.56 - \$8.75)/\$8.75 = 0.093 ≈ 9%.

The Total yield = Dividend yield + Capital gains yield = 6% + 9% = 15%. The total yield must equal the required rate of return. Also, the capital gains yield is not equal to the growth rate during the nonconstant growth phase of a nonconstant growth stock. Finally, the dividend and capital gains yields are not constant until the constant growth phase is reached.

31. c. $V = I(PVIFA_{k,n}) + M(PVIF_{k,n})$

$\$863.731 = \$80(PVIFA_{10\%,n}) + \$1{,}000(PVIF_{10\%,n})$

Now use trial and error to find the value of n for which the equality holds. For n = 12, \$863.731 = \$80(6.8137) + \$1,000(0.3186) = \$863.70. Or using a financial calculator, enter I = 10, PV = -863.731, PMT = 80, FV = 1,000. Solve for n, which equals 12.

32. e.

$$
\begin{aligned}
P_0 &= D_0(1 + g)/(k_s - g) \\
\$45.83 &= \$2.50(1 + g)/(0.16 - g) \\
\$7.33 - \$45.83g &= \$2.50 + \$2.50g \\
\$48.33g &= \$4.83 \\
g &= 0.0999 \approx 10\%.
\end{aligned}
$$

33. b. $\hat{k}_{ps} = D/P_0 = \$12/\$90 = 0.1333 = 13.33\%$,

or Quarterly $\hat{k}_{ps} = \$3/\$90 = 0.0333 = 3.33\%$, and $\hat{k}_{ps} = 4(3.33\%) = 13.33\%$.

34. d. In Problem 33 we calculated the periodic (quarterly) rate to be 3.33 percent. Hence, the effective annual rate is 14.01 percent: $(1.0333)^4 - 1.0 = 14.01\%$.

35. a. $\hat{k}_{psAT} = \hat{k}_{ps}(1 - T) = 13.33\%(1 - 0.28) = 13.33\%(0.72) = 9.60\%$.

36. d. $\hat{k}_{psAT} = \hat{k}_{ps}(1 - 0.30T) = 13.33\%(1 - 0.30(0.35)) = 13.33\%(0.895) = 11.93\%$.

37. b. An investor expects to receive a dividend of \$12 per year for 5 years, and to have the stock redeemed for \$100 after the fifth year.

0	$k_{ps} = ?$	1	2	•••	4	5
-90		12	12		12	12
						100
						112

These cash flows resemble bond cash flows, and the YTM = IRR = $\hat{k}_{ps}$ = 14.98% can easily be found using a financial calculator.

CHAPTER 5
OPTIONS AND OTHER DERIVATIVE SECURITIES

OVERVIEW

In Chapter 4, we discussed how direct claim securities are valued using discounted cash flow analysis. Now, in Chapter 5, we turn to the valuation of options, which are derivative securities. Option theory and valuation are important to financial managers for three reasons. First, two important types of securities issued by firms--warrants and convertibles--have option characteristics. Thus, the valuation of these securities relies on option theory. Second, both debt and equity investment in a firm can be viewed within an option framework, and this can provide insights into the impact of managerial decisions on the values of a firm's stocks and bonds. Finally, some projects undertaken by firms have "strategic value" that is not easily captured by conventional discounted cash flow analysis. This value, which is "above and beyond" the conventional NPV, can often be analyzed within an option framework.

KEY CONCEPTS

An *option* is a contract which gives its holder the right to buy (or sell) an asset at some predetermined price within a specified period of time. *Pure options* are securities that are created outside the firm that have no impact on a firm's financing decisions.

There are many types of options and option markets.

- *Call options* convey the right to buy a share of stock at a set price called the exercise, or striking, price.
- *Put options* give the holder the right to sell the stock at the striking price.
- An option, whether a call or a put, has both a buyer and a seller.
    - The buyer has the right to exercise the option.
    - The seller, who is called the writer, must execute the transaction if the option is exercised.
    - A seller who writes call options on stock he or she holds is said to write covered options. A similar option written without holding the underlying stock is called a naked option.

- If the underlying stock's price is above the exercise price of a call option, the option is said to be in the money. If the underlying stock price is less than the exercise price of a call option, the option is said to be out of the money.

- Corporations on whose stock options are written have nothing to do with the options market--they do not raise money in this market nor do they have any direct transactions in it.

The *formula value* of a call option is defined as follows: Formula value = Current stock price - Exercise price. The formula value can be thought of as the value of the call option if it expired today.

- For example, if a stock sells for $25, and the call option's exercise price is $20, the option's formula value is $25 - $20 = $5.
- However, the actual price as set in the options market generally will be higher than the formula value because there is some probability that the stock price will go higher prior to the expiration of the call option.

One way to visualize the expiration payoffs associated with an option contract is to construct a payoff diagram.

- A profit will be made on the call option transaction only if the stock price is above the exercise price plus the price of the call option.
- The buyer of a put option will earn a gross profit if the price of the underlying asset is below the strike price at expiration. From this gross profit, the original cost of the put option must be subtracted.

Options are attractive to investors because they offer greater leverage and less loss potential than do investments in the underlying stock. However, options are much riskier. For example, an investor who buys the stock and its price stays flat breaks even (not counting transactions costs), while an investor who buys an option on that same stock loses his or her investment.

Options can be used to create hedges which protect the value of an individual stock or portfolio. In addition, by combining different option contracts on the same stock, or by combining options and long or short contracts on the underlying stock, investors can create positions with a wide variety of risk/return tradeoffs. Combination positions include straddles, strips, and straps.

In equilibrium, the prices of put and call options are related to each other (as well as to interest rates and the price of the underlying stock). This relationship is called *put-call parity.*

Put-call parity can be derived by examining a trading strategy that involves (1) buying the underlying stock, (2) selling a call option, and (3) buying a put option on the stock at the same exercise price.

To illustrate put-call parity, consider the following payoff matrix, where P_s is the stock price at expiration and P_x is the exercise price of the options. Note that the options here are European options, and hence can only be exercised at maturity, and that we assume the stock will not pay a dividend during the option period.

	Stock Price at Expiration	
	Less than Exercise Price	Greater than Exercise Price
Value of stock owned	P_s	P_s
Value of put owned	$P_x - P_s$	0
Value of call sold	0	$-(P_s - P_x)$
	P_x	P_x

- Since the value of the above position at expiration is certain (riskless) and is equal to the exercise price, P_x, if markets are efficient then the present value (or cost) of the position must equal P_x discounted at the risk-free rate: $P_s + P_p - P_c = P_x/(1 + k_{RF})^t$.
- This equality leads to the put-call parity equations:

$$P_c = P_s + P_p - P_x/(1 + k_{RF})^t,$$

or

$$P_p = P_c + P_x/(1 + k_{RF})^t - P_s.$$

Here, P_s = stock price at expiration; P_p = put option price; P_c = call option price; k_{RF} = risk-free rate; and t = time to expiration.

- If put and call option prices do not agree with the put-call parity relationship, arbitrageurs can create riskless portfolios of stocks and options that earn a return in excess of the risk-free rate. The process of buying and selling options will force put-call parity to hold.

In addition to the stock price and the exercise price, the price of an option depends on three other factors: (1) the option's term to maturity, (2) the variability of the stock price, and (3) the risk-free rate.

The longer an option has to run, the greater its value and the larger its premium.

An option on an extremely volatile stock will be worth more than one on a very stable stock.

The *Black-Scholes Option Pricing Model (OPM)* provides the relationship between call option value and five relevant factors.

Actual option prices conform reasonably well to the model, and it is widely used by traders.

The model rests on the concept of a riskless hedge. By buying shares of a stock and simultaneously selling call options on that stock, an investor can create a risk-free investment position, where gains on the stock will exactly offset losses on the option, and vice versa.

Black and Scholes made the following assumptions: (1) The stock underlying the call option provides no dividends during the option's life, (2) no transactions costs are incurred, (3) the short-term, risk-free interest rate is known and constant during the option's life, (4) any purchaser of a security may borrow at the short-term, risk-free interest rate, (5) short selling is permitted without penalty, (6) the call option can be exercised only on its expiration date, and (7) stock price moves randomly.

The Black-Scholes model consists of the following three equations:

$$V = P[N(d_1)] - Xe^{-k_{RF}t}[N(d_2)].$$

$$d_1 = \frac{\ln (P/x) + [k_{RF} + (\sigma^2/2)]t}{\sigma\sqrt{t}}.$$

$$d_2 = d_1 - \sigma\sqrt{t}.$$

Here, V = current value of a call option with time t until expiration; P = current price of the underlying stock; $N(d_i)$ = probability that a deviation less than d_i will occur in a standard normal distribution (thus, $N(d_1)$ and $N(d_2)$ represent areas under a standard normal distribution function); X = exercise, or striking, price of the option; $e \approx 2.7183$; k_{RF} = risk-free interest rate; t = time until the option expires (the option period); ln (P/X) = natural logarithm of P/X; and σ^2 = variance of the rate of return on the stock.

The Black-Scholes OPM illustrates that call option prices depend on five factors:

- *Current stock price.* The higher the stock price, the higher the option value, all else the same.
- *Exercise price.* The higher the exercise price, the lower the option value, all else the same.
- *Option period.* The longer the time to maturity, the higher the option value, all else the same.
- *Risk-free rate.* The higher the risk-free rate, the higher the option value, all else the same.

- *Stock return variance.* The higher the variability of returns on the stock, the higher the option value, all else the same.

The equity of a levered firm can be viewed as a call option: When a firm issues debt, this, in a sense, is equivalent to the shareholders selling the assets of the firm to the debtholders, who pay for the assets with cash plus an implied call option whose striking price is equal to the principal value of the debt plus interest. If the company is successful, the stockholders will exercise their call option and "buy the company back" by paying the principal and interest on the debt. Otherwise, the stockholders will default on the debt, which amounts to not exercising their option, and thus the stockholders transfer the company to the debtholders.

To illustrate the usefulness of the concept, consider a company that changes the composition of its assets so that the firm's stand-alone risk (variance) increases, but its market risk (beta) remains constant. Since the equity can be viewed as a call option, the increased variance of returns would increase the market value of the equity without increasing its market risk. However, any gains to the shareholders would come at the expense of the debtholders, since the firm's bankruptcy risk would increase.

Option analysis can also be applied to mergers.

Put and call options represent an important class of derivative securities whose values are derived from other securities. However, there are other types of derivatives, including futures, swaps, structured notes, inverse floaters, and a host of other "exotic" contracts.

Futures are contracts which require the holder to buy or sell some asset at a specified price on a specific future date.

- Futures were originally used for commodities such as wheat.
- Although commodity futures remain important, more trading is done today in foreign exchange and interest rate futures.

In a *swap*, two parties agree to exchange a series of cash flows.

- Most swaps today involve either interest payments or currencies.
- Originally, swaps were arranged between companies by money center banks, who would match counter-parties. Such matching still occurs, but today most swaps are between companies and banks, with the banks then taking steps to insure that their own risks are hedged.

A *structured note* is a debt obligation which is derived from some other debt obligation.

- For example, in the early 1980s investment bankers began buying large blocks of long-term, non-callable, Treasury bonds and then stripping them to create a series of zero coupon bonds corresponding to the Treasury bond payment dates.
- Another example is the *collateralized mortgage obligation (CMO),* in which securities are issued backed by the cash flows from a pool of mortgages. CMOs often consist

of IOs, or interest only notes, which have claim to all interest payments, and POs, or principal only notes, which have claim to all principal payments. Since the timing of refundings in a given pool of mortgages is very difficult to predict, IOs and POs carry a great deal of risk.

Inverse floaters are floating rate notes in which the rate paid on the note moves counter to market rates.

- If interest rates in the economy rise, the interest rate paid on an inverse floater would fall, lowering its cash interest payments. At the same time, the discount rate used to value the inverse floater's cash flows would rise along with other rates.
- The effect of cash flows moving inversely to interest rates makes the value of inverse floaters exceptionally sensitive to changes in interest rates.

Derivatives, including options, are generally used in one of two very different ways.

To speculate: The fact that a relatively small change in the price of an underlying asset produces a much larger change in a derivative's value makes derivatives attractive as speculative securities.

To hedge: Derivatives are often used to protect some underlying position against adverse events. Portfolio managers and corporate financial managers use derivatives to hedge against events such as falling stock prices and rising commodity prices.

The major investment and money center banks have large staffs engaged exclusively in structuring hedges for portfolio managers, corporations, and other investors.

- Often, bankers match risk-averse hedgers with risk-prone speculators.
- In effect, derivatives are used to transfer risk from those who do not want to bear it (hedgers) to those who do (speculators).

Although options, futures, structured notes, and other derivatives serve a valid economic purpose, they can be and are abused at times. Derivatives can be extremely complicated and thus hard to evaluate with respect to risk, return, and suitability for a given investor, and this can lead to problems.

DEFINITIONAL QUESTIONS

1. The formula value of an option equals the _______ price of the stock minus the ________ price of the option.

2. An option's premium above its formula value will decline as the price of the common stock ______.

3. This decline in premium is due to the fact that an increase in stock price reduces the ______ and increases the ______ of the option.

4. The relationship between prices on put and call options on the same stock and their having the same striking price is called ______-______ _____________.

5. A European option is one that can be exercised only on the _____________ ______.

6. If the underlying stock price is above the exercise price of a call option, the option is said to be ______ ______ ____________.

7. A graph of an option's values at expiration at different stock prices is called a ____________ ________________.

8. The equity of a levered firm can be thought of as a ___________ ___________.

9. The __________-____________ __________ _________ ________ is a theoretical model which values call options.

10. All else the same, an increase in a call option's time to expiration will cause the option's value to _______________.

CONCEPTUAL QUESTIONS

11. A naked call option is one that is written without a matching put option.

    a. True   **b.** False

12. The put-call parity relationship makes it possible to value put and call options given the price of the underlying stock.

    a. True   **b.** False

13. An investor would create an option straddle position if he or she thought that a firm's stock price would remain within a narrow range.

    a. True   **b.** False

14. What effect would an increase in the price volatility of an underlying stock have on the value of a call option on that stock?

    a. The option value will decrease.
    b. The option value will increase.
    c. The option value will not change.

15. According to option theory, what would happen to the value of a firm's debt and equity if it sold off its low-risk assets and replaced them with high-risk assets, but its beta remained constant?

    a. The firm's equity value would increase.
    b. The firm's equity value would decrease.
    c. The firm's debt value would increase.
    d. The firm's debt value would decrease.
    e. Statements a and d are both true.

PROBLEM

16. You are evaluating a call option which has a $20 striking price and 3 months to expiration. The underlying stock price is also $20 and its variance is 0.16. The risk-free rate is 12 percent. What is the option's value according to the Black-Scholes OPM?

    a. $1.88 b. $1.99 c. $2.27 d. $2.81 e. $3.65

ANSWERS

1. market (current); exercise (striking)
2. increases
3. leverage; riskiness
4. put-call parity
5. expiration date
6. in the money
7. payoff diagram
8. call option
9. Black-Scholes Option Pricing Model
10. increase

11. b. If the writer sells a call option on a stock that he or she does not own, the seller is said to have written a naked call. If the writer owns the underlying stock, the call option is a covered option.

12. b. Put-call parity gives the relationship between the prices of matching puts and calls, so the price of one of the two options is also required.

13. b. A straddle position makes money only if the underlying stock's price moves outside of the straddle range.

14. b. An increase in price volatility of the underlying asset makes call options more valuable.

15. e. Since the firm's equity can be thought of as a call option, increased risk, and hence volatility, increases its value. Conversely, increased risk increases the chances of financial distress, and hence the firm's debt value falls.

16. a. First, calculate d_1 and d_2:

$$d_1 = \frac{\ln(P/X) + [k_{RF} + (\sigma^2/2]t}{\sigma\sqrt{t}}$$

$$= \frac{\ln(\$20/\$20) + [0.12 + (0.16/2)](0.25)}{0.40(0.50)}$$

$$= \frac{0 + 0.05}{0.20} = 0.25.$$

$$d_2 = d_1 - \sigma\sqrt{t} = 0.25 - 0.20 = 0.05.$$

Next, look up the values for $N(d_1)$ and $N(d_2)$:

$$N(d_1) = N(0.25) = 0.5987.$$

$$N(d_2) = N(0.05) = 0.5199.$$

Finally, use those values to find the option's value:

$$V = P[N(d_1)] - Xe^{-k_{RF}t}N(d_2) = \$20[0.5987] - \$20e^{(-0.12)(0.25)}[0.5199]$$

$$= \$11.97 - \$19.41(0.5199) = \$11.97 - \$10.09 = \$1.88.$$

CHAPTER 6
THE COST OF CAPITAL

OVERVIEW

A firm's cost of capital is critically important for three reasons: (1) Maximizing the value of a firm requires that the costs of all inputs, including capital, be minimized, and to minimize the cost of capital, we must be able to estimate it. (2) Capital budgeting decisions require an estimate of the cost of capital. (3) Many other types of decisions, including those related to public utility regulation, leasing, bond refunding, and working capital, require estimates of capital costs. In this chapter, we discuss the actual process of estimating a firm's overall, or weighted average, cost of capital. Then, in Chapter 10, we discuss the adjustment process used to estimate divisional and project costs of capital.

KEY CONCEPTS

> The primary purpose for estimating a firm's overall, or *weighted average, cost of capital (WACC)* is to establish the opportunity cost of capital for the firm.

The WACC is simply a weighted average of the costs of the various types of capital used by the firm. In general, it can be expressed as follows:

$$\text{WACC} = \sum_{i=1}^{n} w_i k_i.$$

where w_i is the weight, or amount, of each type of capital, k_i is the cost of that capital component, and n is the number of different capital sources used by the firm.

The first decision that must be made is what capital components to include in the WACC estimate.

- That portion of short-term interest-bearing debt that is considered to be permanent financing, all long-term debt, all preferred stock, and all common equity are included in the cost of capital calculations.

- *Non-interest bearing liabilities* such as accounts payable and accruals are netted out in the capital budgeting cash flow estimation process, and hence are excluded from the cost of capital calculations.

The next decision involves the nature of the component costs to be estimated.

- The cost of capital must be developed on an after-tax basis, because after-tax cash flows are the most relevant to investment decisions.
- The relevant component costs are the marginal costs of new funds, and not the historical costs of funds raised in the past.

The following definitions will be used in the cost of capital estimation process:

- k_d = interest rate on new debt, or the before-tax cost of debt.
- $k_d(1 - T)$ = after-tax cost of debt, where T is the marginal tax rate. $k_d(1 - T)$ is the component cost of debt.
- k_{ps} = component cost of preferred stock.
- k_s = component cost of common equity raised by retaining earnings, which equals investors' required rate of return on common stock.
- k_e = cost of common equity raised by issuing additional common stock; it must be distinguished from equity raised through retained earnings due to the flotation costs on a new stock issue.
- WACC = weighted average, or overall, cost of capital.

The relevant cost of debt is the after-tax cost of new debt.

The cost of debt can be adjusted to reflect flotation costs, but since these are typically small on debt issues, most managers neglect flotation costs in their estimates.

The component cost can be found as $k_d(1 - T)$.

- If the bond is callable, then we might want to use the yield to call to estimate the cost of debt.
- Sometimes the effective annual cost of debt can be used in the WACC estimate rather than the nominal cost of debt; however, in view of the uncertainties in cost of capital estimation, most people in industry think it would be pointless to attempt to estimate effective annual cost rates for use in the WACC.
- Flotation costs can be amortized and expensed for tax purposes over the life of the issue. Ignoring this tax savings does not have a material effect on the cost of debt estimate.
- If a firm does not have actively traded debt outstanding nor an ongoing relationship with an investment banker, it is possible to obtain a rough estimate for k_d by examining coupon rates on newly-issued debt of similar companies.
- Note that firms cannot be sure of the exact future benefit of the tax deduction on interest payments, so the true after-tax cost of debt could be higher or lower than the estimated cost.

- Assume that Firm A has k_d = 12% and T = 40%. Then its component cost of debt = $k_d(1 - T) = 12\%(1 - 0.4) = 12\%(0.6) = 7.2\%$.

A number of firms use *preferred stock* as part of their permanent financing mix. Almost all preferred stock in recent years have a *call feature*, a *sinking fund,* or both.

The component cost of perpetual preferred stock, k_{ps}, is the annual preferred dividend, D_{ps}, divided by the price the firm receives net of flotation costs, P_n Thus:

$$\text{Component cost of perpetual preferred stock} = k_{ps} = \frac{D_{ps}}{P_n}.$$

- Note that no tax adjustment is made since preferred stock dividends are paid from after-tax earnings.
- If Firm A's new perpetual preferred stock requires a dividend of \$12 to sell at \$100, and if flotation costs were 5 percent, then $k_{ps} = D_{ps}/P_n$ = \$12/\$95 = 12.6%.

A firm can raise common equity capital in two ways: (1) by retaining earnings and (2) by issuing new common stock.

The cost of equity, k_s, obtained by retaining earnings is the rate of return stockholders require on the firm's common stock. Three approaches are used to estimate k_s.

While the Capital Asset Pricing Model (CAPM) is based on some unrealistic assumptions, the model is often used because of its logical appeal. We assume that the cost of equity is equal to the risk-free rate, k_{RF}, plus a risk premium that is based on the stock's beta coefficient and the market risk premium, $(k_M - k_{RF})b_i$, as set forth in the Security Market Line (SML) equation:

$$k_s = k_{RF} + (k_M - k_{RF})b_i.$$

- The rate on long-term Treasury bonds is the best estimate for the risk-free rate, k_{RF}.
- The market risk premium, $RP_M = k_M - k_{RF}$, can be estimated on the basis of historical (ex post) returns or forward-looking (ex ante) returns.
- Estimate the required rate of return on the market, or an "average" stock, k_M.
- Estimate the beta coefficient by examining historical betas. Three commonly used types of betas are (1) historical betas which are based on a stock's characteristic line using historical data, (2) adjusted betas which account for expected future movement toward 1.0, and (3) fundamental betas which are constantly adjusted to reflect changes in a firm's operations and capital structure. Managers select the appropriate beta given the circumstances at that time.
- Estimate the required rate of return on the firm's stock using the SML.
- If k_{RF} = 10%, k_M = 15%, and the beta of Firm A is 1.3, then

$$k_s = k_{RF} + (k_M - k_{RF})b_i = 10\% + (5\%)1.3 = 16.5\%.$$

The cost of retained earnings, k_s, may also be estimated by the *discounted cash flow (DCF)* approach. If a stock is expected to grow at a constant rate, we can use the constant growth model to estimate the cost of retained earnings:

$$\hat{k}_s = \frac{D_1}{P_0} + g.$$

- The DCF approach assumes that stocks are normally in equilibrium.
- The DCF approach can be applied to nonconstant growth stocks by using the nonconstant growth model.
- The expected growth rate, g, may be based on (1) projections of past growth rates, (2) the retention growth model, or (3) analysts' forecasts.
- The *retention growth model* estimates growth by the equation g = b(r). Here b = expected future retention ratio and r = expected future return on equity (ROE). This model assumes (1) that the retention ratio, b, will remain constant, (2) that the expected return on equity, r, will remain constant, (3) that the firm will not issue new common stock, or that any new stock issued will be priced at book value, and (4) that future projects are expected to have the same degree of risk as the firm's existing assets.
- If Firm A last paid $4.00 in annual dividends, dividends are expected to grow at a constant 10 percent per year, and Firm A's stock is currently selling for $73.33 per share, then

$$k_s = \hat{k}_s = \frac{\$4.00(1.10)}{\$73.33} + 10\% = 6.0\% + 10\% = 16.0\%.$$

The *bond-yield-plus-risk-premium approach* is a third method for estimating k_s. It calls for adding an estimated risk premium to the firm's own bond yield:

$$k_s = \text{Company's own bond yield} + \text{Risk premium}.$$

- Corporate treasurers can easily estimate the firm's bond yield to maturity (before-tax cost of debt), so the real problem occurs in estimating the appropriate risk premium. Risk premiums can be estimated using a market analysts' survey approach or by subtracting the yield on an average (A-rated) bond from the k_M estimate. The risk premium obtained will depend on the company and the state of the economy.
- If Firm A uses an above-own bond yield risk premium of 5 percentage points, then a 12 percent estimate for k_d used earlier results in k_s = 17%:

$$k_s = 12\% + 5\% = 17\%.$$

All three approaches are recommended for estimating the required rate of return on common stock. When different methods produce different results, judgment must be used in selecting the best estimate. In the case of Firm A, the estimates are reasonably consistent, so we could use the average of 16.5 percent as our estimate for the cost of retained earnings.

k_s represents an opportunity cost to the firm--by retaining earnings within the firm rather than paying them out as dividends, stockholders are deprived of the opportunity to invest the earnings in other assets of similar risk that provide a return of 16.5 percent.

The cost of newly issued common stock, or external equity capital, k_e, is higher than the cost of retained earnings, k_s, because of flotation costs on new common stock.

To allow for flotation costs, F, we must adjust the DCF formula for the required rate of return on common stock as follows:

$$k_e = \text{DCF } \hat{k}_e = \frac{D_1}{P_0(1 - F)} + g.$$

If Firm A incurred flotation costs of 10 percent in issuing new common shares, the cost of new stock, according to the DCF model, would be 16.7 percent:

$$k_e = \text{DCF } \hat{k}_e = \frac{\$4.00(1.10)}{\$73.33(1 - 0.10)} + 10\% = 6.7\% + 10\% = 16.7\%.$$

The DCF cost of new common stock is 16.7 percent, while the DCF cost of retained earnings is 16.0 percent. Thus, the flotation premium is 16.7% - 16.0% = 0.7%.

This premium must be added to the final estimate of the cost of retained earnings to obtain the estimate of the cost of new common stock:

$$k_e = k_s + \text{Flotation cost adjustment} = 16.5\% + 0.7\% = 17.2\%.$$

The costs of the individual capital components must be combined to estimate the weighted average cost of capital, WACC.

The formula for the weighted average cost of capital is

$$\text{WACC} = w_d k_d(1 - T) + w_{ps} k_{ps} + w_{ce}(k_s \text{ or } k_e).$$

The WACC is the weighted average cost of each new dollar of capital raised at the margin, and *not* the average cost of all dollars raised in the past nor the average cost of dollars the firm will raise during the current year.

The weights w_d, w_{ps}, and w_{ce} are based on the firm's market value target capital structure and not on book values. Each firm has a target capital structure which minimizes its overall cost of capital, and hence maximizes stock price.

If the target capital structure for Firm A is 30 percent debt, 10 percent preferred stock, and 60 percent common equity, the firm's weighted average cost of capital, using retained earnings as the common equity component, is 13.32 percent:

$$\begin{aligned} \text{WACC} &= w_d k_d(1 - T) + w_{ps}k_{ps} + w_{ce}k_s \\ &= 0.3(12\%)(0.6) + 0.1(12.6\%) + 0.6(16.5\%) \\ &= 2.16\% + 1.26\% + 9.90\% = 13.32\%. \end{aligned}$$

The *marginal cost of capital* is defined as the cost of raising another dollar of new capital. In general, the marginal cost of any factor of production, including capital, will eventually rise as more and more of the factor is used.

Firms raise capital in accordance with their target capital structures.

As companies raise larger and larger sums during a given time period, the component costs begin to rise. This causes an increase in the weighted average cost of each additional dollar of new capital.

Suppose that a firm needs \$500,000 in new capital. Its capital structure is 60 percent common equity, 30 percent debt, and 10 percent preferred stock, and its marginal tax rate is 40 percent. The before-tax cost of debt is 14 percent, and the cost of preferred stock is 12.6 percent. The firm will need to raise 0.6(\$500,000) = \$300,000 in common equity. It expects retained earnings for the year to be \$100,000; therefore, it needs to sell \$300,000 - \$100,000 = \$200,000 of new common stock. The cost of retained earnings is 16.0 percent, but the cost of new equity is 16.8 percent. The weighted average cost of capital, using retained earnings, is:

$$\begin{aligned} \text{WACC} &= w_d k_d(1 - T) + w_{ps}k_{ps} + w_{ce}k_s \\ &= 0.3(14\%)(0.60) + 0.1(12.6\%) + 0.6(16.0\%) = 13.38\%, \end{aligned}$$

while the weighted average cost of capital, using new equity, is:

$$\begin{aligned} \text{WACC} &= w_d k_d(1 - T) + w_{ps}k_{ps} + w_{ce}k_e \\ &= 0.3(14\%)(0.60) + 0.1(12.6\%) + 0.6(16.8\%) = 13.86\%. \end{aligned}$$

The point at which the marginal cost of capital increases is called a *break point*. The retained earnings break point is calculated as Retained earnings/Equity fraction. In this example, the break point is \$100,000/0.6 = \$166,667. That is, when \$166,667 of new capital is raised, the firm will have used 0.6(\$166,667) = \$100,000 of retained earnings. After that, more costly new common equity must be used.

The marginal cost of capital (MCC) schedule shows the relationship between the cost of each dollar raised and the total amount of capital raised during the year.

The optimal capital structure is the one that produces the lowest MCC schedule.

In general, a jump, or break, will occur in the MCC schedule any time the cost of one of the components rises. Firms generally have additional break points beyond that for retained earnings. As more and more securities are issued during the year, the costs of debt, preferred stock, and new common stock will rise.

- The break point is determined by the following equation:

$$\text{Break point} = \frac{\text{Total amount of lower-cost capital of a given type}}{\text{Fraction of this type of capital in the capital structure}}.$$

- If there are no break points, there will be one MCC. If there are n break points, there will be n + 1 different MCCs.

> We have concentrated on retained earnings and new securities as the sources of capital. Actually, companies have other sources--depreciation and deferred taxes--which are often quite large.

Depreciation is a noncash expense; thus, for a profitable firm, depreciation cash flow is available for investment in fixed assets in addition to retained earnings.

- Depreciation cash flow can either be reinvested in the firm or returned to the capital suppliers. If returned, the cash flow would be used to repurchase common and preferred stock, as well as debt, so that the capital structure would not be altered. Thus, depreciation-generated funds have an opportunity cost equal to the firm's WACC prior to the retained earnings break point.
- Depreciation-generated funds push the retained earnings break point out to the right by an amount equal to the depreciation expense.

Deferred taxes arise when a firm uses accelerated depreciation for tax purposes and normal (straight line) depreciation for reporting purposes.

- Like depreciation, deferred taxes represent a noncash charge which provides a source of cash flow.

- Deferred tax cash flows also have an opportunity cost equal to the firm's WACC using retained earnings as the equity component, and they also push the retained earnings break point to the right.

Since the WACC is based strictly on the firm's target capital structure, cash flows from depreciation or deferred taxes are not included in the WACC estimate. However, these flows do affect the point at which the WACC increases.

We have generally incorporated flotation costs into the component costs of capital. The inclusion of flotation costs raises component costs, and hence increases the firm's WACC. An alternative approach to handling flotation costs is to ignore these costs when estimating the firm's WACC, but then, in the capital budgeting process, to allocate dollar flotation costs to the firm's new projects, hence increasing project costs rather than capital costs.

The alternative method amortizes flotation costs over the life of the set of projects currently being evaluated, while the conventional method amortizes flotation costs over an infinite life.

DEFINITIONAL QUESTIONS

1. A firm should calculate its cost of capital as a __________ __________ of the after-tax costs of the various capital components.

2. The cost of retained earnings is defined as the __________ _____ __________ stockholders require on the firm's common stock.

3. __________ approaches can be used to estimate the cost of retained earnings.

4. Assigning a cost to retained earnings is based on the __________ __________ principle.

5. The cost of external equity capital is higher than the cost of retained earnings because of __________ __________.

6. In using the Capital Asset Pricing Model (CAPM), the required rate of return on common stock is found as a function of the _________-____________ __________, the firm's __________ __________, and the required rate of return on an average __________.

7. The cost of retained earnings may also be found by adding a __________ __________ to the interest rate on the firm's own _________-__________ __________.

8. The cost of retained earnings may also be estimated using the DCF method which assumes that markets are in equilibrium and the __________ rate of return equals the ______________ rate of return.

9. The market value proportions of __________ and __________ in the target capital structure should be used to calculate the ________________ ________________ cost of capital.

10. Minimizing the firm's weighted average cost of capital will maximize the firm's __________ __________.

11. A plot of the WACC versus dollars of new capital raised is called the ____________ __________ ___ _______________ schedule.

12. Three commonly used betas are __________, __________, and __________ betas.

13. In estimating the WACC, the weights are based on the firm's __________ __________ target capital structure.

14. __________-________ and __________ __________ funds have a cost equal to the firm's lowest WACC.

Conceptual Questions

15. The preferred proxy for k_{RF} in the CAPM cost of equity estimate is the rate on long-term Treasury bonds, because it relates more closely to common equity costs than does the rate of return on Treasury bills.

 a. True b. False

16. The component costs of capital are based on historical, or embedded, costs.

 a. True b. False

17. The DCF method can only be used for constant growth stocks.

 a. True b. False

18. Funds acquired by the firm through perpetual preferred stock have a cost to the firm equal to the preferred dividend divided by the price investors would pay for one share.

 a. True b. False

19. Which of the following statements *could* be true concerning the costs of debt and equity?

a. The cost of debt for Firm A is greater than the cost of equity for Firm A.
b. The cost of debt for Firm A is greater than the cost of equity for Firm B.
c. The cost of retained earnings for Firm A is less than the external equity cost for Firm A.
d. The cost of retained earnings for Firm A is less than the cost of debt for Firm A.
e. Statements b and c could both be true.

PROBLEMS

20. NBC's next expected dividend, D_1, is \$2.50. The firm has maintained a constant payout ratio of 50 percent during the past 7 years. Seven years ago its EPS was \$1.50. The firm's beta coefficient is 1.2. The required return on an average stock is 13 percent, and the risk-free rate is 7 percent. NBC's A-rated bonds are yielding 10 percent, and its current stock price is \$30. Which of the following values is the most reasonable estimate of NBC's cost of retained earnings, k_s?

a. 10% **b.** 12% **c.** 14% **d.** 20% **e.** 26%

21. The director of capital budgeting for ICU Inc. manufacturers of playground equipment, is considering a plan to expand production facilities in order to meet an increase in demand. The firm's target capital structure calls for a debt/equity ratio of 0.8. ICU currently has a bond issue outstanding which will mature in 25 years and has a 7 percent annual coupon. The bonds are currently selling for \$804. The firm has maintained a constant growth rate of 6 percent. ICU's next expected dividend is \$2 and its current stock price is \$40. Its tax rate is 40 percent. What is the firm's weighted average cost of capital? (Assume that there is no preferred stock outstanding.)

a. 6.5% **b.** 7.5% **c.** 8.5% **d.** 9.5% **e.** 10.5%

22. Midterm Corporation's present capital structure, which is also its target capital structure, calls for 50 percent debt and 50 percent common equity. Midterm expects to retain \$3 million of earnings next year. It can raise new debt at a before-tax cost of 8 percent. The cost of retained earnings is 12 percent, and Midterm can sell any amount of new common stock desired at a cost of new equity of 15 percent. The firm's marginal tax rate is 40 percent. Which of the following statements are correct?

a. Midterm's WACC using retained earnings is 8.4 percent.
b. Midterm's WACC using new common stock is 9.9 percent.
c. Midterm's retained earnings break point is \$6 million.

d. All of the above statements are correct.
e. All of the above statements are incorrect.

23. The management of Florida Phosphate Industries (FPI) is estimating the firm's WACC. FPI projects net income of $10,500, and its payout ratio is 40 percent. The company's earnings and dividends are growing at a constant rate of 5 percent; the last dividend, D_0, was $0.90; and the current equilibrium stock price is $8.59. FPI can raise debt at a 12 percent before-tax cost. If FPI issues new common stock, a 10 percent flotation cost will be incurred. FPI is at its optimal capital structure, which is 40 percent debt and 60 percent equity, and the firm's marginal tax rate is 40 percent. What is FPI's cost of equity when it uses retained earnings and what is the weighted average cost of capital when it uses new common stock?

a. 16.0%; 13.2%
b. 13.2%; 16.0%
c. 12.5%; 11.0%
d. 11.0%; 12.5%
e. 16.6%; 13.2%

The following data apply to the next six problems.

The Richman Corporation's long-term debt currently yields 13 percent. It could sell preferred stock with a $10 annual dividend for $100, but flotation costs would be 5 percent. The firm's beta coefficient is 1.2, the risk-free rate is 10 percent, and the required rate of return on the market is 15 percent. Richman's next dividend is estimated to be $2.00, and it is growing at a constant 5 percent. The firm's stock is currently selling for $20.00. The firm's best estimate of the "over-own-bond" risk premium is 2.5 percentage points. Richman's target capital structure is 40 percent debt, 10 percent preferred stock, and 50 percent equity. Richman expects $40,000 in retained earnings and must incur flotation costs of 10 percent on new common stock sales. Its tax rate is 40 percent.

24. What is the firm's after-tax cost of debt?

a. 7.8% b. 10.5% c. 11.9% d. 12.5% e. 15.5%

25. What is Richman's cost of preferred stock?

a. 7.8% b. 10.5% c. 11.9% d. 12.5% e. 15.5%

26. What is the firm's cost of retained earnings? (Use all three methods.)

a. 11.9% b. 12.5% c. 15.5% d. 16.6% e. 15.0%

27. What is the firm's weighted average cost of capital using retained earnings as the equity component?

a. 11.9% b. 12.5% c. 15.5% d. 16.6% e. 17.0%

28. What is Richman's weighted average cost of capital using new common stock as the equity component?

a. 11.9% b. 12.5% c. 15.5% d. 16.6% e. 17.0%

29. Suppose the firm is forecasting $20,000 in depreciation-generated funds and an additional $5,000 in deferred taxes. What is the cost of these funds?

a. 11.9% b. 12.5% c. 15.5% d. 16.6% e. 17.0%

The following data apply to the next three problems.

Suppose the Martinez Company has this *book value* balance sheet:

Current assets	$22,500,000	Current liabilities	$ 7,500,000
Fixed assets	37,500,000	Long-term debt	22,500,000
		Common equity:	
		Common stock	
		(750,000 shares)	750,000
		Retained earnings	29,250,000
Total assets	$60,000,000	Total claims	$60,000,000

The current liabilities consist entirely of notes payable to banks, and the interest rate on this debt is 10 percent, the same as the rate on new bank loans. The long-term debt consists of 22,500 bonds, each of which has a par value of $1,000, carries an annual coupon interest rate of 6 percent, and matures in 20 years. (Interest is paid annually.) The going rate of interest on new long-term debt, k_d, is 10 percent, and this is the present yield to maturity on the bonds. The common stock sells at a price of $60 per share.

30. What is the market value of the firm's current liabilities (in millions)?

a. $7.33 b. $7.50 c. $8.25 d. $9.22 e. $10.00

31. What is the market value of the firm's common stock (in millions)?

a. $35.0 b. $40.0 c. $45.0 d. $52.5 e. $60.0

32. What is the market value of the firm's long-term debt (in millions)?

a. $23.75 b. $22.5 c. $19.90 d. $17.23 e. $14.84

ANSWERS

1. weighted average
2. rate of return
3. Three
4. opportunity cost
5. flotation costs
6. risk-free rate (k_{RF}); beta coefficient (b); stock (k_M)
7. risk premium; long-term debt
8. required (k_s); expected ($\hat{k}_s$)
9. debt; equity; weighted average
10. stock price
11. marginal cost of capital
12. historical; fundamental; adjusted
13. market value
14. Depreciation-generated; deferred tax

15. a. The rate on long-term Treasury bonds is more logically related to common equity costs.

16. b. The costs reflect the costs of current borrowing, earnings retention, or stock sales.

17. b. The method can also be used for nonconstant growth stocks, but the procedure is more involved.

18. b. Flotation costs must be subtracted from the investor's cost to get the net issuance price.

19. e. If Firm A has significantly more risk than Firm B, Firm A's cost of debt could be greater than Firm B's cost of equity. Also, the cost of retained earnings is less than the cost of external equity because of flotation costs.

20. c. Use all three methods to estimate k_s:

(1) CAPM: $k_s = k_{RF} + (k_M - k_{RF})b = 7\% + (13\% - 7\%)1.2 = 14.2\%$.

(2) Risk premium: k_s = Bond yield + Risk premium = 10% + Approximately 4% = 14%.

(3) DCF: $k_s = D_1/P_0 + g = \$2.50/\$30 + g$, where g can be estimated as follows:

$$\$0.75 = \$2.50(PVIF_{k,7});\quad PVIF_{k,7} = \$0.75/\$2.50 = 0.3000.$$

Thus k, which is the compound growth rate, g, is about 19 percent. Alternatively, using a calculator, input N = 7, PV = -0.75, PMT = 0, and FV = 2.50 to solve for I = 18.8%. Therefore, $k_s = 0.083 + 0.188 = 27.1\%$.

NBC has apparently been experiencing supernormal growth during the past 7 years, and it is not reasonable to assume that this growth will continue. The first two methods yield a k_s of about 14 percent, which appears reasonable.

21. c. Cost of equity = k_s = \$2/\$40 + 0.06 = 0.11 = 11%.

Cost of debt = k_d = Yield to maturity on outstanding issue.

$$V = I(PVIFA_{k_d,n}) + M(PVIF_{k_d,n})$$

$$\$804 = \$70(PVIFA_{k_d,25}) + \$1{,}000(PVIF_{k_d,25}).$$

Solving this gives k_d = 9%. Alternatively, using a financial calculator, input N = 25, PV = -804, PMT = 70, and FV = 1,000 to solve for I = k_d = 9%.

In determining the capital structure weights, note that debt/equity = 0.8 or, for example, 4/5. Therefore, debt/assets is

$$\frac{D}{A} = \frac{\text{Debt}}{\text{Debt} + \text{Equity}} = \frac{4}{4 + 5} = \frac{4}{9}$$

and equity/assets = 5/9. Hence, the weighted-average cost of capital is

$$\begin{aligned}(D/A)(k_d)(1 - T) + (E/A)k_s &= (4/9)(0.09)(1 - 0.4) + (5/9)(0.11)\\ &= 0.024 + 0.061 = 0.085 = 8.5\%.\end{aligned}$$

22. d. WACC = $w_d k_d(1 - T) + w_{ce}(k_s \text{ or } k_e)$

WACC (Retained earnings) = 0.5(8%)(0.6) + 0.5(12%) = 8.4%.

WACC (New common stock) = 0.5(8%)(0.6) + 0.5(15%) = 9.9%.

Now the retained earnings break point is \$3 million/0.5 = \$6 million. Thus, Midterm's overall cost of capital is 8.4 percent up to \$6 million of new capital and 9.9 percent for all new capital above \$6 million.

23. a. The cost of retained earnings is 16.0 percent:

$$k_s = \frac{D_0(1 + g)}{P_0} + g = \frac{\$0.90(1.05)}{\$8.59} + 0.05 = 0.160 = 16\%.$$

The cost of new common equity is 17.2 percent:

$$k_s = \frac{D_0(1 + g)}{P_0(1 - F)} + g = \frac{\$0.90(1.05)}{\$8.59(0.90)} + 0.05 = 17.2\%,$$

and the weighted average cost of capital using new common stock is 13.2 percent:

$$0.4(12\%)(0.6) + 0.6(17.2\%) = 13.2\%.$$

24. a. $k_d(1 - T) = 13\%(0.6) = 7.8\%$.

25. b. $k_{ps} = D_{ps}/P_n = \$10/\$95 = 10.5\%$.

26. c. CAPM: $k_s = k_{RF} + (k_M - k_{RF})b = 10\% + (15\% - 10\%)1.2 = 16.0\%$.

DCF: $k_s = \hat{k}_s = D_1/P_0 + g = \$2.00/\$20.00 + 5\% = 15.0\%$.

Bond yield plus risk premium: 13.0% + 2.5% = 15.5%.

Now judgment must be applied. Since all results are consistent, we could use a weighted average of the three methods, and conclude that $k_S = 15.5\%$.

27. a.
$$\begin{aligned} \text{WACC (RE)} &= w_d k_d(1 - T) + w_{ps}k_{ps} + w_{ce}k_s \\ &= 0.4(13\%)(0.6) + 0.1(10.5\%) + 0.5(15.5\%) = 11.9\%. \end{aligned}$$

28. b. WACC (New CS) = $w_d k_d(1 - T) + w_{ps}k_{ps} + w_{ce}k_e$.

But, we first have to estimate k_e:

$$k_e = \hat{k}_e = \frac{D_1}{P_0(1 - F)} + g = \frac{\$2.00}{\$20(0.9)} + 5\% = 16.1\%.$$

Flotation premium = k_e(DCF) - k_s(DCF) = 16.1% - 15.0% = 1.1%.

Now, add the flotation premium to the judgmental estimate of k_s:

$$k_e = 15.5\% + 1.1\% = 16.6\%.$$

Finally, use this cost in the calculation of WACC:

$$\text{WACC (New CS)} = 0.4(13.0\%)(0.6) + 0.1(10.5\%) + 0.5(16.6\%) = 12.5\%.$$

29. a. Depreciation-generated funds and cash flow from deferred taxes can be reinvested in the firm or returned to the capital suppliers (debtholders, preferred stockholders, and common stockholders). Thus, these funds have an opportunity cost equal to the firm's lowest cost of capital, or WACC (RE) = 11.9%.

30. b. The book and market value of the current liabilities are equal.

31. c. $60 × 750,000 shares = $45,000,000.

32. e. Using a financial calculator, input N = 20, I = 10, PMT = 60, and FV = 1,000 to solve for PV = $659.46 for each bond. Since there are 22,500 bonds, the market value of these bonds is $659.46 × 22,500 = $14,837,793 ≈ $14.84 million.

CHAPTER 7
CAPITAL BUDGETING DECISION METHODS

OVERVIEW

In the last chapter, we discussed the cost of capital. Now, we turn to investment decisions involving fixed assets, or capital budgeting. Here the term capital refers to fixed assets used in production, while a budget is a plan which details projected inflows and outflows during some future period. Thus, the capital budget is an outline of planned expenditures on fixed assets, and capital budgeting is the whole process of analyzing projects and deciding whether they should be included in the capital budget.

KEY CONCEPTS

A number of factors combine to make capital budgeting decisions the most important ones financial managers can make.

Since the results of capital budgeting decisions continue over an extended period, capital budgeting decisions have long-term consequences.

Capital budgeting decisions define the makeup of the firm's assets and, hence, its basic character.

Capital budgeting typically involves large expenditures and, thus, requires extensive planning both for funds acquisition and allocation.

The capital budgeting process involves the same steps that are used in security analysis.

- Cost of the project must be determined.
- Expected cash flows from the project are estimated.
- The riskiness of the projected cash flows is determined and used, along with the firm's WACC, to estimate the project's discount rate, which is called the project cost of capital.
- Cash flows are discounted to their present values.
- The present value of the expected cash flows is compared with the required outlay, or cost, of the project. If the asset's value exceeds its cost, the project should be

accepted. Otherwise, the project should be rejected.

Once cash flow estimates have been made for various projects, different methods can be used to evaluate the proposals and to decide which ones should be accepted for inclusion in the capital budget. The five primary methods used are (1) payback, (2) accounting rate of return (ARR), (3) net present value (NPV), (4) internal rate of return (IRR), and (5) profitability index (PI). A sixth method, the modified IRR (MIRR), will be discussed in a later section.

The *payback period* is defined as the number of years it takes to recover the original investment in the project. It is a type of "breakeven" calculation.

- Its major advantage is that it is easy to calculate and to understand. Its major disadvantages are as follows:
  - It ignores cash flows beyond the payback period. This penalizes long-term projects which may be vital to the firm's long-term success.
  - It ignores the time value of money by assigning equal weight to cash flows in each year during the payback period. However, the discounted payback, which uses discounted cash flows to determine the payback period, does consider the time value of money.
- In spite of its disadvantages, payback continues to be used extensively in capital budgeting decision making. However, it is not used as a primary decision tool, but rather as an indicator of a project's liquidity and risk.

The *accounting rate of return (ARR)* focuses on a project's contribution to the firm's net income rather than its cash flow.

- The ARR is measured as the ratio of the project's average annual expected net income to its average investment.
- Like the regular payback method, the ARR ignores the time value of money. Since none of these procedures provides adequate information on the project's contribution to the firm's value, they could all lead to incorrect capital budgeting decisions.

The *net present value (NPV)* method of evaluating investment proposals is a discounted cash flow (DCF) technique that accounts for the time value of all cash flows from a project.

- The NPV is defined as

$$NPV = \sum_{t=0}^{n} \frac{CF_t}{(1+k)^t}.$$

  Here CF_t is the expected net cash flow in Period t, and k is the project's periodic cost of capital. Project costs, or cash outflows, are treated as negative cash flows and cash inflows are treated as positive flows.
- If the NPV is positive, the project should be accepted; if negative, it should be

rejected.

- If two projects are mutually exclusive (that is, only one can be accepted), the one with the higher NPV should be chosen, assuming that the NPV is positive. If both projects have negative NPVs, neither should be chosen.
- The NPV method is typically regarded by academicians as the best single method because it focuses on the contribution of the project to shareholder wealth. A positive NPV means that an excess exists after the capital contributors have recovered their investments and earned their required rates of return, and this excess accrues solely to the equity holders.

The *internal rate of return (IRR)* is defined as the discount rate that equates the present value of the expected future cash inflows to the present value of the outflows.

- The equation for calculating the IRR is

$$NPV = \sum_{t=0}^{n} \frac{CF_t}{(1 + IRR)^t} = 0.$$

  This is an equation with one unknown, IRR, and we can solve for the value of IRR that forces the equation to equal zero. The solution value is defined as the internal rate of return.
- The IRR formula is simply the NPV formula solved for the particular discount rate that causes the NPV to equal zero.
- The IRR can be found by trial and error, but most financial calculators and computers with financial analysis software can easily calculate IRRs and NPVs.
- Whereas the NPV measures the dollar profitability of a project, the IRR measures the percentage profitability of a project. In effect, the IRR is a project's expected rate of return.
- If the IRR is greater than the project cost of capital, then the project should be accepted; if the IRR is less than the cost of capital, it should be rejected.
- If two projects are mutually exclusive, the IRR rule indicates that the one with the higher IRR should be chosen, assuming that the IRR is greater than the cost of capital.
- Note that the IRR gives some indication of the "safety margin" of a project--a project with an IRR that is far above its cost of capital can tolerate cash flows well below those expected and still be profitable.

Another method that is used to evaluate projects is the *profitability index (PI),* or the benefit/cost ratio, as it is sometimes called.

- The profitability index is defined as

$$PI = \frac{\text{PV benefits}}{\text{PV costs}} = \frac{\sum_{t=0}^{n} \frac{CIF_t}{(1+k)^t}}{\sum_{t=0}^{n} \frac{COF_t}{(1+k)^t}}.$$

  Here CIF_t represents the expected cash inflow in Period t, while COF_t represents the expected cash outflow, or cost, in Period t.
- A project is acceptable if its PI is greater than 1.0, and the higher the PI, the higher is the project's ranking.
- The PI measures a project's relative dollar profitability, or its "bang for the buck."
- Note that, like the IRR, a high PI indicates a high "margin of safety."

So far, we have discussed five possible decision methods.
- Both the payback method and accounting rate of return method have several faults and should not be used as the sole criteria in making capital budgeting decisions.
- The NPV, IRR, and PI methods all recognize time value, all consider the complete set of project cash flows, and all lead to the same accept/reject decisions for independent projects. Thus, any of these methods can be used to choose among independent projects. However, these three methods can give conflicting rankings for mutually exclusive projects.

The net present value profile, which is a plot of a project's NPV versus the discount rate, is a useful tool both in project analysis and in understanding the differences between the NPV and IRR methods.

The NPV profile crosses the Y axis at the undiscounted NPV, while the profile crosses the X axis at the IRR rate.

If two mutually exclusive projects have NPV profiles which intersect in the upper righthand quadrant, then there may be a conflict in rankings between the NPV and IRR methods.

Conflicts can occur under two circumstances.
- The projects differ in scale; that is, one project costs $100,000 while a mutually exclusive project costs $1 million.
- The projects differ in cash flow timing; that is, one project has larger cash flows in its early years, while the other has larger cash flows in its later years. Note that cash flow timing does not refer to project life, but rather to the relative sizes of the flows. Differences in project lives are discussed in the next chapter.

The underlying cause of conflicts in project rankings lies in differing reinvestment rate assumptions.

- The NPV method implicitly assumes that project cash flows are reinvested at the project's cost of capital.
- The IRR method implicitly assumes that project cash flows are reinvested at the project's IRR.
- The opportunity cost of a project's cash flows is the project's cost of capital. If a project's cash inflows were not available to the firm, and if the firm had good investment opportunities, then the funds would be obtained from the firm's capital suppliers, and the cost would be the overall cost of capital. Thus, the assumption of reinvestment at the cost of capital is the correct assumption, and NPV is superior to IRR.

There can also be ranking conflicts between the NPV and PI decision rules. All conflicts should be resolved in favor of the project with the highest NPV.

The conflicts between NPV and IRR, and between NPV and PI, only affect the decisions on mutually exclusive projects. All three methods lead to the same accept/reject decisions on independent projects. Thus, the IRR or PI method can be used in place of the NPV method when evaluating independent projects. (We will use the IRR rule when we find the optimal capital budget.) However, when evaluating mutually exclusive projects, NPV should be used.

A *normal* capital project is one that has one or more cash outflows followed by a series of cash inflows. If, however, a project calls for a large cash outflow either sometime during or at the end of its life, then it is a *nonnormal* project.

Nonnormal projects can present three unique difficulties when evaluated by the IRR criterion: (1) The IRR criterion can lead to an improper decision. (2) The project may have no IRR. (3) The project may have multiple IRRs.

In cases such as these, the NPV criterion can be easily applied, and this method leads to conceptually correct capital budgeting decisions. Also, the MIRR method overcomes the problems inherent in nonnormal projects.

Business executives often prefer to work with percentage rates of return, such as IRR, rather than dollar amounts of NPV. The *modified IRR,* or MIRR, overcomes many of the IRR's disadvantages.

The MIRR is defined as the discount rate which forces

$$\text{PV costs} = \text{PV terminal value},$$

where *terminal value (TV)* is the future value of the inflows. Thus,

$$\sum_{t=0}^{n} \frac{COF_t}{(1+k)^t} = \frac{\sum_{t=0}^{n} CIF_t(1+k)^{n-t}}{(1+MIRR)^n}.$$

$$PV\ costs = \frac{TV}{(1+MIRR)^n}.$$

The MIRR forces cash flow reinvestment at the cost of capital rather than the project's own IRR, making it a better indicator of a project's true profitability.

NPV and MIRR will lead to the same project selection decision for mutually exclusive projects if the two projects are of equal size. However, conflicts between NPV and MIRR can still occur when projects differ in scale, and when this occurs NPV should be used.

MIRR also avoids the problem of multiple IRRs, which can arise when a project is nonnormal. NPV can be easily applied to such situations, but MIRR can also overcome the multiple IRR problem, because there is but one MIRR for any set of cash flows.

The modified IRR is superior to the regular IRR as an indicator of a project's "true" rate of return, or "expected long-term rate of return," but the NPV method is still better for choosing among competing projects that differ in scale, because it provides a better indicator of how much each project increases the value of the firm.

Firms often choose between mutually exclusive projects on the basis of the present value of future costs rather than on the basis of the projects' NPVs or MIRRs.

If the mutually exclusive projects will generate the same revenues, then they can be evaluated on the basis of their costs.

In this situation, each project's costs would be placed on a time line, and the project with the lower (or lowest) present value of costs should be selected.

We have presented six potential capital budgeting decision methods in this chapter, and each has its own set of advantages and disadvantages.

Today, virtually all capital budgeting decisions of importance are analyzed by computer, and hence it is relatively easy to calculate the values for all six methods.

In making the ultimate accept/reject decision, most sophisticated managers would consider all of the measures, because each measure provides a somewhat different piece of relevant information.

If capital costs are expected to change over time, and we can forecast these changes, then the NPV should be calculated using multiple costs of capital.

A project's acceptability can be reversed by changing capital costs.

If capital costs are nonconstant, the rate to which the IRR must be compared to determine project acceptability is unclear, but it would probably be an average of expected future costs.

These points reinforce the preference for the NPV method over the IRR method.

Predicting future capital costs is a difficult undertaking, so firms normally use today's capital costs as the best estimate of future capital costs, and this results in a constant cost of capital for capital budgeting purposes.

DEFINITIONAL QUESTIONS

1. A firm's _________ __________ outlines its planned expenditures on fixed assets.

2. The most difficult step in the analysis of capital expenditure proposals involves estimating future __________ __________.

3. The number of years necessary to return the original investment in a project is known as the ___________ ___________.

4. The primary advantage of payback analysis is its _____________.

5. One important weakness of payback analysis is the fact that _________ ___________ beyond the payback period are _____________.

6. The net present value (NPV) method of evaluating investment proposals is a ____________ cash flow (DCF) technique.

7. A capital investment proposal should be accepted if its NPV is ______________.

8. If two projects are ____________ _____________, the one with the __________ positive NPV should be selected.

9. In the IRR approach, a discount rate is sought which forces the project's NPV to equal ______.

10. The profitability index is also called the __________/______ ratio.

11. A net present value profile shows the relationship between a project's _______ and the _____________ ______ used to calculate the NPV.

12. If a project's ______ is greater than the project's cost of capital, it should be accepted.

13. If a project's _____________ ______ is greater than 1.0, it should be accepted.

14. If two mutually exclusive projects are being evaluated, and one project has a higher, positive NPV while the other project has a higher IRR, the project with the higher, positive ______ should be chosen.

15. The NPV method implicitly assumes reinvestment at the project's _______ _____ ___________, while the IRR method implicitly assumes reinvestment at the _____________ ______ ______ ________________.

16. The MIRR method assumes reinvestment at the __________ _____ __________, making it a better indicator of a project's profitability than IRR.

17. The internal rate of return (IRR) is that ____________ rate which equates the present value of a project's ___________ ___________ with the present value of its __________ ____________.

Conceptual Questions

18. The NPV of a project with cash flows that accrue relatively slowly is more sensitive to changes in the discount rate than is the NPV of a project with cash flows that come in more rapidly.

   a. True **b.** False

19. The NPV method is preferred over the IRR method because the NPV method's reinvestment rate assumption is better.

   a. True **b.** False

20. When you find the yield to maturity on a bond, you are finding the bond's NPV.

a. True b. False

21. Other things held constant, a decrease in the cost of capital (discount rate) will cause an increase in a project's IRR.

a. True b. False

22. The IRR method can be used in place of the NPV method for all independent projects.

a. True b. False

23. The NPV and MIRR methods lead to the same decision for mutually exclusive projects regardless of the projects' relative sizes.

a. True b. False

24. Nonnormal projects sometimes have multiple MIRRs.

a. True b. False

PROBLEMS

25. Your firm is considering a fast-food concession at the upcoming World's Fair. The cash flow pattern is somewhat unusual since you must build the stands, operate them for 2 years, and then tear the stands down and restore the site to its original condition. You estimate the net cash flows to be as follows:

Year	Expected Net Cash Flow
0	($800,000)
1	700,000
2	700,000
3	(400,000)

What is the approximate IRR of this venture?

a. 5% b. 15% c. 25% d. 35% e. 45%

The following data apply to the next three problems.

Toy Motors needs a new machine for production of its forthcoming models. The financial vice president has appointed you to do the capital budgeting analysis. You have identified two different machines that are capable of performing the job. You have completed the cash flow analysis, and the expected net cash flows are as follows:

	Expected Net Cash Flow	
Year	Machine B	Machine O
0	($5,000)	($5,000)
1	2,085	0
2	2,085	0
3	2,085	0
4	2,085	9,677

26. What is the payback period for Machine B?

a. 1.0 years **b.** 2.0 years **c.** 2.4 years **d.** 2.6 years **e.** 3.0 years

27. The cost of capital is uncertain at this time, so you construct NPV profiles to assist in the final decision. The profiles for Machines B and O cross at what cost of capital?

a. 6% **b.** 10% **c.** 18% **d.** 24%
e. They do not cross in the upper righthand quadrant.

28. If the cost of capital for both projects is 14 percent at the time the decision is made, which project would you choose?

a. Project B; it has the higher positive NPV.
b. Project 0; it has the higher positive NPV.
c. Neither; both have negative NPVs.
d. Either; both have the same NPV.
e. Project B; it has the higher IRR.

The following data apply to the next six problems.

The director of capital budgeting for Giant Inc. has identified two mutually exclusive projects, L and S, with the following expected net cash flows:

Year	Expected Net Cash Flow Project L	Project S
0	($100)	($100)
1	10	70
2	60	50
3	80	20

Both projects have a cost of capital of 10 percent.

29. What is the payback period for Project S?

a. 1.6 years **b.** 1.8 years **c.** 2.1 years **d.** 2.5 years **e.** 2.8 years

30. What is Project L's NPV?

a. $50.00 **b.** $34.25 **c.** $22.64 **d.** $18.79 **e.** $10.06

31. What is Project S's PI?

a. 0.96 **b.** 1.03 **c.** 1.12 **d.** 1.15 **e.** 1.20

32. What is Project L's IRR?

a. 18.1% **b.** 19.7% **c.** 21.4% **d.** 23.6% **e.** 24.2%

33. What is Project L's MIRR?

a. 15.3% **b.** 16.5% **c.** 16.9% **d.** 17.1% **e.** 17.4%

34. Plot the NPV profiles for the two projects. Where is the crossover point?

a. 6.9% **b.** 7.8% **c.** 8.7% **d.** 9.6% **e.** 9.9%

ANSWERS

1. capital budget
2. cash flows
3. payback period
4. simplicity
5. cash flows; ignored
6. discounted
7. positive
8. mutually exclusive; higher
9. zero
10. benefit; cost
11. NPV; discount rate
12. IRR
13. profitability index
14. NPV
15. cost of capital; internal rate of return
16. cost of capital

17. discount; cash inflows; cash outflows

18. a. The more the cash flows are spread over time, the greater is the effect of a change in discount rate. This is because the compounding process has a greater effect as the number of years increases.

19. a. Project cash flows are substitutes for outside capital. Thus, the opportunity cost of these flows is the firm's cost of capital, adjusted for risk. The NPV method uses this cost as the reinvestment rate, while the IRR method assumes reinvestment at the IRR.

20. b. The yield to maturity on a bond is the bond's IRR.

21. b. A project's IRR is independent of its cost of capital.

22. a. Both the NPV and IRR methods lead to the same accept/reject decisions for independent projects. Thus, the IRR method can be used as a proxy for the NPV method when choosing independent projects.

23. b. NPV and MIRR may not lead to the same decision when the projects differ in scale.

24. b. Multiple IRRs occur in nonnormal projects, but there is only one MIRR for each project.

25. c. Unless you have a calculator that performs IRR calculations, the IRR must be obtained by trial and error or graphically. (The calculator solution is 25.48 percent.) Note that this project actually has multiple IRRs, with a second IRR at about -53 percent.

26. c. After Year 1, there is \$5,000 - \$2,085 = \$2,915 remaining to pay back. After Year 2, only \$2,915 - \$2,085 = \$830 is remaining. In Year 3, another \$2,085 is collected. Assuming that the Year 3 cash flow occurs evenly over time, then payback occurs \$830/\$2,085 = 0.4 of the way through Year 3. Thus, the payback period is 2.4 years.

27. b. To solve graphically, construct the NPV profiles:

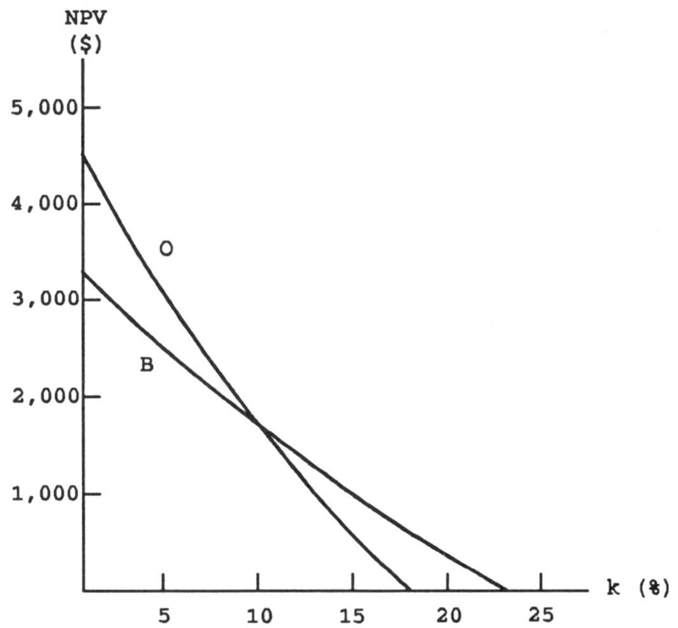

The Y intercept is the NPV when k = 0%. For B, 4($2,085) - $5,000 = $3,340. For O, $9,677 - $5,000 = $4,677. The X intercept is the discount rate when NPV = $0, or the IRR. For B, $5,000 = $2,085($PVIFA_{IRR,4}$); IRR ≈ 24%. For O, $5,000 = $9,677($PVIF_{IRR,4}$); IRR ≈ 18%. The graph is an approximation since we are only using two points to plot lines that are curvilinear. However, it shows that there is a crossover point and that it occurs somewhere in the vicinity of k = 10%. To find the exact value, create a Project D (for delta) which is the difference in the cash flows between the projects.

Year	B	O	Project D (B − O)
0	($5,000)	($5,000)	$ 0
1	2,085	0	2,085
2	2,085	0	2,085
3	2,085	0	2,085
4	2,085	9,677	(7,592)

The IRR of Project D, 10.00 percent, is the crossover point.

28. a. Refer to the NPV profiles. When k = 14%, we are to the right of the crossover point and Project B has the higher NPV. You can verify this fact by calculating the NPVs. NPV_B = $1,075 and NPV_O = $730. Note that Project B also has the higher IRR. However, the

NPV method should be used when evaluating mutually exclusive projects. Note that had the project cost of capital been 8 percent, then Project O would be chosen on the basis of the higher NPV.

29. a. After the first year, there is only \$30 remaining to be repaid, and \$50 is received in Year 2. Assuming an even cash flow throughout the year, the payback period is 1 + \$30/\$50 = 1.6 years.

30. d. $NPV_L = -\$100 + \$10/1.10 + \$60/(1.10)^2 + \$80/(1.10)^3$
$= -\$100 + \$9.09 + \$49.59 + \$60.11 = \$18.79.$

31. e. The present value of the cash outflow is \$100/1.00 = \$100. The present value of the cash inflows is $\$70/1.10 + \$50/(1.10)^2 + \$20/(1.10)^3 = \$63.64 + \$41.32 + \$15.03 = \$119.99$. Thus, the profitability index is \$119.99/\$100 = 1.20.

32. a. We used a calculator to find $IRR_L = 18.1\%$.

33. b.

$$\text{Cost} = \frac{TV}{(1 + MIRR)^n} = \frac{\sum_{t=1}^{n} CIF_t(1 + k)^{n-t}}{(1 + MIRR)^n}.$$

$$\$100 = \frac{\$10(1.10)^2 + \$60(1.10)^1 + \$80(1.10)^0}{(1 + MIRR)^3} = \frac{\$12.10 + \$66.00 + \$80.00}{(1 + MIRR)^3} = \frac{\$158.10}{(1 + MIRR)^3}.$$

$MIRR_L = 16.50\%.$

34. c. The NPV profiles plot as follows:

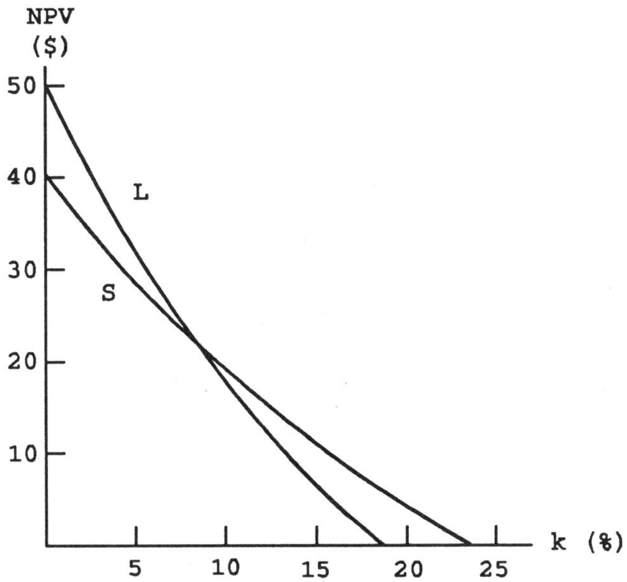

k	NPV_L	NPV_S
0%	$50	$40
5	33	29
10	19	20
15	7	12
20	(4)	5
25	(13)	(2)

Now to find the precise crossover point, determine the cash flows for Project D, which is the difference between the project's cash flows:

Year	L	S	Project D (L - S)
0	($100)	($100)	$ 0
1	10	70	(60)
2	60	50	10
3	80	20	60

The crossover point is the IRR of Project D, or 8.7 percent.

CHAPTER 8
PROJECT CASH FLOW ANALYSIS

OVERVIEW

The basic capital budgeting decision methods were covered in Chapter 7. However, we assumed that the project cash flows were known, so we ignored the most difficult step in capital budgeting -- project cash flow analysis. Now, we examine some cash flow analysis issues, including (1) cash flow estimation, (2) replacement decisions, (3) cash flow estimation bias, (4) managerial option value, (5) mutually exclusive projects with unequal lives, (6) abandonment value, (7) inflation effects, and (8) alternative methods for calculating NPV.

KEY CONCEPTS

The most important step in project analysis is estimating the cash flows. The key concept in the process is to consider only *incremental cash flows*, which are defined as the difference between the firm's cash flows if the project were undertaken and the firm's cash flows without the project.

Cash flow must be distinguished from *accounting income.*

- *Operating cash flow* is, in general, a project's operating income plus depreciation.
- Alternatively, a project's net operating cash flow in any given year can be calculated as

$$NOCF = (R - C)(1 - T) + TD,$$

where R = incremental project revenues, C = incremental project operating costs (less depreciation), T = marginal tax rate, and D = incremental depreciation expense.
- *Interest expense* is not included in a project's operating cash flows, because capital costs are included in the project cost of capital, the discount rate.

In financial analysis, one must be careful to account properly for the timing of cash flows.

In theory, *cash flows* should be forecasted for the entire life of the project; however, for most projects it is very difficult to estimate cash flows beyond the near term.

Many companies have capital budgeting guidelines that limit cash flow forecasts to a set number of years. When cash flows are arbitrarily truncated in the estimation process, there are two approaches to handling the omitted flows:

- All flows beyond the truncation point can be ignored.
- A salvage value can be included in the final year's cash flows that attempts to capture the value of the project at that point in time.

There are three aspects of cash flow estimation which can present problems.

- A *sunk cost* is an outlay that has already occurred or has been committed. Sunk costs are not incremental and hence should not be included in the analysis.
- All relevant *opportunity costs* must be included in the analysis. For example, GM already owns a piece of land suitable for the plant. If the firm were analyzing a project for that land, it must include the current net market value of the land as an opportunity cost. If the project were not undertaken, GM would have the opportunity to sell the land. Note that the relevant opportunity cost is the current net market value, and not the price GM paid to acquire the land.
- The analysis must include *externalities*, which are the effects of a proposed project on the firm's existing projects. If the introduction of a new liquid detergent would reduce sales of a firm's existing line of powder detergents, then the sales reduction must be included in the analysis.

Tax effects can have a major impact on cash flows, and in many cases tax effects can make or break a project. Therefore, it is critical that taxes be dealt with properly when a project's cash flows are being analyzed.

For tax purposes, an asset's depreciation expense is calculated using the *Modified Accelerated Cost Recovery System (MACRS).*

- Assets are categorized into one of several MACRS *recovery periods*.
- Then, the depreciation expense in each year is found by multiplying the asset's depreciable basis by the appropriate recovery allowance percentage. Here are the MACRS recovery allowance percentages for personal property:

	Investment Class			
Year	3-Year	5-Year	7-Year	10-Year
1	33%	20%	14%	10%
2	45	32	25	18
3	15	19	17	14
4	7	12	13	12
5		11	9	9
6		6	9	7
7			9	7
8			4	7
9				7
10				6
11				3

- Under MACRS, the assumption is generally made that property is placed in service in the middle of the first year. Then, the remaining half-year's depreciation is taken at the end. Thus, a 3-year recovery period asset is depreciated over 4 years, and so on.
- The *depreciable basis* is the price of the asset, plus any shipping and installation charges. Note that, under MACRS, the depreciable basis is not reduced by the asset's expected salvage value.

When a depreciable asset is sold, the actual sales price (the realized salvage value) minus the then-existing book value is added to operating income and taxed at the firm's marginal tax rate.

Normally, additional inventories are required to support a new project, and expanded sales also produce additional accounts receivable, both of which must be financed. However, accounts payable and accruals may also increase, and these increases would tend to offset the increases in inventories and receivables.

The difference between the projected increase in current assets and the projected increase in current liabilities is the *projected change in net working capital.*

If the change is positive, additional financing above that required for fixed assets is required, and is added to the project's initial outlay.

Conversely, if the change is negative, the project is generating a cash inflow from working capital changes, and this would reduce the project's initial outlay.

The cash flow analysis on an expansion, or new, project consists of three types of cash flows.

Consider the cash flows which occur at the time the investment is made; we generally call this time t = 0, or Time 0. (For simplicity, we assume that all investment outflows occur at Time 0.)

- Record the purchase price of the asset, plus any transportation and installation costs.
- Show any changes in net working capital.
- The net of these items is the project's Time 0 net investment outlay.

Now consider the future cash flows from operations.

- First, look at the effects of the new equipment on revenues and costs. An incremental increase in revenues would produce a cash inflow, while an incremental increase in costs would produce a cash outflow.
- Then, the depreciation expense in each year must be calculated, and taxes applied.
- The operating cash flows in each year can be structured like an income statement, but without interest expense. Here, the net operating cash flow equals Operating income + Depreciation. Alternatively, the net operating cash flow can be found as the after-tax revenue/cost component, (R - C)(1 - T), plus the depreciation tax savings, TD.

Next, consider the additional cash flows which are projected to occur at the end of the project's life.

- The salvage value represents a cash inflow in the final year. However, any tax effects must also be included.
- Any net working capital change that occurred at Time 0 is offset now. For example, if the project had an increase in net working capital and hence an outflow at Time 0, an equal inflow would be recorded at the end of the project.

Finally, place all the cash flows for each year on a time line and sum to estimate the net cash flows. These are then used to determine the project's NPV, IRR, MIRR, and so on.

The analysis becomes slightly more involved if cash outflows (investment costs) occur over more than one year, but the principles remain the same.

Replacement decision analysis is somewhat more complicated than that for expansion projects, because there are additional cash flows involved.

The following additional cash flows must be considered at Time 0:

- The cash received from the sale of the old equipment is an inflow.
- However, the sale of the old machine will usually have tax effects. If the old equipment is sold below book value, there will be a tax savings; otherwise, taxes must be paid. The tax effect is equal to the loss or gain times the firm's marginal tax rate.

The cash flow from operations calculation must also be modified.

- First, look at the effects of the new equipment on revenues and costs. An incremental increase in revenues would produce a cash inflow, while an incremental increase in costs would produce a cash outflow, just as before. But, the incremental flows must be based on the flows generated by the old asset. After combining the revenue and cost effects into a single incremental cash inflow, multiply by (1 - T) to obtain the after-tax cash inflow.
- The depreciation expense on the new equipment must be compared with the depreciation expense on the old equipment to get the net change in depreciation. This amount is then multiplied by the tax rate to find the tax savings or loss from the change in depreciation.
- Any salvage value on the old machine, including tax effects, must be included as a cash outflow at the end of the old project's life. Accepting the new project causes the firm to forego the old machine's salvage value. Thus, it must be included as an opportunity cost. Of course, any salvage value on the new machine must also be included in the analysis as an inflow, net of taxes.

The analysis here assumes that the replacement project has the same expected life as the expected life of the old machine. If this is not true, an adjustment must be made to account for differing project lives.

> There is a good deal of evidence that suggests that capital budgeting cash flow forecasts are biased; that is, managers tend to be overly optimistic in their forecasts, and, as a result, revenues tend to be systematically overstated and costs tend to be understated.

If bias exists, then the acceptance of a project with a zero estimated NPV will likely result in a realized loss and, hence, a decrease in shareholders' wealth.

A first step to recognizing cash flow estimation bias, especially in projects which are highly profitable, is to ask this question: What is the underlying cause of this project's high profitability?

- If the firm has some inherent advantage in the marketplace, such as patent protection or unique production or marketing expertise, then projects which utilize this advantage may truly be extraordinarily profitable.

- However, in the long run, profitability will probably be eroded by competition, and hence project returns will be driven down to a normal level, which is equal to the firm's cost of capital.

If management believes that cash flow estimation bias exists, and historical performance can be used as an indicator, then those managers' estimates should be adjusted, either by raising the cost of capital or by lowering the cash flow estimates.

Cash flow estimation bias can cause a project's profitability to be overstated, but failure to recognize a project's *managerial options* can cause the project's profitability to be understated.

A project's *managerial option value* is the value of future investment opportunities (future projects) that can only be undertaken if the project currently under consideration is accepted.

A project's managerial option value can be thought of as a call option, and hence option valuation could be applied. However, this is a very difficult process in the real world. Thus, strategic value, the value of a managerial option that involves a company's strategic entry into new products or markets, which increases the value of a project above its calculated NPV, is generally treated subjectively.

If two mutually exclusive projects have different lives, the analysis must compare the projects over a common life.

The *replacement chain (common life)* technique extends one, or both, projects until an equal life is achieved.

- Suppose two mutually exclusive projects are being considered--Project A, with a 2-year life, and Project B, with a 3-year life.
- The projects would be extended to 6 years.
- Project A would have an adjusted NPV equal to the NPV_A plus the NPV_A discounted for 2 years at the project's cost of capital plus the NPV_A discounted for 4 years at the project's cost of capital.
- Project B would have an adjusted NPV equal to the NPV_B plus the NPV_B discounted for 3 years at the project's cost of capital.
- The project with the higher adjusted NPV would be chosen.

Another way to deal with unequal lives is the *equivalent annual annuity (EAA)* method.

- Find each project's NPV over its original life.

- Find the constant annuity cash flow (the equivalent annual annuity) over the life of each project that has the same present value as its NPV. With a financial calculator you would enter the project's original NPV = PV, life = N, k = I, and solve for EAA = PMT.
- The project with the higher NPV would be chosen. Obviously, the project with the higher EAA will have the higher NPV over any common horizon, as long as both projects have the same riskiness and, hence, the same project cost of capital. (The project with the higher EAA will have the higher NPV because each project's common life NPV is simply the present value of its EAA stream.)

As a general rule, the unequal life issue does not arise for independent projects. Also, common life techniques can only be applied when the shorter-life project is actually expected to be replicated.

A serious weakness of the analysis techniques discussed is that changing revenues and/or costs have not been considered. These complications are handled by building the new revenue/cost estimates directly into the cash flow estimates and then using the replacement chain approach.

Thus far, all the capital budgeting examples have been based on a well-defined economic life. However, in most situations, the economic life, or that life which maximizes the project's NPV, is not the same as the physical life of the project. The concept of abandonment value recognizes that abandonment of a project before the end of its physical life can have a significant impact on the project's profitability and risk.

Abandonment value should be considered in the capital budgeting process because there are cases in which recognition of abandonment can make an otherwise unacceptable project acceptable.

Two very different types of abandonment can occur:

- Sale by the original user of a still-valuable asset to some other party who can extract more value from the asset.
- Abandonment of an asset because the project is losing money.

When inflation occurs, the analysis must either explicitly adjust for inflation or treat all variables in real terms.

Investors recognize that inflation erodes purchasing power; they demand an inflation premium in addition to the real required rate of return, and hence they consider expected inflation rates when setting required rates of return. Thus, a firm's market-determined overall cost of capital is a nominal rate.

- Inflation can be explicitly considered in capital budgeting analysis by expressing all cash flows in nominal terms (CF_t) and then using the nominal cost of capital:

$$NPV = \sum_{t=0}^{n} \frac{CF_t}{(1 + k_n)^t}.$$

- The same result can be obtained by expressing all cash flows in real terms (RCF_t) and then by using the real cost of capital:

$$NPV = \sum_{t=0}^{n} \frac{RCF_t}{(1 + k_r)^t}.$$

To produce an unbiased NPV, this second approach requires (1) that all project cash flows, including depreciation, be affected identically by inflation and (2) that this rate of increase equals the inflation rate built into investors' required returns.

Occasionally, the procedures set forth above are violated; that is, real, or constant dollar, cash flows that are not adjusted for inflation are used with the nominal cost of capital. If this occurs, the calculated NPV will be biased downward.

In practice, it is best to express the cash flows in nominal dollars; that is, to include inflation effects in the cash flow estimates and then to discount by the nominal cost of capital. This procedure is preferred because it allows various cash flow components to be adjusted at differing inflation rates.

Inflation adds to the uncertainty, or riskiness, of capital budgeting as well as to its complexity.

DEFINITIONAL QUESTIONS

1. An increase in net working capital would show up as a cash ______ at Time 0, and then again as a cash ______ at the ______ of the project's life.

2. A _______ _______ is a cash outlay which has already occurred or has been committed.

3. In general, a project's operating cash flow in any year is equal to the project's ______ ______ plus its ______ expense.

4. In replacement analysis, two cash flows that occur at t = 0 that are not present in expansion projects are the price received from the sale of the ______ equipment and the ______ effects of the sale.

5. In replacement analysis, the depreciation tax savings or loss is based on the ____________ in depreciation expense between the old and new asset.

6. If two projects are __________, the fact that they have unequal lives will not affect the analysis.

7. If two mutually exclusive projects have unequal lives, either the __________ ______ or __________ ___________ ____________ method may be used for the analysis.

8. In dealing with inflation in capital budgeting, cash flows and cost of capital must both be in _____________ terms or both be in ______ terms.

9. If the cash flows are real, but the cost of capital is nominal, there will be a ____________ bias to the calculated NPV.

10. An ______________ cash flow represents the change in the firm's total cash flow that occurs as a direct result of project acceptance.

CONCEPTUAL QUESTIONS

11. In general, the value of land currently owned by a firm is irrelevant to a capital budgeting decision because the cost of that property is a sunk cost.

    a. True **b.** False

12. McDonald's is planning to open a new location across from the student union. Annual revenues are expected to be $5 million. However, opening the new location will cause annual revenues to drop by $3 million at McDonald's existing stadium location. The relevant revenues for the capital budgeting analysis are $2 million per year.

a. True b. False

13. In a replacement decision, the salvage value of the old asset need not be considered since the current market value of the asset is included in the analysis.

a. True b. False

14. Abandoning a project before the end of its useful physical life may result in a higher NPV for the project.

a. True b. False

PROBLEMS

The following data apply to the next two problems.

Buckeye Foundries builds railroad cars and then leases them to railroads and shippers. The company has some old boxcars which it plans to convert into specialized carriers. Its analysts foresee demand in two areas--cars to carry coal and cars to carry livestock. Each type of car will cost $50,000 per car to convert. Because of the greater weight they will carry, the coal cars will last only 10 years but will provide an after-tax cash flow of $9,500 per year. The livestock cars will last for 15 years, and their annual after-tax cash flow is estimated at $8,140. Buckeye's cost of capital is 10 percent. At the end of each car's original life, it can be rebuilt into "like new" condition at a cost expected to equal the original conversion cost. Also, since Buckeye has only a limited number of cars to convert, regard the two types of cars as being mutually exclusive.

15. Using the replacement chain method of evaluation, find the adjusted NPV for each alternative.

a. $8,373; $11,913
b. $8,373; $14,765
c. $8,373; $16,212
d. $12,846; $11,913
e. $12,846; $14,765

16. Which alternative should be taken according to the equivalent annual annuity method?

a. Livestock cars, since their EAA is $11,913.
b. Coal cars, since their EAA is $8,373.
c. Livestock cars, since their EAA of $1,566 is $203 greater than the EAA of coal cars, which is equal to $1,363.
d. Coal cars, since their EAA is $1,363 which is $100 greater than the EAA of livestock cars, which is equal to $1,263.
e. Neither project should be accepted, as they both have negative NPVs.

17. The capital budgeting director of National Products Inc. is evaluating a new project that would decrease operating costs by $30,000 per year without affecting revenues. The project's cost is $50,000. The project will be depreciated using the MACRS method over its 3-year life. It will have a zero salvage value after 3 years. The marginal tax rate of National Products is 40 percent, and the project's cost of capital is 12 percent. What is the project's NPV?

a. $7,068 b. $8,324 c. $9,432 d. $10,214 e. $12,387

18. Your firm has a marginal tax rate of 40 percent and a cost of capital of 14 percent. You are performing a capital budgeting analysis on a new project that will cost $500,000. The project is expected to have a useful life of 10 years, although its MACRS class life is only 5 years. The project is expected to increase the firm's net income by $61,257 per year and to have a salvage value of $35,000 at the end of 10 years. What is the project's NPV?

a. $48,257 b. $81,359 c. $105,000 d. $132,451 e. $177,902

19. The Board of Directors of Midwest Brewing Inc. is considering the acquisition of a new still. The still is priced at $600,000 but would require $60,000 in transportation costs and $40,000 for installation. The still has a useful life of 10 years but will be depreciated over its 5-year MACRS life. It is expected to have a salvage value of $10,000 at the end of 10 years. The still would increase revenues by $120,000 per year and increase yearly operating costs by $20,000 per year. Additionally, the still would require a $30,000 increase in net working capital. The firm's marginal tax rate is 40 percent, and the project's cost of capital is 10 percent. What is the NPV of the still?

a. $60,892 b. $18,430 c. -$35,821 d. -$130,961 e. -$203,450

The following data apply to the next three problems.

As the capital budgeting director of Union Mills Inc., you are analyzing the replacement of an automated loom system. The old system was purchased 5 years ago for $200,000; it has been depreciated to a zero book value; and it has 5 years of remaining life and a $50,000 salvage value. The market value of the old system is $100,000. The new system has a price of $300,000, plus an additional $50,000 in installation costs. The new system falls into the MACRS 5-year class, has a 5-year economic life, and a $100,000 salvage value. The new system will require a $40,000 increase in the spare parts inventory. The primary advantage of the new system is that it will decrease operating costs by $40,000 per year. Union Mills has a 12 percent cost of capital and a marginal tax rate of 40 percent.

20. What is the net cash investment at Year 0?

a. $350,000 **b.** $340,000 **c.** $330,000 **d.** $40,000 **e.** $23,200

21. What is the annual net operating cash inflow in Year 1?

a. $52,000 **b.** $40,000 **c.** $36,750 **d.** $33,350 **e.** $31,475

22. What is the net cash flow in the final year (Year 5)?

a. $31,360 **b.** $40,000 **c.** $100,740 **d.** $117,800 **e.** $171,000

23. A firm is considering a project with a cost of $5,000 and operating cash flows of $2,000 for 3 years. The expected abandonment cash flows for Years 0, 1, 2, and 3 are $5,000, $3,500, $2,000, and $0, respectively. If the firm's cost of capital is 10 percent, what should the firm do?

a. Do not accept the project.
b. Abandon after Year 1; NPV is $0.
c. Abandon after Year 2; NPV is $56.
d. Abandon after Year 2; NPV is $124.
e. Continue the project until the end of its 3-year physical life.

24. As financial vice president, you are evaluating a potential new project. The VP-manufacturing and VP-sales have provided the following real revenue, operating cost, and depreciation data, all stated in constant Year 0 dollars:

Year	Revenue	Cost	Depreciation
0	$ 0	$90,000	$ 0
1	40,000	10,000	30,000
2	40,000	10,000	30,000
3	40,000	10,000	30,000

The cost of capital to the firm is 14 percent, including the current inflation premium. You estimate that the reported real costs will escalate by 10 percent per year over the project's life, starting at t = 0, while revenues will increase by only 5 percent per year. The firm's marginal tax rate is 40 percent. The $90,000 cost in Year 0 is the net after-tax cost of the project, while the $40,000 annual revenues and $10,000 annual costs are before tax. The project has no salvage value and does not require a change in net working capital. What is the project's NPV?

a. $10,593 **b.** $3,297 **c.** -$5,586 **d.** -$17,689 **e.** -$20,351

ANSWERS

1. outflow; inflow; end
2. sunk cost
3. operating income; depreciation
4. old; tax
5. difference
6. independent
7. replacement chain; equivalent annual annuity
8. nominal; real
9. downward
10. incremental

11. b. The net value of land currently owned is an opportunity cost of the project. If the project is not undertaken, the land could be sold to realize its current market value less any taxes and expenses. Thus, project acceptance means foregoing this cash inflow.

12. a. Incremental revenues, which are relevant in a capital budgeting decision, must consider the effects on other parts of the firm.

13. b. In an incremental analysis, the cash flows assuming replacement are compared with the cash flows assuming the old asset is retained. If the old asset is retained, it will produce a salvage value cash flow which must be included, with tax effects, in the replacement analysis.

14. a. The NPV of a project may be maximized by abandoning at some point, thus making the economic life of the project shorter than the physical life.

15. e. First, find each car's original NPV as follows:

$NPV_C = \$9,500(PVIFA_{10\%,10}) - \$50,000 = \$8,373.$

Alternatively, using a financial calculator, input $CF_0 = -50,000$, $CF_{1-10} = 9,500$, and I = 10 to solve for $NPV_C = \$8,373.39$.

$NPV_L = \$8,140(PVIFA_{10\%,15}) - \$50,000 = \$11,913.$

Alternatively, using a financial calculator, input $CF_0 = -50,000$, $CF_{1-15} = 8,140$, and I = 10 to solve for $NPV_L = \$11,913.49$.

Now look at the projects at a common life of 30 years:

Adjusted $NPV_C = \$8,373 + \$8,373(PVIF_{10\%,10}) + \$8,373(PVIF_{10\%,20}) = \$12,846.$

Adjusted $NPV_L = \$11,913 + \$11,913(PVIF_{10\%,15}) = \$14,765.$

16. c. The original NPVs were calculated above. Now find the EAA as follows:

$EAA_C = \$8,373/PVIFA_{10\%,10} = \$8,373/6.1446 = \$1,363.$

Alternatively, using a financial calculator, input N = 10, I = 10, PV = -8,373.39, FV = 0, and solve for PMT = \$1,362.73.

$EAA_L = \$11,913/PVIFA_{10\%,15} = \$11,913/7.6061 = \$1,566.$

Alternatively, using a financial calculator, input N = 15, I = 10, PV = -11,913.49, FV = 0, and solve for PMT = \$1,366.31.

The difference between the two is \$1,566.31 - \$1,362.73 = \$203.58.

17. c. The only cash outflow is the \$50,000 cost of the project. Cash inflows consist of the reduction in operating costs, equal to \$30,000(0.60) = \$18,000 on an after-tax basis, and depreciation. The value of the depreciation cash flows generated by the project is the amount of tax savings. After-tax depreciation cash flows are found by multiplying the depreciable basis, \$50,000, by the recovery percentage in each year, and then multiplying this product by the tax rate. The allowances in each year are 33, 45, and 15 percent, respectively, and the depreciation tax savings in each year are as follows:

$Dep_1 = \$50,000(0.33)(0.40) = \$6,600.$

$\text{Dep}_2 = \$50{,}000(0.45)(0.40) = \$9{,}000.$

$\text{Dep}_3 = \$50{,}000(0.15)(0.40) = \$3{,}000.$

The project's cash flows are placed on a time line as follows:

0	@12% 1	2	3
(\$50,000)	\$18,000	\$18,000	\$18,000
	6,600	9,000	3,000
			1,400*
\$21,964 ←	\$24,600	\$27,000	\$22,400
21,524 ←		(Year 2)	
15,944 ←			(Year 3)
\$ 9,432			

*Salvage value tax savings. National has taken \$16,500 + \$22,500 + \$7,500 = \$46,500 in total depreciation, and hence the book value at the end of Year 3 is \$50,000 - \$46,500 = \$3,500. Since the salvage value is \$0, National can reduce its taxable income by \$3,500, producing a 0.4(\$3,500) = \$1,400 tax savings.

18. e. In this case, the net income of the project is \$61,257. Net cash flow = Net income + Depreciation = \$61,257 + Depreciation. The depreciation allowed in each year is calculated as follows:

$$\text{Dep}_1 = \$500{,}000(0.20) = \$100{,}000.$$
$$\text{Dep}_2 = \$500{,}000(0.32) = \$160{,}000.$$
$$\text{Dep}_3 = \$500{,}000(0.19) = \$95{,}000.$$
$$\text{Dep}_4 = \$500{,}000(0.12) = \$60{,}000.$$
$$\text{Dep}_5 = \$500{,}000(0.11) = \$55{,}000.$$
$$\text{Dep}_6 = \$500{,}000(0.06) = \$30{,}000.$$
$$\text{Dep}_{7\text{-}10} = \$0.$$

In the final year (Year 10), the firm receives \$35,000 from the sale of the machine. However, the book value of the machine is \$0. Thus, the firm would have to pay 0.4(\$35,000) = \$14,000 in taxes, and the net salvage value is \$35,000 - \$14,000 = \$21,000. The time line is as follows:

0	1	2	3	4	5	6	7	8	9	10
(\$500,000)	\$ 61,257	\$ 61,257	\$ 61,257	\$ 61,257	\$61,257	\$61,257	\$61,257	\$61,257	\$61,257	\$61,257
	100,000	160,000	95,000	60,000	55,000	30,000				21,000
(\$500,000)	\$161,257	\$221,257	\$156,257	\$121,257	\$116,257	\$91,257	\$61,257	\$61,257	\$61,257	\$82,257

The project's NPV can be found by discounting each of the cash flows at the firm's 14 percent cost of capital. The project's NPV, found by using a financial calculator is $177,902.

19. d. The initial net investment is $730,000:

Price	($600,000)
Transportation	(60,000)
Installation	(40,000)
Change in net working capital	(30,000)
Initial net investment	$730,000

The annual net cash flows are equal to the net after-tax increase in revenues, 0.6($120,000 - $20,000) = $60,000, plus the depreciation tax savings. In Year 10, the firm will recover its investment in net working capital and gain the net salvage value. The depreciable basis is $700,000, thus, the annual depreciation tax savings is calculated as follows:

$$Dep_1 = \$700{,}000(0.20)(0.4) = \$56{,}000.$$
$$Dep_2 = \$700{,}000(0.32)(0.4) = \$89{,}600.$$
$$Dep_3 = \$700{,}000(0.19)(0.4) = \$53{,}200.$$
$$Dep_4 = \$700{,}000(0.12)(0.4) = \$33{,}600.$$
$$Dep_5 = \$700{,}000(0.11)(0.4) = \$30{,}800.$$
$$Dep_6 = \$700{,}000(0.06)(0.4) = \$16{,}800.$$
$$Dep_{7\text{-}10} = \$0.$$

The net salvage value is $10,000(0.6) = $6,000. Therefore, the time line is as follows:

0	1	2	3	4	5	6	7	8	9	10
($730,000)	$ 60,000	$ 60,000	$ 60,000	$60,000	$60,000	$60,000	$60,000	$60,000	$60,000	$60,000
										30,000
	56,000	89,600	53,200	33,600	30,800	16,800				6,000
($730,000)	$116,000	$149,600	$113,200	$93,600	$90,800	$76,800	$60,000	$60,000	$60,000	$96,000

The project's NPV using a 10 percent cost of capital is -$130,961.

20. c.

Price of new machine	($300,000)
Installation	(50,000)
Sale of old machine	100,000
Tax on sale	(40,000)*
Increase in net working capital	(40,000)
	($330,000)

*The old machine has been depreciated down to zero, but can be sold for $100,000. The full $100,000 (purchase price minus book value) is treated as ordinary income and is taxed at 40 percent. Thus, Union Mills must pay a tax of 0.4($100,000) = $40,000 on the sale of the old asset.

21. a. The after-tax revenue/cost component is 0.6($40,000) = $24,000. As for the tax savings due to depreciation, the depreciable basis for the new machine is $350,000. Further, the MACRS depreciation allowance for Year 1 of a 5-year class asset is 20 percent. Thus, the depreciation expense on the new machine is 0.20($350,000) = $70,000. The old machine has been fully depreciated, so its depreciation expense in Year 1 is $0, and the change in depreciation due to the replacement decision is an increase of $70,000. The tax savings is 0.4($70,000) = $28,000. Therefore, the Year 1 net cash flow from operations is $24,000 + $28,000 = $52,000.

22. d. In the final year, Year 5, the net cash flow is composed of 0.6($40,000) = $24,000 in after-tax cost decrease and 0.4(0.11)($350,000) = $15,400 in depreciation tax savings, for a total of $39,400, plus the applicable nonoperating cash flows. Thus, we have the following:

From operations	$ 39,400
Salvage value of new machine	100,000
Tax on new machine salvage value	(31,600)
Salvage value of old machine	(50,000)
Tax on old machine salvage value	20,000
Change in working capital	40,000
	$117,800

Note that the salvage value of the old machine is a cash outflow. This is an opportunity cost, since buying the new machine deprives Union Mills of the salvage value of the old machine. Additionally, salvage tax effects must be considered. Also note that the change in working capital considered at t = 0, an outflow, is exactly offset by an inflow at the end of the project. This is because it is assumed that the project will terminate and the increase in working capital is no longer required.

23. d.

Year	Initial Investment and Operating Cash Flow	Abandonment Value in Year t
0	(\$5,000)	\$5,000
1	2,000	3,500
2	2,000	2,000
3	2,000	0

NPV of project:

$$-\$5,000 + \$2,000/(1.10)^1 + \$2,000/(1.10)^2 + \$2,000/(1.10)^3 = -\$26.30.$$

NPV of project if abandoned after Year 1:

$$-\$5,000 + \$2,000/(1.10)^1 + \$3,500/(1.10)^1 = \$0.$$

NPV of project if abandoned after Year 2:

$$-\$5,000 + \$2,000/(1.10)^1 + \$2,000/(1.10)^2 + \$2,000/(1.10)^2 = \$124.$$

24. d. The first step is to recast the given data in nominal terms since the cost of capital is nominal:

Year	Revenue	Cost	Depreciation
0	\$ 0	\$90,000	\$ 0
1	42,000	11,000	30,000
2	44,100	12,100	30,000
3	46,305	13,310	30,000

Now apply standard capital budgeting procedures. The initial investment is \$90,000. The operating cash flows are 0.6(\$42,000 - \$11,000) = \$18,600 for Year 1, 0.6(\$44,100 - \$12,100) = \$19,200 for Year 2, and 0.6(\$46,305 - \$13,310) = \$19,797 for Year 3. The tax savings from depreciation is 0.4(\$30,000) = \$12,000 in Years 1 through 3. Now putting this on a time line gives the following:

```
      0                    1                    2                    3
      |        14%         |                    |                    |
      |--------------------|--------------------|--------------------|
  ($90,000)             $18,600              $19,200              $19,797
                         12,000               12,000               12,000
     26,842◄──────────  $30,600              $31,200              $31,797
     24,007◄─────────────────────────────────────┘                    |
     21,462◄──────────────────────────────────────────────────────────┘
  ($17,689)
```

CHAPTER 9
RISK ANALYSIS IN CAPITAL BUDGETING

OVERVIEW

Risk analysis is important in all financial decisions, especially those relating to capital budgeting. As we saw in Chapters 2 and 3, the higher the risk associated with a security, the higher its required rate of return. This situation is as true for capital projects as it is for securities. This chapter discusses procedures for both assessing risk in a capital budgeting context and for incorporating it into capital budgeting decisions.

KEY CONCEPTS

Three separate and distinct types of project risk can be defined: (1) stand-alone risk, (2) within-firm (corporate) risk, and (3) market risk.

Stand-alone risk is the riskiness of a project in isolation, that is, its riskiness when standing alone. It is an important determinant of both corporate and market risk.

- A project's stand-alone risk is measured by its *variability of profitability*. A common measure is the *standard deviation* of NPV or IRR.
- Although a project's stand-alone risk is relatively easy to measure, projects are not held in isolation--firms hold portfolios of projects, and equity investors hold portfolios of stocks.

Within-firm, or *corporate, risk,* which views the risk of a project within the context of the firm's portfolio of projects, is the contribution of the project to the firm's total risk.

- Conceptually, a project's corporate risk can be found by regressing the project's returns against returns on the firm. In essence, this creates a characteristic line for the project, but the returns on the X axis are firm returns as opposed to market returns, and the slope of this line is the contribution of the project to the firm's riskiness.

- A project's corporate risk is conceptually measured by its *corporate beta*:

$$b_{Corporate} = \left(\frac{\sigma_P}{\sigma_F}\right) r_{P,F} \ .$$

  Here σ_P is the standard deviation of project returns, σ_F is the standard deviation of firm returns, and $r_{P,F}$ is the correlation coefficient between the returns.
- If a project's corporate beta equals 1.0, then the project has the same amount of corporate risk as the firm's other projects. If the beta is greater than 1.0, the project has higher-than-average corporate risk, while the opposite is true if the beta is less than 1.0.

Market risk, which views the risk of a project within the context of an investor's portfolio of stocks, is the contribution of the project to the riskiness of the portfolio.

- Conceptually, a project's market risk can be found by regressing the project's returns against returns on a market portfolio. This creates a standard *characteristic line* for the project, and the *slope* of this line measures the project's market risk.
- A project's market risk is conceptually measured by its *market beta:*

$$b_{Market} = \left(\frac{\sigma_P}{\sigma_M}\right) r_{P,M} \ .$$

- If a project's market beta is equal to the firm's market beta, then the project has the same amount of market risk as the firm's average project. If the beta is greater than the firm's beta, then the project has more market risk, and vice versa if the beta is less than the firm's beta.

Most projects' returns are highly correlated with the returns on the firm's other assets, with the correlation being highest for projects in the firm's core business line. Thus, in general, projects with high stand-alone risk will also have high within-firm risk.

The returns on most projects are also highly correlated with the economy as a whole and, hence, the market. Thus, in general, projects with high stand-alone risk will also have high market risk.

It is occasionally argued that only a project's market risk should be considered, because managers should be acting to maximize shareholder wealth, and the risk that is relevant to shareholders is market risk. Here are some points to consider:

Undiversified stockholders, including owners of small businesses, are more concerned about corporate risk than about market risk.

Many financial theorists argue that even well-diversified stockholders consider corporate risk to be important, because the risk of financial distress is more related to corporate risk than to market risk.

The firm's stability is important to all the firm's stakeholders, including its managers, workers, customers, suppliers, creditors, and even the communities in which it operates.

The starting point for analyzing a project's riskiness is *stand-alone risk analysis,* which involves estimating the uncertainty inherent in the project's cash flows. There are four techniques commonly used to measure stand-alone risk: (1) sensitivity analysis, (2) scenario analysis, (3) Monte Carlo simulation, and (4) decision tree analysis.

Sensitivity analysis is a technique which indicates exactly how much a project's NPV will change in response to a given change in an input variable, other things held constant.

- The analysis begins with expected values for unit sales, sales price, fixed costs, and variable costs to give an expected, or base case, NPV. A series of "what if" questions may then be asked to find the change in NPV, given a change in one of the input variables. Typically, the input values are changed by fixed percentages such as ± 10%, ± 20%, and so on.
- Spreadsheet computer models such as *Lotus 1-2-3* are ideal for performing sensitivity analysis.
- Sensitivity analyses are often plotted; the steeper the plots, the greater the risk.
- Sensitivity analysis is very useful for identifying the critical input variables, but it is less useful for assessing risk, because sensitivity analysis (1) does not consider the inherent uncertainty in the input variable and (2) considers only one risky input variable at a time.
- In general, a project's stand-alone risk depends on both (1) the sensitivity of its NPV to changes in key variables and (2) the range of likely values of these variables as reflected in their probability distributions. Because sensitivity analysis considers only the first factor, it is incomplete.

Scenario analysis provides a more complete analysis, because in addition to the sensitivity of NPV to changes in key variables, it considers the range of likely variable values.

- Most likely, worst, and best case scenarios are estimated and the input values from these scenarios are used to find the corresponding NPVs.
- Probabilities can be assigned to the scenarios, and the NPVs from each scenario used to find the expected NPV, standard deviation of NPV, and coefficient of variation of NPV.
- The project's coefficient of variation of NPV can be compared to the coefficient of variation of NPV on the firm's "average" project to determine the relative stand-alone riskiness of the project.
- Scenario analysis is useful, but it assumes that a project can have only a limited number of outcomes, usually three, while, in reality, there are an almost infinite number of possible outcomes.
- Scenario analysis, as it is commonly applied, assumes that the variables treated as uncertain in the analysis are perfectly positively correlated. That is, all variables assume their worst-case values at the same time and their best-case values at the same time. In reality, the probability that all worst-case and all best-case inputs would occur at the same time is extremely low, so scenario analysis typically overstates the extremes.

Monte Carlo simulation ties together sensitivities and input variable probability distributions. The first step in a simulation is to create a computer model that contains the project's cash flows.

- The computer repeatedly selects a random value for each uncertain variable based on its specified probability distribution, along with values for fixed factors. The end result is a continuous NPV probability distribution.
- Simulation analysis is more comprehensive than scenario analysis, because it considers an infinite number of possible outcomes.
- In spite of its obvious appeal, Monte Carlo simulation has not been as widely used in industry as one might expect. One of the major problems is specifying each uncertain variable's probability distribution and the correlations among the distributions.

Decision tree analysis is often used to evaluate projects that have several decision points. The ability to abandon a project changes the branches of a decision tree, often resulting in decreased stand-alone risk and a higher expected NPV for the project.

Additional points to note concerning decision tree analysis and abandonment possibilities include:

- The cash flows and their associated estimated probabilities are laid out on a grid called a "decision tree."
- The joint probability of each branch is multiplied by the NPV of that branch, and these products are summed to obtain the expected NPV.
- Managers can reduce project risk if they can structure the decision process to include several decision points rather than just one.
- Once production begins, if the firm can shut down or spin off the operation, this could dramatically reduce its risk.
- The cost of abandonment is generally reduced if the firm has alternative uses for the project's assets.
- Capital budgeting is a dynamic process and new information should be used to develop revised probability and cash flow estimates.

Despite the usefulness of scenario and simulation analyses, there are problems with these techniques.

Even when scenario and simulation analyses are completed, no clear-cut decision rule emerges. The analysis provides no mechanism to indicate whether a project's profitability as measured by its expected NPV is sufficient to compensate for its risk as measured by σ_{NPV} or CV_{NPV}.

In addition, scenario and simulation analysis focus on a project's stand-alone risk, so they ignore the effects of diversification, both among projects within the firm and by investors in their personal investment portfolios.

In the previous section, we described four methods for measuring a project's stand-alone risk. However, we know that the type of risk that is most relevant to the firm's managers, employees, creditors, and so on is the project's corporate risk.

Corporate risk is a function of both the project's relative standard deviation and its correlation of returns with the firm's returns.

In practice, it is very difficult to estimate the returns distribution for a project with any confidence, and hence it is difficult to quantify a project's corporate risk.

A subjective assessment is usually made regarding the correlation between the project's returns and the firm's returns. If the correlation is high, then the project's stand-alone risk assessment probably also applies to its corporate risk--high stand-alone risk indicates high corporate risk. If the correlation is zero or negative, then the stand-alone risk assessment overstates the project's corporate risk.

Beta analysis can sometimes be used to determine the appropriate project cost of capital. Conceptually, corporate risk can be thought of within a characteristic line framework. If we consider a firm to be a portfolio of individual assets, then we can think of a project's corporate risk characteristic line as being the plot of the project's returns versus the returns on the entire firm, which are made up of all the firm's individual asset returns, except the project being evaluated.

Because it is difficult to estimate the returns distribution for a single project with any confidence, the corporate risk characteristic line is seldom used for individual projects. However, it is used to estimate the relative risk of divisions within a firm.

> *Market risk* measures risk from the standpoint of an equity investor holding a highly diversified portfolio.

- The required rate of return on equity is equal to the risk-free rate of return plus a risk premium equal to the firm's beta coefficient times the market risk premium:

$$k_s = k_{RF} + (k_M - k_{RF})b.$$

- For example, if a firm has a beta of 0.9, k_M = 12%, and k_{RF} = 7%, then its required rate of return would be k_s = 7% + (5%)0.9 = 11.5%. Stockholders are willing to let the firm invest their money if the firm can earn 11.5 percent on their equity capital.
- If the firm's cost of debt is 8 percent, its marginal tax rate is 40 percent, and its target capital structure is 50 percent debt and 50 percent common equity, then its corporate cost of capital would be 8.2 percent:

$$\text{Corporate } k = w_dk_d(1 - T) + w_sk_s = 0.5(8\%)(0.6) + 0.5(11.5\%) = 8.2\%.$$

Average-risk projects for this firm should be evaluated using an 8.2 percent cost of capital as the discount rate in the NPV method or as the hurdle rate in the IRR and MIRR methods.

The acceptance of a particular capital budgeting project may cause the firm's overall beta to rise or fall, causing a change in the required rate of return.

- The impact of any one project on a firm's beta will depend upon the size of the project relative to its existing "portfolio" of projects.
- Using the Gordon model, $P_0 = D_1/(k_s - g)$, and holding other factors constant, an increase in a firm's beta coefficient will clearly result in a higher required return, k_S,

and hence a decrease in stock price. To maintain a given stock price, there must be an increase in the expected rate of growth, dividends, or both. These factors, in turn, will result in an increase in the expected return. Therefore, an increase in the firm's beta coefficient will cause the stock price to decline unless the increased beta is offset by a higher expected rate of return.

If the beta coefficient for each project can be determined, then individual projects' costs of equity capital can be found as follows:

$$k_{s(Project)} = k_{RF} + (k_M - k_{RF})b_{Project}.$$

High-beta, or high-risk, projects will have a relatively high cost of equity capital, while low-beta projects will have a correspondingly low cost of capital.

A project's cost of equity estimate can then be combined with the firm's cost of debt to find the project's cost of capital. For our illustrative firm, high-beta, high-risk projects would have a project cost of capital above 8.2 percent, while low-risk projects would have a cost less than 8.2 percent. Of course, a project with the same risk as the firm would have a project cost of capital of 8.2 percent.

It is often very difficult to estimate the beta for a particular project, and for some projects, such as a new computer billing system, the beta may not be meaningful.

- One way of estimating project betas is the *pure play method.* Here the firm must find another company which is exclusively engaged in the same business line as the project. Then, the market beta of the "proxy" firm is adjusted for leverage and tax rate differences using the Hamada equation:

$$b_L = b_U[1 + (1 - T)(D/S)],$$

or

$$b_U = \frac{b_L}{1 + (1 - T)(D/S)}.$$

- A second approach to estimating project betas is the *accounting beta method.* Here, a project's (or perhaps a division's) return on assets (ROA) is regressed against the average ROA of a large sample of firms, say the S&P 500. The resulting accounting beta is then used as a proxy for the project's market beta.

The *risk-adjusted discount rate method* discounts expected cash flows at a rate which reflects the riskiness of the flows.

- A firm's weighted average cost of capital may be estimated with a fair degree of accuracy.

- Increasing the discount rate for high-risk projects and lowering it for low-risk projects is a somewhat arbitrary and judgmental process, but it does force managers to consider a project's riskiness.
- Diversified companies with divisions of varying risk may use a two-step process to determine a project's risk-adjusted discount rate.
  - First, divisional costs of capital are established for each of the major operating divisions.
  - Then, within the division, projects classified as high risk would have an increased discount rate while low-risk projects would have a lowered discount rate.

Most firms use the risk-adjusted discount rate method to incorporate differential project risk in the capital budgeting process, but another technique, the certainty equivalent method, can also be used.

The *certainty equivalent method* discounts certainty equivalent cash flows by the risk-free rate.

- The certainty equivalent cash flow is that certain cash flow which is equivalent to the risky cash flow at hand. For example, the certainty equivalent of a risky cash flow with an expected value of $100 would be something less than $100, and the greater the riskiness, the lower the certainty equivalent.
- The certainty equivalent method is conceptually superior to the risk-adjusted discount rate method, because it treats the risk adjustment and the time value of money separately.
- However, the certainty equivalent method is difficult to use in practice because there is no market-determined benchmark that can be used to estimate the certainty equivalent cash flow. Thus, the vast majority of firms use the risk-adjusted discount rate method.

Comparison of the two methods points out an interesting facet of the risk-adjusted discount rate method. Since the risk-adjusted discount rate method combines the risk premium with the time value of money (the risk-free rate), the risk premium is compounded over time, and hence, this method implicitly assumes that a project's cash flows become riskier over time.

Many capital budgeting decisions are based on cost minimization rather than NPV maximization. For example, a firm might be choosing between two production methods. One method could use expensive robotics technology and minimal manpower, while the other method might use few robots but have high labor costs. The revenues, or cash inflows, would be the same under both methods. Thus, the method that minimizes costs will also maximize NPV, and cost minimization could be used as the selection criterion.

If two mutually exclusive projects are being evaluated based on costs alone, the project with the lower present value of costs should be chosen.

If these projects have the same risk as the firm's (or division's) average project, then the discount rate used is the firm's (or division's) marginal cost of capital.

However, if the projects have riskiness other than average, then the risk adjustment procedure is the opposite of that used in the NPV method. That is, projects with above-average risk will have a lower-than-average project cost of capital, while projects that are less risky than average will have a higher-than-average cost of capital.

- This adjustment procedure is followed because projects with above average risk should be penalized, and to do so, the present value of costs must be increased. Decreasing the discount rate causes the project to become less attractive relative to other projects.
- Note that this reverse risk adjustment is also applicable to cash outflows in a normal NPV analysis. For example, a strip mining project might have a large cash outflow at the end of the project's life. If this outflow is riskier than average, then its discount rate must be less than the rate used on the project's other cash flows.

DEFINITIONAL QUESTIONS

1. The _________ the risk associated with an investment, the greater the expected ______ __________ ______ needed to compensate investors.

2. Three types of risk have been identified in capital budgeting decisions: _____________ risk, __________ risk, and ______-______ risk.

3. Measuring stand-alone risk involves determining the uncertainty of a project's ______ ______.

4. Cash flow estimates are really ________ _________ taken from ___________ distributions.

5. A commonly used method of risk analysis is based on constructing optimistic (best case), pessimistic (worst case), and most likely value estimates for the key variables. This method is called __________ ___________.

6. In project analysis, changing one of the key input variables at a time and determining the effect on NPV is known as __________ __________.

7. One purpose of sensitivity analysis is to determine which of the ______ has the ______ influence on the project's NPV.

8. The required rate of return on a company's stock is equal to the _____-_______ rate plus a _________ for risk.

9. The risk premium on a stock is equal to the stock's ______ times the market risk premium.

10. The beta of a portfolio of assets is equal to the __________ __________ of the betas of the individual assets.

11. An increase in the firm's beta coefficient will cause the firm's stock price to ________ unless this increase is offset by a ________ expected rate of return.

12. A project with a high degree of corporate risk will not necessarily affect the firm's ________ risk to any great extent.

13. Within-firm ___________ occurs when returns on various projects' cash flows are not highly ____________ with each other.

14. Firms often measure a project's stand-alone risk, yet a project's market risk is more relevant. Stand-alone risk can also measure market risk if the two are _________ ___________ ___________.

15. Riskier projects should be evaluated with a higher ___________ ______ than average-risk projects.

CONCEPTUAL QUESTIONS

16. Even if the beta of a project being considered has a value of zero, acceptance of the project will affect the market risk of the firm.

    a. True   b. False

17. When projects of different risk are to be considered in capital budgeting, any project will be acceptable to the firm if the project's IRR is greater than the firm's weighted average cost of capital.

    a. True **b.** False

18. When using the pure play approach, the analyzing firm uses a proxy firm's beta as an estimate of the project's beta.

    a. True **b.** False

19. If a cash outflow is judged to be riskier than average, then the firm's marginal cost of capital must be adjusted downward to reflect this differential.

    a. True **b.** False

20. In capital budgeting decisions, corporate risk will be of least interest to

    a. Employees.
    b. Stockholders with few shares.
    c. Institutional investors.
    d. Creditors.
    e. The local community.

PROBLEMS

21. Initially, United Products has a beta of 1.30. The risk-free rate is 12 percent, and the required rate of return on the market is 18 percent. The firm now sells 10 percent of its assets, having a beta of 1.30, and uses the proceeds to purchase a new product line with a beta of 1.00. What is the new overall required rate of return for United Products?

    a. 15.11% **b.** 16.24% **c.** 17.48% **d.** 18.00% **e.** 19.62%

22. Consolidated Inc. uses its marginal cost of capital of 12 percent to evaluate average-risk projects and adds/subtracts two percentage points to evaluate projects of greater/lesser risk. Currently, two mutually exclusive projects are under consideration. Both have a net cost of $200,000 and last 4 years. Project A, which is riskier than average, will produce yearly after-tax net cash flows of $71,000. Project B, which has less-than-average risk, will produce an after-tax net cash flow of $146,000 in Years 3 and 4 only. What should Consolidated do?

a. Accept Project B with an NPV of $9,412.
b. Accept both projects since both NPVs are greater than zero.
c. Accept Project A with an NPV of $6,874.
d. Accept neither project since both NPVs are less than zero.
e. Accept Project A with an NPV of $15,652.

23. Union Industries is considering the purchase of a plant that produces plastic products. The plant is expected to generate a rate of return of 17 percent, and the plant's estimated beta is 2.00. The risk-free rate is 12 percent, and the market risk premium is 6 percent. Union has a target capital structure of 40 percent debt and 60 percent common equity. Its tax rate is 40 percent and its before-tax cost of debt is 14 percent. Union should make the investment.

a. True   b. False

24. Diversified Products (DP) is considering the formation of a new division which will double the assets of the firm. DP is an all-equity firm which has a current required rate of return of 20 percent. The risk-free rate is 10 percent, and the market risk premium is 5 percent. If DP wants to reduce its required rate of return to 18 percent, what is the maximum beta the new division could have?

a. 1.00   b. 1.10   c. 1.20   d. 1.25   e. 1.30

25. Midwest Motors is choosing between two automobile washing/waxing machines on the basis of cost. The expected net costs of the two machines are as follows:

Year	Machine A	Machine B
0	($20,000)	($10,000)
1	(5,000)	(8,000)
2	(5,000)	(8,000)
3	(5,000)	(8,000)
4	(5,000)	(8,000)

The firm's cost of capital is 10 percent. Machine B is judged to be a riskier-than-average project, while Machine A is considered less risky than average. The firm's policy is to add or subtract 2 percentage points to adjust for risk. The firm should choose Machine B.

a. True   b. False

The following data apply to the next two problems.

You are the director capital budgeting for Stanton Publishing Co. (SPC), which publishes romance novels. SPC uses the certainty equivalent approach to capital budgeting decisions.

You are evaluating the acquisition of a new printing press which will increase production by 25 percent and is anticipated to have the following expected net cash flows. Further, you estimate the certainty equivalent cash flows, CE_t, as listed:

Year	Cash Flow	CE_t
0	($30,000)	($30,000)
1	7,500	6,750
2	7,500	6,750
3	7,500	6,750
4	22,500	15,750

You view the Year 4 cash flow as being more risky than Years 1 through 3 because a large proportion of the Year 4 cash flow is salvage value, and SPC's estimates of salvage value are very uncertain. Conversely, you know the cost of the press with certainty, since its manufacturer has given SPC a fixed bid for a 90-day period.

26. Assume the risk-free rate is 4 percent. What is the project's NPV using the certainty equivalent (CE) method?

a. $2,195.03 b. $2,257.48 c. $2,307.31 d. $2,312.89 e. $2,385.11

27. The project has the same risk as the firm's average project, and SPC's WACC is 12 percent. What is the project's NPV using the risk-adjusted discount rate (RADR) method?

a. $2,195.03 b. $2,257.48 c. $2,307.31 d. $2,312.89 e. $2,385.11

The following data apply to the next three problems.

The Clark-Evans Company (CEC) has a target capital structure of 45 percent debt and 55 percent equity, and it will apply this structure to the project under consideration. The firm's beta, which is an average of 7 estimates by financial service firms, is 1.25. Clark-Evans is evaluating a new project which is totally unrelated to its existing line of business. However, it has identified two proxy firms exclusively engaged in this business line. They, on average, have a beta of 1.05 and a debt ratio of 55 percent. Clark-Evans' new project has an estimated IRR of 12 percent. The risk-free rate is 8 percent, and the market risk premium is 5 percent. All three firms have a marginal tax rate of 35 percent. Clark-Evans' before-tax cost of debt is 11 percent.

28. What is the project's unleveraged beta, b_U?

a. 1.250 b. 1.100 c. 0.896 d. 0.775 e. 0.585

29. What is the beta of the project if undertaken by Clark-Evans?

a. 1.250 **b.** 1.100 **c.** 0.896 **d.** 0.775 **e.** 0.585

30. Should the firm accept the project?

a. No; the project's IRR (12%) is less than the project's required rate of return (12.5%).
b. Yes, the project's IRR (12%) is greater than the project's weighted average cost of capital (10.1%).
c. No; the project's IRR (12%) is less than the project's weighted average cost of capital (12.5%).
d. Yes; the project's IRR (12%) is greater than the project's required rate of return (10.1%).
e. The firm is indifferent because the project's IRR (12%) is equal to the project's required rate of return (12%).

ANSWERS

1. higher; rate of return
2. market; corporate (within-firm); stand-alone
3. expected NPV (cash flows)
4. expected values; probability
5. scenario analysis
6. sensitivity analysis
7. variables; greatest
8. risk-free; premium
9. beta
10. weighted average
11. decline; higher
12. market
13. diversification; correlated
14. highly positively correlated
15. discount rate

16. a. The addition of an asset with a beta of zero will lower the beta of the firm, thus lowering the firm's market risk. (We assume that the starting beta of the firm is greater than zero.)

17. b. The only time this statement holds is when all projects being evaluated have the same risk as the firm's current average project. Otherwise, the cost of capital must be adjusted for project risk.

18. a. This is essentially true, but as we will note in Chapter 12, the proxy firm's beta must be adjusted to reflect the analyzing firm's target capital structure and tax rate.

19. a. The present value of a cash outflow (cash cost) must be increased to penalize it for above-average risk, and the present value will be increased only if the discount rate is decreased.

20. c. Institutional investors are well diversified and, therefore, more concerned with market risk.

21. e. New b = 0.9(1.30) + 0.1(1.00) = 1.27.

New k_s = 12% + (18% - 12%)1.27 = 19.62%.

22. a. Look at the time lines:

A:

	0	14%	1	2	3	4
	($200,000)		$71,000	$71,000	$71,000	$71,000
	206,874	←				
	$ 6,874	= NPV				

B:

	0	10%	1	2	3	4
	($200,000)		0	0	$146,000	$146,000
	109,692	←				
	99,720	←				
	$ 9,412	= NPV				

Note that both discount rates are adjusted for risk. Since the projects are mutually exclusive, the project with the higher NPV is chosen.

23. b. The project's required rate of return on equity is 24 percent:

$$k_{s(Project)} = 12\% + (6\%)2 = 24\%.$$

Thus, the project's cost of capital is 17.8 percent:

$$WACC_{Project} = 0.4(14\%)(0.6) + 0.6(24\%) = 17.8\%.$$

Since its expected return is only 17 percent, the plant should not be purchased.

24. c. First, find the current beta of the firm: k = 10% + (5%)b = 20%; thus, b = 2.00.

Now find the beta required to lower the firm's required rate of return to 18 percent:

$$k = 10\% + (5\%)b = 18\%;\ b = 1.60.$$

Finally, if the firm doubles, 50 percent of the expanded firm's assets will be old, while 50 percent will be the new division. Thus, $0.5(2.00) + 0.5(b_{Div}) = 1.60$; $b_{Div} = 1.20$.

25. b. These are cash outflows, so the risk adjustment process is reversed. Thus, the project cost of capital for Machine A is 12 percent, while for B it is 8 percent.

k	PV Costs A	PV Costs B
10%	($35,849)	($35,359)
12	(35,187)	(34,299)
8	(36,561)	(36,497)

We see that with the correct risk adjustment, the PV of costs for Machine A is less than the PV of costs for Machine B, and hence, Machine A should be selected. Note that the normal adjustment for risk would result in an incorrect decision

26. a. The NPV of the project using the CE method is $2,195.03:

$$NPV = -\$30{,}000 + \frac{\$6{,}750}{1.04} + \frac{\$6{,}750}{(1.04)^2} + \frac{\$6{,}750}{(1.04)^3} + \frac{\$15{,}750}{(1.04)^4} = \$2{,}195.03.$$

27. d. The NPV using the RADR method is $2,312.89:

$$NPV = -\$30{,}000 + \frac{\$7{,}500}{1.12} + \frac{\$7{,}500}{(1.12)^2} + \frac{\$7{,}500}{(1.12)^3} + \frac{\$22{,}500}{(1.12)^4} = \$2{,}312.89.$$

28. e. Hamada's equation can be used to estimate the project beta:

$$b_U = \frac{b_L}{1 + (1 - T)(D/S)} = \frac{1.05}{1 + (1 - 0.35)(0.55/0.45)} = \frac{1.05}{1.794} = 0.585.$$

29. c. Another form of the Hamada equation is used to adjust for the firm's leverage:

$$\begin{aligned} b_L &= b_U[1 + (1 - T)(D/S)] \\ &= 0.585[1 + (1 - 0.35)(0.45/0.55)] \\ &= 0.585(1.532) \\ &= 0.896. \end{aligned}$$

30. b. The required rate of return on the project is found using the SML and the WACC:

$$k_{sp} = k_{RF} + (k_M - k_{RF})b_p = 8\% + 5\%(0.896) = 12.48\% \approx 12.5\%.$$

$$\begin{aligned} WACC_p = w_d k_d(1 - T) + w_{ce} k_{sp} &= 0.45(11\%)(1 - 0.35) + 0.55(12.5\%) \\ &= 3.22\% + 6.875\% \\ &= 10.1\%. \end{aligned}$$

Since the project's IRR is 12 percent, $IRR_p > WACC_p$, then the project should be accepted.

CHAPTER 10
THE OPTIMAL CAPITAL BUDGET

OVERVIEW

In Chapter 6, we developed the concept of the corporate cost of capital. Then, in Chapters 7, 8, and 9, we saw how capital projects are evaluated. However, capital budgeting and the cost of capital are actually interrelated--we cannot determine the cost of capital unless we know the size of the capital budget, and we cannot determine the size of the capital budget unless we know the cost of capital. Therefore, as we show in this chapter, the corporate cost of capital and the capital budget must be determined simultaneously.

KEY CONCEPTS

The firm's *investment opportunity schedule (IOS)* plays an important role in determining the optimal capital budget.

The investment opportunity schedule is a plot of the firm's potential projects in descending order of each project's IRR.

If the firm has mutually exclusive projects, then it also has multiple investment opportunity schedules--one for each different combination of projects.

The second element in the optimal capital budget process is the *marginal cost of capital (MCC) schedule.*

The marginal cost of capital schedule is a plot of the firm's weighted average cost of capital against dollars of new capital required.

Suppose that Firm B has a target capital structure of 40 percent debt and 60 percent equity; that its before-tax cost of debt, k_d, is 12 percent; its cost of retained earnings, k_s, is 17.5 percent; and its cost of new common stock, k_e, is 18.2 percent; and that its tax rate, T, is 40 percent.

- Therefore, its WACC using retained earnings as the common stock component is 13.4 percent:

  $$WACC = w_d k_d(1 - T) + w_{ce}(k_s) = 0.4(12\%)(0.6) + 0.6(17.5\%) = 13.4\%.$$

- When new common stock must be used as the equity component, then Firm B's WACC rises to 13.8 percent:

  $$WACC = w_d k_d(1 - T) + w_{ce}(k_e) = 0.4(12\%)(0.6) + 0.6(18.2\%) = 13.8\%.$$

The question now is at what point, or at what amount of new capital raised, does Firm B's WACC increase from 13.4 to 13.8 percent? Of course, the answer is when the firm's retained earnings are exhausted. Suppose Firm B is projecting \$40,000 in retained earnings during the planning period. We know that 60 percent of the capital raised will be raised as equity capital. If X is the total capital raised, then

$$\text{Retained earnings} = 0.6(\text{Total capital}) = 0.6X = \$40,000.$$

Solving for X, which is called the retained earnings break point, we obtain:

$$RE_{BP} = X = \text{Retained earnings}/\%\ \text{Equity} = \$40,000/0.6 = \$66,667.$$

Thus, Firm B can raise \$66,667 of new capital before it exhausts its retained earnings. Of the \$66,667, 0.6(\$66,667) = \$40,000 represents retentions and 0.4(\$66,667) = \$26,667 represents debt financing.

Firm B also has \$100,000 in depreciation cash flow, and, as we learned in Chapter 6, depreciation-generated cash flow and deferred taxes cash flow push the retained earnings break point to the right. Thus, considering both retentions and depreciation cash flows, Firm B's retained earnings breakpoint occurs at \$66,667 + \$100,000 = \$166,667.

The MCC schedule is merely a plot of a firm's WACCs against dollars of new capital required, and Figure 1 shows the MCC schedule for Firm B.

Figure 1
MCC Schedule

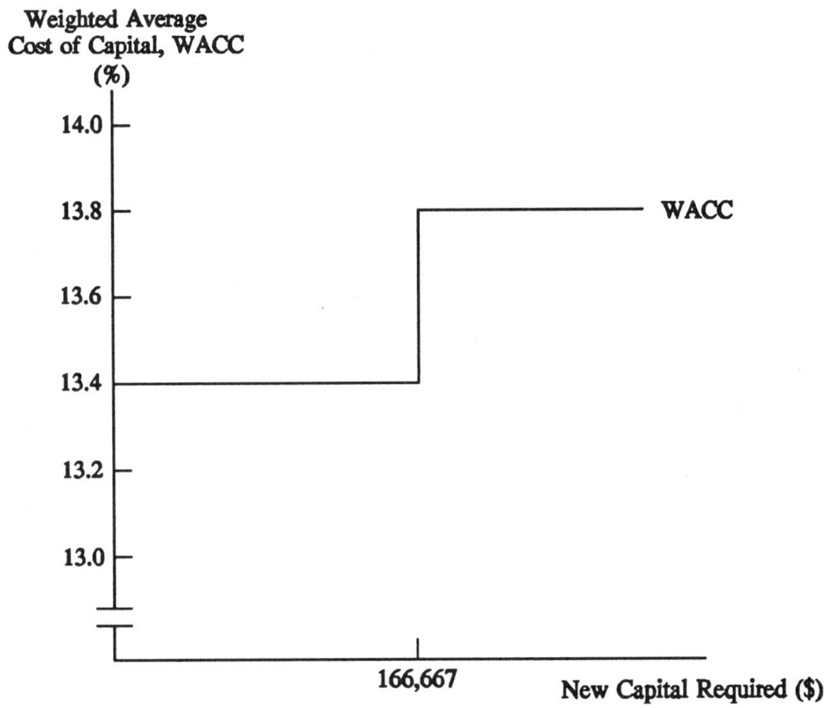

In general, firms have additional break points from the retained earnings break point. As more and more securities are issued during any planning period, the costs of debt, preferred stock, and new common stock will rise, creating additional break points in the MCC.

It is very difficult to precisely identify the new cost levels and break points. Thus, most firms do not attempt to quantitatively define the MCC schedule beyond what is shown above. However, firms will judgmentally increase the WACC if new capital requirements are extraordinarily large.

> The optimal capital budget, along with the firm's marginal cost of capital, is found by combining the IOS and MCC schedules.

The intersection of the IOS and MCC schedules defines the firm's corporate cost of capital.

If the corporate cost of capital is used as the hurdle rate for average risk projects, then the firm will make correct accept/reject decisions, and its level of financing and investment will be optimal. If it uses any other rate, its capital budget will not be optimal.

- The only exception to this general rule is situations where a large project is at the margin, and this project would require capital at different rates. Then, the average cost of capital needed for the marginal project would be used.
- All projects that have average risk should be evaluated at the corporate cost of capital. Note that for independent projects, the IRR method can be used as a proxy for the NPV method since both lead to the same accept/reject decision for independent projects. Thus, all independent projects of average risk with IRRs exceeding the firm's corporate cost of capital should be accepted.
- However, for mutually exclusive projects, the NPV method should be used, and the appropriate discount rate for average-risk projects is the firm's corporate cost of capital.
- Riskier-than-average projects have a higher cost of capital, while those that are less risky than average have a lower cost of capital. The size of the adjustment is arbitrary and is normally set by company policy.
- Alternatively, risk adjustments can be made to the IOS schedule. If this procedure is used, the IRRs of high-risk projects would be lowered and the IRRs of low-risk projects would be raised.

> The procedures set forth above are conceptually correct, and it is important that you understand the logic of this process. However, most companies use a more judgmental, less quantitative process for establishing their optimal capital budgets.

The approximate size of the capital budget is compared with the firm's capital costs to get a reasonably good approximation of the corporation's corporate cost of capital.

The corporate cost of capital is scaled up or down to reflect each division's target capital structure and riskiness.

Each project within each division is classified into one of three risk groups: high, low, or average risk.

Each project's NPV is determined, using its risk-adjusted project cost of capital. All independent projects with positive risk-adjusted NPVs are accepted. For mutually exclusive projects, the highest positive risk-adjusted NPV projects are accepted.

Capital budgeting is normally an application of a classic economic principle: A firm should expand to the point where its marginal profits equal its marginal costs. In other words, keep accepting projects as long as the benefits exceed the costs. However, some firms set an absolute limit on the size of their capital budgets. This is called *capital rationing.*

The principal reason for capital rationing is that some firms are reluctant to engage in external financing. The reasons vary from fear of debt financing to fear of losing control, but the end result is that firms that ration capital grow more slowly than they would under normal capital budgeting practices.

Under capital rationing, the correct objective is to maximize total NPV subject to the constraint that the capital ceiling not be exceeded. Thus, in theory, the manager merely selects that set of projects from the proposed set which maximizes NPV without exceeding the capital constraint. However, in practice, the task is difficult.

- Large firms have hundreds of projects, and it would require linear programming to identify the value-maximizing set of projects.
- The task is made more difficult by the fact that the projects have varying risk.
- Capital rationing usually persists over time, and hence the problem becomes one of choosing the optimal set of projects today for some number of years.

Usually, capital rationing occurs when the firm believes that it will encounter severe problems if it attempts to raise capital beyond some specified amount. Such situations can be rationally handled by increasing the assigned cost of capital as the amount of capital raised increases.

Both practitioners and financial theorists have noted that other factors also influence the firm's capital budgeting decisions. These other factors include: stable earnings per share growth, project maturity, and strategic considerations.

If managers strive to maximize the present value of investment projects subject to the constraint that the earnings of the company should grow at a specified rate, then the set of projects selected may not necessarily be the set that maximizes the firm's long-run value. This implies a situation where investors do not correctly perceive the true long-term value of investment projects.

For most capital budgeting projects, term structure considerations are not important -- the relevant cost of capital is the long-term cost, even if the project has a relatively short physical life.

A great deal of corporate investment is made on the basis of strategic considerations. Strategic investments generally have two common elements:

- Immediate cash flow benefits are hard to identify, and those that can be identified are often insufficient to justify the project.
- Strategic investments offer insurance against the chance that "the regular way of doing business" will not be viable in the future.

Definitional Questions

1. The ___________ ___________ ____________ is a plot of the firm's proposed projects, ranked in descending order of IRR, versus the dollars of new capital required.

2. The marginal cost of capital schedule is a plot of the firm's ___________ ___________ ___________ _____ ___________ versus the dollars of new capital required.

3. The retained earnings break point is the point in the firm's MCC schedule at which the WACC ________ due to the fact that retained earnings are exhausted.

4. The firm's ____________ ________ _____ _____________ is defined by the intersection of the MCC and IOS schedules.

5. All projects of ________ risk should be evaluated at the firm's corporate cost of capital.

6. In general, projects can be evaluated using the IRR method, however, ____________ ____________ projects must be evaluated by the NPV method.

7. Risk adjustments may be made by either adjusting the firm's MCC or by adjusting each project's ________.

8. ___________ ____________ occurs when a firm sets an absolute limit on the dollar amount of investment capital.

Conceptual Questions

9. The firm's corporate cost of capital is determined by the intersection of the MCC and IOS schedules.

   a. True b. False

10. All independent projects with IRRs that exceed the firm's cost of capital should be accepted.

a. True b. False

11. Which of the following steps are commonly used in practice to establish a firm's optimal capital budget?

a. Rough estimates of the MCC and IOS schedules are used to estimate the firm's corporate cost of capital.
b. The corporate cost of capital is scaled up or down to reflect each division's capital structure and risk characteristics.
c. Each division's cost of capital is scaled up or down to reflect differential project risk.
d. Each project's NPV is then determined using its appropriate risk-adjusted cost of capital.
e. All the above steps are used.

PROBLEMS

12. Consolidated Industries' overall corporate cost of capital (WACC) is 10 percent. Division HR is riskier than average, Division AR has average risk, and Division LR is less risky than average. Consolidated adjusts for risk by adding or subtracting 2 percentage points. What is the risk-adjusted project cost of capital for a low-risk project in the HR division?

a. 6% b. 8% c. 10% d. 12% e. 14%

The following data apply to the next three problems.

The Braxton Corporation has the following investment opportunities in the coming planning period:

Project	Net Investment	IRR
F	$300,000	18%
G	100,000	15
H	200,000	13
H*	200,000	12
I	100,000	10

Projects H and H are mutually exclusive. The firm's MCC schedule is 10 percent up to $500,000 of new capital, and 11 percent thereafter.

13. What is the firm's corporate cost of capital?

a. 10% **b.** 11% **c.** 12% **d.** 13% **e.** 15%

14. Assume that all projects have average risk. What is the dollar total of the firm's optimal capital budget?

a. $300,000 **b.** $400,000 **c.** $500,000 **d.** $600,000 **e.** $700,000

15. Now assume that Project F is riskier than average and that Project I is less risky than average. The remaining projects have average risk. Braxton's policy is to adjust the corporate cost of capital up or down by 2 percentage points to account for risk. What is the effect of differential risk on Braxton's optimal capital budget?

a. The capital budget is not changed.
b. Project F is now unacceptable.
c. The capital budget is now $700,000.
d. Project I becomes acceptable.
e. Both c and d are correct.

The following data apply to the next four problems.

The management of Wald Enterprises Inc. (WEI) is planning next year's capital budget. WEI expects its net income to be $18,333 next year, and its payout ratio is 40 percent. The company's earnings and dividends are growing at a constant rate of 5 percent; the last dividend, D_0, was $1.58; and the current equilibrium stock price is $15.03. WEI can raise up to $15,000 of debt at a 10 percent before-tax cost, the next $15,000 will cost 12 percent, and all debt after $30,000 will cost 14 percent. If WEI issues new common stock, a 15 percent underwriting cost will be incurred. WEI can sell the first $20,000 of new common stock at the current market price, but to sell any additional new stock, WEI must lower the price to $13.35. WEI is at its optimal capital structure, which is 40 percent debt and 60 percent equity, and the firm's marginal federal-plus-state tax rate is 40 percent. WEI has the following independent, indivisible, and equally risky investment opportunities:

Project	Cost	IRR
A	$25,000	17%
B	35,000	14
C	25,000	16
D	20,000	15

16. What is WEI's cost of retained earnings?

a. 14.24% **b.** 15.41% **c.** 16.00% **d.** 18.00% **e.** 19.62%

17. What is WEI's retained earnings break point?

a. $11,000 **b.** $18,333 **c.** $20,000 **d.** $31,000 **e.** $37,500

18. What is WEI's corporate cost of capital?

a. 12.00% **b.** 13.20% **c.** 13.68% **d.** 14.65% **e.** 15.13%

19. What is WEI's optimal capital budget?

a. $25,000 **b.** $50,000 **c.** $70,000 **d.** $75,000 **e.** $105,000

ANSWERS

1. investment opportunity schedule
2. weighted average cost of capital (WACC)
3. increases
4. corporate cost of capital
5. average
6. mutually exclusive
7. IRR
8. Capital rationing

9. a. This intersection determines the corporate cost of capital for projects with average risk. The corporate cost of capital is a function of the size of the capital budget, the firm's marginal capital component costs, and the firm's target capital structure.

10. b. This statement would be true if all projects had the same risk as the firm's average project, but this condition seldom holds. In general, the firm's corporate cost of capital would have to be scaled up or down to reflect differential risk.

11. e. In fact, responses (a) through (d) are the steps normally followed, in the correct sequence.

12. c. k_{HR} = 10% + 2% = 12%. $k_{Project}$ = 12% - 2% = 10%.

13. b. First, plot the MCC and IOS schedules:

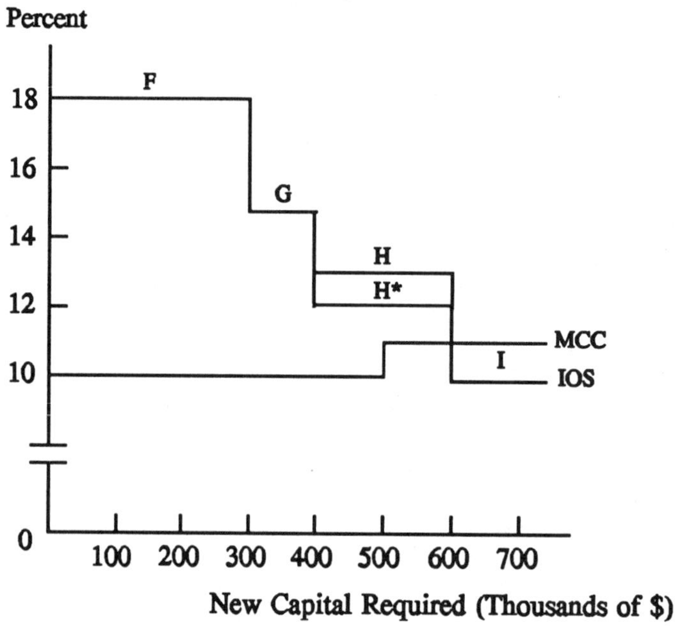

The intersection of the schedules defines the firm's marginal cost of capital. Thus, Braxton's corporate cost of capital is 11 percent.

14. d. Since all projects have average risk, they are all evaluated at a project cost of capital of 11 percent. Clearly, Projects F and G are acceptable since their IRRs exceed 11 percent. (Since they are independent projects, it is permissible to use the IRR method as a proxy for the NPV method.) The decision between Projects H and H* must be made according to the NPV rule. Since we do not know the project cash flows, we cannot calculate their NPVs. However, one of the two would be chosen since both will have positive NPVs. Thus, the optimal capital budget consists of Projects F and G, and either Project H or H*, and totals $600,000.

15. e. Since Project F is riskier than average, its cost of capital must be adjusted upward to 11% + 2% = 13%. However, its IRR is 18 percent so Project F remains acceptable. On the other hand, Project I's cost of capital is adjusted downward to 9 percent, and hence it becomes acceptable. Thus, the optimal capital budget increases to $700,000. Note that Braxton's corporate cost of capital remains at 11 percent.

16. c.

$$k_s = \frac{D_0(1+g)}{P_0} + g = \frac{\$1.58(1.05)}{\$15.03} + 0.05 = 0.16 = 16\%.$$

17. b. BP_{RE} = \$18,333(0.6)/0.6 = \$18,333.

18. d. Work the problem in the following steps:

First, look only at debt:

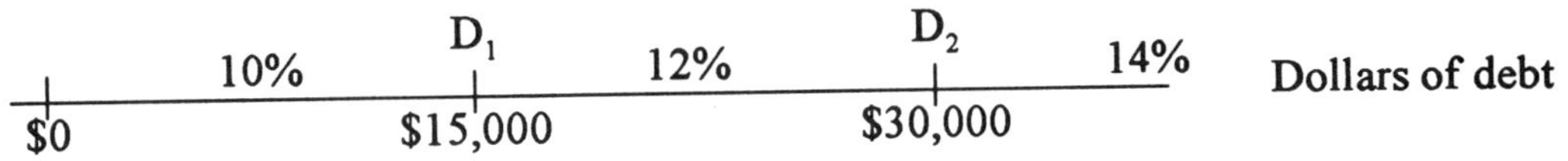

Now look only at equity:

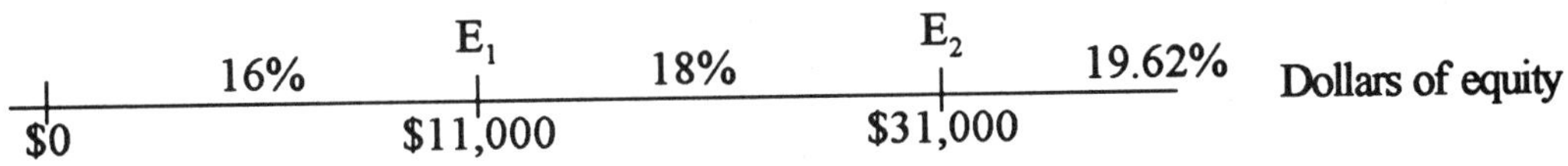

Retained earnings are forecast to be \$18,333(0.6) = \$11,000. The cost of retained earnings is as follows:

$$k_s = \frac{D_0(1+g)}{P_0} + g = \frac{\$1.58(1.05)}{\$15.03} + 0.05 = 0.16 = 16\%.$$

The cost of new equity is as follows:

$$k_{e1} = \frac{D_0(1+g)}{P_0(1-F)} + g = \frac{\$1.58(1.05)}{\$15.03(1-0.15)} + 0.05 = 0.1799 = 18.00\%.$$

$$k_{e2} = \frac{\$1.58(1.05)}{\$13.35(1-0.15)} + 0.05 = 0.1962 = 19.62\%.$$

Now combine debt and equity and look at total capital:

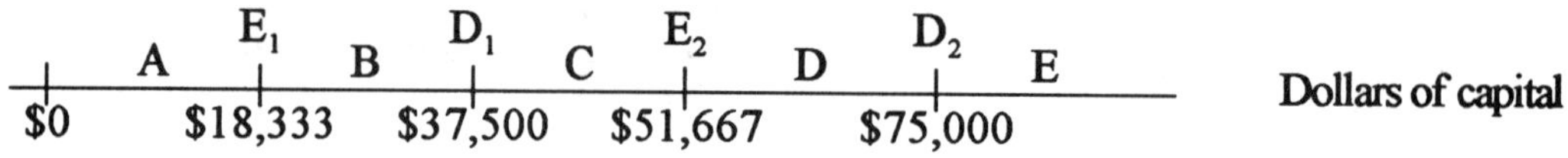

The break points are calculated as follows:

E_1 = $11,000/0.60 = $18,333.
D_1 = $15,000/0.40 = $37,500.
E_2 = $31,000/0.60 = $51,667.
D_2 = $30,000/0.40 = $75,000.

Now determine the weighted average cost of capital for intervals A through E:

$$WACC = w_d k_d(1 - T) + w_{ce} k_s \text{ (or } k_e)$$

A = 0.4(10%)(0.6) + 0.6(16.00%) = 12.00%.
B = 0.4(10%)(0.6) + 0.6(18%) = 13.20%.
C = 0.4(12%)(0.6) + 0.6(18%) = 13.68%.
D = 0.4(12%)(0.6) + 0.6(19.62%) = 14.65%.
E = 0.4(14%)(0.6) + 0.6(19.62%) = 15.13%.

Finally, graph the MCC and IOS schedules:

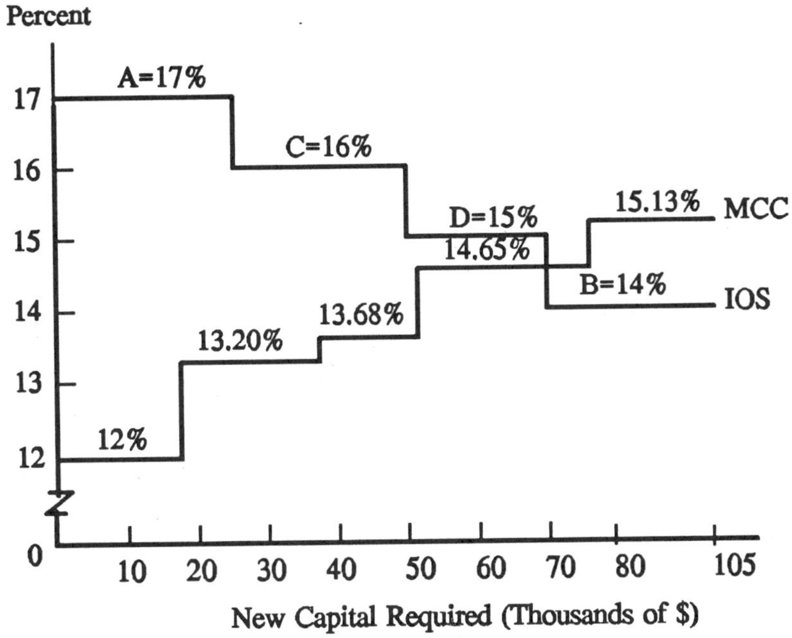

The MCC and IOS schedules intersect at a corporate cost of capital of 14.65 percent and an optimal capital budget of $70,000.

19. c. As shown in the diagram, the MCC and IOS schedules intersect at an optimal capital budget of $70,000, so Projects A, C, and D should be accepted. Project B, with an IRR of 14 percent, would not be acceptable because the corporate cost of capital, 14.65 percent, is greater than its IRR.

CHAPTER 11
CAPITAL STRUCTURE DECISIONS: PART 1

OVERVIEW

One of the most perplexing issues facing financial managers is the relationship between capital structure, which is the mix of debt and equity financing, and stock prices. Should different industries and different firms within industries have different capital structures, and, if so, what are the factors that lead to these differences?

In Chapters 11 and 12, we will discuss both the theories that underlie capital structure decisions and more pragmatic approaches to the problem. Although the capital structure decision is far from precise, an understanding of Chapters 11 and 12 will help you deal with the issues involved.

KEY CONCEPTS

Business risk is the riskiness of the firm's assets if it uses no debt. In a stand-alone risk sense, business risk is a function of the uncertainty inherent in projections of a firm's future rate of return on assets (ROA).

If the firm uses no debt, then its interest payments will be zero, its assets will be all-equity financed, and its return on invested capital will equal its return on assets and its return on equity.

Business risk varies not only from industry to industry but also among firms in a given industry. Further, business risk can change over time.

Business risk depends on several factors.

- Demand variability
- Sales price variability
- Input cost variability
- Competitive factors

- Product liability suits
- Operating leverage, that is, the extent to which costs are fixed.

Operating leverage is the degree to which a firm uses fixed cost inputs (as opposed to variable cost inputs) in its production processes.

- Firms that have a higher percentage of fixed costs are said to have a high degree of operating leverage.
- High operating leverage implies that a relatively small change in sales will result in a large change in ROE.
- In general, the higher a firm's operating leverage, the greater the firm's business risk as measured by the standard deviation of its expected ROE.
- Production technology limits control over the amount of fixed costs and hence operating leverage. However, firms do have some control over the type of production processes they employ. Therefore, a firm's capital budgeting decisions will have an impact on its business risk.
- Once a corporation's operating leverage has been established, this factor exerts a major influence on its capital structure decision.

Financial risk is the additional risk placed on the common stockholders as a result of the decision to use debt and/or preferred stock.

The use of financial leverage concentrates the firm's inherent business risk on a smaller equity base.

The standard deviation of the return on equity for the unleveraged firm, $\sigma_{ROE(U)}$, is a measure of the firm's business risk.

The σ_{ROE} at any debt level is a measure of the stand-alone risk borne by the common stockholders.

If the firm does not use any financial leverage, then $\sigma_{ROE} = \sigma_{ROE(U)}$.

However, if the firm does use financial leverage, then $\sigma_{ROE} > \sigma_{ROE(U)}$, and the difference is a measure of financial risk:

$$\text{Financial risk} = \sigma_{ROE} - \sigma_{ROE(U)}.$$

Financial leverage will be "favorable" and, hence, "leverage up" shareholder returns if the return on assets measured as EBIT/Total assets is greater than the cost of debt. However, the total risk to common stockholders will also increase as leverage increases.

Operating and financial leverage work in the same way; they generally both increase expected ROE, but they also increase the risk borne by stockholders. Operating leverage affects the firm's business risk, financial leverage affects the firm's financial risk, and both influence the firm's stand-alone risk.

Beginning in 1958, *Modigliani and Miller (MM)* addressed the capital structure issue in a rigorous, scientific fashion. The result is the well-known MM propositions.

MM began with a set of assumptions including constant debt costs, zero brokerage costs, perpetual cash flows, and zero growth. Initially, they also assumed zero taxes. MM used an arbitrage proof to develop two propositions.

- Proposition I:

$$V_L = V_U = EBIT/WACC = EBIT/k_{sU}.$$

  where V_L = value of a leveraged firm, and V_U = value of an unleveraged firm in the same risk class, and k_{sU} = the required rate of return for an unleveraged, or all-equity, firm.
  - Proposition I tells us that the value of a firm is established by capitalizing the expected net operating income at the firm's weighted average cost of capital which is a constant equal to the cost of equity of an unleveraged (zero debt) firm. Thus, Proposition I implies that the value of a firm is independent of its leverage.
  - Proposition I also implies (1) that a firm's WACC is the same whether the firm is leveraged or not and (2) that it is equal to the cost of equity to an unleveraged firm in the same risk class.
- Proposition II:

$$k_{sL} = k_{sU} + (k_{sU} - k_d)(D/S).$$

  Here we see that the cost of equity to a leveraged firm, k_{sL}, is equal to the cost of equity to an unleveraged firm in the same risk class, k_{sU}, plus a risk premium whose size depends on both the differential between the costs of equity and debt to an unleveraged firm and the amount of leverage used.
- Taken together, the two MM propositions imply that the inclusion of more debt in the capital structure will not increase a firm's value because the benefits of lower cost debt will be exactly offset by an increase in the cost of equity. Thus, MM without taxes states that both the value of a firm and its WACC are completely unaffected by its capital structure, and its prescription for managers is that one capital structure is as good as another.

MM reworked their theory in 1963 by adding corporate taxes. Here are the MM propositions assuming that corporations are subject to income taxes:

Proposition I:

$$V_L = V_U + TD = EBIT(1 - T)/k_{sU} + TD.$$

- Thus, the value of a leveraged firm is equal to the value of the unleveraged firm in the same risk class plus the gain from leverage, which is the value of the tax savings due to debt financing and which equals the corporate tax rate times the amount of debt used.
- Note that for an unleveraged firm with perpetual cash flows, EBIT(1 - T) = Net income = Total dividends. Thus, the value of the unleveraged firm is equal to the perpetual dividend divided by k_{sU}.
- Also note that the differential between V_U and V_L increases as the firm's use of debt increases, so a firm's value is maximized at virtually 100 percent debt financing.

Proposition II:

$$k_{sL} = k_{sU} + (k_{sU} - k_d)(1 - T)(D/S).$$

- Now, the cost of equity for a leveraged firm is still equal to the cost of equity for an unleveraged firm plus a risk premium, but the risk premium is reduced by the term (1 - T).
- Thus, when corporate taxes are introduced, the cost of equity rises at a slower rate than it did in the absence of corporate taxes. Further, the cost of debt is reduced by the tax deductibility of interest payments. These two factors combine to produce the increase in firm value which is shown by Proposition I.

MM's model with corporate taxes leads to the conclusion that firms should use almost 100 percent debt. However, firms do not follow this prescription, and hence theorists have been searching for other models which better describe actual behavior.

In our previous discussion of business and financial risk, we focused on stand-alone risk. Now we shift our focus from stand-alone risk to *market risk.*

Robert Hamada, using the Capital Asset Pricing Model (CAPM) and the MM with corporate taxes model, developed an expression for the cost of equity to a leveraged firm:

k_{sL} = Risk-free rate + Business risk premium + Financial risk premium

$$= k_{RF} + (k_M - k_{RF})b_U + (k_M - k_{RF})b_U(1 - T)(D/S).$$

By equating the SML equation with Hamada's equation for k_{sL}, we ultimately obtain:

$$b = b_U[1 + (1 - T)(D/S)].$$

Thus, under the MM and CAPM assumptions, the beta of any firm is equal to the beta the firm would have if it used zero debt, adjusted upward by a factor that depends on (1) the corporate tax rate and (2) the amount of financial leverage employed.

A firm's market risk, which is measured by b, depends on both the firm's business risk as reflected by b_U, and its financial risk as reflected by its leverage ratio, D/S, and its tax rate, T.

Within a market risk context, a firm's business risk is measured by its unleveraged beta, b_U, its stand-alone risk is measured by its leveraged beta, b, and its financial risk is measured by the difference, $b - b_U$.

The Hamada relationship can also be used to estimate the cost of equity for a firm or division by leveraging up or down the betas of comparable proxy firms to reflect the firm's or division's capital structure and tax rate.

In 1976, Miller presented a capital structure model which includes not only corporate taxes, but personal taxes as well.

Proposition I of the Miller model takes this form:

$$V_L = V_U + \left[1 - \frac{(1 - T_c)(1 - T_s)}{(1 - T_d)}\right]D.$$

- Here T_c is the corporate tax rate, T_s is the personal tax rate on stock income, and Td is the personal tax rate on bond income.
- The term in brackets, multiplied by D, is the gain from leverage. The bracketed term replaces the factor $T = T_c$ in the MM model with corporate taxes.
- If all taxes are ignored, then $T_c = T_s = T_d = 0$, and the model reduces to the original MM zero taxes model.
- If we ignore personal taxes, then $T_s = T_d = 0$, and the model reduces to the MM with corporate taxes model.

The gain from leverage in the Miller model depends on the values of T_c, T_s, and T_d as well as the amount of debt financing.

- Because taxes on capital gains are deferred (and capped at 28 percent), the effective tax rate on stock income is normally less than the effective tax rate on bond income.
- When $T_s < T_d$, the bracketed term is less than T_c, and the value of financial leverage is less than it would be in the absence of personal taxes.

Thus, Miller's model confirms the earlier MM conclusion that the use of corporate debt increases the value of a firm, but the advantage is clearly less than TD, and hence personal taxes reduce the benefits of corporate debt. Note, however, that the Miller model still prescribes close to 100 percent debt as the value-maximizing capital structure.

While the conclusions of the two MM models and the Miller model follow logically from the initial assumptions, these theories lack support because (1) their assumptions do not reflect actual market conditions, and (2) more important, their prescriptions are not followed. Here are some of the main objections.

Both MM and Miller assumed that personal and corporate leverage are perfect substitutes.

Brokerage costs are assumed away, making the switch from leveraged to unleveraged companies costless.

To reach the conclusions of MM and Miller, one must assume that both corporations and investors can borrow at the same rate.

Miller concluded that equilibrium would be reached, but to reach equilibrium the tax benefit from corporate debt must be the same for all firms and must be constant for an individual firm regardless of the amount of leverage used.

MM and Miller assumed that there are no financial distress and agency costs.

A potential problem with the MM and Miller models is that they ignore financial distress and agency costs. Quite a few firms go bankrupt every year, and the costs of financial distress, as well as agency costs, can be significant.

Actual bankruptcy results in extraordinary costs such as forced sale of assets at below-market prices, deterioration of property, and court and administrative costs. The threat of financial distress also involves costs, since managers must spend more time on fending off bankruptcy than on making good operating decisions, as well as taking costly actions in an attempt to ward off financial distress. In general, the probability of financial distress increases as more debt is used. An increase in the probability of future financial distress lowers the current value of a firm and raises its cost of capital.

Agency costs, which were discussed in Chapter 1, also tend to increase as more and more debt is used.

When these costs are considered, MM's Proposition I, with corporate taxes, becomes

$$V_L = V_U + TD - \text{PV of expected financial distress and agency costs.}$$

This relationship is shown in Figure 1.

Figure 1
Debt Usage versus Firm Value

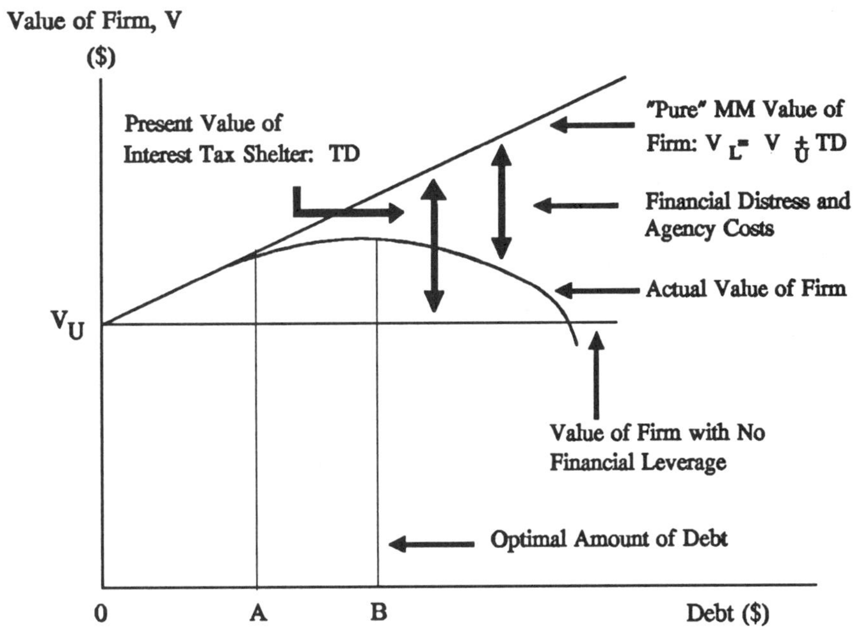

Here we see that the tax shelter effect dominates until debt reaches Point A. After Point A, the financial distress and agency costs begin to offset the tax advantages of debt financing. At Point B, the marginal tax benefits of debt are exactly offset by the marginal financial distress and agency costs, and beyond Point B, the disadvantages of using debt outweigh the benefits. However, the financial distress and agency costs cannot be estimated easily, and it is very difficult, if not impossible, to identify Point B in practice with any precision.

Note that financial distress and agency costs can also be added to the Miller model. When these are added, the relationship between value and debt is the same as when these costs are added to the MM with corporate taxes model, except that the gain from leverage term, TD, would reflect the addition of personal taxes. However, the "Pure MM Value of Firm" line would be less steep under Miller since the value of debt financing is reduced. Further, the Y intercept would be lowered because the addition of personal taxes reduces the value of the unleveraged firm.

The addition of financial distress and agency costs to either the MM tax model or the Miller model results in a trade-off model of capital structure. The optimal capital structure can be visualized as a trade-off between the benefit of debt financing and the costs of debt financing.

DEFINITIONAL QUESTIONS

1. Determination of the __________ capital structure requires consideration of both __________ and __________.

2. A firm's __________ capital structure is generally equal to its estimated optimal structure.

3. Business risk, in a stand-alone risk sense, is a function of the uncertainty inherent in projections of a firm's future _______ _____ __________ ______ __________.

4. The factors that influence a firm's business risk include (1) demand variability, (2) sales price variability, (3) input cost variability, (4) competitive factors, (5) product liability suits, and (6) __________ __________ (the extent to which costs are fixed).

5. Business risk represents the riskiness of the firm's operations if it uses no __________; financial risk represents the risk concentrated on the common stockholders as a result of using __________.

6. Common stockholders are compensated for bearing financial risk by a higher __________ __________.

7. Up to some point, EPS __________ as the debt/assets ratio increases.

8. Firms that have a high ratio of fixed to variable costs are said to operate with a high degree of __________ __________.

9. Operating leverage refers to the use of __________ __________.

10. Financial leverage refers to the use of __________ financing.

11. Hamada's equation gives the relationship between business risk and financial risk in a __________ risk sense.

12. Debt has a __________ advantage over equity in that __________ is a deductible expense while __________ are not.

13. In their 1958 paper, MM prove that a leveraged firm's cost of equity is equal to the cost of equity to an unleveraged firm plus a __________ __________.

14. The MM without taxes model implies that debt financing does not increase the value of the firm because the benefits of lower cost debt are offset exactly by increases in the __________ _____ __________.

15. When MM added corporate taxes to their model, they found that the cost of equity to a leveraged firm rises at a __________ rate than it did in their original model.

16. MM's model with corporate taxes prescribes that firms should use almost ______ __________ financing.

17. The results of the MM model with corporate taxes are drastically changed when __________ __________ and __________ costs are introduced.

18. Miller's 1976 model differs from the earlier MM model in that __________ __________ are added.

19. Considering U.S. tax rates, the Miller model leads to the conclusion that corporate debt is __________ valuable when personal taxes are considered.

20. The same debt ratio that maximizes firm value also __________ the firm's cost of capital.

21. The MM/Miller theories with financial distress and agency costs added are examples of __________ __________ that balance the tax shield benefits of leverage against the costs of leverage.

CONCEPTUAL QUESTIONS

22. Firm A has higher business risk than Firm B. Firm A can offset this by increasing its operating leverage.

a. True **b.** False

23. Two firms, although operating in different industries, have the same expected ROE and the same standard deviation of expected ROE. Thus, in a stand-alone sense, the two firms must have the same financial risk.

a. True **b.** False

24. Two firms could have identical financial and operating leverage yet have different degrees of total risk.

a. True **b.** False

25. Assume a firm has zero debt. The use of some debt is bound to increase ROE.

a. True **b.** False

26. Strong empirical support is evident for the tradeoff models.

a. True **b.** False

27. The propositions that MM derive in their model with corporate taxes are:
I: $V_L = V_U + TD$, and II: $k_{sL} = k_{sU} + (k_{sU} - k_d)(D/S)$.

a. True **b.** False

28. The Miller model, which adds personal taxes, leads to the conclusion that debt does not matter. That is, there is no optimal capital structure.

a. True **b.** False

29. A decrease in the debt ratio will have no effect on

a. Financial risk.
b. Stand-alone risk.
c. Business risk.
d. Market risk.
e. Company-specific risk.

30. The main objections to the capital structure theories are:

a. Personal and corporate leverage are assumed to be perfect substitutes.
b. Brokerage costs are not accounted for.
c. They assume corporations and investors borrow at the same rate.
d. Financial distress costs are assumed to be zero.
e. All of the above.

PROBLEMS

31. The Fisher Company will produce 50,000 10-gallon aquariums next year. Variable costs will equal 40 percent of dollar sales, while fixed costs total $100,000. At what price must each aquarium be sold for the firm's EBIT to be $90,000?

a. $5.00 b. $5.33 c. $5.50 d. $6.00 e. $6.33

32. The Diamond Company has identified two methods of producing playing cards. One method involves using a machine having a fixed cost of $20,000 and variable costs of $1.00 per deck. The other method would use a less expensive machine having a fixed cost of $5,000, but it would require variable costs of $2.00 per deck. If the selling price per deck will be the same under each method, at what level of output would the two methods produce the same net operating income (EBIT)?

a. 5,000 b. 10,000 c. 15,000 d. 20,000 e. 25,000

The following data apply to the next two problems.

A firm with no debt financing has a firm value of $20 million. It has a corporate marginal tax rate of 34 percent. The firm's investors are estimated to have marginal tax rates of 33 percent on interest income and a weighted average of 28 percent on stock income. The firm is planning to change its capital structure by issuing $10 million in debt, and repurchasing $10 million of common stock.

33. According to the Modigliani-Miller view with corporate taxes, what is the value of the leveraged firm?

a. $20.00 million
b. $22.44 million
c. $23.40 million
d. $26.40 million
e. $30.00 million

34. According to the Miller view with corporate and personal taxes, what is the gain from leverage?

a. $0.00
b. $2.91 million
c. $4.60 million
d. $6.40 million
e. $8.00 million

The following data apply to the next three problems.

The Ensyder Trading Company (ETC) is a zero growth firm with an EBIT of $250,000 and corporate tax rate of 40 percent. ETC uses $1 million of debt financing, and the cost of equity of an unleveraged firm in the same risk class is 15 percent. The personal tax rates of ETC's investors are 30 percent on interest income and 20 percent (on average) on income from common stocks.

35. What is the value of ETC according to MM with corporate taxes?

a. $1,000,000 b. $1,114,000 c. $1,314,000 d. $1,400,000 e. $2,000,000

36. What is ETC's value according to Miller (including personal taxes)?

a. $1,000,000 b. $1,114,000 c. $1,314,000 d. $1,600,000 e. $2,000,000

37. Suppose that the present value of financial distress costs is estimated to be $800,000, and that, at a debt level of $1 million, ETC has a 20 percent probability of going bankrupt. Further, assume that the present value of agency costs are $50,000 at a $1,000,000 debt level. What is the firm value if these costs are added to the Miller model?

a. $904,000 b. $1,114,000 c. $1,314,000 d. $1,600,000 e. $2,000,000

The following data apply to the next five problems.

Unleveraged Corporation (Firm U) has a total market value of $500,000, a tax rate of 40 percent, and earnings before interest and taxes (EBIT) of $100,000. Leveraged Corporation (Firm L) is identical in all respects to Firm U, but Firm L has $200,000 market (and book) value of debt outstanding. Firm L pays total annual interest of $16,000 on this debt. Both firms satisfy the MM assumptions.

38. What is the value of Firm L according to MM's Proposition I?

a. $500,000 b. $520,000 c. $540,000 d. $560,000 e. $580,000

39. What is Firm U's cost of equity?

a. 10.00% **b.** 10.34% **c.** 11.00% **d.** 12.00% **e.** 13.26%

40. What is Firm L's cost of equity?

a. 10.00% **b.** 10.34% **c.** 11.00% **d.** 12.00% **e.** 13.26%

41. What is Firm L's weighted average cost of capital?

a. 10.00% **b.** 10.34% **c.** 11.00% **d.** 12.00% **e.** 13.26%

42. An alternative equation for a firm's cost of capital is

$$WACC = \frac{EBIT(1 - T)}{V}.$$

What is Firm L's weighted average cost of capital according to this formula?

a. 10.00% **b.** 10.34% **c.** 11.00% **d.** 12.00% **e.** 13.26%

ANSWERS

1. optimal; risk; return
2. target
3. rate of return on assets
4. operating leverage
5. debt (leverage); debt (leverage)
6. expected return
7. increases
8. operating leverage
9. fixed assets
10. fixed-charge (debt)
11. market
12. tax; interest; dividends
13. risk premium
14. cost of equity
15. slower
16. all debt
17. financial distress; agency
18. personal taxes
19. less
20. minimizes
21. tradeoff models

22. b. Increasing operating leverage will increase Firm A's business risk.

23. b. The two firms would have the same stand-alone risk. Each could have different combinations of business and financial risk.

24. a. Stand-alone risk = Business risk + Financial risk. Business risk consists of several elements in addition to operating leverage (for example, sales variability).

25. b. Debt financing only increases ROE if the cost of the debt is less than the return on the assets.

26. b. Empirical evidence is not strong, suggesting other factors not incorporated into these models are also at work.

27. b. Proposition I is correct as stated; that is, the value of a leveraged firm is equal to the value of the unleveraged firm plus the value of debt financing, TD. However, Proposition II is incorrectly stated. With corporate taxes,

$$k_{sL} = k_{sU} + (k_{sU} - k_d)(1 - T)(D/S).$$

Here the risk premium added to k_{sU} is reduced by the factor (1 - T). It is the reduced level of k_{sL}, plus the reduction in k_d, which produces the benefit from debt financing given by Proposition I.

28. b. The addition of personal taxes reduces the value of corporate debt financing and hence reduces the gain from leverage. However, debt financing is still advantageous, and firms should use some debt financing according to the Miller model, even with financial distress costs included.

29. c. Business risk is solely dependent upon the basic riskiness of the assets, and not the financing mix.

30. e. Many people argue that the theories are based on assumptions which do not reflect actual market conditions.

31. e.

$$\begin{aligned} EBIT &= PQ - VQP - F \\ \$90{,}000 &= P(50{,}000) - 0.4(50{,}000)P - \$100{,}000 \\ 30{,}000P &= \$190{,}000 \\ P &= \$6.33. \end{aligned}$$

32. c. For the first method: EBIT = PQ - \$1.00Q - \$20,000.
For the second method: EBIT = PQ - \$2.00Q - \$5,000.

Now, equate the EBITs:

PQ - \$1.00Q - \$20,000 = PQ - \$2.00Q - \$5,000; \$1.00Q = \$15,000; Q = 15.000.

33. c. $V_L = V_U + TD$ = \$20 + 0.34(\$10) = \$20 + \$3.4 = \$23.4 million.

34. b. Gain from leverage $= [1 - \frac{(1 - T_c)(1 - T_s)}{(1 - T_d)}]D = [1 - \frac{(1 - 0.34)(1 - 0.28)}{(1 - 0.33)}]\$10$

$$= [1 - 0.709]\$10 = 0.291(\$10) = \$2.91 \text{ million.}$$

Note that the gain from leverage is reduced when personal taxes are added.

35. d. $V_L = V_U + TD = \frac{EBIT(1 - T)}{k_{sU}} + TD$

$$= \frac{\$250{,}000(0.6)}{0.15} + 0.4(\$1{,}000{,}000) = \$1{,}000{,}000 + \$400{,}000 = \$1{,}400{,}000.$$

36. b. $V_L = V_U + [1 - \frac{(1 - T_c)(1 - T_s)}{(1 - T_d)}]D$

$$= V_U + [1 - \frac{0.6(0.8)}{0.7}]\$1{,}000{,}000 = V_U + 0.314(\$1{,}000{,}000) = \$314{,}000.$$

Now, the addition of personal taxes also reduces the value of V_U:

$$V_U = \frac{EBIT(1 - T_c)(1 - T_s)}{k_{sU}} = \frac{\$250{,}000(0.6)(0.8)}{0.15} = \$800{,}000.$$

Thus, $V_L = \$800{,}000 + \$314{,}000 = \$1{,}114{,}000.$

37. a. $V_L = V_{Miller}$ - PV (Financial distress costs) - PV (Agency costs)

$$= \$1{,}114{,}000 - 0.2(\$800{,}000) - \$50{,}000 = \$904{,}000.$$

38. e. $V_L = V_U + TD = \$500{,}000 + 0.4(\$200{,}000) = \$500{,}000 + \$80{,}000 = \$580{,}000.$

39. d. $V_U = \frac{EBIT(1 - T)}{k_{sU}}$; $\$500{,}000 = \frac{\$100{,}000(0.6)}{k_{sU}}$; $k_{sU} = \frac{\$60{,}000}{\$500{,}000} = 12.0\%.$

40. e. First, note that Firm L's cost of debt is 8.0 percent:

$$k_d = \$16,000/\$200,000 = 8.0\%.$$

Next, note that V_L = \$580,000 and D = \$200,000. Thus, Firm L's equity value is S = \$580,000 - \$200,000 = \$380,000. Finally,

$$k_{sL} = k_{sU} + (k_{sU} - k_d)(1 - T)(D/S)$$

$$= 12.0\% + (12.0\% - 8.0\%)(0.6)(\$200,000/\$380,000)$$

$$= 12.0\% + 1.26\% = 13.26\%.$$

41. b. $WACC = w_d k_d(1 - T) + w_s k_s$

$$= (\$200,000/\$580,000)(8.00\%)(0.6) + (\$380,000/\$580,000)(13.26\%) = 10.34\%.$$

42. b. WACC = EBIT(1 - T)/V = \$100,000(0.6)/\$580,000 = 10.34%.

CHAPTER 12
CAPITAL STRUCTURE DECISIONS: PART 2

OVERVIEW

We began our discussion of capital structure decisions in Chapter 11. We discovered that using debt concentrates a firm's business risk on its stockholders, but it also increases the expected return on equity.

We also discussed three important capital structure theories: MM with zero taxes, MM with corporate taxes, and Miller (corporate and personal taxes). Although these models provide insights into the value of debt financing, their prescriptions (either that debt does not matter or 100 percent debt is optimal) are simply not followed by managers. However, when financial distress and agency costs are considered along with taxes, the models lead to the more reasonable conclusion that some debt is good, but too much debt is bad. Now we expand our discussion of capital structure decisions.

KEY CONCEPTS

Both the MM with corporate taxes and Miller models modified to include financial distress and agency costs can be described as trade-off models. That is, the optimal capital structure is found by balancing the tax shield benefits of leverage against the costs of leverage, and hence the costs and benefits are "traded off" against one another.

The *tradeoff models* are not capable of specifying precisely optimal capital structures, but they do lead to three important insights about debt usage.

- Firms with inherently risky assets experience higher variability of returns and therefore face a greater probability of financial distress at any debt level. Given the higher probability of financial distress at any level of debt, firms with higher business risk should borrow less than firms with lower business risk.

- Specialized assets, intangible assets, and growth opportunities lose more value in financial distress than tangible assets, so firms using these types of assets should use less debt than firms employing standardized, tangible assets.
- Firms paying taxes at the highest rates gain the most benefit from debt financing and, hence, should carry more debt than firms in lower tax brackets.

Although the tradeoff models present a logical framework for thought, empirical support for the tradeoff models is not strong, suggesting that factors that are not incorporated into the model are at work.

The *asymmetric information theory* of capital structure was developed in an attempt to reconcile the MM/Miller theories with the pecking order method of financing observed by Professor Gordon Donaldson. By allowing that asymmetric (or different) information exists for different groups of market participants, certain actions may be implied for corporate financial policy.

Donaldson observed that there is a "pecking order" of financing, not the balanced approach that would result if the trade-off models accurately described real-world behavior.

The asymmetric information theory attempts to explain this "pecking order."

- Information asymmetries often exist between managers and investors.
- When such situations exist, a firm will issue new stock only when its stock price is overvalued by the market. If its stock is undervalued, the firm will issue debt.
- Because investors recognize this, they tend to mark down a company's share price when it announces plans to issue new stock, since chances are that the announcement is *signaling* bad news, not good news.
- If managers believe that new stock sales will be regarded as negative signals, then they should maintain some *reserve borrowing capacity*, so they can always issue debt on favorable terms if external financing is needed.

Industries which hold a significant amount of proprietary information, such as pharmaceutical or semiconductor industries, will have a higher degree of asymmetric information than retailing or trucking industries. Although asymmetric information theory is applicable to all firms, its impact on managerial decisions varies from firm to firm.

The tradeoff models are summarized graphically below:

- The left-hand graph shows the relationship between the debt ratio and capital costs. Both the cost of equity and cost of debt rise steadily with increasing leverage, but the rate of increase accelerates sharply at higher debt levels. The weighted average cost of capital first declines, then hits a minimum, and then begins to rise. Note, however,

The great contribution of the tradeoff models of MM and Miller is that these models identified the specific costs and benefits of using debt financing. Prior to these models, no capital structure theory existed, and we had no systematic approach to analyzing the effects of financial leverage.

Figure 1
The Effects of Debt Financing

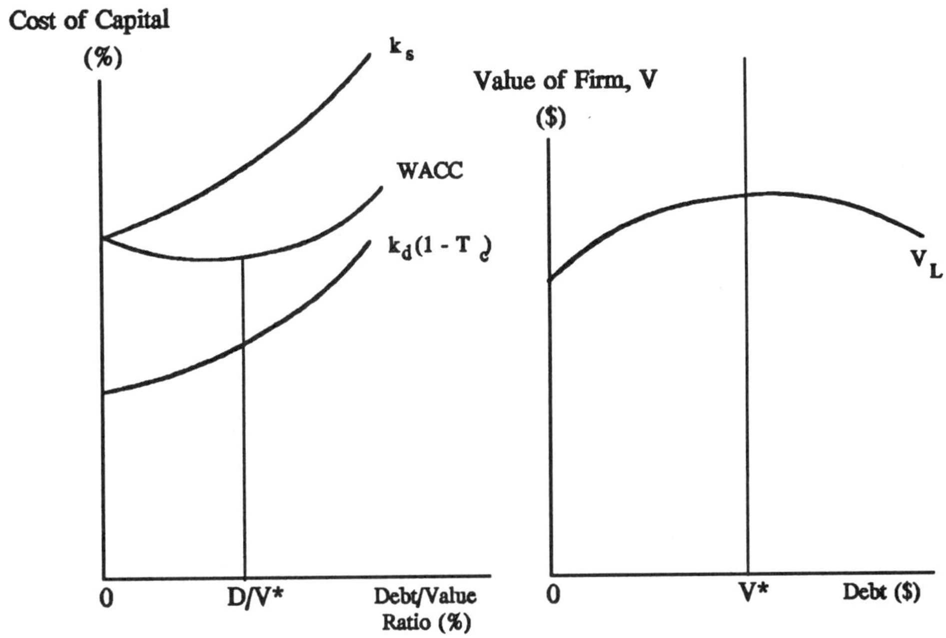

that the WACC curve is shallow, indicating the debt ratio does not have a pronounced effect on WACC over a fairly wide range of values.

- The right-hand graph shows that firm value first rises with debt usage, hits a peak, and then falls. Again, the relationship is such that small deviations from the optimal debt ratio do not have a large impact on value.
- Note in the figure that the same debt ratio that minimizes the cost of capital also maximizes firm value. Thus, the optimal capital structure can be defined in terms of either cost minimization or value maximization because the same capital structure does both.

Little disagreement exists in either business or academic circles that the general situation described above is correct. However, details can only be discovered by empirical testing. Unfortunately, firms which differ only in capital structure do not exist, and future earnings are not known with any certainty. Thus, empirical tests have not produced conclusive results.

We believe that there is a net benefit to debt financing, at least out to some point, but we also believe that firms should maintain a borrowing reserve. Thus, firms use debt on the basis of their tax rates, asset structures, and inherent riskiness, but they also try to maintain the ability to issue new debt at favorable rates if it becomes necessary to raise external capital when chaotic market conditions exist.

The *optimal capital structure* is that structure which will maximize the value of the firm and, for zero-growth firms, can be obtained by quantitative analysis.

- First, the costs of debt and equity are estimated for different levels of debt, holding total assets constant.
- As more debt is used, the estimated costs of debt and equity will rise, because the riskiness of these capital components is increasing.
- The estimated component costs are then combined to find the weighted average cost of capital at each debt level.
- The amount of debt which produces the lowest overall weighted average cost of capital (WACC) is optimal, and this is the firm's target capital structure, because that capital structure which minimizes a firm's weighted average cost of capital also maximizes its stock price.
- For a complete description of the calculations, see text Chapter 12.
- Using leverage also involves a risk/return tradeoff for EPS. Higher leverage increases expected earnings per share, but using more leverage also increases the firm's risk of low or even negative earnings per share.
- Price per share and EPS will not both be maximized at the same level of debt. Since management is primarily interested in maximizing shareholder wealth, the optimal capital structure should be based on value, or share price, and not on EPS.
- Although conceptually simple, it is impossible to place much faith in the results, since it is just not possible to estimate the values for k_d and k_s at different debt levels with any degree of precision and the models are very sensitive to input estimates.

Since we cannot determine precisely the optimal capital structure, managers must apply judgment along with quantitative analysis. The judgmental analysis involves many different factors, and in one situation a particular factor might have great importance, while the same factor might be relatively unimportant in another situation. Here is a listing of the more important judgmental factors.

Long-run viability. Managers of large firms, especially those providing vital services such as utilities, have a responsibility to provide continuous service. Thus, these firms must refrain from using leverage to the point where the firm's long-run viability is endangered.

Managerial conservatism. Well-diversified investors have eliminated most, if not all, of the company-specific risk from their portfolios. However, managers generally view potential bankruptcy with more concern since their career earnings could be seriously affected if the firm fails. Thus, managers might be more "conservative" in their use of leverage and might set a lower target capital structure than the one which maximizes stock price.

Lender and rating agency attitudes. Regardless of managers' own analyses of the proper amounts of leverage, there is no question that lenders' and rating agencies' attitudes are frequently important determinants of financial structures.

- Lenders and rating agencies generally focus on the risk of default. Accordingly, they place considerable importance on a firm's times-interest-earned (TIE) ratio:

$$\text{TIE} = \text{EBIT/Interest charges.}$$

- Another measure that is often used to estimate default probability is the fixed charge coverage (FCC) ratio:

$$\text{FCC} = \frac{\text{EBIT} + \text{Lease payments}}{\text{Interest charges} + \text{Lease payments} + \dfrac{\text{Sinking fund payments}}{1 - T}}.$$

Sinking fund payments are mandatory payments made to redeem debt. Note that this definition "grosses up" the sinking fund payments in recognition of the fact that these payments are made with after-tax dollars. Also note that lump-sum principal repayments might be included along with the sinking fund payments.

Reserve borrowing capacity and financing flexibility. As indicated by the asymmetric information theory, firms often maintain the ability to issue debt at all times in order to assure access to relatively low-cost, "safe" financing. This means they would generally use less debt than an MM-type analysis would suggest.

Control. If a firm's management just barely has voting control, then there could be an inclination to use more debt financing. Conversely, excessive use of debt coupled with an economic downturn could lead to excessive influence by creditors. In general, control considerations do not necessarily suggest the use of debt or equity, but the effects of capital structure on control will certainly be considered.

Additional considerations:

- *Asset structure.* Firms with assets that are suitable as collateral for loans tend to use more debt than firms without such assets.
- *Growth rate.* Firms with high growth rates need lots of capital. Since flotation costs are generally considerably lower for debt than for equity, high-growth firms tend to use more debt than do slow-growth firms.
- *Profitability.* Firms that are highly profitable often have very low debt ratios. Although there is no theoretical justification, such firms simply do not need to sell much debt--they can do most of their financing through retained earnings.
- *Taxes.* The higher the firm's marginal tax rate, the greater the advantage of using debt.

A spreadsheet forecasting model can be used to assess the effects of capital structure changes on a firm's profitability and financial condition.

The financial manager begins by entering base year values and data on expected unit sales growth rates, expected inflation rates, and other known or estimated operating input data.

Next, the debt/equity mix, the debt maturity mix, and the component costs of the capital must be entered. Note that the component costs must reflect the particular capital structure being analyzed--the higher the debt ratio, the higher the component costs.

The model then forecasts balance sheets and income statements, as well as ROE, EPS, DPS, WACC, and projected stock prices for a specified number of years.

Finally, the model can be used to analyze alternative scenarios by changing the financing and/or operating input values.

The optimal capital structure should be thought of in market value rather than in book value terms, even though managers often seem to focus on book values.

Definitional Questions

1. The addition of financial distress and agency costs leads to a WACC curve which first __________, then reaches a __________, and then __________.

2. The optimal capital structure is that structure at which the marginal __________ of leverage equal the marginal __________.

3. The asymmetric information theory relaxes the MM models' assumption that __________ __________ exists.

4. By allowing for asymmetric information, Donaldson's __________ __________ method of financing can be explained.

5. Difficulties in estimating the relationship between __________ ratios and the costs of __________ and __________ have made some managers reluctant to rely heavily on quantitative analysis to set the target capital structure.

6. Conservative financial managers may try to maintain a target capital structure that is __________ than optimal.

7. The __________ ratio and the __________ __________ __________ ratio give some indication of a firm's ability to cover its fixed charges, and hence its default risk.

8. External capital is particularly important to firms with high __________ __________.

9. Owner/managers may prefer additional __________ as opposed to common stock in order to maintain __________ of the company.

10. A firm's cost of capital should be based on __________ __________ weights. However, these weights are based on its __________ capital structure rather than its current capital structure.

Conceptual Questions

11. While asymmetric information theory applies to all firms, its impact on managerial decisions varies from firm to firm.

    a. True b. False

12. As a general rule, the capital structure which maximizes stock price (firm value) also

a. Maximizes earnings per share.
b. Minimizes the probability of financial distress.
c. Minimizes both the cost of equity and the cost of debt.
d. Answers a, b, and c above are all correct.
e. Answers a, b, and c above are all incorrect.

13. Firms should use more debt if

a. They are in a lower tax bracket.
b. They have stable expected returns on their assets (low business risk).
c. They employ standardized, tangible assets.
d. Answers b and c above are correct.
e. Answers a, b, and c above are correct.

14. If information asymmetries exist, then management is motivated to issue new stock only if the stock is

a. Overvalued.
b. Undervalued.
c. Fairly valued.

PROBLEMS

The following data apply to the next six problems.

United Producers (UP), an unlevered firm, has a total market value of $10 million, consisting of 500,000 shares of common stock selling at $20 per share. Management is considering issuing $2 million of debt at a before-tax cost of 12 percent, and using the proceeds to repurchase stock at the new equilibrium market price. If the plan is carried out, the required rate of return on equity will increase by 2 percentage points to 16 percent. UP's marginal tax rate is 40 percent. The firm pays out all earnings as dividends.

15. What are UP's earnings before interest and taxes (EBIT)?

a. $1.4 million
b. $2.3 million
c. $3.0 million
d. $3.6 million
e. $4.2 million

16. Regardless of your answer to Question 15, assume that UP's EBIT is $2,800,000. What is the value of the firm if the restructuring occurs?

a. $ 9.76 million
b. $10.00 million
c. $10.56 million
d. $11.00 million
e. $11.60 million

17. Suppose a tax law change occurs which causes UP's marginal tax rate to decline to 30 percent. UP's EBIT remains at $2.8 million. Under these conditions, what is the value of the firm at zero debt?

a. $10 million
b. $11 million
c. $12 million
d. $13 million
e. $14 million

18. Under the conditions of Problem 17, what is the value of the firm if restructuring occurs?

a. $13.2 million
b. $14.0 million
c. $14.2 million
d. $14.6 million
e. $14.8 million

19. Disregard the tax change in Problem 17 and refer back to the data in the original problem. Assume these data are correct, including the implied EBIT of $2.8 million, except that use of financial leverage will increase the required rate of return on equity to only 15 percent, rather than 16 percent. What is the value of the firm if the restructuring occurs?

a. $ 9.4 million
b. $10.0 million
c. $12.2 million
d. $13.0 million
e. $13.1 million

20. Under the conditions of Problem 19, what will be the new number of shares outstanding if the restructuring occurs?

a. 500,000 b. 478,642 c. 438,231 d. 418,301 e. 396,547

The following data apply to the next four questions.

Union Brick Inc. (UBI) has a total market value of $200 million, consisting of 2 million shares of common stock selling for $50 per share and $100 million of 10 percent perpetual bonds currently selling at par. UBI pays out all earnings as dividends, and its marginal tax rate is 40 percent. The firm's earnings before interest and taxes (EBIT) are $30 million. Management is considering increasing UBI's debt to $140 million. The additional funds will be used to repurchase stock at the new equilibrium price. At a debt level of $140 million

UBI's cost of debt is estimated at 12 percent and its cost of equity is estimated to be 15 percent.

21. What is UBI's current (debt = $100 million) required rate of return on equity?

a. 11.0% b. 12.0% c. 13.0% d. 14.0% e. 15.0%

22. Assume that UBI will increase its outstanding debt by calling in the old debt and issuing new debt, resulting in a debt level of $140 million. What would be UBI's new firm value?

a. $ 52.8 million
b. $100.0 million
c. $140.0 million
d. $192.8 million
e. $200.0 million

23. Refer to Problem 22. What would be UBI's new stock price?

a. $40.00 b. $46.40 c. $50.00 d. $50.40 e. $52.60

24. Now assume that UBI will increase its outstanding debt by issuing $40 million of new debt--the debt outstanding will not be called. What would be UBI's new stock price?

a. $40.00 b. $46.40 c. $50.00 d. $50.40 e. $52.60

ANSWERS

1. declines; minimum; rises
2. benefits; costs
3. perfect information
4. pecking order
5. debt; debt; equity
6. less
7. times-interest-earned; fixed charge coverage
8. growth rates
9. debt; control
10. market value; target

11. a. This statement is correct.

12. e. The capital structure which maximizes stock price also minimizes the firm's weighted average cost of capital. The probability of financial distress is minimized at zero debt. Also, note that neither the cost of debt nor the cost of equity is minimized at the optimal capital structure.

13. d. Firms gain the most benefits from using debt when they are in the highest tax bracket. Firms with highly variable expected returns and intangible, specialized assets should use lower levels of debt.

14. a. Management will want to issue new stock only if the excess value will benefit the existing stockholders and not be passed on to new investors.

15. b. $V_0 = S_0 = 500{,}000(\$20) = \$10{,}000{,}000.$

$$S_0 = \frac{(EBIT - k_dD)(1 - T)}{k_s} = \frac{EBIT(1 - T)}{k_s}.$$

Thus,

$$\$10{,}000{,}000 = \frac{EBIT(0.6)}{0.14}$$
$$0.6(EBIT) = \$1{,}400{,}000$$
$$EBIT = \$2{,}333{,}333.$$

16. e.

$$S_1 = \frac{(EBIT - k_dD)(1 - T)}{k_s}$$
$$= \frac{[\$2{,}800{,}000 - 0.12(\$2{,}000{,}000)]0.6}{0.16} = \$9{,}600{,}000.$$
$$V_1 = D_1 + S_1 = \$2{,}000{,}000 + \$9{,}600{,}000 = \$11{,}600{,}000.$$

17. e.

$$S_0 = \frac{(EBIT - k_dD)(1 - T)}{k_s}$$
$$= \frac{(\$2{,}800{,}000 - \$0)(0.7)}{0.14} = \$14{,}000{,}000 = V_0.$$

Now, less money is paid in taxes, more remains for the shareholders, and the value of the firm is higher.

18. a.

$$S_1 = \frac{(EBIT - k_dD)(1 - T)}{k_s}$$

$$= \frac{[\$2{,}800{,}000 - 0.12(\$2{,}000{,}000)]0.7}{0.16} = \$11{,}200{,}000.$$

$$V_1 = D_1 + S_1 = \$2{,}000{,}000 + \$11{,}200{,}000 = \$13{,}200{,}000.$$

19. c.

$$S_1 = \frac{(EBIT - k_dD)(1 - T)}{k_s}$$

$$= \frac{[\$2{,}800{,}000 - 0.12(\$2{,}000{,}000)]0.6}{0.15} = \$10{,}240{,}000.$$

$$V_1 = D_1 + S_1 = \$2{,}000{,}000 + \$10{,}240{,}000 = \$12{,}240{,}000.$$

20. d. First, find the equilibrium stock price:

$$P = \frac{V_1 - D_0}{n_0} = \frac{\$12{,}240{,}000 - \$0}{500{,}000} = \$24.48.$$

Then, find the number of shares repurchased:

$$\text{Shares repurchased} = \frac{\$2{,}000{,}000}{\$24.48} = 81{,}699.$$

Finally, determine the shares remaining:

$$\text{Shares remaining} = 500{,}000 - 81{,}699 = 418{,}301.$$

21. b.

$$k_s = \frac{(EBIT - k_dD)(1 - T)}{S} = \frac{[\$30 - 0.10(\$100)]0.6}{\$100} = 12.0\%.$$

22. d.

$$S_1 = \frac{(EBIT - k_dD)(1 - T)}{k_s} = \frac{[\$30 - 0.12(\$140)]0.6}{0.15} = \$52.8 \text{ million}.$$

$$V_1 = D_1 + S_1 = \$140 + \$52.8 = \$192.8 \text{ million}.$$

23. b.

$$P = \frac{V_1 - D_0}{n_0} = \frac{\$192.8 - \$100}{2} = \$46.40.$$

Note that stock price decreases with the increase in leverage. Thus, the change should not be made.

24. d.

$$S_1 = \frac{(EBIT - k_d D - k_{d1} D_1)(1 - T)}{k_s}$$

$$= \frac{[\$30 - 0.10(\$100) - 0.12(\$40)]0.6}{0.15} = \$60.8 \text{ million}.$$

$$V_1 = S_1 + D_0 + D_1.$$

But the value of the old debt, D_0, decreases because its riskiness has increased:

$$D_0 = \frac{0.1(\$100)}{0.12} = \$83.33 \text{ million}.$$

Thus, V_1 = \$60.8 + \$83.33 + \$40 = \$184.13 million. Finally

$$P = \frac{V_1 - D_0}{n_0} = \frac{\$184.13 - \$83.33}{2} = \$50.40.$$

Note that the change should be made under these circumstances. Here some of the wealth of the old bondholders is being transferred to the shareholders.

CHAPTER 13
DIVIDEND POLICY

OVERVIEW

Dividend policy, which is the decision whether to pay out earnings as dividends or to retain and reinvest them in the firm, has three key elements: (1) What fraction of earnings should be paid out, on average, over time? This is the target payout policy decision. (2) Should the firm attempt to maintain a steady, stable dividend growth rate, or should it vary its dividend payments from year to year depending on its internal need for funds and on its cash flows? (3) What dollar amount should the firm pay in current dividends? These three elements are the primary focus of this chapter. We also examine two related issues: stock repurchases and stock splits.

KEY CONCEPTS

Dividend policy theories attempt to establish the relationship between a firm's payout policy and its value. In essence, they attempt to determine whether investors prefer dividends or capital gains.

Modigliani and Miller (MM) argue that a firm's value is determined solely by its basic earnings power and its risk class. Thus, the value of the firm depends on asset investment policy only, and not how the firm's net income is split between dividends and retained earnings. This is called *dividend irrelevance.*

- MM prove their proposition, but only under a set of restrictive assumptions, including (1) zero taxes, (2) zero flotation and transactions costs, (3) independence between dividend policy and equity costs, and (4) symmetric information.
- Obviously, firms and investors do pay taxes, and firms do incur flotation costs. Thus, the MM conclusions on dividend irrelevance may not be valid under real-world conditions.

Another theory, the *bird-in-the-hand theory,* has been proposed by Myron Gordon and John Lintner.

- Gordon and Lintner argue that k_s increases as the dividend payout is reduced because investors view dividend payments as more certain than the capital gains that presumably result from retained earnings.
- MM call the Gordon-Lintner argument the "bird-in-the-hand theory" because, in MM's view, most investors are going to reinvest their dividends in the same or similar firms, and the riskiness of the firm's cash flows to investors in the long run is solely a function of the riskiness of the firm's assets.

A third theory, the *tax preference theory*, is based on the fact that capital gains are effectively taxed at a lower rate than dividend income because taxes on capital gains are deferred until the end of the holding period.

- Because of the tax deferral feature on capital gains (and the fact that capital gains taxes are capped at 28 percent), investors should require higher rates of return on high dividend yield stocks than they do on low dividend yield stocks, other things held constant.
- Under the old tax laws before 1986, capital gains were taxed at a significantly lower rate as well as deferred, making the yield differentials even more pronounced.

Note that each of these theories leads to a different prescription for financial managers.

- According to MM, there is no optimal dividend payout policy.
- Gordon and Lintner argue that firms should set high dividend payout ratios to maximize stock price.
- The tax preference theory leads to the opposite conclusion that firms should set low dividend payout ratios.

Unfortunately, empirical testing has not produced definitive results regarding which theory is correct.

> There are three other issues which have a bearing on optimal dividend policy.

It has been observed that an announcement of a dividend increase is often accompanied by an increase in the price of the stock.

- This might be interpreted by some that investors prefer dividends over capital gains, thus supporting the Gordon-Lintner hypothesis.
- However, MM argue that a dividend increase is a "signal" to investors that the firm's management forecasts good future earnings. Thus, MM argue that investors' reactions to dividend announcements do not necessarily show that investors prefer dividends to retained earnings. Rather, the fact that the stock price changes merely indicates that there is an important *information*, or *signaling*, content in dividend announcements.

MM also suggest that a *clientele effect* might exist.

- Some stockholders prefer current income; they would want the firm to pay out a high percentage of its earnings.
- Other stockholders have no need for current income; they would simply reinvest any dividends received, after first paying income taxes on the dividend income. These stockholders would want the firm to retain most of its earnings.
- Thus, a firm attracts a specific clientele that is drawn to its dividend policy.
- Empirical evidence supports the contention that a clientele effect does exist, but MM argue that one clientele is as good as another, so the existence of clienteles does not imply that one payout policy is better than another. However, MM offer no proof that the aggregate makeup of investors permits firms to disregard clientele effects.

The relationship between dividend policy and agency costs has a bearing on the optimal dividend policy. One of the most perplexing issues in dividend policy is why firms pay dividends and then issue new securities.

- One potential answer is the signaling value inherent in dividends. However, it is hard to imagine that the value that arises from signaling is greater than the costs associated with new security issues.
- A second explanation for paying dividends relates to agency costs. An agency conflict exists between managers and stockholders, and because of this potential agency conflict, stockholders are willing to incur agency costs to monitor managerial actions. The monitoring problem is substantially reduced when firms must consistently raise external capital.
- For any given level of investment, the higher the dividend payout, the more frequently the firm must issue new securities. A higher payout policy thus forces firms to undergo the frequent scrutiny of the capital markets, and this appraisal process mitigates the agency problem. If the costs of paying dividends (which includes flotation for additional securities) is less than the value inherent in the additional monitoring, then large dividend payouts make sense.

As we noted at the beginning of the chapter, the decision as to how stable over time a firm's dividend should be is an important issue.

Firm's profits and cash flows vary over time, as do their investment opportunities. Taken alone, this suggests that corporations should vary their dividends over time.

However, many stockholders rely on dividends to meet expenses. Further, dividend cuts are usually interpreted by investors as signals of bad news.

How should the balance be struck; that is, how stable and dependable should a firm attempt to make its dividends? Although it is impossible to give a definitive answer to this question, the following points are relevant:

- Virtually every corporation (and analysts) makes a 5- or 10-year financial forecast, including projected earnings, cash flow, and dividends. For a "normal" company, such forecasts typically project higher earnings and dividends.
- Years ago, when inflation was not persistent, the term "stable dividend policy" meant a policy of paying the same dollar dividend year after year. Today, most companies and stockholders expect earnings and dividends to grow over time as a result of both inflation and retentions. Thus, today a stable dividend policy generally means increasing the dollar dividend at a reasonably steady rate.
- Companies with volatile earnings and cash flows would be reluctant to make a commitment to increase the dividend each year, but they would still plan to increase dividends when the situation warrants.

Dividend stability has two components:
- How dependable is the growth rate?
- How dependable is the current dividend; that is, can investors at least count on receiving the current dividend in the future?

Most observers believe that dividend stability is desirable, even though statistical problems prevent empirical tests from proving the point. If this position is correct, then:
- Investors would prefer a stock that pays more predictable dividends to one that has the same expected present value of dividends but pays them in a more erratic manner.
- This means that the cost of equity would be minimized, and shareholder wealth maximized, if a firm stabilizes its dividends as much as possible, given its requirements to support capital growth.

> In the preceding sections we have seen that investors may or may not prefer dividends to capital gains, but they do seem to prefer predictable to unpredictable dividends. Given this situation, how should firms set their basic dividend policies?

The residual dividend model is based on the premise that investors prefer to have a firm retain and reinvest earnings rather than pay them out in dividends if the rate of return the firm can earn on reinvested earnings exceeds the rate of return investors can obtain for themselves on other investments of comparable risk. Further, it is less expensive for the firm to use retained earnings than it is to issue new common stock. A firm using the residual model would follow these four steps:
- Determine the optimal capital budget.
- Determine the amount of equity required to finance the optimal capital budget, recognizing that the funds used will consist of both equity and debt to preserve the optimal capital structure.
- To the extent possible, use retained earnings to supply the equity required.

- Pay dividends only if more earnings are available than are needed to support the optimal capital budget.

Since both investment opportunities and earnings vary from year to year, strict adherence to the residual dividend model would result in dividend variability--one year the firm might declare zero dividends because investment opportunities were good (or profitability poor), and the next year it might pay a large dividend because investment opportunities were poor (or profitability good).

Because annual use of the residual model leads to unstable dividends, it is not used to set annual dividend payments. However, it is used, in conjunction with a firm's 5-year forecast, to determine a long-run target payout ratio.

Note that dividends are paid from cash flow, and not from earnings, so target payout ratios are set more on the basis of cash flows than on earnings.

The actual payment procedure is as follows:

- On the declaration date the directors meet and declare the regular dividend.
- At the close of the business on the holder-of-record date, the company closes its stock transfer books and makes up a list of shareholders as of that date.
- The securities industry has set up a convention of declaring that the right to the dividend remains with the stock until four business days prior to the holder-of-record date. The date when the right to the dividend leaves the stock is called the ex-dividend date.
- The company actually mails the checks to the holders of record on the payment date.

During the 1970s, most large companies instituted *dividend reinvestment plans (DRIPs),* whereby stockholders can automatically reinvest their dividends in the stock of the paying corporation.

There are two types of dividend reinvestment plans:

- In an old stock plan, a bank (acting as trustee) takes the total amount of dividends designated for the plan, purchases the company's stock on the open market, and distributes the shares to the investors on a pro rata basis. The transactions costs are low because of the large transaction, and hence, the participating shareholders benefit.
- In a new stock plan, the company merely issues stock to investors in the plan in lieu of cash dividends. Often, the stock is offered at a 3 to 5 percent discount from market price.

Companies may change from one type of DRIP to the other, depending on their needs for additional equity capital.

In addition to the theories and issues discussed so far, a number of other factors influence the dividend decision.

Bond indentures often contain provisions that restrict dividend policy.

Typically, common dividends cannot be paid if the company has omitted (passed) its preferred dividend.

Dividend payments cannot exceed the balance sheet value for retained earnings. This restriction, called the impairment of capital rule, is designed to protect creditors.

Dividends must be paid with cash, and hence, a cash shortage may restrict dividends.

The IRS can penalize a firm if it believes that the firm is withholding dividends for the sole purpose of investor tax avoidance.

If management is concerned about control, then it may be reluctant to sell new common stock, and hence may retain more earnings than it otherwise would, rather than pay dividends. In general, managers do not want to issue new common stock because new common stock requires issuance costs and new common stock sales are generally perceived as negative signals.

Setting dividend policy is truly an exercise in informed judgment, and not a decision that can be based on a precise mathematical model. In practice, dividend policy is not an independent decision--the dividend decision is made jointly with the capital structure and capital investment decisions.

In setting dividend policy, managers first consider the firm's future investment opportunities, expected internal cash flows, and target capital structure. This gives them an idea of the residual earnings that might be available for dividends. In effect, managers use the residual dividend model, but applied to a long planning period.

An actual dollar dividend per share is then selected so that there is an extremely low probability that the dividend, once set, will have to be lowered, or worse yet, omitted.

If there is a great deal of uncertainty in the forecasted inflows and required outflows of the firm, a conservative dividend policy (low dollar dividend and low projected growth rate) will be adopted.

Firms may distribute income to stockholders by *repurchasing* their own stock. These repurchased shares are called treasury stock.

When outstanding shares are repurchased, the earnings per share on the remaining shares will increase, resulting in a higher market price per share. Capital gains have been substituted for dividends.

Many very large repurchase programs are part of a general corporate restructuring plan whereby excess capital from asset sales or the issuance of new debt is distributed to stockholders through a major one-time stock repurchase. A "regular" stock repurchase is merely a substitute for cash dividends.

The advantages to repurchases include:

- Repurchase announcements are viewed as positive signals because the repurchase is often motivated by management's belief that the firm's shares are undervalued.
- Stockholders have a choice when the firm repurchases stock, while they must accept dividend payments and pay the resulting tax.
- Repurchases can remove a large block of stock that is overhanging the market and keeping the price per share down.
- If the excess cash flow is believed to be temporary, management can make the distribution in the form of share repurchase rather than declare an increased cash dividend that cannot be maintained.
- Repurchases can be used to produce large-scale changes in capital structures.

Disadvantages to repurchases include:

- The stock price may benefit more from cash dividends than from repurchases because stockholders may not be indifferent between dividends and capital gains.
- Selling stockholders may not be fully aware of all the implications of a repurchase.
- The corporation may pay too high a price for the repurchased stock, to the disadvantage of remaining stockholders.

There are pros and cons regarding stock repurchases:

- Because of uncertainties about their tax treatment, repurchases on a regular, systematic, dependable basis are probably not a good idea.
- However, repurchases do offer investors an opportunity to save taxes, and, for this reason, they should be given careful consideration.
- Repurchases can be especially valuable to a firm that wants to make a large shift in its capital structure within a short period of time.

Stock dividends and stock splits are often used to lower a firm's stock price and, at the same time, to conserve its cash resources.

The effect of a stock split is an increase in the number of shares outstanding and a reduction in the par, or stated, value of the shares. For example, if a firm had 1,000 shares of stock outstanding with a par value of $100 per share, a 2-for-1 split would reduce the par value to $50 and increase the number of shares to 2,000.

- The total net worth of the firm remains unchanged.
- The stock split does not involve any cash payment, only additional certificates representing new shares.

Although the economic effects of stock splits and stock dividends are virtually identical, accountants treat them somewhat differently. For a discussion of the accounting treatment, see any financial accounting text.

Stock dividends and splits "divide a given amount of pie into smaller slices."

The rationale behind using stock splits and dividends to reduce share prices lies in the belief in an "optimal trading range" within which large numbers of investors will be able to purchase the stock and the price will be maximized.

Unless the total amount of dividends paid on shares is increased, any upward movement in the stock price following a stock split or dividend is likely to be temporary. The price will normally fall in proportion to the dilution in per share earnings and dividends unless earnings and dividends rise.

DEFINITIONAL QUESTIONS

1. MM argue that a firm's dividend policy has ______ ______ on shareholder wealth.

2. Gordon and Lintner hypothesize that investors value a dollar of ______ more highly than a dollar of expected ______ ______.

3. The tax differential theory implies that firms should set ______ dividend payout ratios.

4. A company may be forced to increase its ______ ratio in order to avoid a tax on retained earnings deemed to be unnecessary for the conduct of the business.

5. Some stockholders prefer dividends to ______ ______ because of a need for current ______.

6. If the ______ of a firm's stock increases with the announcement of an increase in dividends, investors may be reacting to the ______ content in the dividend announcement rather than to a preference for dividends over capital gains.

7. The hypothesis that some investors prefer a high dividend payout while others prefer a low payout is called the ______ effect.

8. The residual dividend policy is based on the fact that new common stock is ______ ______ than retained earnings.

9. The policy of using "extra" dividends is most appropriate for a firm with ______ earnings.

10. The stock transfer books of a corporation are closed on the ____________________ date, and ___________ are paid to shareholders as of that date.

11. The _____________ date occurs four business days prior to the ____________________ date and provides time for stock transfers to be recorded on the books of the firm.

12. Actual payment of a dividend is made on the ____________ date as announced by the firm's _______ ___ __________ .

13. Many firms have instituted ______ ______ plans whereby stockholders purchase additional shares of the company's stock in lieu of receiving dividends.

14. Stock repurchases substitute ___________ ___________ for cash dividends.

15. Firms often repurchase stock with funds from the sale of _________ or the issuance of new ____________ when restructuring occurs.

16. A stock split involves a reduction in the ________ ________ of the common stock, but no accounting transfers are made between accounts.

CONCEPTUAL QUESTIONS

17. If investors are indifferent between dividends and capital gains, the farther to the left the IOS and MCC schedule intersect, the *higher* the dividend payout ratio should be.

    a. True **b.** False

18. An increase in cash dividends will result in an increase in the price of the common stock because D_1 will increase in the stock valuation model.

a. True   b. False

19. Which of the following is a possible disadvantage to stock repurchases?

a. The shareholder may or may not decide to sell.
b. The price of the stock may be undervalued.
c. EPS will increase.
d. The repurchase may be viewed as a signal of poor growth opportunities.
e. All of the above.

20. If investors prefer dividends to capital gains, then

a. The required rate of return on equity, k_s, will not be affected by a change in dividend policy.
b. The cost of capital will not be affected by a change in dividend policy.
c. k_s will increase as dividends are reduced.
d. k_s will decrease as the retention rate increases.
e. A policy conforming to the residual theory of dividends will maximize stock price.

PROBLEMS

21. Express Industries' expected net income for next year is $1.0 million. The company's target, and current, capital structure is 40 percent debt and 60 percent common equity. The optimal capital budget for next year is $1.2 million. If Express uses the residual dividend policy to determine next year's dividend payout, what is the expected payout ratio?

a. 0%   b. 10%   c. 28%   d. 42%   e. 56%

22. Amalgamated Shippers has a current, and target, capital structure of 30 percent debt and 70 percent equity. This past year Amalgamated, which uses the residual dividend policy, had a dividend payout ratio of 47.5 percent and net income of $800,000. What was Amalgamated's capital budget?

a. $400,000   b. $500,000   c. $600,000   d. $700,000   e. $800,000

ANSWERS

1. no effect
2. dividends; capital gains
3. low
4. payout
5. capital gains; income
6. price; information
7. clientele
8. more costly
9. volatile
10. holder-of-record; dividends
11. ex-dividend; holder-of-record
12. payment; board of directors
13. dividend reinvestment
14. capital gains
15. assets; debt
16. par value

17. a. If investors are indifferent, firms should follow the residual theory. Thus, the smaller the optimal capital budget, the higher the dividend payout ratio.

18. b. A dividend increase could also be perceived by investors as leading to lower growth in future earnings, thus reducing g in the model. The net effect on stock price is uncertain.

19. d. From the shareholder's point of view, the repurchase may signal that the stock is undervalued and will therefore rise in price, providing a capital gain. It is an advantage to the stockholder to have the option to sell or not. Repurchases will increase EPS to the remaining shareholders, but a repurchase could be viewed as a signal that the firm has limited growth opportunities available.

20. c. This is the Gordon-Lintner hypothesis. If investors view dividends as being less risky than potential capital gains, then the cost of equity is inversely related to the payout ratio.

21. c. The $1,200,000 capital budget will be financed using 40 percent debt and 60 percent equity. Therefore, the equity requirement will be 0.6($1,200,000) = $720,000. Since the expected net income is $1,000,000, $280,000 will be available to pay as dividends. Thus, the payout ratio is expected to be $280,000/$1,000,000 = 0.28 = 28%.

22. c. Of the $800,000 in net income, 0.475($800,000) = $380,000 was paid out as dividends. Thus, $420,000 was retained in the firm for investment. This is the equity portion of the capital budget, or 70 percent of the capital budget. Therefore, the total capital budget was $420,000/0.7 = $600,000.

CHAPTER 14
COMMON STOCK AND THE INVESTMENT BANKING PROCESS

OVERVIEW

This chapter is more descriptive than analytical, but financial managers do need a working knowledge of the issues covered. Common stock constitutes the ownership position in a firm. As owners, the common stockholders have certain rights and privileges, including (1) the right to control the firm through election of directors and (2) the right to the residual earnings of the firm.

Firms generally begin their corporate life as closely held companies, with all the common stock held by the founding managers. Then, as the company grows, it is often necessary to sell stock to the general public (that is, go public) to raise more funds. At this point, the firm's managers must be familiar with securities markets, including their regulation by the Securities and Exchange Commission (SEC). Eventually, the firm may choose to list its stock on one of the organized exchanges.

KEY CONCEPTS

> *Common equity* is the sum of the firm's common stock, paid-in capital, and retained earnings, which equals the common stockholders' total investment in the firm.

Legal and accounting terminology is important in analyzing the owners' position in a business firm.

- Shares of common stock are authorized by the owners of a business and issued by management.
- *Par value* is essentially the minimum price at which new shares can be sold.
- Any difference between the par value and what stockholders paid for common stock sold by the company is shown on the balance sheet as *additional paid-in capital.*
- *Retained earnings* represent the net income earned over the years that has been reinvested in the business rather than paid out as dividends.

- The *book value per share* is equal to the company's *net worth,* or common equity (stockholder's equity), consisting of the sum of common stock, retained earnings, and paid-in capital, divided by the number of shares of common stock outstanding.

The corporation's common stockholders have certain rights and privileges.

- Common stockholders have control of the firm through their election of the firm's directors, who in turn select officers to manage the business.
    - In a large, publicly owned firm, neither the managers nor any individual shareholder normally has the 51 percent necessary for absolute control of the company.
    - Thus, stockholders must vote for directors, and the voting process is regulated by both state and federal laws.
    - Stockholders who are unable to attend annual meetings may still vote by means of a proxy. Proxies can be solicited by any party seeking to control the firm.
- The preemptive right gives the current shareholders the right to purchase any new shares issued, in proportion to their current holdings.
    - The preemptive right may or may not be required by state law.
    - When granted, the preemptive right enables current owners to maintain their proportionate share of ownership and control of the business.
    - It also prevents the sale of shares at low prices to new stockholders, which would dilute the value of the previously issued shares.

Special classes of common stock are sometimes created by a firm to meet special needs and circumstances. If two classes of stock were desired, one would normally be called "Class A" and the other "Class B."

- Class A might be entitled to receive dividends before dividends can be paid on Class B stock.
- Class B might have the exclusive right to vote.
- Note that Class A and Class B have no standard meanings.
- Founders' shares are stock owned by the firm's founders that have sole voting rights but restricted dividends for a specified number of years.

> The United States has highly developed markets for buying and selling common stocks. Institutional investors have long dominated the bond market, and in recent years they have become a major factor in the stock market. Pension funds and other institutional investors now own about 40 percent of the stock of large, publicly held firms, but they represent about 80 percent of the trading volume.

The stocks of smaller companies are generally owned by management groups, or only a few people, and are referred to as closely held, or privately owned, corporations. The stocks of larger firms are generally held by a large number of investors. These companies are called publicly held corporations.

Stock market transactions may be separated into three distinct categories.

- The primary market handles initial public offerings (IPOs) of shares in firms that were formerly closely held. Here, capital for a firm can be raised by going public, and this market is often termed the new issue market.
- The primary market also handles additional shares sold by established, publicly owned companies. Companies can raise additional capital by selling in this market.
- The secondary market deals with trading in previously issued, or outstanding, shares of established, publicly owned companies. The company receives no new money when sales are made in the secondary market.

Going public has the following advantages:

- The original owners are able to diversify their holdings by selling some of their stock in a public offering.
- Public ownership increases the liquidity of the stock.
- New corporate cash is more easily raised by a publicly owned company.
- Going public establishes the firm's value in the marketplace.

Going public has the following disadvantages:

- A publicly owned company must file quarterly and annual reports with various governmental agencies.
- Publicly owned firms must disclose operating and ownership data.
- The opportunities for owners/managers to engage in questionable, but legal, self-dealings are reduced.
- If a publicly held firm is very small, and if its shares will be traded infrequently, then its stock will not really be liquid, and the market price may be lower than the stock's true value.
- Managers of publicly owned firms with less than 50 percent control must be concerned about tender offers and proxy fights. This sometimes leads to operating decisions that are not in the best long-run interests of the shareholders.

Stocks traded on organized exchanges are called *listed stocks.* While the decision to go public is significant, the decision to list is not a major event. In order to have its stock listed, a company must apply to an exchange, pay a relatively small fee, and meet the exchange's minimum requirements.

The company will have to file a few new reports with an exchange.

It will have to abide by the rules of the exchange.

Firms benefit from listing their stock by gaining liquidity, status, and free publicity. These factors may cause the value of the stock to be increased.

If stock is to be sold to raise new capital, the new shares may be sold in one of five ways:

If stockholders have a *preemptive right*, or if the firm chooses to do so, it can sell the additional stock to existing stockholders as a rights offering. Each shareholder is issued an option to buy a certain number of new shares, and the terms of the option are listed on a certificate called a stock purchase right, or simply a right.

If the preemptive right does not exist, the company can choose between a *rights offering* and a *public offering*. Procedures for public offerings are discussed later in the chapter.

In a *private placement*, securities are sold to one or a few investors, generally institutional investors. The primary advantages are lower flotation costs and greater speed, since the shares will not have to go through the SEC registration process.

Many companies have plans that allow employees to purchase stock on favorable terms.

- First, under executive incentive stock option plans, key managers are given options to purchase stock. If they perform well, the stock will go up, and the options will become valuable.
- Second, there are plans for lower-level employees. For example, at IBM employees can allocate part of their salary to buy newly issued shares at less than market price.
- A third type of plan is an *Employee Stock Ownership Plan (ESOP)*, in which the stock bought for the employees is purchased out of a share of the company's profits. ESOPs have the following potential advantages: (1) tax breaks, (2) anti-takeover defense, (3) pension cost control, and (4) productivity enhancement. Potential disadvantages are: (1) no productivity enhancement, (2) the balance of power is altered, (3) legal considerations, and (4) retiree benefits.

Companies can issue new stock through dividend reinvestment plans, which were discussed in Chapter 13.

Common stock financing has the following advantages and disadvantages:

Financing with common stock has the following advantages to the corporation:

- Common stock does not obligate the firm to make fixed payments to investors.
- Common stock financing carries no fixed maturity date; it is permanent capital which does not have to be "paid back."

- Common stock increases the creditworthiness of the firm, thus increasing the future availability of debt at a lower cost and establishing a reserve borrowing capacity.
- Common stock can often be sold more easily than debt if the firm's prospects look potentially good, but risky.

Financing with common stock has the following disadvantages to the corporation:
- Issuing common stock extends voting rights, and thus control, to new stockholders.
- Common stock means that more stockholders share in the firm's net profits rather than receiving a fixed payment as with creditors.
- The cost of underwriting and distributing common stock is high. Furthermore, the announcement of a new common stock issue may depress the firm's stock price.

In a *going private transaction*, the entire equity of a publicly held firm is purchased by a small group of investors that usually includes the firm's current senior management.

Such deals almost always involve substantial borrowing and thus are commonly known as *leveraged buyouts (LBOs)* or *leveraged managerial buyouts (MBOs).*

The primary advantages to going private are:
- Administrative cost savings because the firm does not have stockholder servicing costs, and top management is free from meetings with security analysts, government hearings, and so on.
- An even larger potential gain comes from the improvement in the incentives for high-level managerial performance. Heavy interest payments combined with a knowledge that success will bring large wealth does a lot to improve decisions.
- The increased flexibility available to managers of private firms.
- An increase in shareholder participation in corporate decision making.
- The increased use of financial leverage, which of course reduces taxes.

Not all firms are privately held, because the advantages of access to public capital markets dominate the advantage of going private for most firms.

Most participants in the securities markets, including the organized exchanges, brokers, investment bankers, and dealers, are regulated by the federal government through the Securities and Exchange Commission (SEC) and also by state governments.

The SEC has jurisdiction over all interstate offerings to the public in amounts of $1.5 million or more.

New issues must be registered at least 20 days before they are offered to the public. A prospectus describing the company and the securities to be offered must be sent to prospective purchasers of the new issue. The registration statement provides financial, legal, and technical information about the company to the SEC.

The SEC also regulates all national security exchanges. Firms listed on these exchanges must file financial reports with both the SEC and the exchanges.

The Federal Reserve System controls the flow of credit (margin credit) that may be used in purchasing securities.

The SEC also monitors the stock transactions of corporate insiders.

The securities industry realizes the importance of stable markets, sound brokerage firms, and the absence of stock manipulation. Therefore, the various exchanges and trade organizations work closely with the regulatory agencies to police the markets and protect customers.

The purpose of regulation is to ensure that adequate and accurate information is available concerning securities offered to the public and to prevent fraud. Regulation cannot ensure that investments will be successful or that investors will exercise good judgment.

> The financial manager must have a knowledge of the investment banking process, the process by which new securities are issued. Investment banking decisions take place in two stages.

At Stage I, the firm makes some initial, preliminary decisions on its own.

- The dollar amount of new capital required is established.
- The type of securities to be offered is specified. Further, if common stock is to be issued, managers must decide whether a rights offering should be used.
- The basis on which to deal with the investment bankers, either by a competitive bid or a negotiated deal, is determined.
- Finally, the investment banking firm must be selected.

The Stage II decisions are made jointly by the firm and the selected investment banker.

- First, the two parties will reevaluate the Stage I decisions.
- The firm and its investment banker must decide whether the banker will work on a "best efforts" basis or will "underwrite" the issue.
  - On a best efforts sale, the banker does not guarantee that the securities will be sold or that the company will get the cash it needs.

- On an underwritten issue, the company does get a guarantee. Essentially, the banker purchases the issue from the company, then resells the securities at a higher price. The banker bears significant risks in underwritten offerings.

- The investment banker's compensation must be negotiated.
- The offering price must be set. The investment banker will have an easier job if the issue is priced relatively low, while the issuer naturally wants as high a price as possible.
- If pressure from the new shares and/or negative signaling effects drives down the price of the stock, all shares outstanding, not just the new shares, are affected.

> Once the company and its investment banker have decided how much money to raise, the type of securities to issue, and the basis for pricing the issue, they will prepare and file an SEC Registration statement and a prospectus.

If the sum of money involved is large and the risk of a price fluctuation is substantial, investment bankers form underwriting syndicates in an effort to minimize the risk each banker carries. The banking house which sets up the deal is called the lead, or managing, underwriter.

A new selling procedure has recently emerged. It's called an unsyndicated stock offering, and it does not require an underwriting syndicate. The managing underwriter, acting alone, sells the issue entirely to institutional investors, thus bypassing both retail stockbrokers and individual investors.

For new issues involving small companies, the investment banker will normally maintain a market in the shares after the public offering. This is done in order to provide liquidity for the shares and to maintain a good relationship with both the issuer and the investors who purchased the shares.

> Large well-known public companies which issue securities frequently may file a master registration statement with the SEC and then update it with a short-form statement just prior to each individual offering.

This procedure is known as a shelf registration because, in effect, the company puts its new securities on the "shelf," and then sells them to investors when it feels the market is right.

Shelf registrations have two advantages over standard registrations:

- Lower flotation costs.
- More control over the timing of the issue.

DEFINITIONAL QUESTIONS

1. Ownership interest in a corporation is reflected on the balance sheet by the ______ ______ accounts.

2. Amounts paid by stockholders in excess of the par value are shown as "additional _______-___ _________."

3. One of the fundamental rights of common stockholders is to elect a firm's ___________, who in turn elect the operating management.

4. If a stockholder cannot vote in person, participation in the annual meeting is still possible through a ________.

5. The preemptive right protects stockholders against loss of _________ of the corporation as well as _________ of market value from the sale of new shares below market value.

6. Firms may find it desirable to separate the common stock into different __________. Generally, this classification is designed to differentiate stock in terms of the right to receive _______ and the right to ______.

7. A ______ ______ or ______ ______ corporation is one whose stock is held by a small group, normally its management.

8. The trading of previously issued shares of a corporation takes place in the ________ market, while new issues are offered in the ________ market.

9. ______ ______ refers to the sale of shares of a closely held business to the general public. Such a sale is also called an ______ ______ ______.

10. Going public establishes the firm's ________ in the marketplace.

11. Securities traded on an organized exchange are known as __________ securities.

12. Before an interstate issue of stock amounting to $1.5 million or more can be sold to the public, it must be _________ with and approved by the ________.

13. Setting the ________ price for an issue of stock may present a conflict of interest between the issuer and the ________ ________.

14. In order to spread the risk of underwriting a sizable common stock issue, investment bankers will form an ______ ______.

15. Credit used to buy stock is known as ________ credit, and its use is controlled by the ________ ________ ________.

CONCEPTUAL QUESTIONS

16. A firm may go public, yet the firm itself may not receive any additional funds in the process.

a. True **b.** False

17. Flotation costs are generally higher for bond issues than for stock issues.

a. True **b.** False

18. When new shares are being sold, if it appears that the investment bankers will be unable to sell the entire issue at the initial offering price, the only way the entire issue can be sold is to lower the price.

a. True **b.** False

19. A change in the dividend payout ratio will have the most direct (most immediate) effect on a firm's

a. Common stock account.
b. Earnings per share.
c. Paid-in capital account.
d. Net operating income.
e. Retained earnings account.

20. When stockholders assign their right to vote to another party, this is called

a. A privilege.
b. A preemptive right.
c. An ex right.
d. A proxy.
e. A prospectus.

21. In a going private transaction, the entire equity of a publicly held firm is purchased by a small group of investors. Such deals which involve substantial borrowing to purchase the equity are called

a. Initial public offerings (IPOs).
b. Leveraged buyouts (LBOs).
c. Rights offerings.
d. ESOPs.
e. None of the above.

PROBLEMS

The following data apply to the next three problems.

McCollough Company
Stockholders' Equity Accounts

Common stock (100,000 shares authorized 80,000 shares outstanding, $1 par)	$ 80,000
Additional paid-in capital	720,000
Retained earnings	1,200,000
Total common stockholders' equity	$2,000,000

22. If all 80,000 shares outstanding were sold at one offering, how much did McCollough receive for each share?

a. $1 **b.** $5 **c.** $10 **d.** $20 **e.** $25

23. What is the current book value per share?

a. $1 **b.** $5 **c.** $10 **d.** $20 **e.** $25

24. Suppose the firm sold the remaining authorized shares and netted $20.00 per share from the sale. What is the new book value per share?

a. $23 **b.** $24 **c.** $25 **d.** $26 **e.** $27

ANSWERS

1. stockholders' equity (common equity)
2. paid-in capital
3. directors
4. proxy
5. control; dilution
6. classes; dividends; vote
7. closely held; privately owned
8. secondary; primary
9. Going public; initial public offering (IPO)
10. value
11. listed
12. registered; SEC
13. offering; investment banker
14. underwriting syndicate
15. margin; Federal Reserve Board

16. a. An example, that of the Ford Foundation selling stock to the general public, is given in the text. Also, a firm may go public if its managers sell off a portion of their stock holdings. Then, the funds obtained go to the managers rather than the firm.

17. b. The investment banker normally must expend greater effort in selling stocks, thus must charge a higher fee. Also, a new common stock issue may lower stock price because of negative signaling effects and/or supply/demand price pressure.

18. b. The investment bankers may be able to increase the demand for the stock by "promoting" the issue. If not, then a price reduction may be required.

19. e. Although a change in the dividend payout would, in the long run, affect every item listed, retained earnings would be affected most directly.

20. d. Recently, there has been a spate of proxy fights, whereby a dissident group of stockholders solicits proxies in competition with the firm's management. If the dissident group gets a majority of the proxies, then it can gain control of the board of directors and oust existing management.

21. b. Leveraged buyouts often involve up to 90 percent debt financing.

22. c. The offering of 80,000 shares resulted in the firm collecting $80,000 in par value and $720,000 in additional paid-in capital for a total of $800,000. Thus, each share must have brought the firm $800,000/80,000 = $10.

23. e. The total common equity of $2,000,000 represents the total investment of the 80,000 shares outstanding. Thus, the book value per share is $2,000,000/80,000 = $25.

24. b. The firm now sells the remaining 20,000 shares and nets $20 per share for a total of $400,000. Thus, the new total common equity is $2,400,000, and 100,000 shares are outstanding. The new book value per share is $2,400,000/100,000 = $24. Note that selling new shares below book value results in a lower book value on all shares. The opposite holds if new shares are sold above book value.

CHAPTER 15
LONG-TERM DEBT

OVERVIEW

As noted in Chapters 11 and 12, the use of debt financing is generally required to maximize the value of the firm. In this chapter, we discuss long-term debt, including its different forms, typical provisions in debt contracts, securitization, bond ratings, and the various factors that influence a firm's decision to use debt financing at a particular point in time.

KEY CONCEPTS

> There are many types of long-term debt. In this section, we briefly review the traditional long-term debt instruments.

A *term loan* is a contract under which a borrower agrees to make a series of interest and principal payments, on specific dates, to a lender.

- Term loans are negotiated directly between the borrowing firm and a financial institution -- generally a bank, an insurance company, or a pension fund.
- The *maturity* of a term loan is generally from 3 to 15 years, but it may be as short as 2 or as long as 30 years.
- Term loans have several advantages over publicly issued securities: speed, flexibility, and low issuance costs. Also, because they are negotiated directly between lender and borrower, formal documentation is minimized.
- The interest rate on a term loan can be either fixed for the life of the loan or variable. If fixed, the rate will be close to the rate on bonds of equivalent maturity for companies of comparable risk. If variable, it is usually set at a certain number of percentage points over the prime rate, the commercial paper rate, the T-bill rate, or the London Interbank Offered Rate (LIBOR).
- Term loans are actually *private placements* of debt, as opposed to public offerings of bonds. Private placements are often called *story credit,* because each placement has a "story" explaining the company's need for funds.

A *bond* is also a long-term debt contract, but it differs from a term loan in that it is generally offered to the public rather than to a single lender or a small group of lenders. Most bonds are issued with maturities from 20 to 50 years, though some are as short as 7 to 10 years. Unlike term loans, a bond's interest is generally fixed.

- When real estate or other property is pledged as collateral for a bond issue, the bond is referred to as a *mortgage bond.* In case of bankruptcy, the mortgage bondholders have first claim on the proceeds from the sale of the pledged assets.
- A *debenture* is an unsecured bond, and its holders are general creditors of the corporation. The use of debentures depends on the firm's general credit strength and the nature of its assets.
- *Subordinated debt* has claims on assets, in the event of bankruptcy, only after senior debt as named in the subordinate debt's indenture has been paid off. *Second mortgage bonds* are subordinate to first mortgage bonds. Also, subordinated debentures may be subordinated to designated notes payable or to all other debt.
- There are several other important types of bonds.
    - *Convertible bonds* are securities that can be converted into a fixed number of shares of common stock at the option of the bondholder.
    - Bonds issued with *warrants* provide the investor with an option to buy the common stock of the firm at a stated price. The warrants are detachable from the bonds, and the bonds remain outstanding even after the warrants have been exercised.
    - *Income bonds* pay interest only when covered by the earnings of the firm.
    - *Indexed bonds* have their coupon rates tied to an inflation index, such as the consumer price index.
    - *Tax-exempt bonds* can be issued by industrial development agencies and pollution control agencies, which are set up by state and local governments in the public interest.

> The last 15 years witnessed many innovations in long-term debt financing. We discuss six of these in this section.

Zero (or *very low*) *coupon bonds* pay no interest but are offered at a substantial discount below their par values, and hence provide capital appreciation rather than interest income. These bonds are commonly called "zeros" or *original issue discount bonds (OIDs).*

- The advantages to the issuer are as follows:
    - No cash outlays are required until maturity.
    - These bonds often have a lower required rate of return than coupon bonds.
- The advantages for investors are as follows:
    - There is little danger of a call.
    - Zero coupon bonds guarantee a "true" yield to maturity since there is no reinvestment rate risk.

When interest rates are volatile, lenders are reluctant to lend long term. Thus, they charge very high maturity risk premiums. On the other hand, borrowers, in general, would rather borrow long term so that they do not have to worry about having to continually refund their debt. The answer to the dilemma is long-term *floating rate debt.*

- The debt may have a 5- or 10-year maturity, but the interest rate changes periodically to reflect current market conditions.
- Floating rate debt is advantageous to lenders because it causes the market value of the debt to be stabilized, and it provides lenders with more income to meet their own obligations should interest rates rise.
- Floating rate debt is also advantageous to corporations because they can obtain debt with a long maturity without committing themselves to paying an historically high rate of interest for the entire term of the loan. However, if interest rates rise, borrowers will face increasing interest expense.

Bonds that are redeemable at par at the holder's option also protect the holder against changes in interest rates.

- Typically, these bonds are not callable by the company, but holders can turn them in for redemption at any time during the first 5 or so years.
- Poison put bonds are bonds that are redeemable at par if the company restructures or engages in a leveraged buyout that significantly lowers the credit rating of the debt. The risk of an event of this nature is called event risk.

Another type of bond is the *junk bond,* a high-risk, high-yield bond issued by troubled companies or issued to finance a leveraged buyout or a merger.

- Junk bonds are rated below investment grade, or below triple-B.
- Junk bonds may be bonds that at one time had a higher rating and were originally sound; these are called *fallen angels.* Junk bonds may slo be bonds that were originally issued as junk.
- Holders of junk bonds must bear almost as much risk as stockholders do and therefore receive substantially higher yields than holders of other types of bonds.
- Junk bonds and their development illustrate the flexibility and adaptability of the investment banking industry to the needs and new trends in capital markets.
- Junk bonds are somewhat controversial: Junk bonds have been accused of fueling the fires of financial speculation, particularly LBOs and hostile takeovers. On the other hand, the broad and deep junk market has allowed companies that would otherwise be unable to issue debt to obtain bond financing.

Project financing is another type of debt that has been used extensively in recent years.

- In project financing, the holders of the debt generally have claims only against the sponsor's equity in the project and the cash flows generated from the project, and not against the firm or firms that own the project (the sponsors).
- Project financings increase the number and type of investment opportunities; hence, they make capital markets "more complete."

- Project financing is often used in conjunction with joint ventures and other types of business combinations where more than one firm is involved.

As the term is generally used, a *security* refers to a publicly traded financial instrument. Thus securities tend to have high liquidity. In recent years, various types of debt have been *securitized*, which means turned into liquid securities.

- Securitization has occurred in two major ways:
  - Some debt instruments that were formerly never traded are now being widely traded. Examples are commercial paper and junk bonds.
  - In asset securitization, individual assets are pledged as collateral but then typically combined into pools to reduce risk. The oldest type of asset securitization is the mortgage-backed security, but today, such things as accounts receivable and automobile loans are also used as collateral.
- The process of securitization has, in general, lowered costs and increased the availability of funds to borrowers, decreased risks to lenders, and created new investment opportunities for many investors.

A firm's managers are most concerned about (1) the effective cost of debt and (2) any provisions which might restrict the firm's future actions. The following features address both of these concerns.

An *indenture* is the legal document which spells out the rights of both the bondholders and the issuing corporation. It contains the basic terms of the issue as well as any special provisions such as restrictive covenants, call provisions, and sinking funds. A trustee, an official who represents the bondholders, makes sure that the terms of the indenture are carried out.

A *restrictive covenant* is a provision in a bond issue that requires the issuer to meet certain stated conditions.

- Standard provisions typically include minimum levels for the current ratio and the debt-to-assets ratio.
- These requirements are designed to help insure that the credit standing of the firm and the bond issue remains high.

A *call provision* gives the issuing corporation the right to call a bond (or preferred stock) for redemption.

- When a bond is called, the company must normally pay an amount greater than the par value. This extra payment over par is referred to as a call premium.
- Bonds are frequently called when the issuing firm can refund the issue at a lower interest rate. The call premium is thus a penalty for depriving investors of the higher rate of interest.

A *sinking fund provision* requires that a firm retires a portion of a bond issue each year. Its purpose is like that of an amortization schedule for a term loan.

- Failure to make a sinking fund payment constitutes technical default, so lenders can require immediate payment on the entire issue and possibly force the firm into bankruptcy.
- Generally, sinking funds permit the firm to call a specific number of bonds for redemption or to buy the required number of bonds in the open market. The firm will select whichever method is the least costly.
- Note that a sinking fund call involves a small percentage of the issue, say one-thirtieth of a 30-year issue, while a regular call involves the entire issue. Further, no premium is paid on sinking fund calls, the bonds are redeemed at par.

In many bonds and term loans, the borrower pledges specific assets of the firm as *collateral.* The pledging of collateral reduces the riskiness of the loan to lenders because they have the right to recover the pledged assets in case of default. Collateralized debt is often called secured debt.

Bond issues are normally assigned quality ratings by both Moody's Investors Service and Standard & Poor's Corporation. These ratings reflect the probability that a bond will go into default. Aaa (Moody's) and AAA (S&P) are the highest ratings.

Bond ratings influence investors' perceptions of default risk and therefore have an impact on the interest rate paid and hence on the firm's cost of capital.

Institutions are often limited to investing in investment grade securities, that is, those rated BBB or Baa, or higher. It is important, therefore, that a firm maintains a good quality rating on its bond issues.

Rating assignments are based on qualitative and quantitative factors, including the firm's debt/assets ratio, current ratio, and coverage ratios.

Rating agencies review outstanding bonds on a periodic basis and occasionally upgrade or downgrade a bond as the issuer's circumstances change. Also, if a company issues more bonds, this will trigger a review by the rating agencies.

A change in a firm's bond rating will have a significant effect on its ability to borrow long-term capital, and on the cost of that capital.

Long-term debt has several advantages and disadvantages to the issuer.

The major advantages are as follows:

- The cost of debt is independent of earnings, so debtholders do not participate in the gains if profits soar. Conversely, if profits fall, the bondholders must still be paid their interest.
- Because of tax effects, the risk-adjusted component cost of debt is lower than that of common stock.
- The corporate owners do not have to share control when debt financing is used.

The major disadvantages are as follows:

- Since debt service (interest plus scheduled principal repayments) is a fixed charge, a reduction in revenues may result in insufficient cash flow to meet debt service requirements. This could lead to bankruptcy.
- Financial leverage increases the riskiness of the firm and hence increases the costs of both debt and equity.
- Debt has a fixed maturity, and hence, the firm must repay the principal at some future date.
- Long-term debt indenture agreements are relatively restrictive compared to other sources of financing.
- Widely accepted credit standards dictate the maximum amount of debt that is considered "reasonable," and the cost of debt beyond this limit becomes exorbitant.

Long-term financing decisions are difficult because they are influenced by many factors, most of which are subjective. These factors vary among firms at any point in time and for any given firm over time.

One of the most important considerations in any financing decision is the way the firm's actual capital structure compares with its target capital structure.

- Over the long haul, firms try to maintain their target structures.
- However, from year to year, firms may stray from the target to minimize flotation costs, to take advantage of market conditions, or to deal with their own internal situation. As examples, a firm would not want to issue long-term debt if it was convinced that its bond rating would be upgraded in the near future, and it would not want to issue stock if it felt that its earnings were about to rise sharply and more than the public anticipated.

Firms also must consider the maturity of the assets being financed.

- If a firm uses 30-year bonds to finance 10-year assets, the bond payments would continue long after the asset was retired.
- If a firm uses 10-year bonds to finance 30-year assets, it would have to "roll over" the debt after 10 years.
- Each of the above strategies involves significant risks. In general, the best all-around strategy is to match the maturity of the debt to the maturity of the assets being financed.

Current interest rate levels and forecasts of future interest rates also play an important role in the financing decision.

- If current rates are high, and are expected to drop, it might be wise to use short-term financing until rates drop, and then lock in the lower rates with long-term financing.
- Conversely, if current rates are low and expected to rise, use long-term financing now to lock in the rates.
- However, interest rates are difficult, if not impossible, to forecast. Thus, pursuing one of the above strategies could prove to be disastrous if the forecasts were wrong.

The firm's current condition and earnings outlook also have an effect on the choice of securities.

- A firm may delay debt financing which would trigger a review by the rating agencies.
- Debt issued when in a poor financial condition would probably cost more and have more severe restrictive covenants.

The amount of financing required and the availability of assets which could be pledged as collateral also impact the financing decision.

DEFINITIONAL QUESTIONS

1. A _______ loan is a contract to pay _______ and _______ on specific dates to a lender.

2. Term loans are generally negotiated directly with a _______, _______ _______, or _______ _______. They are not sold to the _______ at large.

3. The process of paying off a term loan in equal __________ over the life of the loan is called __________.

4. _______ _______ _____ are offered at a discount below their par values and pay no coupon payments.

5. A high yield, high risk bond is called a _______ _______.

6. The oldest type of asset securitization is the _________________ __________.

7. A ______ is a long-term contract that is generally offered to the public and under which the ______ agrees to make payments of interest and principal to the holders.

8. The legal document setting forth the terms and conditions of a bond issue is known as the ______.

9. The ______ represents the bondholders and sees that the terms of the indenture are carried out.

10. A bond secured by real estate is known as a __________ bond.

11. Failure to make a sinking fund payment places the company in ________ ________, and could ultimately lead to ______.

12. In meeting its sinking fund requirements, a firm may ______ the bonds or purchase them on the ______ ______.

13. Except when the call is for sinking fund purposes, when a bond issue is called, the firm must pay a ______ ______, or an amount in excess of the ________ value of the bond.

14. A restrictive _________ is a provision in the bond's ______ which requires the issuer to meet certain stated conditions.

15. Firms issue various securities because investors have different _______/_________ trade-offs.

16. Over the long run, a firm should finance in accordance with its ______ ________ ___________.

17. The least risky financing strategy is to match the ______ of the debt with the ______ of the asset being financed.

18. It is very __________, if not __________, to forecast interest rates.

Conceptual Questions

19. The "penalty" for having a low bond rating is less severe when the Security Market Line is relatively steep than when it is not so steep.

   a. True **b.** False

20. There is a direct relationship between bond ratings and the required rate of return of bonds; that is, the higher the rating, the higher is the required rate of return.

a. True **b.** False

21. Which of the following would tend to increase the coupon interest rate on a bond that is to be issued?

a. Adding a sinking fund.
b. Adding a restrictive covenant.
c. Adding a call provision.
d. A change in the bond's rating from Aa to Aaa.
e. Both a and c above.

22. Zero coupon bonds have become quite popular over the last several years. These bonds are advantageous to the issuer because

a. The bond is, in effect, not callable.
b. These bonds generally have a higher yield to maturity than normal coupon bonds.
c. The bond's cash outflows are spread over the life of the bond.
d. The bonds are initially sold above par value.
e. None of the above statements is correct.

PROBLEMS

23. J. C. Nickel is planning a zero coupon bond issue. The bond has a par value of $1,000, matures in 10 years, and will be sold at an 80 percent discount, or for $200. The firm's marginal tax rate is 40 percent. What is the annual after-tax cost of debt to Nickel on this issue? (Assume that the discount can be amortized on a straight line basis over the life of the bond and deducted from taxable income.)

a. 9.59% **b.** 10.00% **c.** 11.62% **d.** 14.79% **e.** 17.46%

The following data apply to the next two problems.

Ten years ago, the Privy Company issued a 10-year bond with a 10 percent annual coupon. The $100,000 issue sold at its par value of $1,000 per bond. The indenture had a sinking fund provision which stipulated that one-tenth of the issue must be redeemed at the end of each year.

24. Assume that interest rates fell after the issue date, causing the market value of the bonds to rise, and that Privy exercised the sinking fund provision by calling one-tenth of the issue (10 bonds) each year. What was the realized before-tax cost of the issue?

a. 8.0%   b. 9.2%   c. 10.0%   d. 11.2%   e. 12.0%

25. Now assume that interest rates rose after the issue date, causing the market value of bonds to fall, and that the firm retired the issue over time by buying 10 of the bonds outstanding each year on the open market. Further, assume that Privy repurchased each bond (with a face value of $1,000) for $950, so its total expenditure to purchase 10 bonds was $9,500. Now what was the realized before-tax cost of the issue?

a. 8.0%   b. 9.2%   c. 10.0%   d. 11.2%   e. 12.0%

ANSWERS

1. term; interest; principal
2. bank; insurance company; pension fund; public
3. installments (amounts); amortization
4. Zero coupon bonds
5. junk bond
6. mortgage-backed security
7. bond; borrower
8. indenture
9. trustee
10. mortgage
11. technical default; bankruptcy
12. call; open market
13. call premium; par
14. covenant; indenture
15. risk/return
16. target capital structure
17. maturity; maturity
18. difficult; impossible

19. b. A steeper SML implies a higher risk premium on risky securities, and thus a greater "penalty" on lower-rated bonds.

20. b. The relationship is inverse. The higher the rating, the lower is the default risk, and hence the lower is the required rate of return. Aaa/AAA is a high rating, and as we go down the alphabet, the ratings are lower.

21. c. Sinking funds, restrictive covenants, and an improvement in the bond rating all indicate lower risk for the bond, and hence would lower the coupon rate.

22. e. The primary advantages to the issuer are (1) that zero coupons have a lower required rate of return, and (2) that annual interest payments are avoided.

23. a. Look at the cash flows to the firm. At Year 0, the firm receives $200. At Year 10, the firm must pay out $1,000. For each of the 10 years, Nickel is declaring a ($1,000 - $200)/10 = $80 interest expense, even though it is not actually paying interest in the interim period. The tax benefit of that expense is 0.40($80) = $32. Putting these cash flows on a time line, we get the following:

0	1	9	10
$200	$32	$32	$ 32
			(1,000)
			($ 968)

The cost of debt to the firm is that discount rate which equates the present values of the cash inflows and outflows, or the IRR. (The calculator solution is 9.59 percent.)

24. c. Each year, Privy retired $10,000 face value in bonds. Thus, its interest expense also decreased by one-tenth each year:

Year	Debt Outstanding at Beginning of Year	Interest Expense
1	$100,000	$10,000
2	90,000	9,000
--	---	---
9	20,000	2,000
10	10,000	1,000

Thus, Privy paid 10 percent on the outstanding balance throughout the life of the issue and it was retired at par value. Thus, its realized before-tax cost was also 10 percent.

25. b. To answer this, you must lay out the cash flows over the life of the issue:

Year	Debt Outstanding at Beginning of Year	Interest Expense	Sinking Fund Expense	Total Service Requirement
1	$100,000	$10,000	$9,500	$19,500
2	90,000	9,000	9,500	18,500
3	80,000	8,000	9,500	17,500
4	70,000	7,000	9,500	16,500
5	60,000	6,000	9,500	15,500
6	50,000	5,000	9,500	14,500
7	40,000	4,000	9,500	13,500
8	30,000	3,000	9,500	12,500
9	20,000	2,000	9,500	11,500
10	10,000	1,000	9,500	10,500

Now, the firm received $100,000 at Time 0, and paid out the cash flows shown above in the right-hand column. The IRR of this cash flow stream, 9.2 percent, was Privy's realized before-tax cost of debt in this case. The ability to repurchase the bonds at less than par reduced the cost of the issue. (Note that Privy would not actually be able to repurchase the final $10,000 worth of bonds for $9,500. At maturity, it must pay the full par value. This would change the total service requirement in Year 10 to $11,000, and the resultant before-tax cost of debt would increase slightly from 9.196% to 9.248%.)

CHAPTER 16
HYBRID FINANCING: PREFERRED STOCK, WARRANTS, AND CONVERTIBLES

OVERVIEW

In the two preceding chapters, we examined the use of common stock and various types of long-term debt. In this chapter, we examine three other sources of long-term capital: preferred stock, which is a hybrid security that represents a cross between debt and equity financing; warrants, which are derivative (option) securities that are issued by firms; and convertibles, which are hybrids between debt or preferred stock and warrants. In discussing warrants and convertibles, we will be using many of the option concepts discussed in Chapter 5.

KEY CONCEPTS

Preferred stock is a hybrid--it is similar to bonds in some respects and to common stock in others. Preferred stock resembles bonds in that it has a par value, and like a bond's coupon payments, preferred dividends are fixed in amount and must be paid before common stock dividends. On the other hand, if earnings are not sufficient to cover the preferred dividend, the directors can omit the dividend without subjecting the company to potential bankruptcy.

Accountants generally view preferred stock as equity and show it on the balance sheet as an equity account. Financial managers view preferred stock as being somewhere between debt and common equity -- it imposes a fixed charge and thus increases the firm's financial leverage, yet if the preferred dividend is omitted, the company may not be forced into bankruptcy.

Some of the major provisions of preferred stock issues are featured below.

- Preferred stockholders have priority over common stockholders with regard to earnings and assets.

- Preferred stock has an established par value which represents the amount due the preferred stockholders in the event of liquidation.
- Most preferred stock provides for cumulative dividends, whereby all preferred dividends in arrears must be paid before common dividends can be paid.

Occasionally other provisions are encountered in preferred stock issues.

- Preferred stockholders are generally given voting rights after management has missed a specified number of dividend payments.
- Most newly issued preferred stocks now have sinking funds and/or call provisions.
- Because of these provisions, most preferred stocks now have finite maturity dates and hence are not perpetual.
- Preferred stock may be convertible into common stock.

Two important innovations in preferred stock financing have occurred in recent years.

- *Floating*, or *adjustable rate, preferred stocks (ARPs)* tie their dividends to the rate on Treasury securities instead of paying fixed dividends.
- *Money market,* or *market auction, preferred stocks* are, from the investor's point of view, a low risk 7-week maturity security which can be sold between auction dates at close to par value.

Preferred stock financing has both advantages and disadvantages.

- By using preferred, the firm can avoid sharing either control or earnings with new investors, yet limit the possibility of bankruptcy if earnings are not sufficient to meet the dividend payment.
- However, since preferred dividends are not tax deductible, preferred stock usually has a higher after-tax cost than debt financing.

Preferred stock also has its benefits and drawbacks to investors.

- Because 70 percent of preferred dividends received by corporations are exempt from taxes, preferred stock offers high after-tax returns to corporations, and hence, most nonconvertible preferred stock is owned by corporations.
- For the individual investor, after-tax bond yields are generally higher than those of riskier preferred stock.

> A *warrant* is a call option issued by a company which gives the holder the right to buy a stated number of shares of the company's stock at a specified price.

Often warrants are attached to debt instruments as an incentive for investors to buy the combined issue at a lower interest rate than would otherwise be the case. Additionally, warrants may eliminate the need for extremely restrictive indenture provisions.

Warrants were originally used as "sweeteners" by small, risky firms to make their bonds or preferred stocks more attractive. However, after AT&T became the first large and financially strong corporation to use warrants, their use by such firms became commonplace.

Most warrants are *detachable* and can be traded separately from the bond or preferred stock with which they were issued.

Warrants generate additional equity capital when they are exercised.

- The *exercise price* on warrants is generally set 10 to 30 percent above the market price of the stock at the time the warrant is issued.
- If the market price is above the exercise price, and the warrants are about to expire, holders will exercise their options and purchase stock.
- Since warrants pay no dividends, holders will be inclined to exercise them and obtain common stock as the common dividend is increased.
- A stepped-up exercise price will also induce holders to exercise their warrants.

Warrants generally produce needed funds as the company grows and as the stock price increases over the exercise price.

The component cost of an issue with warrants can be estimated by placing the expected cash flows associated with the issue on a time line and then calculating the IRR of the stream.

Although the interest rate on the bond will be less than the rate on a similar straight debt issue, the total cost rate of the issue, including the opportunity cost of the warrants, will usually be somewhere between the firm's costs of straight debt and equity because the riskiness of a bond with warrants falls between that of debt and equity.

Convertible securities are bonds or preferred stocks which can be exchanged for common stock at the option of the holder and under specified terms and conditions.

Conversion of a bond or preferred stock, unlike the exercise of a warrant, does not produce additional funds for the firm. However, conversion does lower the debt ratio.

The *conversion ratio (CR)* specifies the number of common shares that will be received for each bond or share of preferred stock that is converted.

The *conversion price,* P_c, is the effective price paid for the common stock when conversion occurs. For example, if a bond is issued at its par value of $1,000 and can be converted into 40 shares of common stock, the conversion price would be

$$P_c = \$1,000/CR = \$1,000/40 = \$25 \text{ per share.}$$

Someone buying the bond and then converting it would, in effect, be paying \$25 per share for the stock.

The conversion price of a bond is typically set at about 10 to 30 percent above the market price of common stock when the bond is sold. Thus, if the common stock is selling for \$20.83 at the time the convertible is issued, the conversion price might be set at 1.2(\$20.83) = \$25. This would produce a conversion ratio of CR = 40:

$$CR = \$1{,}000/P_c = \$1{,}000/\$25 = 40.$$

Convertible issues have certain advantages and disadvantages to the issuing corporation.

- By giving investors an opportunity to realize capital gains, a firm can sell debt with a lower interest rate or preferred stock with a lower dividend yield.
- Convertibles provide a way of selling common stock in the future at prices higher than those currently prevailing.
  - However, if the stock price does not increase, investors will not convert and the company will be stuck with debt (or preferred) rather than equity in its capital structure. However, the interest rate on this debt will be comparatively low.
  - If the stock price does rise, the company can force conversion by including a call feature in the bond's indenture or on the preferred stock.
- Note that if the firm's stock price rises sharply, it would have been better off to have waited and sold the common shares at the higher price.

The actual market price of a convertible bond will always be equal to or greater than the higher of its straight debt value or its conversion value. The higher of those two values is called the floor price.

Like a bond with warrants, the expected cost rate on convertible debt can be estimated by placing the issue's expected cash flows on a time line. Also, like debt with warrants, the costs should lie between the issuing firm's cost of straight debt and its cost of common stock, because, from the investors' viewpoint, a convertible is riskier than straight debt but less risky than common stock.

Firms with warrants or convertible securities outstanding must reflect these securities when they report earnings per share to stockholders. A firm could report earnings per share in one of three ways:

Simple EPS, where earnings available to common stockholders are divided by the average number of shares actually outstanding during the period.

Primary EPS, where earnings available are divided by the average number of shares that would be outstanding if those warrants and convertibles likely to be exercised or converted had actually been exercised or converted.

Fully diluted EPS, which is similar to primary EPS except that all warrants and convertibles are assumed to be exercised or converted regardless of the likelihood of this occurring.

For firms with large amounts of warrants and/or convertibles outstanding, there can be substantial differences between EPS calculations. Thus, the SEC requires that both primary and fully diluted earnings be shown.

> Securities innovation is the development of new securities that not only are different but also enable issuers or investors to do something they could not do before, or to do the same thing in a more cost-effective way.

Value can be created in several ways by securities innovation:

- Reallocation of risk from one class of investors to another class that is less risk sensitive.
- Reduction of transactions costs paid to third parties, or increased liquidity for investors.
- Reduction of investors' taxes without increasing the corporate tax rate liability, or vice versa.

Definitional Questions

1. Preferred stock has characteristics similar to both _______ and ________ ________.

2. The _______ ________ feature means that preferred stockholders must receive all dividends in arrears before common dividends may be paid.

3. Warrants and convertibles may make a company's securities more attractive to a broader range of ________ and hence lower its ________ ________ ________.

4. A ________ is an option to buy a stated number of shares of __________ ________ at a specified _________.

5. Warrants are often attached to a ________ issue in order to make it salable at a relatively low ________ rate.

6. Warrants are ________ options as opposed to ________ options.

7. The ________ price of a warrant is generally set at about ______ to ______ percent above the market price of the stock.

8. When they are exercised, warrants add additional ________ ________ to a firm's capital structure.

9. Warrants will certainly be exercised if the stock price is above the ________ price and the warrant is about to ________.

10. Holders of warrants will have an extra incentive to convert to ________ ________ as the company increases the ________ on its common shares.

11. Almost all warrants are __________ and can be traded separately from the debt or preferred stock with which they were issued.

12. Convertible bonds or preferred stocks may be exchanged for ________ ________ at the option of the ________.

13. The ________ ________ specifies the number of shares of common stock that will be received for each bond that is converted.

14. The ________ ________ is the effective price paid for one share of common stock upon conversion.

15. When a convertible bond is issued, the conversion price is determined by dividing the ________ ________ of the bond by the number of shares received on conversion.

16. Selling a convertible issue may have the effect of selling ________ ________ at a price higher than the market price prevailing at the time the convertible is issued.

17. If a firm's stock price does increase, the company can force ________ of convertible bonds by including a _______ _______ in the bond indenture.

18. It may be unwise for a firm to sell a convertible issue if it anticipates that its ________ _________ will increase rapidly in the near future.

19. In reporting its earnings, a firm with warrants and convertible securities must report both ________ EPS and ________ ________ EPS.

Conceptual Questions

20. Preferred stock is generally viewed as equity by bondholders and as debt by common stockholders.

    a. True b. False

21. The coupon interest rate on convertible bonds is generally set higher than the rate on similar nonconvertible issues.

    a. True b. False

22. Primary EPS shows what EPS would have been if all warrant and convertibles had been converted prior to the reporting date.

    a. True b. False

23. Investors are willing to accept lower interest (or dividend) yields on convertible securities in the hopes of later realizing capital gains.

    a. True b. False

24. The conversion of a convertible bond replaces debt with common equity on a firm's balance sheet, but it does not bring in any additional capital.

    a. True b. False

25. The market price of a warrant may be substantially above its expiration value.

    a. True b. False

26. The advantage to the corporation of using preferred stock financing is:

    a. Preferred dividends are tax deductible.
    b. Preferred stockholders bear no risk of ownership.
    c. The returns on preferred stock are always higher than on bonds.
    d. The firm can retain control and limit the profit sharing of new investors.
    e. Preferred stockholders always have voting rights.

PROBLEMS

27. The Clayton Corporation has warrants outstanding that permit the holder to purchase one share of common stock per warrant at $30. What is the expiration value of Clayton's warrants if the common stock is currently selling at $20 per share?

a. -$20 **b.** -$10 **c.** $5 **d.** $10 **e.** $20

28. Refer to Problem 27. Calculate the expiration value if the common stock is now selling at $40 per share.

a. -$20 **b.** -$10 **c.** $0 **d.** $10 **e.** $20

29. White Corporation has just sold a bond issue with 10 warrants attached to each bond. The bonds have a 20-year maturity, an annual coupon rate of 12 percent, and they sold at the $1,000 initial offering price. The current yield to maturity on bonds of equal risk, but without warrants, is 15 percent. What is the value of each warrant?

a. $22.56 **b.** $21.20 **c.** $20.21 **d.** $19.24 **e.** $18.78

The following data apply to the next four problems.

Central Food Brokers is considering issuing a 20-year convertible bond that will be priced at its par value of $1,000 per bond. The bonds have a 12 percent annual coupon interest rate, and each bond could be converted into 40 shares of common stock. The stock currently sells at $20 per share, has an expected annual dividend of $3.00, and is growing at a constant 5 percent per year. The bonds are callable after 10 years at a price of $1,050, with the price declining by $5 per year thereafter. If, after 10 years, the conversion value exceeds the call price by at least 20 percent, management will call the bonds.

30. What is the conversion price?

a. $20 **b.** $25 **c.** $33 **d.** $40 **e.** $50

31. If the yield to maturity on similar nonconvertible bonds is 16 percent, what is the straight-debt value?

a. $1,000.00 **b.** $907.83 **c.** $812.22 **d.** $762.85 **e.** $692.37

32. What is the conversion value in Year 10?

a. $800.73 **b.** $1,000.50 **c.** $1,148.01 **d.** $1,222.18 **e.** $1,303.12

33. If an investor expects the bond issue to be called in Year 10, and he plans on converting it at that time, what is the investor's expected rate of return upon conversion?

a. 12.0% **b.** 12.2% **c.** 13.6% **d.** 14.4% **e.** 15.3%

ANSWERS

1. bonds (debt); common stock (equity)
2. cumulative dividends
3. investors; cost of capital
4. warrant; common stock; price
5. debt; interest
6. call; put
7. exercise (striking); 10; 30
8. common equity
9. exercise (striking); expire
10. common stock; dividend
11. detachable
12. common stock; holder
13. conversion ratio
14. conversion price
15. par value
16. common stock
17. conversion; call provision
18. stock price
19. primary; fully diluted

20. a. Preferred stock is treated as debt by common stockholders since preferred dividends must be paid before common dividends. Bondholders have a priority claim on cash flows over preferred stockholders and also priority in the event of liquidation and therefore view preferred stock as equity.

21. b. The coupon interest rate is lower because investors expect some capital gains return upon conversion. Note, however, that the overall required rate of return is higher for the convertible issue.

22. b. Primary EPS includes only those shares from warrants and convertibles likely to be converted in the near future. Fully diluted EPS includes all shares.

23. a. However, the investor is including the expected capital gain as part of his required return, so the total required return on convertibles is higher than on a straight security with similar other features.

24. a. The bond is turned in to the company and replaced with common stock. No cash is exchanged.

25. a. A warrant is a call option, and hence its value depends not only on its expiration value, but also on its time to maturity, the price volatility of the underlying stock, and the risk-free rate.

26. d. By setting a fixed dividend, management can limit the degree of profit sharing by preferred stockholders and also retain control since preferred stockholders normally do not have voting rights.

27. b. Expiration value = Market price - Exercise price. When P_0 = \$20, the Expiration value = \$20 - \$30 = -\$10.

28. d. When P_0 = \$40, the Expiration value = \$40 - \$30 = \$10.

29. e. First, find the straight-debt value:

$$V = I(PVIFA_{k,n}) + M(PVIF_{k,n}) = \$120(PVIFA_{15\%,20}) + \$1,000(PVIF_{15\%,20}) = \$812.22.$$

Thus the value of the attached warrants is \$1,000 - \$812.22 = \$187.78. Since each bond has 10 warrants, each warrant must have a value of \$18.78.

30. b. P_c = Par value/Shares received = \$1,000/40 = \$25.00.

31. d. $V = I(PVIFA_{k,n}) + M(PVIF_{k,n}) = \$120(PVIFA_{16\%,20}) + \$1,000(PVIF_{16\%,20}) = \$762.85.$

32. e. $C_t = P_tCR$; $C_{10} = P_{10}CR = \$20(1.05)10(40) = \$1,303.12.$

33. c. This is solved by finding the value of k_c in the equation:

$$\text{Price paid} = I(PVIF_{k_c,n}) + \text{Expected conversion value}(PVIF_{k_c,n})$$

$$\$1,000 = \$120(PVIF_{k_c,n}) + \$1,303.12(PVIF_{k_c,n})$$

$$k_c = 13.6\%.$$

CHAPTER 17
LEASE FINANCING

OVERVIEW

Firms generally own fixed assets and hence report them on their balance sheets, but it is the use of the fixed assets that is important, not their ownership. One way of obtaining the use of facilities and equipment is to buy them, but an alternative is to lease them. Prior to the 1950s, leasing was generally associated with real estate (land and buildings). Today, however, it is possible to lease virtually any kind of asset, and about one-third of all new capital equipment acquired by businesses is financed through lease arrangements.

KEY CONCEPTS

There are two parties (at least) to every lease agreement, and there are several different types of *leases*.

The *lessor* is the owner of the leased property. The lessor receives the tax benefit of ownership through depreciation tax savings.

The *lessee* buys the right to use the property by making lease payments to the lessor.

There are four common types of leasing arrangements.

- *Operating leases*. These leases include both financing and maintenance services.
    - Operating leases ordinarily call for the lessor to maintain the equipment; the cost of maintenance is built into the lease payments.
    - The lease contract is written for less than the useful life of the equipment; that is, the lease is not fully amortized.
    - The lessor expects to recover the cost of the equipment through lease renewal payments or through disposal of the leased equipment.

- Operating leases often contain a cancellation clause to protect the lessee against obsolescence.

- *Financial,* or *capital, leases.* These leases are fully amortized; however, they do not provide for maintenance and are not cancelable.
  - They differ from a sale and leaseback in that the equipment is new.
  - Equipment is purchased by the lessor from the manufacturer or distributor, and the lessee simultaneously executes an agreement to lease the equipment from the financial institution.
- *Sale and leaseback.* In this type of lease, a firm owning an asset sells the property to a leasing company and simultaneously leases it back for a specified period at specific terms.
  - The sale and leaseback is an alternative to simply borrowing against the property on a mortgage loan basis.
  - The seller receives the purchase price but retains the use of the property in exchange for rental payments.
  - The lease payments are sufficient to return the purchase price to the lessor plus provide a specified return on the investment.
- *Combination leases.* This type of lease contains features of both operating and financial leases.

> Lease payments are deductible expenses for income tax purposes, provided the IRS agrees that the contract is a genuine lease and not an installment loan called a lease.

The IRS restrictions prevent a company from using a lease arrangement to depreciate equipment over a much shorter period than its MACRS class life, and hence gain undeserved tax benefits.

A lease that complies with all the IRS requirements for a genuine lease is called a *guideline,* or *tax-oriented, lease.* The main points of the tax guidelines are as follows:

- The lease term must not exceed 80 percent of the estimated useful life of the equipment at the commencement of the lease transaction.
- The equipment's estimated residual value at the expiration of the lease must equal at least 20 percent of its value at the start of the lease.
- Neither the lessee nor any related party can have the right to purchase the property from the lessor at a fixed price predetermined at the lease's inception.
- Neither the lessee nor any related party can pay or guarantee payment of any part of the price of the leased equipment.
- The leased equipment must not be "limited use" property, defined as equipment that can only be used by the lessee or a related party at the end of the lease.

In a guideline lease, the tax benefits of ownership belong to the lessor, and the lessee can deduct the full amount of the lease payment.

A lease that does not meet the tax guidelines is called a non-tax-oriented lease. For this type of lease, the tax benefits of ownership accrue to the lessee, but the lessee can only deduct the implied interest portion of each lease payment.

> Lease financing is financially comparable to debt financing because both subject the firm to a contractual series of payments and failure to make these payments could lead to bankruptcy.

Leasing is sometimes referred to as *off balance sheet financing* because often neither the leased assets nor the lease liabilities appear directly on the firm's balance sheet.

A firm with extensive lease arrangements would have both its assets and its liabilities understated in comparison with a firm which borrowed to purchase the assets, and hence, the firm that leases would show a lower debt ratio. Note, however, that lease obligations must be shown in the notes to the financial statements.

FASB #13 requires firms to capitalize certain financial leases and thus to restate their balance sheets.

- Ownership of the property is effectively transferred from the lessor to the lessee.
- The lessee can purchase the property at less than its true market value when the lease expires.
- The lease runs for a period equal to or greater than 75 percent of the asset's life.
- The present value of the lease payments is equal to or greater than 90 percent of the initial value of the asset.

When a lease is capitalized, leased assets must be reported under fixed assets, and the present value of future lease payments must be shown as a debt obligation.

Leased assets are equivalent to assets purchased using all debt financing. Suppose a firm's target capital structure is 50 percent debt and 50 percent equity. Further, assume that 50 percent of the firm's assets are leased. Then, to maintain its target capital structure, the firm must use all-equity financing for the nonleased assets.

The lease decision is a financing decision, and not a capital budgeting decision. Thus, lease analysis is not generally conducted unless the decision has already been made to acquire the asset.

Leases must be evaluated by both the lessee and the lessor. For the lessee, the analysis focuses on whether leasing the asset is less costly than borrowing and buying the asset.

In an NPV-type analysis, the lessee estimates the cost of leasing and the cost of owning, assuming that the asset is financed solely with debt. If the cost of leasing is less than the cost of owning, the asset should be leased.

- All cash flows must reflect tax effects.
- Since leasing is a substitute for debt financing, and since lease cash flows have approximately the same risk as debt cash flows, the appropriate discount rate is the after-tax cost of debt.
- In a lease analysis, the NPV of the lease is often called the ***net advantage to leasing (NAL).***

The lease versus purchase decision can also be analyzed using an IRR approach.

- The IRR of the lease is the after-tax cost rate of the lease.
- The asset should be leased if the IRR of the lease is less than the after-tax cost of debt.
- If the cost of leasing is less than the cost of debt, the overall cost of capital for an asset with lease financing would be less than that for a nonleased asset of similar risk. Thus, assets that were marginally unacceptable could have a positive NPV if lower cost lease financing were available.

The final way to analyze a lease from the lessee's perspective is through the *equivalent loan method.* With this method the lessee considers the dollar amount of the loan that it could obtain if it paid the cash flows to a lender instead of the lessor. The difference in the financing amounts is equal to the NAL.

The lessor views the lease transaction as an investment, and hence, the lessor's analysis focuses on the return on the lease transaction.

The lessor compares the return on the lease with the return available on alternative investments of similar risk. If the return expected on the lease is greater than that available on alternatives of similar risk, the lease should be written.

The analysis is similar to that of the lessee, in that the cash flows are laid out on a time line.

- All tax effects must be considered.
- If the lessor's NPV is positive, then the lease should be written.

- The lessor's IRR can also be examined, and if it is greater than the after-tax return on comparable investments, the lease transaction should be completed.

When the lessor borrows to purchase the leased property, the lease is called a *leveraged lease.*

- Whether or not a lease is leveraged is unimportant from the lessee's standpoint.
- Typically, leveraged leases provide the lessor with higher NPVs per dollar of invested capital than unleveraged leases. However, the riskiness to the lessor is increased by the leveraging.

Other issues often arise in leasing decisions.

The value of the asset at lease termination is called its *residual value.*

- It might first appear that assets with large residual values would most likely be owned since the owner gets the residual value.
- However, competition among leasing companies forces lease contracts to reflect expected residual values. Thus, large residual value assets are not necessarily more suitable for buying than for leasing.

It is sometimes argued that firms which lease a significant portion of their assets can get more favorable debt terms than firms which do not.

- This premise rests upon the assumption that credit analysts do not recognize the full impact of leasing on a firm's financial strength.
- However, this contention is of questionable validity for firms with audited financial statements.

Tax considerations are an important motive behind many nonoperating leases that are written today.

- A firm that is unprofitable, or that is expanding rapidly and generating large depreciation writeoffs, cannot immediately use the full tax benefits of ownership.
- On the other hand, firms in the highest marginal tax bracket gain the most tax benefits from owning.
- Therefore, companies that make extensive use of lease financing are typically doing poorly and are unable to effectively use tax benefits, while lessors include highly profitable companies which can fully use the tax benefits.

The ability to structure leases that are advantageous to both lessor and lessee depends in large part on tax laws. The four major factors that influence leasing are (1) investment tax credits, (2) depreciation rules, (3) tax rates, and (4) alternative minimum taxes.

- The *investment tax credit (ITC)* is a direct reduction of taxes that occurs when a firm purchases new capital equipment.
- Owners recover their investments in capital assets through *depreciation*, which is tax deductible. Recent tax laws have tended to slow depreciation write-offs and, hence, to reduce the value of ownership.
- The value of depreciation depends on the firm's *tax rate*, because the depreciation tax savings equals the amount of depreciation multiplied by the tax rate. Higher tax rates mean greater ownership tax savings, and hence more incentive for tax-driven leases.
- The *alternative minimum tax (AMT)* also impacts leasing activity.
  - Previously, some corporations were able to pay little or no taxes by using accelerated depreciation for tax purposes and yet report high earnings to stockholders by using straight line depreciation. The AMT now requires companies to pay a minimum tax equal to approximately 20 percent of their reported earnings.
  - A company can reduce its reported income, and hence its AMT liability, by using short-term, fully amortized leases on long-term assets—such leases need not meet the requirements for ordinary tax deductibility.

In addition to tax motivations, there are many other reasons why firms might lease assets rather than purchase them.

Many assets are leased, particularly through operating leases, because it is less risky for the firm to lease the asset than to commit to ownership.

- Assets that face rapid and uncertain technological obsolescence are often leased. Lessees benefit because they are more easily able to acquire the most advanced equipment. Although the risk of obsolescence is passed to the lessor, lessors may be better able to bear this risk because of (1) diversification across a wide variety of assets and (2) being better able to assess residual values and market the used assets.
- If the life of the project is in doubt, then it may be better to lease the asset, since it might be easier to dispose of the asset in the event of premature termination of the project.

DEFINITIONAL QUESTIONS

1. Conceptually, leasing is similar to __________, and it provides the same type of financial ____________.

2. Under a __________ _____ ____________ arrangement, the seller receives the purchase price of the asset but retains the ______ of the property.

3. _____________ leases include both financing and maintenance arrangements.

4. A(n) __________, or __________, lease is similar to a sale and leaseback arrangement, but generally applies to the purchase of ___________ equipment directly from the manufacturer.

5. The IRS would disallow a "lease" which pays for the asset in a relatively ______ period, and then permits the lessee to retain the asset for a ___________ payment.

6. If the IRS allows the lease, then the ______ ___________ is fully deductible.

7. FASB #13 requires that firms ___________ certain financial leases and hence restate their ___________ ______.

8. Capitalizing a lease requires that the asset be listed under ______ ______, and that the ___________ ______ of the future lease payments be shown as ___________.

9. The value of an asset at the end of the lease term is referred to as its ________ ______.

10. ___________ among leasing companies will tend to force leasing rates down to the point where __________ values are fully reflected in the lease rates.

11. Since some leases do not appear on the _________ ______, a firm may be able to use more ___________ than if it did not lease.

12. The leasing decision is a __________ decision rather than a __________ __________ decision.

13. Both the lessee and the lessor can use the ______ or ______ technique to evaluate a lease.

14. ______ _______________ are often an important motive behind financial leases.

15. The ____________ ____________ ______ is designed to insure that corporations reporting high earnings will pay some taxes.

CONCEPTUAL QUESTIONS

16. Capital leases typically include both financing and maintenance arrangements.

a. True **b.** False

17. Leveraged leases typically provide the lessor with higher NPVs per dollar of investment than do unleveraged leases.

a. True **b.** False

18. When one is evaluating a lease proposal, cash flows should be discounted at a relatively high rate because lease flows are fairly certain.

a. True **b.** False

19. Generally, operating leases are fully amortized, and the lease is written for the expected life of the asset.

a. True **b.** False

20. A firm which uses extensive lease financing may have a substantially lower reported debt ratio than a firm which borrows to finance its assets.

a. True **b.** False

21. Firms may or may not capitalize a financial lease.

a. True **b.** False

22. The more stringent alternative minimum tax (AMT) has generated new leasing business.

a. True **b.** False

23. Which of the following statements is most *correct*?

a. Some years ago leasing was called "off balance sheet financing" because the leased asset and the corresponding lease obligation did not appear directly on the balance sheet. Today, though, that situation has changed materially because *all leases* must be capitalized and reported on the balance sheet, along with the value of the leased asset.

b. In a lease versus purchase analysis, cash flows should generally be discounted at the weighted average cost of capital (WACC).
c. Each of the above statements is true.
d. Each of the above statements is false.

PROBLEMS

The following data apply to the next four problems.

Treadmill Trucking Company is negotiating a lease for five new tractor/trailer rigs with Leasing International. Treadmill has received its best offer from Betterbilt Trucks for a total price of $1 million. The terms of the lease offered by International Leasing call for a payment of $205,000 at the beginning of each year of the 5-year lease. As an alternative to leasing, the firm can borrow from a large insurance company and buy the trucks. The $1 million would be borrowed on an amortized term loan at a 10 percent interest rate for 5 years. The trucks fall into the MACRS 5-year class and have an expected residual value of $100,000. Maintenance costs would be included in the lease. If the trucks are owned, a maintenance contract would be purchased at the beginning of each year for $10,000 per year. Treadmill plans to buy a new fleet of trucks at the end of the fifth year. Leasing International has a 40 percent federal-plus-state marginal tax rate, while Treadmill Trucking has a total tax rate of 20 percent.

24 What is Treadmill's present value of the cost of owning?

a. $802,468 b. $805,265 c. $807,189 d. $817,197 e. $829,668

25. What is Treadmill's present value of the cost of leasing?

a. $702,468 b. $705,265 c. $707,189 d. $729,668 e. $735,419

26. Treadmill should lease the trucks.

a. True b. False

27. Assume that the lessor's alternative to leasing is to invest in a 5-year certificate of deposit which pays 9 percent before taxes. The lessor should

a. Write the lease; it has an IRR of 3 percent.
b. Not write the lease; it has an IRR of 3 percent.
c. Write the lease; its NPV is $78,625.

d. Not write the lease; its NPV is -$78,625.
e. Be indifferent between the lease and the alternative investment.

The following data apply to the next four problems.

Walton Publishing Company (WPC) is evaluating a potential lease agreement on a printing press that costs $250,000 and falls into the MACRS 3-year class. The loan rate would be 8 percent if WPC decided to borrow and buy rather than lease. The press has a 4-year economic life, and its estimated residual value is $25,000 at the end of Year 4. If WPC buys the press, it would purchase a maintenance contract which costs $5,000 per year, payable at the beginning of each year. The lease terms, which include maintenance, call for a $71,000 lease payment at the beginning of each year. WPC's tax rate is 40 percent. (Hint: Use a financial calculator.)

28. Should the firm lease or buy?

a. Lease; it costs $842 less than buying.
b. Lease; it costs $1,576 less than buying.
c. Buy; it costs $1,576 less than leasing.
d. Buy; it costs $842 less than leasing.
e. Neither lease nor buy; the truck's NPV is negative.

29. Assume that the lessor is in the 40 percent tax bracket. Further, the lessor's investment alternatives of similar risk yield 8 percent before taxes. Should the lessor write the lease?

a. Yes; its NPV is $1,577.
b. No; its NPV is -$1,577.
c. Yes; its NPV is $842.
d. No; its NPV is -$842.
e. The lessor is indifferent.

30. At what lease payment would the lessee be indifferent between owning and leasing?

a. $42,178 b. $68,348 c. $69,572 d. $70,898 e. $70,296

31. Assume that the lessor's NPV on the lease investment is $1,600. Further, assume that the lessor could obtain financing on 80 percent of his cost of $250,000. If the lessor leverages, assume his NPV on the lease investment would drop to $800. Should the lessor leverage the lease?

a. Yes b. No

ANSWERS

1. borrowing; leverage
2. sale and leaseback; use
3. Operating
4. financial; capital; new
5. short; small (nominal)
6. lease payment
7. capitalize; balance sheets
8. fixed assets; present value; debt (liability)
9. residual value
10. Competition; residual
11. balance sheet; leverage (debt)
12. financing; capital budgeting
13. NPV; IRR
14. Tax considerations
15. alternative minimum tax

16. b. Operating leases include both financing and maintenance arrangements, while financial, or capital, leases typically do not provide maintenance services. However, many leases written today are combination leases, which combine some of the features of both operating and financial leases.

17. a. However, this only holds true if the cost of leveraging is less than the return on the lease. Further, note that leveraging increases the lessor's risk.

18. b. The cash flows are fairly certain, so they should be discounted at a relatively low rate, generally, the after-tax cost of debt.

19. b. Operating leases are not fully amortized. The lessor expects to recover all costs either in subsequent leases or through the sale of the used equipment at its residual value.

20. a. But analysts would recognize that leases are as risky as debt financing and thus include the impact of lease financing on the firm's debt costs and capital structure.

21. b. FASB #13 spells out in detail the conditions under which leases must be capitalized.

22. a. Firms have been seeking ways to lower their AMT liability. Leasing for short periods and hence making high lease payments will reduce the company's reported earnings and meet this need.

23. d. Statement a is false; only certain leases that meet the FASB #13 criteria for capitalization have to be reported on the balance sheet. Statement b is false; the discount rate in a borrow-versus-lease decision is the after-tax cost of debt because the cash flows are fairly certain. Therefore, statement d is the correct choice.

24. d. Place the cash flows associated with ownership on a time line:

	0	1	2	3	4	5
	8%					
Outlay	-1,000,000					
Dep. tax savings[a]		40,000	64,000	38,000	24,000	22,000
Maintenance (AT)[b]	-8,000	-8,000	-8,000	-8,000	-8,000	
Residual value (AT)[c]						92,000
	-1,008,000	32,000	56,000	30,000	16,000	114,000

[a]Depreciation schedule:

Year	Factor	Depreciation Expense	Tax Savings
1	0.20	$ 200,000	$ 40,000
2	0.32	320,000	64,000
3	0.19	190,000	38,000
4	0.12	120,000	24,000
5	0.11	110,000	22,000
6	0.06	60,000	12,000
		$1,000,000	$200,000

[b]After-tax maintenance cash flow = $10,000(1 - T) = $8,000.

[c]Net residual value = $100,000 - ($100,000 - $60,000)(T) = $92,000.

PV cost of owning at the firm's 8 percent after-tax cost of debt is $817,197.

25. c. Place the cash flows associated with leasing on a time line:

	0	1	2	3	4	5
	8%					
Lease payments (AT)[a]	-164,000	-164,000	-164,000	-164,000	-164,000	

[a]$205,000(1 - T) = $164,000.

PV cost of leasing at the firm's 8 percent after-tax cost of debt is $707,189.

26. a. The Net Advantage to Leasing (NAL) is $817,197 - $707,189 = $110,008; hence, the trucks should be leased.

27. d. Place the lessor's cash flows on a time line:

	0	1	2	3	4	5
	5.4%					
Outlay[a]	-1,000,000					
Dep. tax savings[b]		80,000	128,000	76,000	48,000	44,000
Lease payment (AT)[c]	123,000	123,000	123,000	123,000	123,000	
Residual value (AT)[d]						84,000
Maintenance (AT)[e]	-6,000	-6,000	-6,000	-6,000	-6,000	
	-883,000	197,000	245,000	193,000	165,000	128,000

[a]Cost of purchasing the trucks.

[b]This is each year's depreciation expense times the lessor's tax rate of 40 percent.

[c]After-tax lease payment = $205,000(1 - 0.40) = $123,000.

[d]After-tax residual value = $100,000 - ($100,000 - $60,000)(T) = $84,000.

[e]After-tax maintenance payment = $10,000(1 - T).

The lessor's NPV of the lease investment is the PV of the net cash flows when discounted at the after-tax opportunity cost of capital or 9%(1 - T) = 9%(0.6) = 5.4%. NPV = -$78,625.

28. c. Cost of owning: Net investment = $250,000.

Year	Factor	Depreciation
1	0.33	$ 82,500
2	0.45	112,500
3	0.15	37,500
4	0.07	17,500
	1.00	$250,000

	0	1	2	3	4
	4.8%				
Net cost	-250,000				
Maintenance (AT)	-3,000	-3,000	-3,000	-3,000	
Dep. tax savings		33,000	45,000	15,000	7,000
Residual value (AT)					15,000
	-253,000	30,000	42,000	12,000	22,000

PV cost of owning at 4.8% = $157,470.

Cost of leasing:

	0	4.8%	1	2	3	4
Lease payment	-42,600		-42,600	-42,600	-42,600	

PV cost of leasing at 4.8% = $159,046.

Thus, owning is $157,470 - $159,046 = $1,576 less costly than leasing, so the firm should purchase the printing press.

29. a. Lessor's analysis:

	0	1	2	3	4
	4.8%				
Net cost	-250,000				
Maintenance	-3,000	-3,000	-3,000	-3,000	
Dep. tax savings		33,000	45,000	15,000	7,000
Net residual value					15,000
Lease payment	42,600	42,600	42,600	42,600	
	-210,400	72,600	84,600	54,600	22,000

The lessor's NPV at 4.8 percent = -$1,577.

30. e. The lessee would be indifferent if the cost of leasing were equal to $157,470, the PV of owning. Thus,

$$\$157{,}470 = PMT(PVIFA_{4.8\%,4})(1.048)$$
$$PMT = \$42{,}177.74.$$

Lease payment = $42,177.74/0.6 = $70,296.23 ≈ $70,296.

31. a. If the lessor can finance 80 percent of his cost, the lease would only require an investment of 0.2($250,000) = $50,000. Thus, the lessor could write 5 leases for the same $250,000 original investment, and his total NPV would be 5($800) = $4,000, which is significantly higher than the assumed $1,600 NPV available on the $250,000 unleveraged lease.

CHAPTER 18
FINANCIAL STATEMENT ANALYSIS

OVERVIEW

Financial analysis is of vital concern to corporate managers, security analysts, investors, and lenders, all of whom use it for a variety of purposes. The scope of any financial analysis depends on its purpose, which may range from a total analysis of a firm's strengths and weaknesses to a relatively simple analysis of its short-term liquidity. Since the foundation of most types of financial analyses is the firm's financial statements, we focus on financial statement analysis in this chapter. Note, though, that financial statements reflect what has happened in the past, yet the really interesting question is where the firm is going in the future. Therefore, analysts generally use the types of analyses discussed in this chapter as a springboard for predicting and planning for the future, which is the subject of the next chapter.

KEY CONCEPTS

A firm's annual report to shareholders presents two important types of information. The first is a verbal statement of the company's recent operations and its expectations for the coming year. The second is a set of quantitative financial statements which report what actually happened to the firm's financial position, earnings, and dividends over the past few years.

The *income statement* summarizes the firm's revenues and expenses over the past year. Earnings per share (EPS) is called "the bottom line," denoting that of all the items on the income statement, EPS is the most important.

The *balance sheet* shows the firm's assets and the claims against those assets. It portrays the financial condition at a point in time.

- Assets, found on the left-hand side of the balance sheet, are typically shown in the order of their liquidity. Claims, found on the right-hand side, are generally listed in the order in which they must be paid.
- Only cash represents actual money. Noncash assets should produce cash flows eventually, but they do not represent cash in hand.

- Claims against the assets consist of liabilities and stockholders' equity. Thus, Assets – Liabilities – Preferred stock = Common stockholders' equity (Net worth).
- The common equity section of the balance sheet is divided into three accounts: common stock, paid-in capital, and retained earnings. Common stock and paid-in capital accounts arise from the issuance of stock to raise capital. Retained earnings are built up over time as the firm "saves" a part of its earnings rather than paying all earnings out as dividends.
- Companies often use the most accelerated permissible method to calculate depreciation for tax purposes but use straight line depreciation, which results in a lower expense, for stockholder reporting.
- The balance sheet may be thought of as a snapshot of the firm's financial position *at a point in time* (for example, end of year), while the income statement reports on operations *over a period of time* (for example, one calendar year).

The *statement of retained earnings* reports changes in the equity accounts between balance sheet dates.

- The balance sheet account "retained earnings" represents a claim against assets, not assets per se.
- Retained earnings as reported on the balance sheet do not represent cash and are not "available" for the payment of dividends or anything else. Retained earnings represent funds which have already been reinvested in operating assets of the firm.

The *statement of cash flows* reports the impact of a firm's operating, investing, and financing activities on cash flows over an accounting period.

- *Free cash flow* is what remains after considering all anticipated cash inflows and outflows, including working capital expenditures, fixed asset additions, and asset sales.
- The bottom line of the statement of cash flows (net cash gain or loss) can be viewed as the firm's base line free cash flow.

> The real value of financial statements is to help predict the firm's future earnings and dividends. From an investor's standpoint, predicting the future is what financial statement analysis is all about. From management's standpoint, financial statement analysis is useful both as a way to anticipate future conditions and, more important, as a starting point for planning actions that will influence the future course of events. An analysis of the firm's ratios is the first step in a financial analysis.

Liquidity ratios are used to measure a firm's ability to meet its current obligations as they come due.

- The *current ratio* measures the extent to which the claims of short-term creditors are covered by short-term assets. It is determined by dividing current assets by current liabilities.

- The *quick,* or *acid test, ratio* is calculated by deducting inventories from current assets and then dividing the remainder by current liabilities. Inventories are excluded because it may be difficult to liquidate them at their full book value.

Asset management ratios measure how effectively a firm is managing its assets and whether or not the level of those assets is properly related to the level of operations as measured by sales.

- The *inventory turnover ratio* is defined as sales divided by inventories. It is often necessary to use the average inventory figure rather than the year-end figure, especially if a firm's business is highly seasonal.
- The *days sales outstanding (DSO)* is used to appraise accounts receivable, and it is calculated by dividing average daily sales into accounts receivable to find the number of days' sales tied up in receivables. Thus, the DSO represents the average length of time that the firm must wait after making a sale before receiving cash.
- The *fixed assets turnover ratio* is the ratio of sales to net fixed assets. It measures how effectively the firm uses its plant and equipment.
- The *total assets turnover ratio* is calculated by dividing sales by total assets. It measures the utilization of all the firm's assets.

Debt management ratios measure the extent to which a firm is using debt financing, or *financial leverage*, and the degree of safety afforded to creditors.

- The *debt ratio*, or ratio of total debt to total assets, measures the proportion of funds provided by creditors. The lower the ratio, the greater the protection afforded creditors in the event of liquidation.
- The *times-interest-earned (TIE) ratio* is determined by dividing earnings before interest and taxes (EBIT) by the interest charges. The TIE measures the extent to which operating income can decline before the firm is unable to meet its annual interest costs.
- The *fixed charge coverage ratio* is similar to the TIE ratio, but it is more inclusive because it recognizes that many firms incur long-term obligations under lease contracts and sinking funds.

Profitability ratios show the combined effects of liquidity, asset management, and debt management on operating results.

- The *profit margin on sales* is calculated by dividing net income by sales.
- The *basic earning power (BEP) ratio* is calculated by dividing earnings before interest and taxes (EBIT) by total assets. It shows the raw earning power of the firm's assets, before the influence of taxes and leverage.
- The *return on total assets (ROA)* is the ratio of net income to total assets; it measures the return on all the firm's assets after interest and taxes.
- The *return on common equity (ROE)* measures the rate of return on the common stockholders' investment. It is equal to net income divided by common equity.

Market value ratios relate the firm's stock price to its earnings and book value per share, and thus give management an indication of what investors think of the company's past performance and future prospects.

- The *price/earnings (P/E) ratio*, or price per share divided by earnings per share, shows how much investors are willing to pay per dollar of reported profits. P/E ratios are higher for firms with high growth prospects, other things held constant, but they are lower for riskier firms.
- The *market/book (M/B) ratio*, defined as market price per share divided by book value per share, gives another indication of how investors regard the company. Higher M/B ratios are generally associated with firms that have a high rate of return on common equity.

Trend analysis looks at the trend of a single ratio over time. Trend analysis can provide clues as to whether the firm's financial situation is improving, holding constant, or deteriorating. Comparative analysis compares the firm's ratios with industry average ratios and/or the ratios of leading competitors. Such analysis provides insights into the firm's relative performance.

The Du Pont equation shows the relationship among four key ratios:

$$\text{ROE} = \text{Profit margin} \times \text{Total assets turnover} \times \text{Equity multiplier}$$

$$= \frac{\text{Net income}}{\text{Sales}} \times \frac{\text{Sales}}{\text{Total assets}} \times \frac{\text{Total assets}}{\text{Common equity}}$$

This relationship allows analysts to easily summarize a firm's financial condition because it decomposes stockholder profitability into three important determinants: (1) expense control, (2) asset utilization, and (3) debt utilization.

Common size analysis is another technique for analyzing a firm's financial statements.

To create common size statements, all income statement items are divided by sales, and all balance sheet items are divided by total assets. Thus, a common size income statement shows each item as a percentage of sales, and a common size balance sheet shows each item as a percentage of total assets.

The advantage of common size statements is that they facilitate comparisons of balance sheets and income statements over time and across companies.

Common size and ratio analyses provide the same types of information about a firm, but, since they look at the data from different perspectives, they should both be used in a complete financial statement analysis, along with a Du Pont analysis.

Percentage change analysis is another technique to help interpret a firm's financial statements. In this analysis, growth rates are calculated for all income statement items and balance sheet accounts.

Industry data to be used in comparative analyses can be found in external sources such as Dun & Bradstreet's Key Business Ratios, Robert Morris Associates' Annual Statement Studies, and *The Value Line Investment Survey*. Larger firms will generally create their own comparative data using a computerized data base supplied by a financial services firm.

Financial statement analysis is useful, but there are a number of limitations which analysts must recognize.

Ratios are often not useful for analyzing the operations of conglomerate firms which oper ate in many different industries because comparative ratios are from single industries.

The use of industry averages may not provide a very challenging target for high-level performance.

Inflation affects depreciation charges, inventory costs, and therefore the value of both balance sheet items and net income. For this reason, the analysis of a firm over time, or a comparative analysis of firms of different ages, can be misleading. Also, ratios may be distorted by seasonal factors.

Different operating policies, such as the decision to lease rather than to buy equipment, may have an impact on financial ratios. Information on the firm's noncapitalized lease agreements, on its pension plan, on its recent acquisitions and divestitures, on its accounting policies, and so forth, can be found in the notes to the financial statements and should be considered by the analyst.

Many ratios can be interpreted in different ways, and whether a particular ratio is "good" or "bad" should be based upon a complete financial analysis rather than the level of a single ratio at a single point in time.

Different accounting practices can distort ratio comparisons. However, most firms in a given industry use similar procedures.

Window dressing is sometimes used to make financial statements look better to analysts.

DEFINITIONAL QUESTIONS

1. Of all its communications with shareholders, a firm's _______ report is generally the most important.

2. The income statement reports the results of operations during the past year, the most important item being __________ _____ ________.

3. The __________ ______ lists the firm's assets as well as claims against those assets.

4. Typically, assets are listed in order of their ______________, while liabilities are listed in the order in which they must be paid.

5. Assets – Liabilities – Preferred stock = ______ worth, or _______ ____________ equity.

6. The three accounts which normally make up the common equity section of the balance sheet are common stock, _____ - ___ capital, and __________ ____________.

7. ___________ ___________ as reported on the balance sheet represent income earned by the firm in past years that has not been paid out as dividends.

8. Retained earnings are generally reinvested in ___________ _______ and are not held in the form of cash.

9. The ___________ ___ __________ __________ is designed to show how the firm's operations have affected its cash position.

10. The three major categories of the Statement of Cash Flows are cash flows associated with ____________ activities, ______-_______ _________ activities, and ____________ activities.

11. The current ratio and acid-test ratio are examples of ______________ ratios. They measure a firm's ability to meet its _______ - ______ obligations.

12. The days sales outstanding (DSO) ratio is found by dividing average sales per day into accounts ______________. The DSO is the length of time that a firm must wait after making a sale before it receives ______.

13. Debt management ratios are used to evaluate a firm's use of financial __________.

14. The debt ratio, which is the ratio of _______ ______ to _______ _______, measures the proportion of funds supplied by creditors.

15. The ______ - _________ - ________ ratio is calculated by dividing earnings before interest and taxes by the amount of interest charges.

16. The combined effects of liquidity, asset management, and debt management are measured by _________________ ratios.

17. Dividing net income by sales gives the _________ __________ on sales.

18. The ________ /________ ratio measures how much investors are willing to pay for each dollar of a firm's current income.

19. Firms with higher rates of return on stockholders' equity tend to sell at relatively high ratios of __________ price to ______ value.

20. Individual ratios are of little value in analyzing a company's financial condition. More important are the _______ of a ratio over time and the comparison of the company's ratios to ______________ average ratios.

21. The ___ ______ equation shows how debt utilization, total assets turnover, and profit margin combine to produce return on equity.

22. Return on assets is a function of two variables, the profit ________ and ________ __________ turnover.

23. Analyzing a particular ratio over time for an individual firm is known as _________ analysis.

24. To create __________ ______ ____________, all income statement items are divided by sales, and all balance sheet items are divided by total assets.

CONCEPTUAL QUESTIONS

25. The equity multiplier can be expressed as 1 – (Debt/Assets).

a. True **b.** False

26. A high quick ratio is *always* a good indication of a well-managed liquidity position.

a. True **b.** False

27. International Appliances Inc. has a current ratio of 0.5. Which of the following actions would improve (increase) this ratio?

a. Use cash to pay off current liabilities.
b. Collect some of the current accounts receivable.
c. Use cash to pay off some long-term debt.
d. Purchase additional inventory on credit (accounts payable).
e. Sell some of the existing inventory at cost.

28. Refer back to Question 27. Assume that International Appliances has a current ratio of 1.2. Now, which of the following actions would improve (increase) this ratio?

a. Use cash to pay off current liabilities.
b. Collect some of the current accounts receivable.
c. Use cash to pay off some long-term debt.
d. Purchase additional inventory on credit (accounts payable).
e. Use cash to pay for some fixed assets.

29. Examining the ratios of a particular firm against the same measures for a group of firms from the same industry, at a point in time, is an example of

a. Trend analysis.
b. Comparative analysis.
c. Du Pont analysis.
d. Simple ratio analysis.
e. Industry analysis.

30. Which of the following statements is most *correct*?

a. Having a high current ratio and a high quick ratio is always a good indication that a firm is managing its liquidity position well.

b. A decline in the inventory turnover ratio suggests that the firm's liquidity position is improving.
c. If a firm's times-interest-earned ratio is relatively high, then this is one indication that the firm should be able to meet its debt obligations.
d. Since ROA measures the firm's effective utilization of assets (without considering how these assets are financed), two firms with the same EBIT must have the same ROA.
e. If, through specific managerial actions, a firm has been able to increase its ROA, then, because of the fixed mathematical relationship between ROA and ROE, it must also have increased its ROE.

31. Which of the following statements is most *correct*?

a. Suppose two firms with the same amount of assets pay the same interest rate on their debt and earn the same rate of return on their assets and that ROA is positive. However, one firm has a higher debt ratio. Under these conditions, the firm with the higher debt ratio will also have a higher rate of return on common equity.
b. One of the problems of ratio analysis is that the relationships are subject to manipulation. For example, we know that if we use some cash to pay off some of our current liabilities, the current ratio will always increase, especially if the current ratio is weak initially, for example, below 1.0.
c. Generally, firms with high profit margins have high asset turnover ratios and firms with low profit margins have low turnover ratios; this result is exactly as predicted by the Du Pont equation.
d. Firms A and B have identical earnings and identical dividend payout ratios. If Firm A's growth rate is higher than Firm B's, then Firm A's P/E ratio must be greater than Firm B's P/E ratio.
e. Each of the above statements is false.

PROBLEMS

The following financial statements apply to the next six problems.

Roberts Manufacturing Balance Sheet
December 31, 1993
(Dollars in Thousands)

Cash	$ 200	Accounts payable	$ 205
Receivables	245	Notes payable	425
Inventory	625	Other current liabilities	115
Total current assets	$1,070	Total current liabilities	$ 745
Net fixed assets	1,200	Long-term debt	420
		Common equity	1,105
Total assets	$2,270	Total liabilities and equity	$2,270

Roberts Manufacturing
Income Statement for Year Ended December 31, 1993
(Dollars in Thousands)

Sales		$2,400
Cost of goods sold:		
Materials	$1,000	
Labor	600	
Heat, light, and power	89	
Indirect labor	65	
Depreciation	80	1,834
Gross profit		$ 566
Selling expenses		175
General and administrative expenses		216
Earnings before interest and taxes (EBIT)		$ 175
Less interest expense		35
Earnings before taxes (EBT)		$ 140
Less taxes (40%)		56
Net income (NI)		$ 84

32. Calculate the liquidity ratios, that is, the current ratio and the quick ratio.

a. 1.20; 0.60 **b.** 1.20; 0.80 **c.** 1.44; 0.60 **d.** 1.44; 0.80 **e.** 1.60; 0.60

33. Calculate the asset management ratios, that is, the inventory turnover ratio, fixed assets turnover, total assets turnover, and days sales outstanding.

a. 3.84; 2.00; 1.06; 36.75 days
b. 3.84; 2.00; 1.06; 35.25 days
c. 3.84; 2.00; 1.06; 34.10 days
d. 3.84; 2.00; 1.24; 34.10 days
e. 3.84; 2.20; 1.48; 34.10 days

34. Calculate the debt management ratios, that is, the debt and times-interest-earned ratios.

a. 0.39; 3.16 **b.** 0.39; 5.00 **c.** 0.51; 3.16 **d.** 0.51; 5.00 **e.** 0.73; 3.16

35. Calculate the profitability ratios, that is, the profit margin on sales, return on total assets, return on common equity, and basic earning power of assets.

a. 3.50%; 4.25%; 7.60%; 8.00%
b. 3.50%; 3.70%; 7.60%; 7.71%
c. 3.70%; 3.50%; 7.60%; 7.71%
d. 3.70%; 3.50%; 8.00%; 8.00%
e. 4.25%; 3.70%; 7.60%; 8.00%

36. Calculate the market value ratios, that is, the price/earnings ratio and the market/book value ratio. Roberts had an average of 10,000 shares outstanding during 1993, and the stock price on December 31, 1993, was $40.00.

a. 4.21; 0.36 **b.** 3.20; 1.54 **c.** 3.20; 0.36 **d.** 4.76; 1.54 **e.** 4.76; 0.36

37. Use the Du Pont equation to determine Roberts' return on equity.

a. 6.90% **b.** 7.24% **c.** 7.47% **d.** 7.60% **e.** 8.41%

38. Lewis Inc. has sales of $2 million per year, all of which are credit sales. Its days sales outstanding is 42 days. What is its average accounts receivable balance?

a. $233,333 **b.** $266,667 **c.** $333,333 **d.** $350,000 **e.** $366,667

39. Southeast Jewelers Inc. sells only on credit. Its days sales outstanding is 60 days, and its average accounts receivable balance is $500,000. What are its sales for the year?

a. $1,500,000 **b.** $3,000,000 **c.** $2,000,000 **d.** 2,750,000 **e.** $3,225,000

40. A firm has total interest charges of $20,000 per year, sales of $2 million, a tax rate of 40 percent, and a profit margin of 6 percent. What is the firm's times-interest-earned ratio?

a. 10 **b.** 11 **c.** 12 **d.** 13 **e.** 14

41. Refer to Problem 40. What is the firm's TIE, if its profit margin decreases to 3 percent and its interest charges double to $40,000 per year?

a. 3.0 **b.** 2.5 **c.** 3.5 **d.** 4.2 **e.** 3.7

42. A fire has destroyed many of the financial records at Anderson Associates. You are assigned to piece together information to prepare a financial report. You have found that the firm's return on equity is 12 percent and its debt ratio is 0.40. What is its return on assets?

a. 4.90% **b.** 5.35% **c.** 6.60% **d.** 7.20% **e.** 8.40%

43. Refer to Problem 42. What is the firm's debt ratio if its ROE is 15 percent and its ROA is 10 percent?

a. 67% **b.** 50% **c.** 25% **d.** 33% **e.** 45%

44. Rowe and Company has a debt ratio of 0.50, a total assets turnover of 0.25, and a profit margin of 10 percent. The president is unhappy with the current return on equity, and he thinks it could be doubled. This could be accomplished (1) by increasing the profit margin to 14 percent and (2) by increasing debt utilization. Total assets turnover will not change. What new debt ratio, along with the 14 percent profit margin, is required to double the return on equity?

a. 0.55 **b.** 0.60 **c.** 0.65 **d.** 0.70 **e.** 0.75

45. Altman Corporation has $1,000,000 of debt outstanding, and it pays an interest rate of 12 percent annually. Altman's annual sales are $4 million, its federal-plus-state tax rate is 25 percent, and its net profit margin on sales is 10 percent. If the company does not maintain a TIE ratio of at least 5 times, its bank will refuse to renew the loan, and bankruptcy will result. What is Altman's TIE ratio?

a. 3.33 **b.** 4.44 **c.** 2.50 **d.** 4.00 **e.** 5.44

46. Refer to Problem 45. What is the maximum amount Altman's EBIT could decrease and its bank still renew its loan?

a. $53,333 **b.** $45,432 **c.** $66,767 **d.** $47,898 **e.** $57,769

47. Pinkerton Packaging's ROE last year was 2.5 percent, but its management has developed a new operating plan designed to improve things. The new plan calls for a total debt ratio of 50 percent, which will result in interest charges of $240 per year. Management projects an EBIT of $800 on sales of $8,000, and it expects to have a total assets turnover ratio of 1.6. Under these conditions, the federal-plus-state tax rate will be 40 percent. If the changes are made, what return on equity will Pinkerton earn?

a. 12.50% b. 13.44% c. 13.00% d. 14.02% e. 14.57%

The following financial statement applies to the next three problems.

Baker Corporation Balance Sheet
December 31, 1995

Cash and marketable securities	$ 50	Accounts payable	$ 250
Accounts receivable	200	Accruals	250
Inventory	250	Notes payable	500
Total current assets	$ 500	Total current liabilities	$1,000
Net fixed assets	1,500	Long-term debt	250
		Common stock	400
		Retained earnings	350
Total assets	$2,000	Total liabilities and equity	$2,000

48. What is Baker Corporation's current ratio as of December 31, 1995?

a. 0.35 b. 0.65 c. 0.50 d. 0.25 e. 0.75

49. If Baker uses $50 of cash to pay off $50 of its accounts payable, what is its new current ratio?

a. 0.47 b. 0.44 c. 0.54 d. 0.33 e. 0.62

50. If Baker uses its $50 cash balance to pay off $50 of its long-term debt, what is its new current ratio?

a. 0.35 b. 0.50 c. 0.55 d. 0.60 e. 0.45

The following financial statements apply to the next problem.

Whitney Inc. Balance Sheet
December 31, 1995

Total current assets	$250	Total current liabilities	$100
Fixed assets	500	Long-term debt	250
		Common stockholders' equity	400
Total assets	$750	Total liabilities and equity	$750

Whitney Inc. Income Statement
for Year Ended December 31, 1995

Sales		$1,000
Cost of goods sold (excluding depreciation)	$550	
Other operating expenses	100	
Depreciation	50	
Total operating costs		700
Earnings before interest and taxes (EBIT)		$ 300
Less interest expense		25
Earnings before taxes (EBT)		$ 275
Less taxes (40%)		110
Net income		$ 165

51. What are Whitney Inc.'s basic earning power and ROA ratios?

a. 30%; 22% **b.** 40%; 30% **c.** 50%; 22% **d.** 40%; 22% **e.** 40%; 40%

The following financial statements apply to the next problem.

Cotner Enterprises Balance Sheet
December 31, 1995

Total current assets	$ 417	Total current liabilities	$ 300
Fixed assets	833	Long-term debt	500
		Common stockholders' equity	450
Total assets	$1,250	Total liabilities and equity	$1,250

Cotner Enterprises Income Statement
for Year Ended December 31, 1995

Sales		$1,700
Cost of goods sold (excluding depreciation)	$1,190	
Other operating expenses	135	
Depreciation	75	
Total operating costs		1,400
Earnings before interest and taxes (EBIT)		$ 300
Less interest expense		54
Earnings before taxes (EBT)		$ 246
Less taxes (34%)		84
Net income		$ 162

52. What are Cotner Enterprise's basic earning power and ROA ratios?

a. 20%; 12.96%
b. 24%; 12.96%
c. 24%; 15.75%
d. 17.5%; 12.96%
e. 24%; 10.5%

53. Dauten Enterprises is just being formed. It will need $2 million of assets, and it expects to have an EBIT of $400,000. Dauten will own no securities, so all of its income will be operating income. If it chooses to, Dauten can finance up to 50 percent of its assets with debt which will have a 9 percent interest rate. Dauten has no other liabilities. Assuming a 40 percent federal-plus-state tax rate on all taxable income, what is the difference between the expected ROE if Dauten finances with 50 percent debt versus the expected ROE if it finances entirely with common stock?

a. 7.2% b. 6.6% c. 6.0% d. 5.8% e. 9.0%

ANSWERS

1. annual
2. earnings per share
3. balance sheet
4. liquidity
5. Net; Common stockholders'
6. paid-in; retained earnings
7. Retained earnings
8. operating assets
9. Statement of Cash Flows
10. operating; long-term investing; financing
11. liquidity; short-term (or current)
12. receivable; cash
13. leverage
14. total debt; total assets
15. times-interest-earned
16. profitability
17. profit margin
18. price/earnings
19. market; book
20. trend; industry
21. Du Pont
22. margin; total assets
23. trend
24. common size statements

25. b. 1 − (Debt/Assets) = Equity/Assets. The equity multiplier is equal to Assets/Equity.

26. b. Excess cash resulting from poor management could produce a high quick ratio. Similarly, if accounts receivable are not collected promptly, this could also lead to a high quick ratio.

27. d. This question is best analyzed using numbers. For example, assume current assets equal $50 and current liabilities equal $100; thus, the current ratio equals 0.5. For answer a,

assume \$5 in cash is used to pay off \$5 in current liabilities. The new current ratio would be \$45/\$95 = 0.47. For answer d, assume a \$10 purchase of inventory on credit (accounts payable). The new current ratio would be \$60/\$110 = 0.55, which is an increase over the old current ratio of 0.5. (Problems 17 through 19 were set up to help visualize this question.)

28. a. Again, this question is best analyzed using numbers. For example, assume current assets equal \$120 and current liabilities equal \$100; thus, the current ratio equals 1.2. For answer a, assume \$5 in cash is used to pay off \$5 in current liabilities. The new current ratio would be \$115/\$95 = 1.21, which is an increase over the old current ratio of 1.2. For answer d, assume a \$10 purchase of inventory on credit (accounts payable). The new current ratio would be \$130/\$110 = 1.18, which is a decrease from the old current ratio of 1.2.

29. b. The correct answer is comparative analysis. A trend analysis compares the firm's ratios over time, while a Du Pont analysis shows the relationships among return on equity, assets turnover, profit margin, and leverage.

30. c. Excess cash resulting from poor management could produce high current and quick ratios; thus statement a is false. A decline in the inventory turnover ratio suggests that either sales have decreased or inventory has increased—which suggests that the firm's liquidity position is *not* improving; thus statement b is false. ROA = Net income/Total assets, and EBIT does not equal net income. Two firms with the same EBIT could have different financing and different taxes resulting in different net incomes. Also, two firms with the same EBIT do not necessarily have the same total assets; thus statement d is false. ROE = ROA × Assets/Equity. If ROA increases because total assets decrease, then the equity multiplier decreases, and depending on which effect is greater, ROE may or may not increase; thus statement e is false. Statement c is correct; the TIE ratio is used to measure whether the firm can meet its debt obligation, and a high TIE ratio would indicate this is so.

31. a. Ratio analysis is subject to manipulation; however, if the current ratio is less than 1.0 and we use cash to pay off some current liabilities, the current ratio will decrease, *not* increase; thus statement b is false. Statement c is just the reverse of what actually occurs. Firms with high profit margins have low turnover ratios and vice versa. Statement d is false; it does not necessarily follow that if a firm's growth rate is higher then its stock price will be higher. Statement a is correct. From the information given in statement a, one can determine that the two firms' net incomes are equal; thus, the firm with the higher debt ratio (lower equity ratio) will indeed have a higher ROE.

32. c. $$\text{Current ratio} = \frac{\text{Current assets}}{\text{Current liabilities}} = \frac{\$1{,}070}{\$745} = 1.44.$$

$$\text{Quick ratio} = \frac{\text{Current assets} - \text{Inventory}}{\text{Current liabilities}} = \frac{\$1{,}070 - \$625}{\$745} = 0.60.$$

33. a. $$\text{Inventory turnover} = \frac{\text{Sales}}{\text{Inventory}} = \frac{\$2{,}400}{\$625} = 3.84.$$

$$\text{Fixed assets turnover} = \frac{\text{Sales}}{\text{Net fixed assets}} = \frac{\$2{,}400}{\$1{,}200} = 2.00.$$

$$\text{Total assets turnover} = \frac{\text{Sales}}{\text{Total assets}} = \frac{\$2{,}400}{\$2{,}270} = 1.06.$$

$$\text{DSO} = \frac{\text{Accounts receivable}}{\text{Sales/360}} = \frac{\$245}{\$2{,}400/360} = 36.75 \text{ days.}$$

34. d. Debt ratio = Total debt/Total assets = \$1,165/\$2,270 = 0.51.

TIE ratio = EBIT/Interest = \$175/\$35 = 5.00.

35. b. $$\text{Profit margin} = \frac{\text{Net income}}{\text{Sales}} = \frac{\$84}{\$2{,}400} = 0.0350 = 3.50\%.$$

$$\text{ROA} = \frac{\text{Net income}}{\text{Total assets}} = \frac{\$84}{\$2{,}270} = 0.0370 = 3.70\%.$$

$$\text{ROE} = \frac{\text{Net income}}{\text{Common equity}} = \frac{\$84}{\$1{,}105} = 0.0760 = 7.60\%.$$

$$\text{BEP} = \frac{\text{EBIT}}{\text{Total assets}} = \frac{\$175}{\$2{,}270} = 0.0771 = 7.71\%.$$

36. e. $$\text{EPS} = \frac{\text{Net income}}{\text{Number of shares outstanding}} = \frac{\$84{,}000}{10{,}000} = \$8.40.$$

$$\text{P/E ratio} = \frac{\text{Price}}{\text{EPS}} = \frac{\$40.00}{\$8.40} = 4.76.$$

$$\text{Market/book value} = \frac{\text{Market price}}{\text{Book value}} = \frac{\$40(10{,}000)}{\$1{,}105{,}000} = 0.36.$$

37. d. $$\text{ROE} = \text{Profit margin} \times \text{Total assets turnover} \times \text{Equity multiplier}$$
$$= \frac{\$84}{\$2{,}400} \times \frac{\$2{,}400}{\$2{,}270} \times \frac{\$2{,}270}{\$1{,}105} = 0.035 \times 1.057 \times 2.054 = 0.0760 = 7.60\%.$$

38. a. $$\text{DSO} = \frac{\text{Accounts receivable}}{\text{Sales/360}}$$
$$42 \text{ days} = \frac{\text{AR}}{\$2{,}000{,}000/360}$$
$$\text{AR} = \$233{,}333.$$

39. b. $$\text{DSO} = \text{Accounts receivable/(Sales/360)}$$
$$60 \text{ days} = \$500{,}000/(\text{Sales}/360)$$
$$60(\text{Sales}/360) = \$500{,}000$$
$$\text{Sales} = \$3{,}000{,}000.$$

40. b. Net income= \$2,000,000(0.06) = \$120,000.
Earnings before taxes = \$120,000/(1 − 0.4) = \$200,000.
EBIT = \$200,000 + \$20,000 = \$220,000.
TIE = EBIT/Interest = \$220,000/\$20,000 = 11.

41. c. Net income= \$2,000,000(0.03) = \$60,000.
Earnings before taxes = \$60,000/(1 − 0.4) = \$100,000.
EBIT = \$100,000 + \$40,000 = \$140,000.
TIE = EBIT/Interest = \$140,000/\$40,000 = 3.5.

42. d. If Total debt/Total assets = 0.40, then Total equity/Total assets = 0.60, and the equity multiplier (Assets/Equity) = 1/0.60 = 1.667.

$$\frac{NI}{E} = \frac{NI}{A} \times \frac{A}{E}$$

$$\begin{aligned} ROE &= ROA \times EM \\ 12\% &= ROA \times 1.667 \\ ROA &= 7.20\%. \end{aligned}$$

43. d.

$$\begin{aligned} ROE &= ROA \times \text{Equity multiplier} \\ 15\% &= 10\% \times \text{TA/Equity} \\ 1.5 &= \text{TA/Equity} \\ \text{Equity/TA} &= 0.67. \end{aligned}$$

Debt/TA = 1 − Equity/TA = 1 − 0.67 = 0.33 = 33%.

44. c. If Total debt/Total assets = 0.50, then Total equity/Total assets = 0.50 and the equity multiplier (Assets/Equity) = 1/0.50 = 2.0.

ROE = PM × Total assets turnover × EM.

Before: ROE = 10% × 0.25 × 2.00 = 5.00%.

After: 10.00% = 14% × 0.25 × EM; thus EM = 2.8571.

$$\begin{aligned} \text{Equity multiplier} &= \frac{\text{Assets}}{\text{Equity}} \\ 2.8571 &= \frac{1}{\text{Equity}} \\ 0.35 &= \text{Equity}. \end{aligned}$$

Debt = Assets - Equity = 100% - 35% = 65%.

45. e. TIE = EBIT/Interest, so find EBIT and Interest.

Interest = $1,000,000(0.12) = $120,000.

Net income = $4,000,000(0.10) = $400,000.

Pre-tax income = $400,000/(1 − T) = $400,000(0.75) = $533,333.

EBIT = $533,333 + $120,000 = $653,333.

TIE = $653,333/$120,000 = 5.44×.

46. a.

$$\begin{aligned} TIE &= EBIT/INT \\ 5 &= EBIT/\$120{,}000 \end{aligned}$$

EBIT = \$600,000.

From Problem 45, EBIT = \$653,333, so EBIT could decrease by \$653,333 − \$600,000 = \$53,333.

47. b. ROE = Profit margin × Total assets turnover × Equity multiplier
= NI/Sales × Sales/TA × TA/Equity.

Now we need to determine the inputs for the equation from the data that were given. On the left we set up an income statement, and we put numbers in it on the right:

Sales (given)	\$8,000
− Cost	NA
EBIT (given)	\$ 800
− Interest (given)	240
EBT	\$ 560
− Taxes (40%)	224
Net income	\$ 336

Now we can use some ratios to get some more data:

Total assets turnover = S/TA = 1.6.

D/A = 50%, so E/A = 50%, and therefore TA/E = 1/(E/A) = 1/0.5 = 2.00.

Now we can complete the Du Pont equation to determine ROE:

ROE = \$336/\$8,000 × 1.6 × 2.0 = 13.44%.

48. c. Baker Corporation's current ratio equals Total current assets/Total current liabilities = \$500/\$1,000 = 0.50.

49. a. Baker Corporation's new current ratio equals (\$500 − \$50)/(\$1,000 − \$50) = \$450/\$950 = 0.47.

50. e. Only the current asset balance is affected by this action. Baker's new current ratio = (\$500 − \$50)/\$1,000 = \$450/\$1,000 = 0.45.

51. d. Whitney's BEP ratio equals EBIT/Total assets = \$300/\$750 = 40%.
Whitney's ROA equals Net income/Total assets = \$165/\$750 = 22%.

52. b. Cotner's BEP ratio equals EBIT/Total assets = \$300/\$1,250 = 24%.
Cotner's ROA equals Net income/Total assets = \$162/\$1,250 = 12.96%.

53. b. Known data: Total assets = \$2,000,000, EBIT = \$400,000, k_d = 9%, T = 40%.

D/A = 0.5 = 50%, so Debt = 0.5(\$2,000,000) = \$1,000,000. Equity = Total assets - Debt = \$2,000,000 - \$1,000,000 = \$1,000,000. At a 9 percent interest rate, INT = 0.09(\$1,000,000) = \$90,000.

	D/A = 0%	D/A = 50%
EBIT	\$400,000	\$400,000
Interest	0	90,000
Taxable income	\$400,000	\$310,000
Taxes (40%)	160,000	124,000
Net income (NI)	\$240,000	\$186,000

For D/A = 0%, ROE = NI/Equity = \$240,000/\$2,000,000 = 12%. For D/A = 50%, ROE = \$186,000/\$1,000,000 = 18.6%. Difference = 18.6% - 12.0% = 6.6%.

CHAPTER 19
LONG-TERM FINANCIAL PLANNING

OVERVIEW

In the last chapter, we saw how one can analyze financial statements to identify a firm's strengths and weaknesses. Now, we consider the actions a firm can take to exploit its strengths and maximize its weaknesses. The key to good planning is a set of projected, or pro forma, financial statements which examine the effects of alternative policies on the financial condition of the firm. However, a good financial plan cannot, by itself, ensure that the firm's goals will be met; the plan must be backed up by a financial control system for monitoring the situation, both to ensure that the plan is carried out properly and to facilitate rapid adjustments if economic and operating conditions change from those projected.

KEY CONCEPTS

Financial planning is a key part of the planning process.

Strategic planning charts the course for a firm over the long term. A *strategic plan* can take many forms, but most include the following elements:

- The *corporate purpose* (also known as corporate vision) defines the overall mission of the firm.
- The *corporate scope* defines a firm's lines of business and geographic areas of operations.
- The corporate purpose and scope outline the general philosophy and approach of the business. Corporate objectives set forth specific goals that management strives to attain.
- Corporate strategies are broad approaches to be taken to meet corporate objectives.

Operating plans provide implementation guidance for management.

- Most firms use a five-year horizon for developing operating plans, with the first year of the plan being the most detailed and with each succeeding year's plan becoming less specific.
- The operating plan explains in considerable detail who is responsible for what particular function and when specific tasks are to be accomplished.

The financial planning process can be broken down into five steps.

Set up a system of projected financial statements which can be used to analyze the effects of the operating plan on projected profits and other financial condition indicators.

Determine the funds needed to support the five-year plan.

Forecast the funds availability over the next five years by estimating the funds generated internally as well as those which must be obtained from external sources.

Establish and maintain a system of controls governing the allocation and use of funds within the firm.

Develop procedures for adjusting the basic plan if the economic forecasts upon which the plan was based do not materialize.

The principal components of the financial plan are: an analysis of the firm's current financial condition, a sales forecast, a capital budget, a cash budget, a set of pro forma financial statements, and the external financing plan.

Well-run companies generally base their operating plans on a set of forecasted financial statements. A sales forecast for the next five years or so is developed, the assets required to meet the sales target are determined, and a decision is made concerning how to finance the required assets. These forecasts represent the "base case" and are a standard by which to judge alternate forecasts.

The *sales forecast* generally begins with a review of sales for the past 5 to 10 years.

If the sales forecast is off, the consequences can be serious. Thus, an accurate sales forecast is critical to the well-being of the firm.

The first step in the financial plan is to develop a set of projected financial statements, with the sales forecast as the key input. To forecast financial statements, the simplest technique is the constant ratio method.

The first step is to forecast next year's income statement.

- A sales forecast is needed.
- Assumptions about the operating cost ratio, the tax rate, interest charges, and the dividend payout ratio are made.
- In the simplest case, costs are assumed to increase at the same rate as sales; in more complicated situations, cost changes are forecasted separately.
- The objective is to determine how much income the company will earn and then retain for reinvestment in the business during the forecasted year.

The second step is to forecast next year's balance sheet.

- All asset accounts can be assumed to vary directly with sales unless the firm is operating at less than full capacity. If the firm is not operating at full capacity, then fixed assets will not vary directly with sales, but the cash, receivables, and inventory accounts will increase in proportion to the increase in sales.
- Liabilities, equity, or both must also increase if assets increase -- asset expansions must be financed in some manner.
- Certain liability accounts, such as accounts payable and accruals, will increase *spontaneously* with sales. Retained earnings will increase, but not proportionately with sales. The new retained earnings will be determined from the projected income statement.
- Other financing accounts, such as short-term debt (notes payable), long-term debt, and common stock, are not directly related to sales. Changes in these accounts result from managerial decisions; they do not increase spontaneously as sales increase.
- The difference between projected total assets and projected liabilities and equity is the amount of *additional funds needed (AFN).*

The third step is the decision on how to finance the additional funds required. Sometimes contractual agreements, such as a limit on the debt ratio, will restrict the firm's financing decisions.

One complexity that arises in financial forecasting relates to *financing feedbacks*, which are the effects on the income statement and balance sheet of actions taken to finance increases in assets. Financing feedbacks are incorporated into the pro forma financial statements through additional calculations, or *passes*, of the projected income statement and balance sheet.

Once the pro forma financial statements have been developed, the key ratios can be analyzed to determine whether the forecast meets the firm's financial targets as specified in the firm's financial plan.

Although most firms' forecasts of capital requirements are made by constructing pro forma financial statements as described above, the following formula also is sometimes used to forecast financial requirements:

The formula is as follows:

$$\begin{array}{c} \text{Additional} \\ \text{funds} \\ \text{needed} \end{array} = \begin{array}{c} \text{Required} \\ \text{increase} \\ \text{in assets} \end{array} - \begin{array}{c} \text{Spontaneous} \\ \text{increase} \\ \text{in liabilities} \end{array} - \begin{array}{c} \text{Increase in} \\ \text{retained} \\ \text{earnings} \end{array},$$

or

$$\text{AFN} = (\text{A*/S})\Delta\text{S} - (\text{L*/S})\Delta\text{S} - \text{MS}_1(1 - \text{d}).$$

Here, A*/S = assets that must increase if sales are to increase, expressed as a percentage of sales, or the required dollar increase in assets per $1 increase in sales; L*/S = liabilities that increase spontaneously with sales as a percentage of sales, or spontaneously generated financing per $1 increase in sales; S_1 = total expected sales for the year in question (note that S_0 = last year's sales); ΔS = change in sales = $S_1 - S_0$; M = profit margin, or rate of profits after taxes per $1 of sales; and d = the percentage of earnings paid out in dividends (dividend payout ratio).

Inherent in the formula is the assumption that each asset item must increase in direct proportion to sales increases and that designated liability accounts also grow at the same rate as sales. Obviously, these assumptions do not always hold, so its results are not always reliable. Thus, the formula is often used as a supplement to the constant ratio method.

The faster a firm's growth rate in sales, the greater its need for additional financing.

- Higher growth rates require managers to plan very carefully to decide if the additional financing needed is actually available to the firm. Otherwise, they may need to reconsider their projected growth rate.
- Dividend policy as reflected in the payout ratio also affects external capital requirements: the higher the payout ratio, the smaller the addition to retained earnings, and hence the greater the requirements for external capital. Dividend policy may be changed to satisfy internal financing requirements, but this may have a negative impact on stock price and may be met with resistance from investors.
- The amount of assets required per dollar of sales, A*/S, is often called the *capital intensity ratio*. This factor has a major effect on capital requirements per unit of sales

growth. If the capital intensity ratio is low, then sales can grow rapidly without much outside capital. However, if a firm is capital intensive, even a small growth in output will require a great deal of outside capital.

- Profit margin, M, also has an effect on capital requirements. The higher the profit margin, the lower the funds requirement; and the lower the profit margin, the higher the requirement. Thus, highly profitable firms can raise most of their capital internally.

> The forecasting process is greatly complicated if the ratios of balance sheet items to sales are not constant at all levels of sales.

Where *economies of scale* occur in asset use, the ratio of that asset to sales will change as the size of the firm increases.

Technological considerations sometimes dictate that fixed assets be added in large, discrete units, often referred to as *lumpy assets.* This automatically creates excess capacity immediately after a plant expansion.

Forecasting errors can cause the actual asset/sales ratio for a given period to be quite different from the planned ratio. This situation can result in excess capacity.

Since excess capacity may exist in fixed assets, projected sales levels need to be adjusted downward since they were estimated on the assumption of full capacity of fixed assets.

- Full capacity sales is defined as actual sales divided by the percentage of capacity at which the fixed assets operated to achieve these sales:

$$\text{Full capacity sales} = \frac{\text{Actual sales}}{\begin{array}{c}\text{Percentage of capacity at which}\\ \text{fixed assets were operated}\end{array}}.$$

- The target fixed assets to sales ratio is equal to the current year's fixed assets divided by full capacity sales:

$$\text{Target fixed assets/Sales ratio} = \frac{\text{Actual fixed assets}}{\text{Full capacity sales}}.$$

- The required level of fixed assets is equal to the target fixed assets to sales ratio times projected sales:

$$\text{Required level of fixed assets} = \frac{\text{Target fixed assets}}{\text{Sales}}(\text{Projected sales}).$$

If any of the above conditions apply (economies of scale, lumpy assets, or excess capacity), the A*/S ratio will not be a constant, and the constant ratio technique should not be used. Rather, other techniques must be used to forecast asset levels to determine additional financing requirements. Several methods are discussed below:

If we assume that the relationship between a certain item or account and sales is linear, then we can use simple linear regression techniques to estimate the item or account level for any given sales increase. An estimated regression equation is determined which provides an estimated relationship between a given asset account and sales.

If the relationship between a certain item or account and sales is not linear, *curvilinear regression* might be used to make the forecast. If the relationship has points that are widely scattered about the regression line, and it does not appear to be curvilinear, then the best forecast may be obtained using *multiple regression.* In this case, there is a good chance that other factors affect the level of the variable.

A final approach to forecasting, the one generally used in practice, is to develop a specific model for each income statement and balance sheet variable to be forecasted. This method is called *specific variable forecasting,* because each income statement item and balance sheet account is forecasted independently, given the sales forecast.

Although the type of financial forecasting described in this chapter can be done with a hand calculator, virtually all corporate forecasts are made using computerized forecasting models. Most models are based on spreadsheet programs. These programs are easy to construct for forecasts extending over several years, and they are useful for instantaneously recomputing projected statements and ratios when one of the input variables is changed.

Financial forecasting and planning are vital to corporate success, but planning is for nought unless the firm has a control system (1) that ensures implementation of the planned policies and (2) that provides an information feedback loop which permits rapid adjustments if the market conditions upon which the plan is based change.

In a financial control system, the key question is "How is the firm doing in 199X as compared with our forecasts, and if actual results differ from the budget, what can we do to get back on track?"

The basic tools of financial control are *budgets* and *pro forma financial statements*. These express management's targets and are compared with actual corporate performance to determine *variances*, the difference between actual and target values.

By focusing on variances, managers can *manage by exception,* concentrating on those variables that are most in need of improvement and leaving alone those operations that are running smoothly.

DEFINITIONAL QUESTIONS

1. __________ plans lay out the firm's long-term purpose, scope, objectives, and strategies.

2. Most firms' operating plans have a ___-_______ horizon.

3. One of the key sections of the operating plan is the ___________ plan.

4. The most important element in financial planning is the _____ forecast.

5. If various asset items increase, ___________ and/or ______ ______ must also increase.

6. Typically, certain liabilities will rise ____________ with sales. These include accounts __________ and ______.

7. _______-________ ________ and ______ ______ are examples of liability and equity accounts that do not increase spontaneously with higher levels of sales.

8. ______ ____________, or projected, financial statements provide the foundation for financial planning.

9. As the dividend ______ ______ is increased, the amount of earnings available to finance sales growth is ____________.

10. Retained earnings depend not only on sales level and dividend payout ratio, but also on the __________ ___________.

11. The amount of assets required per dollar of sales is often called the ___________ _________ ratio.

12. A capital intensive industry will require large amounts of ____________ capital to finance increased growth.

13. The percentage of sales method assumes that the ______ of balance sheet items to ______ is ____________ at all levels of sales.

14. If the relationship is linear, but not proportional, ______ ___________ ____________ may be used to forecast financial statement items.

15. Considerable managerial ____________ is required to properly evaluate the output generated by computerized financial planning models.

16. Planning models are especially useful because they permit managers to see the effects of changing basic ___________ assumptions or specific ____________ policies.

CONCEPTUAL QUESTIONS

17. An increase in a firm's inventories will call for external financing unless the increase is matched by an equal or larger decrease in some other asset account.

    a. True   **b.** False

18. If the capital intensity ratio of a firm actually decreases as sales increase, use of the constant ratio method will typically *overstate* the amount of external funds required, other things held constant.

    a. True   **b.** False

19. If the dividend payout ratio is 100 percent, the financial ratios are held constant, and the firm is operating at full capacity, any increase in sales will require external financing.

    a. True   **b.** False

20. One of the first steps in the constant ratio method of forecasting is to identify those asset and liability accounts which increase spontaneously with retained earnings.

a. True b. False

21. Which of the following would reduce the external funds required if all other things are held constant?

a. An increase in the dividend payout ratio.
b. A decrease in the profit margin.
c. An increase in the capital intensity ratio.
d. An increase in the expected sales growth rate.
e. A decrease in the firm's tax rate.

PROBLEMS

The following data apply to the next two problems.

Union Inc. has the following balance sheet:

Current assets	$ 5,000	Accts. payable	$ 1,000
Net fixed assets	5,000	Notes payable	1,000
		Long-term debt	4,000
		Common equity	4,000
Total assets	$10,000	Total claims	$10,000

Business has been slow; therefore, fixed assets are vastly underutilized. Management believes they can double sales next year with the introduction of a new product. No new fixed assets will be required, and management forecasts that no earnings will be retained next year.

22. What is next year's external financing requirement according to the constant ratio method?

a. $0 b. $4,000 c. $9,000 d. $13,000 e. $19,000

23. Now assume that fixed assets are currently being utilized to capacity. What is the external financing requirement for this situation?

a. $0 b. $4,000 c. $9,000 d. $13,000 e. $19,000

24. The 1995 balance sheet for American Pulp and Paper is shown below (millions of dollars):

Cash	$ 3.0	Accounts payable	$ 2.0
Accounts receivable	3.0	Notes payable	1.5
Inventory	5.0	Long-term debt	3.0
Current assets	$11.0	Common equity	7.5
Fixed assets	3.0		
Total assets	$14.0	Total claims	$14.0

In 1995, sales were $60 million. Management believes that sales will increase in 1996 by 20 percent to a total of $72 million. The profit margin is expected to be 5 percent, and the dividend payout ratio is targeted at 40 percent. The firm has excess capacity and no increase in fixed assets will be required. What is the external financing requirement for 1993?

a. $0.36 million **b.** $0.24 million **c.** $0 million **d.** -$0.24 million **e.** -$0.36 million

ANSWERS

1. Strategic
2. 5-year
3. financial
4. sales
5. liabilities; net worth (common equity)
6. spontaneously; payable; accruals
7. Long-term debt; common stock
8. Pro forma
9. payout ratio; decreased
10. profit margin
11. capital intensity
12. external (additional)
13. ratio; sales; constant
14. simple linear regression
15. judgment
16. economic; financial

17. a. When an increase in an asset account is not offset by an equivalent decrease in an asset account, then financing is needed to reestablish equilibrium on the balance sheet.

18. a. A decreasing capital intensity ratio means that fewer assets are required, proportionately, as sales increase. Thus, the external funding requirement is overstated by the constant ratio method.

19. a. With no retained earnings, any growth in assets must be matched by a growth in spontaneous liabilities to avoid external financing. When operating at full capacity, all assets are spontaneous, but all liabilities cannot be spontaneous since a firm must have common equity. Thus, the growth in assets cannot be matched by a growth in spontaneous liabilities and external financing will be required.

20. b. The first step is to identify those accounts which increase spontaneously with sales.

21. e. All other statements would cause the external funding requirement to increase.

22. b. Look at next year's balance sheet:

Current assets	$10,000	Accounts payable	$ 2,000
Net fixed assets	5,000	Notes payable	1,000
		Long-term debt	4,000
		Common equity	4,000
	$15,000		$11,000

With no retained earnings next year, the common equity account remains at $4,000. Thus, the external financing requirement is $15,000 - $11,000 = $4,000.

23. c. In this situation, net fixed assets, like current assets, would double, and total assets would equal $20,000. Thus, the external financing requirement would be $20,000 - $11,000 = $9,000.

24. e. Since fixed assets are sufficient to absorb the increase in sales, this item is not included in the computation. Therefore, only $11 million of the $14 million in total assets will increase spontaneously with sales. None of the items on the right side of the balance sheet rises spontaneously with sales except accounts payable. Therefore, with a sales increase of $72 -$60 = $12 million, assets will increase by ($11/$60)($12) = $2.2 million, while spontaneous liabilities will increase by ($2/$60)($12) = $0.4 million. Finally, the firm will generate (0.05)($72)(0.6) = $2.16 million, and hence the need for external financing is

$$\$2.2 - \$0.4 - \$2.16 = -\$0.36 \text{ million.}$$

This means that the increased profits and spontaneously generated liabilities are sufficient to support the external assets required. Thus, no external funds will be required. In fact, there will be an internally generated surplus of funds of $360,000.

CHAPTER 20
SHORT-TERM FINANCIAL PLANNING AND BUDGETING

OVERVIEW

Although long-term financial planning is an essential part of good management, such planning does not include the detail necessary for businesses to operate efficiently in the short run. In this chapter, we discuss short-term planning and budgeting, which involves making sure that the firm has the short-term asset--primarily cash and inventories--necessary to conduct day-to-day operations. If cash is not available to pay employees, suppliers, and tax collectors, or if inventories are not on hand to make or sell products, the company will grind to a halt.

KEY CONCEPTS

It is useful to begin by reviewing some basic definitions and concepts.

Working capital, sometimes called *gross working capital*, is defined as current assets, while *net working capital* is current assets minus current liabilities.

The *current ratio*, which is current assets divided by current liabilities, is intended to measure a firm's liquidity. The *quick ratio*, which also attempts to measure liquidity, is current assets less inventories, divided by current liabilities.

The most comprehensive picture of a firm's liquidity is obtained by examining its *cash budget*, which forecasts a firm's cash inflows and outflows and thus focuses on what really counts, the firm's ability to generate the cash inflows required to meet its required cash outflows.

Working capital policy refers to the firm's basic policies regarding target levels for each category of current assets and how current assets will be financed.

Working capital management involves the administration of current assets and current liabilities.

A firm's current asset levels and financing requirements rise and fall with business cycles and seasonal trends. At the peak of such cycles, businesses carry their maximum amounts of current assets. Similar fluctuations in financing needs can occur over these cycles; typically, financing needs contract during recessions, and they expand during booms.

The *cash conversion cycle* focuses on the conversion of operating events to cash flows. It measures the length of time between when the company makes payments and when it receives cash inflows.

The following terms and definitions are used:

- *Inventory conversion period*, which is the average length of time required to convert materials into finished goods and then to sell these goods.

$$\text{Inventory conversion period} = \frac{\text{Inventory}}{\text{Sales per day}}.$$

- *Receivables collection period*, or *days sales outstanding,* which is the average length of time required to convert the firm's receivables into cash, that is, to collect cash following a sale.

$$\text{Receivables collection period} = \text{DSO} = \frac{\text{Receivables}}{\text{Sales}/360}.$$

- *Payables deferral period*, which is the average length of time between the purchase of raw materials and labor and the payment of cash for them.

$$\text{Payables deferral period} = \frac{\text{Payables}}{\text{Cost of goods sold}/360}.$$

- *Cash conversion cycle*, which nets out the three periods just defined, and which therefore equals the average length of time between the firm's actual cash expenditures on productive resources and its own cash receipts from the sale of its products. Thus, the cash conversion cycle equals the average length of time the firm has funds tied up in current assets.

Using these definitions, the cash conversion cycle is defined as follows:

$$\begin{matrix}\text{Inventory} & & \text{Receivables} & & \text{Payables} & & \text{Cash} \\ \text{conversion} & + & \text{collection} & - & \text{deferral} & = & \text{conversion}. \\ \text{period} & & \text{period} & & \text{period} & & \text{cycle}\end{matrix}$$

To illustrate, suppose it takes a firm an average of 72 days to convert raw materials and labor to widgets and to sell them, and it takes another 24 days to collect on receivables, while 30 days normally lapse between receipt of materials (and work done) and payments for materials and labor. In this case, the cash conversion cycle is 72 days + 24 days - 30 days = 66 days.

A firm should shorten its cash conversion cycle as much as possible *without increasing costs or depressing sales.* This would maximize profits because the longer the cash conversion cycle, the greater the need for external financing--and such financing has a cost.

> The zero working capital concept has the goal of improving both financial and production efficiency by reducing working capital holdings.

Proponents claim that it not only generates cash, but it also speeds up production, which helps businesses operate more efficiently.

Reducing working capital, and hence increasing turnover, has two major financial benefits.

- Every dollar freed up results in a one-time dollar contribution to cash flow.
- The quest for zero working capital permanently raises a company's earnings.

> Working capital policy involves two basic decisions: (1) What is the appropriate level for current assets, and (2) how should current assets be financed?

There are three alternative policies regarding the total amount of current assets carried. Each policy differs in that different amounts of current assets are carried to support a given level of sales.

- A *relaxed current asset investment (or "fat cat") policy* is one in which large amounts of cash, marketable securities, and inventories are carried and where sales are stimulated by the use of a liberal credit policy.
- A *restricted current asset investment (or "lean-and-mean") policy* is one in which holdings of cash, securities, inventories, and receivables are minimized.
- A *moderate current asset investment policy* is between the two extremes.
- Generally, the decision on current assets levels involves a risk/return trade-off. The relaxed policy minimizes risk, but it also has the lowest expected return. On the

other hand, the restricted policy offers the highest expected return coupled with the highest risk.

The second short-term financial decision is how to finance current assets.

- The *maturity matching, or "self-liquidating," approach* matches asset and liability maturities. Defined as a moderate current asset financing policy, this would use permanent financing for permanent assets (permanent current assets and fixed assets) and use short-term financing to cover seasonal and/or cyclical temporary assets (fluctuating current assets).
- The *aggressive approach* is used by a firm which finances all of its fixed assets with long-term capital but part of its permanent current assets with short-term, nonspontaneous credit.
- A *conservative approach* would be to use permanent capital to meet some of the cyclical demand and then to hold the temporary surpluses as marketable securities at the trough of the cycle. Here, the amount of permanent financing exceeds permanent assets.

There are advantages and disadvantages to the use of short-term financing.

A short-term loan can be obtained much faster than long-term credit.

Short-term debt is more flexible than long-term debt since it may be repaid if the firm's financing requirements decline. Long-term debt can be retired, but this will probably involve a prepayment penalty.

Short-term interest rates are normally lower than long-term rates. Therefore, financing with short-term credit usually results in lower interest costs.

Short-term debt is generally more risky than long-term debt for two reasons.

- Short-term interest rates fluctuate widely, while long-term rates tend to be more stable and predictable, and hence the interest rate on short-term debt could increase dramatically over a short period.
- Short-term debt comes due every few months. If a firm does not have the cash to repay debt when it comes due, and if it cannot refinance the loan, it may be forced into bankruptcy.

The cash budget shows the firm's projected cash inflows and outflows over some specified period. It provides much more detailed information concerning a firm's future cash flows than do the forecasted financial statements.

The *cash budget* is useful in determining when cash surpluses or shortages will occur. Plans can then be made to borrow to cover shortages or to invest surpluses.

The *target cash balance* is the desired cash balance that a firm plans to maintain in order to conduct business. It can rise and fall with seasonal patterns and long-term changes in the scale of the firm's operations.

Improved forecasts of cash inflows and outflows permit a firm to hold a smaller cash balance.

DEFINITIONAL QUESTIONS

1. Current assets are also referred to as __________ ____________.

2. ______ working capital is defined as __________ assets minus current ____________.

3. The ______ ____________ __________ is the average length of time the firm has funds tied up in current assets.

4. In the maturity matching approach to working capital financing, permanent assets should be financed with __________ capital, while __________ assets should be financed with short-term credit.

5. Some firms use short-term financing to finance permanent assets. This approach maximizes __________ __________ but also involves the most ______.

6. Short-term borrowing provides more ____________ for firms that are uncertain about their future borrowing needs.

7. Short-term borrowing will be less expensive than long-term borrowing if the yield curve is ___________ sloping.

8. Short-term interest rates fluctuate ______ than long-term rates.

9. A cash budget reflects the effects of future operations on the firm's ______ ______.

10. A good cash budgeting system improves __________ of cash inflows and outflows and permits firms to hold ________ cash balances.

11. __________ ____________ ________ refers to the firm's basic policies regarding target levels for each category of current assets and how current assets will be financed.

12. __________ ____________ ________ is the average length of time required to convert materials into finished goods and then to sell these goods.

13. __________ ____________ ________, or DSO, is the average length of time required to convert the firm's receivables into cash, that is, to collect cash following a sale.

14. __________ ____________ ________ is the average length of time between the purchase of raw materials and labor and the payment of cash for them.

15. A ___________ current asset investment policy is one in which large amounts of cash, marketable securities, and inventories are carried and where sales are stimulated by the use of a liberal credit policy.

16. A __________ current asset investment policy is one in which holdings of cash, securities, inventories, and receivables are minimized.

CONCEPTUAL QUESTIONS

17. The matching of asset and liability maturities is considered desirable because this strategy minimizes price risk.

    a. True **b.** False

18. Other things held constant, an increase in the payables deferral period will lead to a reduction in the need for nonspontaneous funding.

    a. True **b.** False

19. Generally, a firm should use short-term debt, rather than long-term financing, to minimize its interest expense.

    a. True **b.** False

PROBLEMS

20. Price Industries Inc. has an inventory conversion period of 60 days, a receivables collection period of 35 days, and a payments cycle of 28 days. What is the length of the firm's cash conversion cycle?

a. 67 days **b.** 82 days **c.** 95 days **d.** 104 days **e.** 117 days

21. Refer to Problem 20. If Price's sales are $972,000 annually, what is the firm's investment in accounts receivable?

a. $72,450 **b.** $79,600 **c.** $85,300 **d.** $94,500 **e.** $100,000

22. A firm sells $1 million in merchandise a month on average. It keeps inventory equal to its monthly sales on hand at all times. If the firm analyzes its accounts using a 360-day year, what is the firm's inventory conversion period?

a. 360 days **b.** 180 days **c.** 60 days **d.** 30 days **e.** 15 days

23. A firm purchases raw materials on June 1st. It converts the raw materials into inventory by the last day of the month, June 30th. However, it pays for the materials on June 20th. On July 10th, it sells the finished goods for inventory. Then the firm collects cash from the sale one month later on August 10th. If this sequence accurately represents the firm's average working capital cycle, what is the firm's cash conversion cycle?

a. 45 days **b.** 51 days **c.** 61 days **d.** 107 days **e.** 30 days

The following data apply to the next three problems.

The Cairn Corporation is trying to determine the effect of its inventory turnover ratio and days sales outstanding (DSO) on its cash flow cycle. Cairn's sales (which were all on credit) were $750,000, and it earned a net profit of 12 percent, or $90,000. It turned over its inventory 9 times during the year, and its DSO was 45 days. The firm had fixed assets totaling $60,000. Cairn's payables deferral period is 30 days.

24. What is Cairn's cash conversion cycle?

a. 40 days **b.** 42 days **c.** 55 days **d.** 37 days **e.** 45 days

25. Assume that Cairn holds negligible amounts of cash and marketable securities. What are its total assets turnover and ROA?

a. 3.16; 32.45%
b. 3.55; 37.96%
c. 3.55; 25.87%
d. 3.16; 30.00%
e. 3.16; 37.96%

26. Suppose Cairn's managers believe that the inventory turnover can be raised to 12 times. Assuming that all other facts remain the same, what would Cairn's cash conversion cycle, total assets turnover, and ROA have been if the inventory turnover had been 12?

a. 45; 3.00; 45.00%
b. 40; 3.47; 41.62%
c. 45; 3.47; 41.62%
d. 40; 3.00; 45.00%
e. 45; 3.47; 45.00%

27. Matthew and Sarah Weisner recently leased space in the Plaza Shopping Center and opened a new business, Weisner's Ice Cream Shop. Business has been good but the Weisners frequently run out of cash. This has necessitated late payment on certain ice cream orders, which in turn is beginning to cause a problem with suppliers. The Weisners plan to borrow from a bank to have cash ready as needed, but first they need to forecast how much cash will be needed. Therefore, they have decided to prepare a cash budget for June, July, and August to determine their cash needs. Ice cream sales are made on a cash basis only. The Weisners must pay for their ice cream orders 1 month after the purchase. Rent is $1,000 per month, and they pay themselves a combined salary of $2,400 per month. In addition, they must make a tax payment of $6,000 in June. The current cash on hand (June 1) is $200, but the Weisners have decided to maintain a target cash balance of $3,000. Estimated ice cream sales and purchases for June, July, and August are given below. May purchases amounted to $70,000.

	Sales	Purchases
June	$80,000	$ 20,000
July	20,000	20,000
August	30,000	20,000

What amount of money will the Weisners need to borrow or have in surplus in each of the months in the budget period (June, July, and August)?

a. $2,200; $5,600; ($1,000)*
b. $2,700; $5,600; ($1,000)*
c. $2,200; $9,400; ($1,000)*
d. ($1,000)*; $4,700; $500
e. $2,200; $5,600; $2,000

*The firm projects a cash surplus in this month.

ANSWERS

1. working capital
2. Net; current; liabilities
3. cash conversion cycle
4. permanent (long-term); temporary
5. expected returns; risk
6. flexibility
7. upward
8. more
9. cash flows
10. forecasts; smaller
11. Working capital policy
12. Inventory conversion period
13. Receivables collection period
14. Payables deferral period
15. relaxed
16. restricted

17. b. The matching of maturities minimizes default risk, or the risk that the firm will be unable to pay off its maturing obligations, and reinvestment rate risk, or the risk that the firm will have to roll over the debt at a higher rate.

18. a. This statement is correct.

19. a. Generally, the yield curve slopes upward, making the statement true. Even when the curve slopes downward, this suggests that rates are likely to fall, in which case interest expenses will fall if the firm uses short-term debt, but rates will be locked in (at a high level) if it uses long-term debt. Of course, if interest rates rise, the firm which financed with short-term debt may end up paying far more interest than a firm which obtained long-term funds when rates were lower.

20. a. Cash conversion cycle = Inventory conversion period + Receivables collection period − Payables deferral period = 60 days + 35 days − 28 days = 67 days.

21. d.

$$\text{DSO} = \frac{\text{Receivables}}{\text{Sales}/360}$$

$$35 = \frac{\text{Receivables}}{\$972{,}000/360}$$

$$\text{Receivables} = \$94{,}500.$$

22. d. Inventory conversion period = Inventory/(Sales/360).

Annual sales = \$1 million × 12 = \$12 million. Inventory = \$1 million.

Inventory conversion period = \$1,000,000/(\$12,000,000/360) = 30 days.

23. b. Payables deferral period = 20 days (June 1 to June 20).

Inventory conversion period = 40 days (June 1 to July 10).

Receivables collection period = 31 days (July 10 to August 10).

Cash conversion cycle = 40 + 31 - 20 = 51 days.

24. c. Sales = \$750,000; Sales/Inventory = 9; DSO = 45 days; Payables deferral period = 30 days.

Inventory conversion period = Inventory/(Sales/360) = Inventory/Sales × 360.

We know that Sales/Inventory = 9, so Inventory/Sales = 1/9.

Inventory conversion period = 1/9 × 360 = 40 days.

Cash conversion cycle = Inventory conversion period + Receivables collection period − Payables deferral period = 40 days + 45 days − 30 days = 55 days.

25. e. We need to calculate receivables and inventory to determine total assets.

$$\text{DSO} = \frac{\text{Receivables}}{\text{Sales}/360}$$

$$45 = \frac{\text{Receivables}}{\$750{,}000/360}$$

$$\text{Receivables} = \$93{,}750.$$

$$9 = \frac{\text{Sales}}{\text{Inventory}}$$

$$9 = \frac{\$750{,}000}{\text{Inventory}}$$

$$9(\text{Inventory}) = \$750{,}000$$

$$\text{Inventory} = \$83{,}333.$$

Total assets = Cash + Marketable securities + Receivables + Inventories + Fixed assets = \$0 + \$0 + \$93,750 + \$83,333 + \$60,000 = \$237,083.

Now calculate Total assets turnover = Sales/Total assets and ROA = Net income/Total assets:

Sales/Total assets = \$750,000/\$237,083 = 3.16.

ROA = Net income/Total assets = $90,000/$237,083 = 37.96%.

26. c. Sales/Inventory = 12; $750,000/Inventory = 12; Inventory = $62,500.

$$\text{Inventory conversion period} = \frac{\text{Inventory}}{\text{Sales}/360} = \frac{\$62{,}500}{\$750{,}000/360} = 30 \text{ days.}$$

Cash conversion cycle = 30 + 45 − 30 = 45 days.

Total assets = Cash + MS + Receivables + Inventories + Fixed assets
= $0 + $0 + $93,750 + $62,500 + $60,000
= $216,250.

Sales/Total assets = $750,000/$216,250 = 3.47.

ROA = Net income/Total assets = $90,000/$216,250 = 41.62%.

27. a.

Worksheet	June	July	August
Sales	$80,000	$20,000	$30,000
Purchases	20,000	20,000	20,000
Payments for purchases	70,000	20,000	20,000
Cash budget			
Receipts from sales	$80,000	$20,000	$30,000
Payments:			
Purchases	$70,000	$20,000	$20,000
Salaries	2,400	2,400	2,400
Rent	1,000	1,000	1,000
Taxes	6,000		
Total payments	$79,400	$23,400	$23,400
Net cash gain (loss)	$ 600	($ 3,400)	$ 6,600
Cash at start of month	200	800	(2,600)
Cumulative cash	$ 800	($ 2,600)	$ 4,000
Less: Target cash balance	3,000	3,000	3,000
Surplus cash or total loans to maintain $3,000 target cash balance	($ 2,200)	($ 5,600)	$ 1,000

CHAPTER 21
CASH MANAGEMENT AND SHORT-TERM FINANCING

OVERVIEW

Approximately 1.5 percent of the average industrial firm's assets are held as cash, which is defined as demand deposits plus currency. In addition, sizable holdings of near-cash short-term marketable securities such as Treasury bills are often reported on corporations' financial statements. However, cash and marketable securities balances vary widely across industries, between firms within a given industry, and within a given firm over time. Thus, firms often use short-term financing as a cash management tool when needed to supplement cash from operations. In this chapter, we analyze the factors that determine firms' cash and marketable securities balances, we describe the most commonly used types of marketable securities, and we discuss the use and sources of short-term financing.

OUTLINE

Cash is a nonearning asset. Excessive cash balances reduce the rate of return on equity and hence the value of a firm's stock. Thus, the goal of cash management is to minimize the amount of cash the firm must hold in order to conduct its normal business activities, yet, at the same time, maintain sufficient cash balances to take trade discounts, to maintain its credit rating, and to meet unexpected cash needs.

Firms hold cash for two primary reasons:

- *Transactions balances* are held to provide the cash needed to conduct normal business operations.
- *Compensating balances* are often required by banks for providing loans and services.

Two secondary reasons are also cited:

- *Precautionary balances* are held in reserve for random fluctuations in cash inflows and outflows.
- *Speculative balances* are held to enable the firm to take advantage of bargain purchases.

Most firms do not segregate funds for each of these motives, but they do consider them in setting their overall cash positions.

An ample cash balance should be maintained to take advantage of trade discounts and favorable business opportunities, to help the firm maintain its credit rating, and to meet emergency needs.

Cash management has changed significantly over the last two decades as a result of relatively high interest rates during most of the 1980s and emergence of new technologies.

New technology, particularly computerized electronic funds transfer mechanisms, has improved cash management efficiency.

Cash management techniques fall generally into five categories: (1) synchronizing cash flow, (2) using float, (3) accelerating collections, (4) getting available funds to where they are needed, and (5) controlling disbursements.

Synchronizing cash inflows and outflows permits a reduction in the firm's cash balances, decreases its bank loans, lowers its interest expense, and boosts profits.

A firm's *float* is defined as the difference between the balance shown in a firm's checkbook and the balance on the bank's records. A firm's *net float* is a function of its ability to speed up collections on checks received (*collections float*) and to slow down collections on checks written (*disbursement float*).

Several techniques are now used to speed collections and to get funds where they are needed.

A *lockbox plan* is a procedure which speeds up collections and reduces collections float through the use of post office boxes in payers' local areas.

- Customers mail checks to a post office box in a specified city. A local bank then collects the checks, deposits them, starts the clearing process, and notifies the selling firm that payment has been received.
- Processing time is further reduced because it takes less time for banks to collect local checks.

A *pre-authorized debit* allows funds to be automatically transferred from a customer's account to the firm's account on specified dates.

- These transactions are known as "paperless" transactions.
- With a pre-authorized debit, the payer loses his disbursement float.

Concentration banking mobilizes funds from decentralized receiving locations into one or more central cash pools. The cash manager then uses the pools for short-term investing or reallocation among the firm's other banks. Concentration banking allows firms to take maximum advantage of economies of scale in cash management and investment. Two commonly used transfer tools are *depository transfer checks* and *electronic depository transfers*. In addition to the automated clearinghouses, the Federal Reserve wire system can be used for cash concentration or other cash transfers.

Accelerating collections represents one side of cash management; the other side is controlling funds outflow, or disbursement control.

No single action controls cash outflows more effectively than *centralization of payables*, which permits the financial manager to evaluate the payments coming due for the entire firm and to schedule cash transfers to meet these needs on a company-wide basis.

Zero-balance accounts (ZBAs) are special disbursement accounts having a zero-dollar balance on which disbursement checks are written. Typically, firms establish several zero-balance accounts in their concentration bank and then fund ZBAs from a master account. As checks are presented to a ZBA for payment, funds are automatically transferred from the master account.

Controlled disbursement accounts are similar to ZBAs, except that controlled disbursement accounts can be set up at any bank. Typically, these accounts are established at remote locations. These accounts are not funded until the day's checks have been presented against the account.

Firms often maintain bank balances in excess of transactions needs as a means of compensating the bank for various services. These balances are called compensating balances. The banks in turn earn income on these funds by lending them to their borrowing customers.

Compensating balances also are required by some bank loan agreements. Compensating balances may be established as an absolute minimum or as a minimum average balance over some time period, generally a month.

Because of the growing number of services offered by banks to their customers, many firms want to choose only certain services from among the set offered. Thus, many banks now charge fees for each service rendered instead of requiring an overall compensating balance.

From a company's point of view, fees for services are generally favored over compensating balances for several reasons:

- Fees are a tax-deductible expense, while interest forgone on compensating balances is not.
- Fees are generally fixed over some period, so they can be easily budgeted and monitored. The costs associated with compensating balances are much more uncertain.
- It's more practical for companies to "shop" for cash management services when fees are charged, because it is easier to compare the fees of competing banks than to compare compensating balance requirements.

From a bank's point of view, compensating balances are often preferred for several reasons:

- Compensating balances increase the bank's total deposits.
- Compensating balances create additional security for the bank if the company defaults on a bank loan.
- Compensating balances are available to banks to relend to another customer.

In developing cash management systems, a manager must make sure the system's benefit outweighs the cost.

Marketable securities typically provide lower yields than a firm's operating assets, yet they are often held in sizable amounts.

Marketable securities are held for two basic reasons: as a *substitute for cash balances,* and as a *temporary investment.* The securities are sold when cash is needed for transactions.

- Seasonal or cyclical operations may generate surplus cash at some times and deficits at other times. Marketable securities may be built up during one phase of the cycle and then liquidated to cover forecasted deficits.
- Marketable securities may be used to accumulate funds for a known financial requirement such as a bond redemption or a major tax payment.

A wide variety of marketable securities, differing in terms of risk and expected rate of return, are available. The risks inherent in securities are defined below:

- *Default risk* is the risk that a borrower will not be able to make promised interest payments or to repay principal amounts on schedule.

- The probability that some event, such as a recapitalization or leveraged buyout, will occur which suddenly increases a firm's credit risk, and hence lowers the value of its outstanding bonds, is called *event risk.*
- *Price risk* involves the changes in security prices that occur with changes in interest rates.
- *Inflation,* or *purchasing power, risk* is the risk that inflation will reduce the purchasing power of a given sum of money.
- *Liquidity,* or *marketability, risk* refers to whether an asset can be quickly sold at or near its current market value.
- Most firms emphasize safety in their marketable securities portfolios even though such an investment policy requires a sacrifice in terms of the *rates of return* earned on the portfolios.

Many types of securities are available for investment of surplus cash. Among those most suitable for holding as *near-cash reserves* are U.S. Treasury bills, commercial paper, negotiable certificates of deposit, money market mutual funds, floating rate preferred stock, and Eurodollar time deposits.

One of the key elements in a firm's cash budget is the target cash balance. The target cash balance is normally set as the larger of the firm's transactions balances plus precautionary balances or its required compensating balances. The Baumol model provides some insights into the process, while Monte Carlo simulation is often used to set target cash balances in practice.

The Baumol model applies inventory methodology (EOQ model) to cash balances.

- The optimal cash holdings to be transferred from marketable securities or to be borrowed, C*, can be found by the equation:

  $$C* = \sqrt{\frac{2(F)(T)}{k}}.$$

  Here, F = fixed costs of borrowing or of converting marketable securities into cash; T = total amount of net new cash needed for transactions over the entire period, usually a year; and k = the opportunity cost of holding cash.
- Assuming no precautionary balances, the optimal average cash balance is C*/2.
- The Baumol model is simplistic in many respects, but it can provide a useful starting point for establishing a target cash balance.
- To illustrate, suppose F = \$150, T = \$5,200,000, and k = 15%. Then,

$$C^* = \sqrt{\frac{2(\$150)(\$5,200,000)}{0.15}} = \$101,980.$$

- Therefore, the firm should sell securities (or borrow) in the amount of \$101,980 when its cash balance approaches zero. If we divide T by C*, we have the number of transactions per year; \$5,200,000/\$101,980 ≈ 51, or about once a week. The firm's average cash balance would be \$101,980/2 ≈ \$51,000.
- Note that safety stocks could be added to the Baumol model, just as with the EOQ model. Also note that there are economies of scale in cash holdings according to the Baumol model; a doubling of cash needs would increase the average cash balance by only 41 percent.

Monte Carlo simulation is often used to set the target cash balance. The simulation is applied to the cash budget, and cash balance targets can be set to provide some statistical measure of safety--perhaps the cash balance would be set so that there is only a 10 percent probability of running out of cash.

Short-term financing allows a firm to raise funds externally to meet its cash budget shortfalls. There are four primary sources of short-term financing: accruals, accounts payable, bank loans, and commercial paper.

Accrued wages and taxes increase and decrease spontaneously as a firm's operations expand and contract. This type of debt is "free" in the sense that no interest is paid on funds raised through accruals. However, a firm cannot ordinarily control its accruals.

Accounts payable, or trade credit, is the largest single category of short-term debt. Trade credit is a spontaneous source of funds in that it arises from ordinary business transactions. Most firms make purchases on credit, recording the debt as an account payable.

An increase in sales will be accompanied by an increase in inventory purchases, which will automatically generate additional financing.

The cost of trade credit is made up of discounts lost by not paying invoices within the discount period.

- For example, if credit terms are 2/10, net 30, the cost of 20 additional days' credit is 2 percent of the dollar value of the purchases made.
- The following equation may be used to calculate the approximate percentage cost of not taking discounts:

$$\text{Approximate percentage cost} = \frac{\text{Discount \%}}{100 - \text{Discount \%}} \times \frac{360}{\text{Days credit is outstanding} - \text{Discount period}}.$$

- For example, the approximate annual cost of not taking the discount when the credit terms are 2/10, net 30, is

$$\text{Approximate percentage cost} = \frac{2}{98} \times \frac{360}{30 - 10} = 0.0204(18) = 0.367 = 36.7\%.$$

- Note that the first term on the right-hand side of the equation is the periodic cost, and the second term is the number of periods per year. In effective annual interest terms, the rate is even higher. Thus, the *effective annual rate* is $(1.0204)^{18} - 1.0 = 1.439 - 1.0 = 43.9\%$.

Trade credit can be divided into two components: *Free trade credit* is that credit received during the discount period. *Costly trade credit* is obtained by foregoing discounts. This costly component should be used only when it is less expensive than funds obtained from other sources.

- Financial managers should always use the free component, but they should use the costly component only after analyzing the cost of this capital to make sure that it is less than the cost of funds which could be obtained from other sources.
- Competitive conditions may permit firms to do better than the stated credit terms by taking discounts beyond the discount period or by simply paying late. Such practices, called *stretching accounts payable*, reduce the cost of trade credit, but they also result in poor relationships with suppliers.

> Bank loans appear on a firm's balance sheet as notes payable and represent another important source of short-term financing. Bank loans are not generated spontaneously but must be negotiated and renewed on a regular basis.

About two-thirds of all bank loans mature in a year or less, although banks do make longer-term loans.

When a firm obtains a bank loan, a *promissory note* specifying the following items is signed: the amount borrowed, the percentage interest rate, the repayment schedule, any collateral offered as security, and other terms of the loan.

Banks normally require regular borrowers to maintain *compensating balances* equal to 10 to 20 percent of the face value of loans. Such required balances generally increase the effective interest rate on the loan.

A *line of credit* is an informal understanding between the bank and the borrower concerning the maximum loan balance the bank will allow.

A *revolving credit agreement* is a formal line of credit often used by large firms. Normally, the borrower will pay the bank a commitment fee to compensate the bank for guaranteeing that the funds will be available. This fee is paid on the unused balance of the commitment in addition to the regular interest charge on funds actually borrowed. Unlike a line of credit, the bank has a legal obligation to honor a revolving credit agreement.

Choosing a bank involves an analysis of the following variables:

Willingness to assume risks. Some banks are quite conservative, while others are more willing to make risky loans.

Advice and counsel. A bank's ability to provide counsel is particularly important to firms in their formative years.

Loyalty to customers. This variable deals with a bank's willingness to support customers during difficult economic times.

Specialization. A bank may specialize in making loans to a particular type of business. Firms should seek out a bank which is familiar with their particular type of business.

Maximum loan size. This is an important consideration for large companies when establishing a borrowing relationship because most banks cannot lend to a single customer more than 15 percent of the total amount of the bank's capital.

Merchant banking. Originally the term applied to banks which not only loaned depositors' money but also provided its customers with equity capital and financial advice. In recent years, commercial banks have been attempting to get back into merchant banking, in part because of their foreign competitors.

Other services. The availability of services such as lockbox systems and electronic funds transfers should also be taken into account when selecting a bank.

Commercial paper, another source of short-term credit, is an unsecured promissory note. It is generally sold to other business firms, to insurance companies, to banks, and to money market mutual funds. Only large, financially strong firms are able to tap the commercial paper market.

Maturities of commercial paper range from a few days to nine months, with an average of about five months.

Interest rates on prime commercial paper generally range from 1½ to 3 percentage points below the stated prime rate, and about 1/8 to 1/2 of a percentage point above the T-bill rate. However, rates fluctuate daily with supply and demand conditions in the marketplace, and since no compensating balance is required, the effective cost is even lower in comparison to bank loans.

A disadvantage of the commercial paper market vis-a-vis bank loans is that the impersonal nature of the market makes it difficult for firms to use commercial paper at times when they are in temporary financial distress.

For a strong firm, borrowing on an unsecured basis is generally cheaper and simpler than on a secured loan basis because of the administrative costs associated with the use of security. However, lenders will refuse credit without some form of collateral if a borrower's credit standing is questionable.

Most secured short-term business borrowing involves the use of accounts receivable and inventories as collateral.

The legal procedures for establishing loan security have been standardized and simplified in the *Uniform Commercial Code.*

Accounts receivable financing involves either the pledging of receivables or the selling (factoring) of receivables.

The *pledging of accounts receivable* is characterized by the fact that the lender not only has a claim against the receivables but also has recourse to the borrower. If the person or firm that bought the goods does not pay, the selling firm must take the loss. Thus, the risk of default on the pledged accounts receivable remains with the borrower.

Factoring, or *selling accounts receivable,* involves the purchase of accounts receivable by the lender, generally without recourse to the borrower, which means that if the purchaser of the goods does not pay for them, the lender rather than the seller of the goods takes the loss.

A substantial amount of credit is secured by business inventories.

The *inventory blanket lien* gives the lending institution a lien against all of the borrower's inventories. However, the borrower is free to sell inventories, which reduces the value of the collateral.

A *trust receipt* is an instrument acknowledging that the goods are held in trust for the lender. The borrower may keep the goods in his possession, but he must remit the proceeds of the sale of the specific goods to the lender at the end of each day.

Like trust receipts, *warehouse receipt financing* uses inventory as security.

DEFINITIONAL QUESTIONS

1. The goal of cash management is to ____________ the amount of ______ the firm must hold in order to conduct its normal business activities.

2. Precautionary balances are maintained in order to allow for random, unforeseen fluctuations in cash ___________ and ___________.

3. The _________ _________, which is similar to the EOQ inventory model, is used to establish the target cash balance.

4. ___________ balances are maintained to pay banks for services they perform.

5. Efficient cash management is often concerned with speeding up the ___________ of checks received and slowing down the __________ of checks issued.

6. One method for speeding the collection process is the use of a ____________ system.

7. The most effective method of controlling cash outflows is ______________ ____ ______________.

8. The difference between a firm's balance on its own books and its balance as carried on the bank's books is known as ___________.

9. In a cash-gathering system, local depository banks channel funds to a regional ______________ bank.

10. Three mechanisms by which firms transfer funds between accounts at different banks are ___________ ___________ ______, ___________ checks, and _________ transfers.

11. As a general rule, a firm should invest in cash management operations so long as the marginal ____________ on the cash saved exceeds the marginal ______ of freeing this cash.

12. Business firms subject to __________ patterns of cash flows may invest surplus funds in short-term securities and then liquidate them when cash ___________ occur.

13. ___________ risk refers to an issuer's inability to make interest payments or to repay the ____________ at maturity.

14. The prices of ______ - ______ bonds are much more sensitive to changes in interest rates than are the prices of ________ - ______ bonds.

15. ___________ wages and taxes are a common source of short-term credit. However, most firms have little control over the ______ of these accounts.

16. Accounts payable, or ___________ _________, is the largest single source of short-term credit for most businesses.

17. Trade credit is a(n) ______________ source of funds in the sense that it automatically increases when sales increase.

18. Trade credit can be divided into two components: __________ trade credit and ___________ trade credit.

19. Free trade credit is that credit received during the ___________ period.

20. ___________ trade credit should only be used when the cost of the trade credit is less than the cost of alternative sources.

21. The instrument signed when bank credit is obtained is called a(n) _____________ ______. Among the items it specifies are the amount borrowed and the percentage interest rate.

22. Many banks require borrowers to keep ______________ _____________ on deposit with the bank equal to 10 or 20 percent of the face value of the loan.

23. Maturities on commercial paper generally range from ______ to ______ months, with interest rates set about 1 ½ to 3 percentage points __________ the __________ rate.

24. A(n) ___________ loan is one where collateral such as __________ or _____________ have been pledged in support of the loan.

25. A(n) __________ ____ ___________ is an informal understanding between a bank and a borrower as to the maximum loan that will be permitted.

26. The fee paid to a bank to secure a revolving credit agreement is known as a(n) _______________ fee, and it is paid on the unused balance in addition to the regular interest charge on funds actually borrowed.

27. Commercial paper can only be issued by ________, ______________ ________ firms.

28. ________ occurs when accounts receivable are purchased by the lender, generally without recourse to the borrower, which means that if the purchaser of the goods does not pay for them, the lender rather than the seller of the goods takes the loss.

29. A(n) ____________ ___________ lien gives the lender a lien against all inventories of the borrower.

Conceptual Questions

30. Money market mutual funds are suitable vehicles for investment of surplus cash, especially for small firms.

a. True **b.** False

31. The term *price risk* refers to the probability that a firm will be unable to continue making interest payments on its debt.

a. True **b.** False

32. Accruals are "free" in the sense that no interest must be paid on these funds.

a. True **b.** False

33. The effect of compensating balances is to decrease the effective interest rate of a loan.

a. True **b.** False

34. Which of the following actions would not be consistent with good cash management?

a. Increasing the synchronization of cash flows.
b. Using ZBA accounts in disbursing funds.
c. Using lockboxes in funds collection.
d. Maintaining an average cash balance equal to that required as a compensating balance or that which minimizes total cost.

e. Minimizing the use of float.

35. Which of the following investments is not likely to be a proper investment for temporarily idle cash?

  a. Commercial paper.
  b. Treasury bills.
  c. Recently issued long-term AAA corporate bonds.
  d. Treasury bonds due within one year.
  e. AAA corporate bonds due within one year.

36. Which of the following statements concerning commercial paper is *correct*?

  a. Commercial paper is secured debt of large, financially strong firms.
  b. Commercial paper is sold primarily to individual investors.
  c. Maturities of commercial paper generally exceed nine months.
  d. Commercial paper interest rates are typically 1.25 to 1.50 percentage points above the stated prime rate.
  e. None of the above statements is correct.

37. Which of the following statements is most *correct*?

  a. Due to the existence of positive maturity risk premiums, at most times short-term debt carries lower interest rates than long-term debt. Therefore, if a company finances primarily with short-term as opposed to long-term debt, its expected TIE ratio, hence, its overall riskiness, will be lower than if it finances with long-term debt. Therefore, the more conservative the firm, the greater its reliance on short-term debt.
  b. If a firm buys on terms of 2/10, net 30, and pays on the 30th day, then its accounts payable may be thought of as consisting of some "free" and some "costly" trade credit. Since the percentage cost of the costly trade credit is lowered if the payment period is reduced, the firm should try to pay earlier than on Day 30, say, on Day 25.
  c. Suppose a firm buys on terms of 2/10, net 30, but it normally pays on Day 60. Disregarding any "image" effects, it should, if it can borrow from the bank at an effective rate of 14 percent, take out a bank loan and start taking discounts.
  d. Each of the above statements is false.
  e. Each of the above statements is true.

PROBLEMS

38. The Mill Company has a daily average collection of checks of $250,000. It takes the company 4 days to convert the checks to cash. Assume a lockbox system could be employed which would reduce the cash conversion period to 3 days. The lockbox system would have a net cost of $25,000 per year, but any additional funds made available could be invested to net 8 percent per year. Should Mill adopt the lockbox system?

    a. Yes; the system would free $250,000 in funds.
    b. Yes; the benefits of the lockbox system exceed the costs.
    c. No; the benefit is only $10,000.
    d. No; the firm would lose $5,000 per year if the system were used.
    e. The benefits and costs are equal; hence, the firm is indifferent toward the system.

39. The Ryder Company has been practicing cash management for some time by using the Baumol model to determine cash balances. Recently, when the interest rate on marketable securities was 10 percent, the model called for an average cash balance of $1,000. A rapid increase in interest rates has driven this rate up to 15 percent. The firm incurs a cost of $20 per transaction. Ryder does not carry any precautionary balances. What is the appropriate average cash balance now?

    a. $596.97 b. $604.73 c. $816.50 d. $1,632.99 e. $1,333.33

The following data apply to the next three problems.

Stanton Industries projects that cash outlays of $1.5 million will occur uniformly throughout the year. Stanton plans to meet its cash requirements by periodically selling marketable securities from its portfolio. The firm's marketable securities are invested to earn 9 percent, and the cost per transaction of converting securities to cash is $18.

40. Using the Baumol model, what is the optimal transaction size for transfers from marketable securities to cash?

    a. $24,495 b. $33,271 c. $20,876 d. $23,154 e. $27,989

41. What will be Stanton's average cash balance?

    a. $13,994.50 b. $16,635.50 c. $11,577.00 d. $10,438.00 e. $12,247.50

42. How many transfers per year will be required?

a. 45.08 **b.** 61.24 **c.** 53.59 **d.** 71.85 **e.** 64.78

The following data apply to the next three problems.

A firm buys on terms of 2/10, net 30, but generally does not pay until 40 days after the invoice date. Its purchases total $1,080,000 per year.

43. How much "non-free" trade credit does the firm use on average each year?

a. $120,000 **b.** $90,000 **c.** $60,000 **d.** $30,000 **e.** $20,000

44. What is the *approximate* cost of the "non-free" trade credit?

a. 16.2% **b.** 19.4% **c.** 21.9% **d.** 24.5% **e.** 27.4%

45. What is the *effective* cost rate of the costly credit?

a. 16.2% **b.** 19.4% **c.** 21.9% **d.** 24.5% **e.** 27.4%

The following data apply to the next two problems.

Douglas Industries needs an additional $500,000, which it plans to obtain through a factoring arrangement. The factor would purchase Douglas's accounts receivable and advance the invoice amount, minus a 4 percent commission, on the invoices purchased each month. Douglas sells on terms of net 30 days. In addition, the factor charges a 14 percent annual interest rate on the total invoice amount, to be deducted in advance.

46. What amount of accounts receivable must be factored to net $500,000?

a. $527,241 **b.** $515,464 **c.** $530,441 **d.** $525,367 **e.** $518,989

47. If Douglas can reduce credit expenses by $10,000 per month and avoid bad debt losses of 3.5 percent on the factored amount, what is the total annual dollar cost of the savings that results from the use of the factoring arrangement?

a. $12,353 **b.** $11,076 **c.** $14,544 **d.** $13,767 **e.** $11,841

ANSWERS

1. minimize; cash
2. inflows; outflows
3. Baumol model
4. Compensating
5. collection; payment (disbursement)
6. lockbox
7. centralization of payables
8. float
9. concentration
10. depository transfer checks; electronic; wire
11. return (benefit); cost
12. seasonal; shortages
13. Default; principal
14. long-term; short-term
15. Accrued; size (amount)
16. trade credit
17. spontaneous
18. free; costly
19. discount
20. Costly
21. promissory note
22. compensating balances
23. one; nine; below; prime
24. secured; receivables; inventories
25. line of credit
26. commitment
27. large; financially strong
28. Factoring
29. inventory blanket

30. a. They offer safety and liquidity, the two most important factors in choosing marketable securities.

31. b. Price risk stems from the loss of a security's value if interest rates rise. Default risk refers to the probability of missing interest payments.

32. a. Neither workers nor the IRS require interest payments on wages and taxes that are not paid as soon as they are earned.

33. b. Compensating balances increase the effective rate because the firm is required to maintain excess non-interest-bearing balances.

34. e. Management should try to maximize float.

35. c. Long-term bonds have too much price risk for the firm's liquid asset portfolio.

36. e. Commercial paper is the unsecured debt of strong firms. It generally has a maturity from one to nine months and is sold primarily to other corporations and financial institutions. Rates on commercial paper are typically below the prime rate.

37. c. Statement a is false; short-term debt fluctuates more than long-term debt; thus, the greater the firm's reliance on short-term debt, the riskier the firm. Statement b is false; it makes no difference in the cost if the firm pays on Day 25 versus Day 30 in this

instance. Statement c is true; if the firm can "stretch" its payables the approximate cost is 14.69% (the effective cost is 15.66%). Thus, the firm should obtain the 14% bank loan to take discounts as this is the lowest cost to the firm. Obviously, statements d and e are false.

38. d. Currently, Mill has 4($250,000) = $1,000,000 in unavailable collections. If lockboxes were used, this could be reduced to $750,000. Thus, $250,000 would be available to invest at 8 percent, resulting in an annual return of 0.08($250,000) = $20,000. If the system costs $25,000, Mill would lose $5,000 per year by adopting the system.

39. c. The model is

$$C* = \sqrt{\frac{2(F)(T)}{k}}.$$

Initially, the average cash balance, C*/2, is $1,000; thus, C* = $2,000. Therefore,

$$\begin{aligned} \$2{,}000 &= \sqrt{\frac{2(\$20)(T)}{0.10}} \\ \$4{,}000{,}000 &= \frac{2(\$20)(T)}{0.10} \\ \$4{,}000{,}000 &= \$400T \\ \$10{,}000 &= T. \end{aligned}$$

Therefore, the new average cash balance is

$$\begin{aligned} C^* &= \sqrt{\frac{2(\$20)(\$10{,}000)}{0.15}} \\ C^* &= \$1{,}632.99 \\ C^*/2 &= \$816.50. \end{aligned}$$

40. a. $C* = \sqrt{\frac{2(F)(T)}{k}}$ = Optimal transaction size.

F = $18; T = $1,500,000; k = 9%.

$$C* = \sqrt{\frac{2(\$18)(\$1{,}500{,}000)}{0.09}} = \$24{,}494.90 \approx \$24{,}495.$$

41. e. Average cash balance = $24,495/2 = $12,247.50.

42. b. Transfers per year = \$1,500,000/\$24,495 = 61.24.

43. b. \$1,080,000/360 = \$3,000 in purchases per day. Typically, there will be \$3,000(40) = \$120,000 of accounts payable on the books at any given time. Of this, \$3,000(10) = \$30,000 is "free" credit, while \$3,000(30) = \$90,000 is "non-free" credit.

44. d.

$$\text{Approximate cost} = \frac{\text{Discount \%}}{100 - \text{Discount \%}} \times \frac{360}{\text{Days credit is outstanding} - \text{Discount period}}$$

$$= \frac{2}{100 - 2} \times \frac{360}{40 - 10} = \frac{2}{98} \times \frac{360}{30} = 24.5\%.$$

45. e. The periodic rate is 2/98 = 2.04%, and there are 360/30 = 12 periods per year. Thus, the effective annual rate is 27.4 percent:

$$\left(1 + \frac{k_{Nom}}{m}\right)^{12} - 1.0 = (1.0204)^{12} - 1.0$$

$$= 1.2743 - 1.0 = 0.2743 = 27.4\%.$$

46. a.

$$\text{Accounts receivable needed to factor} = \frac{\$500{,}000}{1 - \left(\frac{0.14}{12} + 0.04\right)} = \$527{,}241.$$

47. c. Monthly costs:

Commission = \$527,241(0.04) =	\$21,090
Interest = \$527,241(0.14/12) =	6,151
	\$27,241

Monthly savings:

Credit expense	\$10,000
Bad debt losses = \$527,241(0.035) =	18,453
	\$28,453

The factoring arrangement will result in a savings of \$28,453 – \$27,241 = \$1,212 per month, or \$1,212(12) = \$14,544 per year.

CHAPTER 22
INVENTORIES

OVERVIEW

Inventory management techniques are covered in depth in production management courses. Still, most firms typically have about 20 percent of their assets in inventories, so they represent a significant investment. Since financial managers have a responsibility both for raising the capital needed to carry inventories and for the overall profitability of the firm, it is essential that finance students understand the basics of inventory management.

KEY CONCEPTS

> Inventories are essential to the operation of most businesses.

Inventories are commonly classified into three categories.

- Raw materials
- Work-in-process
- Finished goods

Inventories are greatly influenced by the level of sales. Since inventories are acquired before sales can take place, an accurate sales forecast is critical to effective inventory management.

> When finished goods are sold, the firm must assign a *costs of goods sold.* The cost of goods sold appears on the income statement as an expense for the period, and the balance sheet inventory account is reduced by a like amount.

Four methods can be used to value the cost of goods sold and, hence, to value remaining inventory.

- Under *specific identification*, a unique cost is attached to each item of inventory. This method is used only when items are high cost and move relatively slowly.
- In the *first-in, first-out (FIFO)* method, the units sold during a given period are assumed to be the first units that were placed in inventory.
- The *last-in, first-out (LIFO)* method is the opposite of FIFO. Here the cost of goods sold is based on the last units placed in inventory.
- The *weighted average* method involves the computation of the weighted average unit cost of goods in inventory, and this average value is then applied to each unit sold to determine the cost of goods sold.

The *inventory valuation method* used affects the firm's reported profitability, taxes, and ending inventory values.

- If costs are constant (zero inflation), all four methods would produce the same cost of goods sold, ending inventory, taxes, and cash flows.
- In an inflationary period, LIFO provides the greatest cost of goods sold, and hence the highest tax deductibility, which results in the greatest cash flow. Since inflation has been a fact for the past 30 years, most firms use LIFO to take advantage of its greater tax benefits and cash flow. Note, however, that the higher cost of goods sold produces the lowest reported income and lowest ending inventory.

> The goal of inventory management is to provide at the lowest total cost the inventories required to sustain operations. The first step in inventory management is to identify all the costs involved in purchasing and maintaining inventories.

Carrying costs generally rise in direct proportion to the average amount of inventory held.

- Carrying costs include the following:
    - Cost of the capital tied up in inventories
    - Storage and handling costs
    - Insurance costs
    - Property taxes
    - Depreciation and obsolescence
- If TCC = total carrying cost, C = annual carrying cost as a percentage of inventory value, P = purchase price per unit of inventory, and A = average number of units held in inventory, then

$$TCC = (C)(P)(A).$$

Ordering costs, which are considered to be fixed costs, decline as average inventories increase, that is, as the number of orders decrease.

- Ordering costs include the costs of placing and receiving orders.

- If TOC = total ordering cost, F = fixed cost associated with placing and receiving an order, and N = the number of orders placed per year, then

$$TOC = (F)(N).$$

The costs of running short of inventory, or stock-out costs, may well be the most important element of inventory costs. These costs will be added later, when safety stocks are discussed.

Total inventory costs, TIC, equal the sum of total carrying cost and total ordering cost:

$$TIC = TCC + TOC = (C)(P)(A) + (F)(N).$$

- Now recognize that if Q units are ordered each time an order is placed, and assuming that inventories are used evenly over the year and inventory levels are run down to zero immediately prior to receipt of the next order, then the average inventory level is one-half the number ordered:

$$A = Q/2.$$

- Further, if Q units are ordered each time, and S units are required over the year, then

$$N = S/Q.$$

- Using these relationships for A and N, the total inventory cost equation can be rewritten as

$$TIC = (C)(P)\left(\frac{Q}{2}\right) + \frac{(F)(S)}{Q}.$$

Inventories are obviously necessary, but it is equally obvious that inventory levels that are too high or too low are costly to the firm.

The *Economic Ordering Quantity (EOQ)* model minimizes total inventory costs.

The model, which is derived by minimizing total inventory costs, is

$$EOQ = \sqrt{\frac{2(F)(S)}{(C)(P)}},$$

where:

- EOQ is the optimal quantity to be ordered each time an order is placed.
- F = fixed costs of placing and receiving an order.
- S = annual sales in units.
- C = carrying cost expressed as a percentage of inventory value.
- P = purchase price the firm must pay per unit of inventory.

The assumptions of the model are as follows:

- There is no uncertainty in sales forecasts.
- Inventory usage is evenly distributed over time.
- Orders are received without delay.
- All carrying costs are completely variable and all ordering costs are completely fixed.

With instantaneous order delivery, the order point is zero. However, if the instantaneous order delivery assumption is dropped, the order point is found as follows:

- Find the daily rate of usage.
- The lead time is the number of days required to place an order and receive delivery.
- Order point equals daily usage times lead time.

Demand, rate of usage, and order lead time cannot always be known with certainty. Therefore, firms add a safety stock to their inventories to avoid running out of inventory and suffering stock-out costs.

- At the optimal level of safety stock, the probable cost of running out of inventory is just offset by the cost of carrying the additional inventory.
- The costs of a stock-out include the following:
    - Customer ill will
    - Production delays
    - Lost sales
- The probability of a stock-out is influenced by fluctuations in usage rate and delivery time.
- Inclusion of a safety stock does not affect the EOQ.
    - The average inventory with the safety stock is

$$A = (EOQ/2) + \text{Safety stock}.$$

    - The order point is increased by the amount of the safety stock.
    - Total inventory costs are increased by the carrying cost of the safety stock.

Suppliers often offer discounts for ordering large quantities; such discounts are called quantity discounts. To evaluate taking or not taking a quantity discount, the savings of the quantity discount is compared against the increased costs of ordering (and holding) a nonoptimal amount.

Inflation impacts the EOQ both by raising carrying costs and by increasing the value of the inventory and, hence, on average, has minimal impact on optimal holdings.

For most firms, it is unrealistic to assume that demand for an inventory item is uniform throughout the year. Thus, the EOQ model cannot be used on an annual basis, but it can be used on a seasonal basis, with inventories either run down or built up during the transition between seasons.

Small deviation from the EOQ quantity do not appreciably increase the cost of ordering and carrying inventories, and hence, the optimal ordering quantity concept should be viewed more as a range than as a single value.

The EOQ model, together with safety stock analysis, can be used to establish the proper inventory level, but inventory management also involves the establishment of an *inventory control system*.

Inventory control systems can be very simple to extremely complex, depending on the size of the firm and the nature of the inventories.

- One simple control procedure is the *red-line method*. A red line is drawn inside the bin where the inventory is stocked. When the red line shows, an order is placed.
- The *two-bin method* has inventory items stocked in two bins. When the working bin is empty, an order is placed and inventory is drawn from the second bin.
- Large companies employ much more sophisticated *computerized inventory control systems*.
- *Just-in-time* systems coordinate a manufacturer's production with suppliers' so that raw materials arrive from suppliers just as they are needed in the production process.

Another important development related to inventories is *out-sourcing*, which is the practice of purchasing components rather than making them in-house. Out-sourcing is often combined with just-in-time systems to reduce inventory levels.

A final point relating to inventory levels is the relationship between production scheduling and inventory levels. Inventory policy must be coordinated with the firm's manufacturing and procurement policies, because the ultimate goal is to minimize total production and distribution costs, and inventory costs are just one part of the picture.

DEFINITIONAL QUESTIONS

1. Inventories are usually classified as _______ _____________, _______-____-__________, and ____________ ________.

2. The goal of inventory management is to provide the inventories needed for operations at the _________ _________.

3. Storage costs, obsolescence, and other costs that ________ with larger inventories are known as __________ costs.

4. Ordering and receiving costs are __________ related to average inventory size.

5. The ________ __________ quantity minimizes the total costs of ordering and holding inventories.

6. When the level of inventories reaches the ________ _________, the EOQ amount should be ordered.

7. ______ ______must be maintained in order to allow for shipping delays and uncertainty in the rate of ______.

8. Running out of an item of inventory is called a ________-______.

9. Inventory control systems that require suppliers to deliver items as they are needed are called _________-____-________ systems.

10. The optimal ordering quantity should be thought of more as a ____________ than as a point value.

CONCEPTUAL QUESTIONS

11. The economic ordering quantity is the order quantity that provides the minimum total cost; that is, both the ordering and carrying cost components are minimized.

    a. True   b. False

12. The costs of a stock-out do not include

a. Disruption of production schedules.
b. Loss of customer goodwill.
c. Depreciation and obsolescence.
d. Loss of sales.
e. Answers c and d above.

13. The addition of a safety stock to the EOQ model

a. Increases the EOQ proportionately.
b. Raises the order point.
c. Lowers the order point.
d. Does not change the total inventory costs.
e. Results in greater variability in the time required to receive deliveries.

PROBLEMS

The following data apply to the next four problems.

The South Florida Lawn Supply Company is reviewing its inventory policy regarding lawn seed. The following relationships and conditions exist:

(1) Orders must be placed in multiples of 100 bags.
(2) Requirements for the year are 16,200 bags.
(3) The purchase price per bag is $5.00.
(4) The carrying cost is 20 percent of inventory value.
(5) The fixed costs per order are $25.
(6) The desired safety stock is 300 units; this amount is on hand initially.
(7) Five days are required for delivery.
(8) Assume 360 days per year.

14. What is the economic ordering quantity?

a. 600 bags **b.** 700 bags **c.** 800 bags **d.** 900 bags **e.** 1,000 bags

15. How many orders should South Florida Lawn Supply place each year?

a. 22 **b.** 20 **c.** 18 **d.** 16 **e.** 14

16. What is the reorder point?

a. 750 bags   b. 525 bags   c. 345 bags   d. 300 bags   e. 225 bags

17. What is the average inventory level?

a. 750 bags   b. 525 bags   c. 345 bags   d. 300 bags   e. 225 bags

The following data apply to the next six problems.

The Magnuson Company is trying to determine its optimal inventory policy. The following relationships and conditions exist for the firm:

(1) Annual sales are 120,000 units.
(2) The purchase price per unit is $500.
(3) The carrying cost is 20 percent of inventory value.
(4) The fixed costs per order are $600.
(5) The optimal safety stock is 500 units, which are already on hand.
(6) Assume 360 days per year.

18. What is the economic ordering quantity?

a. 600 units   b. 800 units   c. 1,000 units   d. 1,200 units   e. 1,400 units

19. What is the maximum inventory the company will hold?

a. 1,300 units   b. 1,400 units   c. 1,500 units   d. 1,600 units   e. 1,700 units

20. What is the average inventory the company will hold?

a. 600 units   b. 850 units   c. 1,100 units   d. 1,200 units   e. 1,700 units

21. How often will the company order?

a. Every 2.0 days
b. Every 3.60 days
c. Every 5.25 days
d. Every 2 weeks
e. Continually

22. What are the firm's annual total inventory costs disregarding the safety stock?

a. $50,000   b. $120,000   c. $150,000   d. $170,000   e. $200,000

23. What are the annual total inventory costs including the safety stock?

a. \$50,000 **b.** \$120,000 **c.** \$150,000 **d.** \$170,000 **e.** \$200,000

Answers

1. raw materials; work-in-process; finished goods
2. lowest cost
3. increase; carrying
4. inversely
5. economic ordering
6. order point
7. Safety stocks; usage
8. stock-out
9. just-in-time
10. range

11. b. The total cost, or sum of ordering and carrying costs, is minimized, but neither of the component costs is minimized. For example, to minimize carrying costs, no inventory would be kept on hand at all.

12. c. Depreciation and obsolescence are inventory carrying costs.

13. b. The addition of a safety stock increases the order point by the amount of the safety stock.

14. d.

$$\text{EOQ} = \sqrt{\frac{2(F)(S)}{(C)(P)}} = \sqrt{\frac{2(\$25)(16{,}200)}{0.20(\$5)}} = \sqrt{\frac{\$810{,}000}{\$1.00}} = 900 \text{ bags.}$$

15. c.

$$\frac{16{,}200 \text{ units per year}}{900 \text{ units per order}} = 18 \text{ orders per year.}$$

16. b. Daily rate of use = 16,200/360 = 45 bags. Reorder point = 300 + 5(45) = 525 bags.

Thus, South Florida Lawn Supply Company will have 1,200 bags on hand immediately after a shipment is received, will use 45 bags per day, will reorder when the stock is down to 525 bags (which is 5 days' requirement, plus the safety stock), and will be down to 300 bags just before a shipment arrives.

17. a. Average inventory level = EOQ/2 + Safety stock = 900/2 + 300 = 750 bags.

Note that the inventory fluctuates between 1,200 and 300 bags.

18. d.

$$EOQ = \sqrt{\frac{2(F)(S)}{(C)(P)}} = \sqrt{\frac{2(\$600)(120{,}000)}{0.20(\$500)}} = \sqrt{\frac{\$144{,}000{,}000}{\$100}} = 1{,}200 \text{ units.}$$

19. e. Maximum inventory = EOQ + Safety stock = 1,200 + 500 = 1,700 units.

20. c. Average inventory = EOQ/2 + Safety stock = 600 + 500 = 1,100 units.

21. b.

$$\frac{120{,}000 \text{ units per year}}{1{,}200 \text{ units per order}} = 100 \text{ orders per year.}$$

$$\frac{360 \text{ days per year}}{100 \text{ orders per year}} = 3.60 \text{ days.}$$

The firm must place one order every 3.60 days.

22. b.

$$TIC = (C)(P)(Q/2) + \frac{(F)(S)}{Q} = 0.2(\$500)(1{,}200/2) + \frac{\$600(120{,}000)}{1{,}200}$$

$$= \$60{,}000 + \$60{,}000 = \$120{,}000.$$

Note that total carrying cost equals total ordering cost at the EOQ.

23. d. Now, the average inventory is EOQ/2 + Safety stock = 1,100 units rather than EOQ/2 = 600 units.

$$TIC = 0.2(\$500)(1{,}100) + \frac{\$600(120{,}000)}{1{,}200} = \$110{,}000 + \$60{,}000 = \$170{,}000.$$

Another way of looking at this is

TIC = Cost of working inventory + Cost of safety stock

= \$120,000 + 500(\$500)(0.2) = \$120,000 + \$50,000 = \$170,000.

CHAPTER 23
RECEIVABLES AND CREDIT POLICY

OVERVIEW

Firms would, in general, rather sell for cash than on credit, but competitive pressures force most firms to offer credit. Thus, goods are shipped, inventories are reduced, and an account receivable is created. Eventually, the customer will pay the account, at which time the firm will receive cash and its receivables will decline. Carrying receivables has both direct and indirect costs, but it also has an important benefit--granting credit will increase sales. The optimal credit policy is the one which maximizes the firm's net cash flows over time, giving consideration to the risk assumed.

KEY CONCEPTS

The effective management of receivables is important to the profitability and risk level of the firm.

Accounts receivable are created when a firm sells goods or performs services on credit rather than on a cash basis. When cash is received, accounts receivable are reduced by the same amount.

The total amount of accounts receivable outstanding is determined by (1) the volume of credit sales and (2) the average length of time between sales and collections.

The investment in receivables, like any asset, must be financed in some manner.

Receivables must be actively managed to insure that the firm's receivables policy is effective. There are three commonly used methods to monitor a firm's receivables.

One method used is the *days sales outstanding (DSO),* also sometimes called the average collection period (ACP).

- The DSO measures the average length of time it takes a firm's customers to pay off their credit purchases.
- The DSO is calculated by dividing the receivables balance by average daily credit sales.
- The DSO can be compared with the industry average and the firm's own credit terms to get an indication of how well customers are adhering to the terms prescribed and how customers' payments, on average, compare with the industry average.

A second method used to monitor a firm's receivables position is the *aging schedule.*

- An aging schedule breaks down a firm's receivables by the ages of the accounts.
- An aging schedule points out the percentage of receivables value attributable to late paying customers.

Both the DSO and aging schedule can be misleading if sales are seasonal and/or cyclical. The *payments pattern approach* is a receivables monitoring method which overcomes this deficiency.

- The main tool in the payments pattern approach is the uncollected balances schedule.
- This schedule focuses on each month's Receivables/Sales ratio. If customers follow a constant payments pattern, then the firm's Receivables/Sales ratios will remain constant over time even when sales fluctuate.
- The payments pattern approach is also useful for forecasting future receivables balances.

The major controllable variables that affect sales are sales price, product quality, advertising, and the firm's *credit policy.* The credit policy consists of (1) the credit period, (2) credit standards, (3) collection policy, and (4) discounts.

The *credit period* is the length of time for which credit is granted. Increasing the credit period often stimulates sales, but there is a cost involved in carrying the increased rceeivables.

Credit standards relate to decisions about who will be granted credit. If the firm extended credit sales to only the strongest of customers, it would never have bad debt losses. On the other hand, it would probably be losing sales.

- Two major sources of external credit information are available: credit associations and credit-reporting agencies such as Dun & Bradstreet.
- Modern credit managers classify customers into five or six categories according to degree of risk. Then, the credit manager concentrates his time and attention on the weakest customers. This is referred to as management by exception.
- *Credit scoring systems* use multiple discriminant analysis to assess credit risk in a quantitative manner.

Collection policy refers to the procedures the firm follows to collect past-due accounts. The collection process can be expensive in terms of both direct costs and lost goodwill, but at least some firmness is needed to prevent an undue lengthening of the collection period and to minimize outright losses.

The last variable in the credit policy decision is the firm's *cash discount policy.* Cash discounts attract customers and encourage early payment but reduce the dollar amount received on each discount sale.

It is possible sometimes to sell on credit and assess a carrying charge on the receivables that are outstanding, making credit sales more profitable than cash sales.

It is illegal to offer more favorable credit terms to one customer or class of customers than to another, unless the differences are cost justified.

Customers' response to credit policy can sometimes force companies to reconsider the credit terms that they have established.

When offering credit, a seller can choose from a variety of credit instruments based on the type of trade and one's confidence in the buyer's ability to pay.

An *open account* is used for most credit. With this instrument, the only formal evidence of credit is an invoice which accompanies the shipment and which the buyer signs to indicate that goods have been received.

A *promissory note* may be used as evidence of the credit obligation. Promissory notes are useful if the order is very large, if the seller anticipates the possibility of having trouble collecting, or if the buyer wants a longer-than-usual time in which to pay for the order.

A *draft* is a cross between a check and promissory note. A specific type of draft is chosen based on the seller's objectives. The common types are as follows:

- Commercial draft
- Sight draft
- Time draft or trade acceptance
- Banker's acceptance

With a conditional sales contract, the seller retains legal ownership of the goods until the buyer has completed payment.

> Changes in credit policy must be analyzed. For example, easing the credit policy normally stimulates sales. As sales rise, costs also rise (1) to produce the extra required goods, (2) to carry the additional receivables outstanding, and (3) because bad debt expenses may rise.

The question to answer when considering a credit policy change, therefore, is whether sales revenues will rise more than costs.

One way to answer this question is to compare projected income statements and, hence, focus on the incremental changes in expected sales revenues and costs that would result from a proposed change in the credit policy.

- In this analysis, determine the firm's cost of carrying receivables before and after the change in credit policy.
- The cost of carrying receivables is the product of the days sales outstanding, sales per day, the variable cost ratio, and the cost of funds.

$$\text{Cost of carrying receivables} = \text{DSO} \times \text{Sales per day} \times \text{Variable cost ratio} \times \text{Cost of funds}.$$

- Only variable costs are considered because only this portion needs to be financed; the remainder is profit.
- The change in the level of bad debt losses and the dollar value of the discounts taken must also be determined.
- If expected sales revenues less expected expenses are greater after the proposed change in credit policy than before, the change in credit policy should be undertaken, unless the riskiness of the change is disproportionate to the benefits.

The second approach to analyzing changes in credit policy, the incremental analysis approach, uses a set of algebraic equations which focus directly on the incremental changes.

- The following equations are used:

Sales increase: $\Delta I = [(DSO_N - DSO_0)(S_0/360)] + V[(DSO_N)(S_N - S_0)/360]$.

Sales decrease: $\Delta I = [(DSO_N - DSO_0)(S_N/360)] + V[(DSO_0)(S_N - S_0)/360]$.

$\Delta P = (S_N - S_0)(1 - V) - k(\Delta I) - (B_N S_N - B_0 S_0) - (D_N S_N P_N - D_0 S_0 P_0)$.

- The symbols used, as well as the application of these equations, are discussed fully in the text.

There is quite a bit of uncertainty in credit policy change analysis because the variables are very difficult to estimate. Further, the end result depends on the reactions of competitors. Thus, the final decision is based on the quantitative analysis plus a great deal of informed judgment.

DEFINITIONAL QUESTIONS

1. ______ ______ are created when goods are sold or services are performed on credit.

2. A firm's outstanding accounts receivable will be determined by the ______ of credit sales and the length of time between __________ and __________.

3. Sales volume and the collection period will be affected by a firm's ______ ______.

4. Extremely strict credit standards will result in lost ______.

5. Effective credit standards require a balance between the ______ costs of credit and the marginal ______ on increased sales.

6. Credit terms generally specify the ______ for which credit is granted and any ______ ______ that is offered for early payment.

7. The optimal credit terms involve a tradeoff between increased ______ and the cost of carrying additional ______ ______.

8. ______ policy refers to the manner in which a firm tries to obtain payment from past-due accounts.

9. Two popular methods for monitoring receivables are ______ ______ and the ______ ______ ______.

10. The best method for monitoring receivables is the ______ ______ approach which focuses on the ______ ______ schedule.

11. Credit sales may be especially profitable if a ______ charge is assessed on accounts receivable.

12. ______ ______ are local groups which meet to exchange credit information.

13. Most credit is offered on ______ ______, which means that the only formal evidence of credit is the invoice.

14. If a seller wants a stronger legal claim against a creditor, the seller will require the buyer to sign a ______ ______.

CONCEPTUAL QUESTIONS

15. A firm changes its credit policy from 2/10, net 30, to 3/10, net 30. The change is to meet competition, so no increase in sales is expected. The firm's average investment in accounts receivable will probably increase as a result of the change.

    a. True **b.** False

16. An aging schedule is constructed by a firm to keep track of when its accounts payable are due.

    a. True **b.** False

17. If a credit policy change increases the firm's accounts receivable, the entire increase must be financed by some source of funds.

    a. True **b.** False

18. The goal of credit policy is to

    a. Minimize bad debt losses.
    b. Minimize DSO.
    c. Maximize sales.
    d. Minimize collection expenses.
    e. Extend credit to the point where marginal profits equal marginal costs.

PROBLEMS

The following data apply to the next three problems.

Simmons Brick Company sells on terms of 3/10, net 30. Gross sales for the year are $1,200,000, and the collections department estimates that 30 percent of the customers pay on the tenth day and take discounts; 40 percent pay on the thirtieth day; and the remaining 30 percent pay, on average, 40 days after the purchase. Assume 360 days per year.

19. What is the days sales outstanding?

a. 10 days **b.** 13 days **c.** 20 days **d.** 27 days **e.** 40 days

20. What is the current receivables balance?

a. $60,000 **b.** $70,000 **c.** $75,000 **d.** $80,000 **e.** $90,000

21. What would be the new receivables balance if Simmons toughened up on its collection policy, with the result that all nondiscount customers paid on the thirtieth day?

a. $60,000 **b.** $70,000 **c.** $75,000 **d.** $80,000 **e.** $90,000

The following data apply to the next three problems.

Furston Inc., a retail firm, currently has sales of $1 million. Its credit period and days sales outstanding are both 30 days, and 1 percent of its sales end up as bad debts. Furston's credit manager estimates that if the firm extends its credit period to 45 days, sales will increase by $100,000, but its bad debt losses on the incremental sales would be 3 percent. Variable costs are 40 percent, and the cost of carrying receivables, k, is 15 percent. Assume a tax rate of 40 percent and 360 days per year.

22. What would be the incremental investment in receivables if the change were made?

a. $3,250 **b.** $41,667 **c.** $21,667 **d.** $50,000 **e.** $56,667

23. What would be the incremental cost of carrying receivables?

a. $5,000 **b.** $3,250 **c.** $8,250 **d.** $10,000 **e.** $0

24. What would be the incremental change in net income?

a. $32,250 **b.** $26,875 **c.** $20,000 **d.** $10,550 **e.** $15,875

The following data apply to the next two problems.

Hodes Furniture currently has annual sales of $2,000,000. Its days sales outstanding is 40 days, and bad debts are 5 percent of sales. The credit and collection manager is considering instituting a stricter collection policy, whereby bad debts would be reduced to 2 percent of total sales, and the days sales outstanding would fall to 30 days. However, sales would also fall by an estimated $250,000 annually. Variable costs are 60 percent of sales and the cost of carrying receivables is 12 percent. Assume a tax rate of 40 percent and 360 days per year.

25. What would be the incremental change in receivables investment if the change were made?

a. -$16,667 **b.** -$27,167 **c.** -$48,611 **d.** -$45,833 **e.** -$72,431

26. What would be the incremental change in profits?

a. -$16,667 **b.** -$17,700 **c.** -$20,250 **d.** -$25,750 **e.** -$15,000

ANSWERS

1. Accounts receivable
2. volume; sales; collections
3. credit policy
4. sales
5. marginal; profits
6. period; cash discount
7. sales; accounts receivable
8. Collection
9. aging schedules; days sales outstanding (DSO)
10. payments pattern; uncollected balances
11. carrying
12. Credit associations
13. open account
14. promissory note

15. b. No new customers are being generated. The current customers pay either on Day 10 or Day 30. The increase in trade discount will induce some customers who are now paying on Day 30 to pay on Day 10. Thus, the days sales outstanding is shortened which, in turn, will cause a decline in accounts receivable.

16. b. The aging schedule breaks down accounts receivable according to how long they have been outstanding.

17. b. Receivables are based on sales price which presumably includes some profit. Only the actual cash outlays associated with receivables must be financed. The remainder, or profit, appears on the balance sheet as an increase in retained earnings.

18. e. The goal of credit policy is to maximize overall profits. This is achieved when the marginal profits equal the marginal costs.

19. d. 0.3(10 days) + 0.4(30 days) + 0.3(40 days) = 27 days.

20. e. Receivables = (DSO)(Sales/360) = 27($1,200,000/360) = $90,000.

21. d. New days sales outstanding = 0.3(10) + 0.7(30) = 24 days.

Sales per day = $1,200,000/360 = $3,333.33; Receivables = $3,333.33(24) = $80,000.00.

Thus, the average receivables would drop from $90,000 to $80,000. Furthermore, sales may decline as a result of the tighter credit and reduce receivables even more. Also, some additional customers may now take discounts, which would further reduce receivables.

22. c. The incremental receivable investment is calculated as follows:

$$\text{Old credit policy: DSO} \times \begin{matrix}\text{Sales}\\ \text{per day}\end{matrix} \times \begin{matrix}\text{Variable}\\ \text{cost ratio}\end{matrix}$$

$$(30)\left(\frac{\$1,000,000}{360}\right)(0.4) = \$33,333.$$

$$\text{New credit policy: DSO} \begin{matrix}\text{Sales}\\ \text{per day}\end{matrix} \times \begin{matrix}\text{Variable}\\ \text{cost ratio}\end{matrix}$$

$$(45)\left(\frac{\$1,100,000}{360}\right)(0.4) = \$55,000.$$

The incremental investment in receivables is $55,000 - $33,333 = $21,667.

23. b. The incremental cost of carrying receivables would be calculated as follows:

$$\text{Old credit policy: DSO} \times \begin{matrix}\text{Sales}\\ \text{per day}\end{matrix} \times \begin{matrix}\text{Variable}\\ \text{cost ratio}\end{matrix} \times \begin{matrix}\text{Cost of}\\ \text{funds}\end{matrix}.$$

New credit policy:

$$(45)\left(\frac{\$1{,}100{,}000}{360}\right)(0.4)(0.15) = \$8{,}250.$$

or

$$\$55{,}000(0.15) = \$8{,}250.$$

Thus, the incremental cost is \$8,250 - \$5,000 = \$3,250.

24. a.

	Income Statement under Current Policy	Effect of Change	Income Statement under New Policy
Gross sales	\$1,000,000	\$ 100,000	\$1,100,000
Less discounts	0	0	0
Net sales	\$1,000,000	\$ 100,000	\$1,100,000
Production costs	400,000	40,000	440,000
Profit before credit costs and taxes	\$ 600,000	\$ 60,000	\$ 660,000
Credit related costs:			
Cost of carrying receivables	5,000	3,250	8,250
Collection expenses			
Bad debt losses	10,000	3,000	13,000
Profit before taxes	\$ 585,000	\$ 53,750	\$ 638,750
Taxes (40%)	234,000	21,500	255,500
Net income	\$ 351,000	\$ 32,250	\$ 383,250

25. d. The incremental change in receivable investment would be calculated as follows:

$$\text{Old credit policy: DSO} \times \frac{\text{Sales}}{\text{per day}} \times \frac{\text{Variable}}{\text{cost ratio}}$$

$$\text{New credit policy:} \quad DSO \times \frac{\text{Sales}}{\text{per day}} \times \frac{\text{Variable}}{\text{cost ratio}}$$

$$(30)\left(\frac{\$1{,}750{,}000}{360}\right)(0.6) = \$87{,}500.$$

The incremental change in receivables is $87,500 - $133,333 = -$45,833.

26. b.

	Income Statement under Current Policy	Effect of Change	Income Statement under New Policy
Sales	$2,000,000	($250,000)	$1,750,000
Less discounts	0	0	0
Net sales	$2,000,000	($250,000)	$1,750,000
Production costs	1,200,000	150,000	1,050,000
Profit before credit costs and taxes	$ 800,000	($100,000)	$ 700,000
Credit related costs:			
Cost of carrying receivables	16,000	(5,500)	10,500
Collection expenses			
Bad debt losses	100,000	(65,000)	35,000
Profit before taxes	$ 684,000	($ 29,500)	$ 654,500
Taxes (40%)	273,600	(11,800)	261,800
Net income	$ 410,400	($ 17,700)	$ 392,700

CHAPTER 24
CORPORATE RESTRUCTURING: MERGERS, LBOs, AND DIVESTITURES

OVERVIEW

Most corporate growth occurs through internal expansion, which takes place when the firm's existing divisions grow through normal capital budgeting activities. However, the most dramatic examples of growth, and often the largest increases in stock prices, are the result of *mergers*, the first topic in this chapter. *Leveraged buyouts*, or *LBOs*, occur when a firm's stock is acquired by a small group of investors rather than by another company. Since LBOs are similar in many respects to mergers, they too are covered in this chapter. The conditions of corporate life do change over time, and, as a result, firms occasionally find it desirable to divest, or sell off, major divisions to other firms that can better utilize the divested assets. *Divestitures* are also covered in the chapter.

KEY CONCEPTS

Several reasons have been proposed to justify corporate mergers.

One major reason for mergers is *synergy*.

- If Companies A and B merge to form Company C, and if C's value exceeds that of A and B taken separately, then synergy is said to exist.
- Synergism can arise from four sources:
  - Operating economies
  - Financial economies
  - Differential management efficiency
  - Increased market power

- Operating and financial economies, as well as increases in managerial efficiency, are socially desirable. However, mergers that reduce competition are both undesirable and illegal.

Tax considerations can provide an incentive for mergers.

- A highly profitable firm might merge with a firm which has accumulated tax losses so as to put these losses to immediate use.
- A firm with excess cash and a shortage of internal investment opportunities might seek a merger rather than pay the cash out as dividends, which would result in the shareholders paying immediate taxes on the distribution.

Occasionally, a firm will merge with another because it thinks it has found a "bargain," that is, *assets can be purchased below their replacement cost.*

- However, if the capital markets are efficient, stock prices represent the fair market value of the underlying assets.
- The fact that a firm's market value is far below its replacement or book value does not, in itself, make the firm an attractive acquisition candidate.

Diversification is often cited by managers as a rationale for mergers.

- Diversification may bring some real benefits to the firm, especially by reducing the variability of the firm's earnings stream, which benefits the firm's managers, creditors, and other stakeholders.
- However, by simply holding portfolios of stocks, stockholders can generally diversify more easily and efficiently than can firms.

Financial economists like to think that business decisions are based only on economic considerations. However, some business decisions are based more on managers' personal motivations than on economic factors.

- Some mergers occur because managers want to increase the size of their firms, and hence gain more power, prestige, and monetary compensation.
- Other mergers occur because managers want to keep their jobs, so they merge with other firms to make the firm less attractive to hostile suitors. This type of merger is called a *defensive merger*.

Firms are generally valued in the markets as ongoing firms. However, some firms are worth more if they are broken up and then sold off in pieces. Thus, some acquisitions are motivated by the fact that a firm's *breakup value* is greater than its current market value.

Economists classify mergers into four groups:

A *horizontal merger* occurs when one firm combines with another in the same line of business.

A *vertical merger* exists when firms combine in a producer-supplier relationship.

A *congeneric merger* occurs when the merging companies are somewhat related, but not to the extent required for a horizontal or vertical merger.

A *conglomerate merger* occurs when completely unrelated enterprises combine.

The high level of merger activity in the 1980s was sparked by several factors:

The relatively depressed condition of the stock market that existed prior to 1983.

The unprecedented level of inflation that existed during the 1970s and early 1980s, which increased the replacement value of firms' assets even while a weak stock market reduced their market value.

The Reagan administration's view that "bigness is not necessarily badness," which resulted in a more tolerant attitude toward large mergers.

The general belief among the major natural resource companies that it is cheaper to "buy reserves on Wall Street" than to explore and find them in the field.

The development of an active junk bond market which helped finance many takeovers.

Attempts to ward off raiders by use of defensive mergers.

The decline of the dollar, which made U. S. companies relatively cheap to foreign acquirers.

It appears that a new merger wave is beginning, but now the major driving force is strategic realignment in industries such as health care, communications, and entertainment.

In most mergers, one company, the *target company*, is acquired by another, the *acquiring company.*

In a *friendly merger*, the management of the target company approves the merger and recommends it to their stockholders.

- Under these circumstances a suitable price is determined, and the acquiring company will simply buy the target company's shares through a friendly *tender offer*.
- Payment will be made either in cash, or in the stock or debt of the acquiring firm.

A *hostile merger* is one in which the target firm's management resists the takeover. The target firm's management either believes the price offered is too low, or it may simply want to remain independent.

- Under these circumstances, the acquiring company may make a hostile tender offer for the target company's shares. This is a direct appeal to the target firm's stockholders asking them to exchange their shares for cash, bonds, or stock in the acquiring firm.
- The number of hostile tender offers has increased greatly during the past several years.

Mergers are regulated by both the state and federal governments.

Federal laws place three major restrictions on acquiring firms.

- Acquirers must disclose their current holdings and future intentions within 10 days of amassing at least 5 percent of a company's stock, and they must disclose the source of the funds to be used in the acquisition.
- Target shareholders must be given at least 20 days to tender their shares.
- If the tender price is increased during the 20 day open period, all shareholders who tendered prior to the new offer must receive the higher price.

Many states now have merger laws which restrict the actions that can be taken by raiders.

- One such law restricts the ability of a raider to vote the shares they have acquired; that is, the merger must be approved by disinterested shareholders.
- Other state laws limit the use of golden parachutes, onerous debt-financing plans, and some types of poison pills to protect target stockholders from their own managers.

While merger analysis may appear simple, there are a number of complex issues involved.

The acquiring company must estimate the cash flows that will result from the acquisition. It must also determine what effect, if any, the merger will have on its own required rate of return on equity. The acquiring company also must decide how to pay for the merger -- with cash, its own stock, or some other type or package of securities; and having estimated the benefits of the merger, the acquiring and target firms' managers and stockholders must bargain (or fight) over how to share these benefits.

The terms of a merger include three important elements:

- *Postmerger control of the firm*, which is of great interest to managers due to their concern for their jobs.
- *The price to be paid* determines whether the shareholders of the acquiring company or the shareholders of the target company reap the greater benefits from the merger.
- *The structure of the offer* is how to pay for the merger -- in cash, in securities of the acquiring firm, or in some combination of the two.

The acquiring firm must perform a capital budgeting-type analysis. If it appears that the target firm can be purchased for less than its intrinsic value, then the offer should be made.

However, the target firm's shareholders must believe that a "fair" price is being offered. Otherwise, they will not tender their shares.

From a financial standpoint, there are two basic types of mergers:

- *Operating mergers*, where the operations of two companies are combined in hopes of synergistic gains.
- *Financial mergers*, where the two operations are not combined and where no operating economies are expected.

The primary expected benefit of an operating merger is higher cash flows. Financial mergers may result in a greater ability to employ leverage, greater liquidity for the stock, or a matching of capital needs and resources.

The valuation of the target firm involves two key items: (1) a set of pro forma financial statements, and (2) a discount rate to apply to the projected cash flows.

In a pure financial merger, the expected post-merger cash flows of the acquired firm are the same as if the firm remained independent.

In an operating merger, cash flow projections are more difficult, but essential to the merger analysis. Synergistic effects may result in greater cash flows than would have been achieved if the target firm had remained independent. For example, economies of scale may result in lower operating costs per unit of production, and hence, higher cash flows.

Merger cash flows, unlike capital budgeting cash flows, must include interest expense.

- The target firm usually has embedded debt that will be assumed by the acquiring company.
- This debt does not generally have the same cost as marginal debt.
- Thus, debt costs must be explicitly included in the cash flow analysis.

In essence, we are using the equity residual method to value the target firm. With debt costs included in the cash flow analysis, the resulting net cash flows accrue solely to the equity holders of the acquiring firm. Thus, the *appropriate discount rate is a cost of equity* rather than an overall cost of capital. The cost of equity used must reflect the underlying riskiness of the target company's assets and the riskiness of the financing mix used for the acquisition.

Hamada's equation, which was developed in Chapter 11, can be used to adjust the beta of the target firm to reflect the tax and leverage consequences of the merger. The Security Market Line can then be used to determine the target firm's post-merger cost of equity.

The present value of the incremental merger cash flows is the maximum price that the acquiring firm should pay for the target company. The larger the synergistic benefits, the more room for bargaining, and the higher the probability that the merger will actually be consummated.

Once the value of the target is estimated, the acquiring firm must decide on the *structure of the takeover bid.*

The structure of the bid is extremely important since it affects:

- The capital structure of the postmerger firm.
- The tax treatment of both the acquiring firm and the target firm's stockholders.
- The ability of the target firm's stockholders to reap the rewards of future merger-related gains.
- The types of federal and state regulations that apply to the merger.

Target shareholders do not have to pay taxes on their takeover proceeds if their shares are paid for by stock in the acquiring firm (at least 50 percent of the payment must be in stock--either common or preferred). If the offer is predominantly cash or debt securities, taxes will have to be paid.

If the acquiring firm elects to write up the target company's assets for tax purposes, the target company must pay a capital gains tax on the write-up. However, it can then depreciate the assets from their new, higher value.

Investment bankers play an important role in merger activities.

The major investment banking firms have merger and acquisition (M&A) departments which help to match merger partners.

These same investment bankers can also help a firm fend off an unwanted suitor.

- Sometimes a *white knight* will be lined up to acquire a firm that is trying to avoid being taken over by an unfriendly suitor.
- In other situations, a *white squire* may be sought to buy shares in the target firm, hold them, and then vote in favor of current management.
- Investment bankers can also recommend *poison pills*, which are actions that effectively destroy the value of the firm in the event of a merger, and hence drive off unwanted suitors.

Investment bankers are often used to help establish the offering price. Generally, both the acquiring and target firms will use investment bankers to help establish a price and also to participate in the negotiations.

Investment banking firms also engage in *risk arbitrage*, which means speculating in the stocks of companies that are likely takeover targets. They also help to finance mergers.

The latest merger wave has sparked a great deal of research to answer this question: "Do corporate acquisitions really create value, and if so, how is this value shared between the parties involved?

Researchers attempt to answer questions such as this by examining the relative stock price performance of merging firms around the merger announcement date.

On average, the stock prices of target companies have increased by 20-30 percent upon the merger announcement.

However, the stock prices of acquiring firms have tended to remain unchanged.

Thus, the evidence strongly indicates that acquisitions do create value, but that shareholders of target firms reap virtually all of the benefits.

> Mergers are one way for two companies to completely join assets and management, but many firms are striking cooperative deals which fall short of merging. Such cooperative amalgamations are called *corporate alliances*, and they occur in many forms.

Joint ventures are an important type of alliance.

- Joint ventures are controlled by a combined management team formed by the parent companies.
- Joint ventures are operated independently from the parent companies.

> In a *leveraged buyout (LBO)*, a small group of equity investors, usually including current top management, acquires a firm in a transaction financed largely by debt.

The debt is serviced by the cash flows generated by the acquired company's operations and by the sale of some of its assets.

- Often, some of the assets must be sold to service the debt.
- The heavy debt burden forces management to operate very efficiently.

Usually, after several years of being privately held, the firm has been streamlined and made more efficient. Then, the owners recover their equity investment by going public again.

> Although corporations do more buying than selling of productive assets, selling, or *divestiture*, does take place.

There are three primary types of *divestitures*:

- A division may be *sold to another firm*. This is the most common form of divestiture.
- In a *spin-off*, a division may be set up as a corporation, with the parent firm's stockholders then being given stock in the new corporation on a pro rata basis.
- In a *liquidation*, the assets of a division are sold off piecemeal, rather than as a single entity.

There are a variety of reasons cited for divestitures:

- It appears that, on occasion, investors do not properly value some assets when they are part of a large conglomerate. Thus, divestiture can occur to enhance firm value.
- Often, firms will need to raise large amounts of cash to finance expansion in their core business, or to reduce an onerous debt burden, and divestitures can raise the needed cash.
- Sometimes, assets are just no longer profitable and must be liquidated.
- Firms that are struggling against bankruptcy often have to divest profitable divisions just to stay alive.
- The government sometimes mandates divestiture on antitrust grounds.

A *holding company* is a firm that holds large blocks of stock in other companies and exercises control over those firms. The holding company is often called the parent company and the controlled companies are known as subsidiaries or operating companies. Holding companies may be used to obtain some of the same benefits that could be achieved through mergers and acquisitions. However, the holding company device has some unique disadvantages as well as unique advantages.

Advantages of holding companies include the following:

- *Control with fractional ownership.* Effective control of a company may be achieved with far less than 50 percent ownership of the common stock.
- *Isolation of risks.* Claims on one unit of the holding company may not be liabilities to the other units. Each element of the holding company organization is a separate legal entity.
- *Legal separation.* Certain regulated companies such as utilities and banks find it easier to operate as holding companies in order to separate those assets under the control of regulators from those not subject to regulation.

Disadvantages of holding companies include the following:

- *Partial multiple taxation.* Consolidated tax returns may be filed only if the holding company owns 80 percent or more of the voting stock of the subsidiary. Otherwise, intercorporate dividends will be taxed. Note, though, that firms that own over 20 percent but less than 80 percent of another corporation can deduct 80 percent of the dividends received from taxable income, while firms that own less than 20 percent may deduct only 70 percent of the dividends received.
- *Ease of enforced dissolution.* It is much easier for the Justice Department to require disposal of a stock position than to demand the separation of an integrated business operation.

The holding company device can be used to control large amounts of assets with a relatively small equity investment. The substantial leverage involved in such an operation may result in high returns, but it also involves a high degree of risk.

DEFINITIONAL QUESTIONS

1. If the value of two firms, in combination, is greater than the sum of their separate values, then __________ is said to exist.

2. Synergistic effects may result from either _________ economies or __________ economies.

3. The Justice Department may be concerned about the _____________ implications of a proposed merger.

4. A(n) ___________ merger takes place when two firms in the same business combine, while the combination of a steel company with a coal company would be an example of a ___________ merger.

5. The merger of two completely unrelated enterprises is referred to as a(n) _________ merger.

6. A firm which seeks to take over another company is commonly called the ____________ company, while the firm it seeks to acquire is referred to as the _____________ company.

7. A merger may be described as "friendly" or "hostile," depending upon the attitude of the _____________ of the target company.

8. A(n) _________ __________ is a request by the acquiring company to the target company's ____________ to submit their shares in exchange for a specified price or specified number of shares of stock.

9. A(n) ____________ merger combines the business activity of the two firms with the expectation of ____________ benefits.

10. _____________ mergers do not combine the business operations of two firms, and no operating economies are expected.

11. Merger analysis is very similar to ____________ ____________ analysis.

12. In valuing the target firm, the analysis focuses on the cash flows that accrue to the stockholders of the ______________ firm.

13. A(n) __________ __________ occurs when two firms combine parts of their companies to accomplish specific, limited objectives.

14. A pro rata distribution of stock in a new firm which was formerly a subsidiary is called a(n) __________.

15. Unless a holding company owns at least ______ percent of the share of a subsidiary company, it may be subject to multiple __________ on a portion of any intercorporate __________.

CONCEPTUAL QUESTIONS

16. In a financial merger, the expected post-merger cash flows are generally the sum of the cash flows of the separate companies.

    a. True **b.** False

17. Interest expense must be explicitly included in the incremental cash flow analysis for a merger.

    a. True **b.** False

18. The holding company device can be used to take advantage of the principle of financial leverage. Thus, the holding company can control a great deal of assets with a limited amount of top-tier equity.

    a. True **b.** False

PROBLEMS

The following data apply to the next four problems.

TransCorp, a large conglomerate, is evaluating the possible acquisition of the Chip Company, a transistor manufacturer. TransCorp's analyst projects the following postmerger incremental cash flows (in millions of dollars):

	1996	1997	1998	1999
Net sales	$200	$230	$250	$270
Cost of goods sold	130	140	145	150
Selling/administrative expense	20	25	30	32
EBIT	$ 50	$ 65	$ 75	$ 88
Interest	10	12	13	14
EBT	$ 40	$ 53	$ 62	$ 74
Taxes	16	21	25	30
Net income	$ 24	$ 32	$ 37	$ 44
Retained earnings	12	13	14	15
Cash available to stockholders	$ 12	$ 19	$ 23	$ 29
Terminal value				400
Net CF	$ 12	$ 19	$ 23	$429

The acquisition, if made, would occur on January 1, 1996. All cash flows above are assumed to occur at end-of-year. Chip currently has a market value capital structure of 10 percent debt, but TransCorp would increase the debt to 50 percent if the acquisition were made. Chip, if independent, pays taxes at 30 percent, but its income would be taxed at 40 percent if consolidated. Chip's current market-determined beta is 1.80.

The cash flows above include the additional interest payments due to increased leverage and asset expansion, and the full taxes paid by TransCorp on the Chip income stream. Depreciation-generated funds would be used to replace worn-out equipment, so they would not be available to TransCorp's shareholders. Retained earnings would be used, in addition to new debt, to finance required asset expansion. Thus, the net cash flows are the flows that would accrue to TransCorp's stockholders. The risk-free rate is 10 percent and the market risk premium is 5 percent.

19. What is the appropriate discount rate for valuing the acquisition?

a. 10.00% **b.** 15.00% **c.** 19.00% **d.** 21.75% **e.** 23.35%

20. What is the value (in millions of dollars) of the Chip Company to TransCorp?

a. $197.73 **b.** $206.42 **c.** $219.78 **d.** $322.85 **e.** $429.00

21. Chip has 5 million shares outstanding. Chip's current market price is $32.50. What is the maximum price per share that TransCorp should offer?

a. $32.50 **b.** $37.50 **c.** $41.37 **d.** $43.96 **e.** $46.93

22. TransCorp should offer Chip's stockholders $32.625 per share.

a. True **b.** False

ANSWERS

1. synergy
2. operating; financial
3. antitrust
4. horizontal; vertical
5. conglomerate
6. acquiring; target
7. management
8. tender offer; stockholders
9. operating; synergistic
10. Financial
11. capital budgeting
12. acquiring
13. joint venture
14. spinoff
15. 80; taxation; dividends

16. a. In a financial merger, no synergistic effects are anticipated.

17. a. The target firm generally has embedded debt that is being assumed by the acquiring firm. Since these costs are not marginal, they must be specifically included in the analysis.

18. a. This statement is true, but the leveraging which occurs in a holding company organization significantly increases the riskiness of the firm.

19. e. $$b_U = \frac{b_L}{1 + (1 - T)(D/E)} = \frac{1.80}{1 + (1 - 0.30)(0.1/0.9)} = \frac{1.80}{1.08} = 1.67.$$

$$b_L = b_U[1 + (1 - T)(D/E)] = 1.67[1 + (1 - 0.40)(0.5/0.5)]$$
$$= 1.67(1.6) = 2.67.$$

$$k_s = 10\% + 2.67(5\%) = 23.35\%.$$

20. c. $$V = \frac{\$12 \text{ million}}{(1.2335)^1} + \frac{\$19 \text{ million}}{(1.2335)^2} + \frac{\$23 \text{ million}}{(1.2335)^3} + \frac{\$429 \text{ million}}{(1.2335)^4} = \$219.78 \text{ million}.$$

21. d. \$219.78 million/5 million = \$43.96.

22. b. It does not make sense to offer Chip's shareholders just a little above the current market price. Not enough shares would be tendered to gain control, the expenses would be for nought, and other firms could be induced to make competing bids.

CHAPTER 25
CORPORATE RISK MANAGEMENT

OVERVIEW

Risk management can mean many things, but in business it generally involves the management of unpredictable events that have adverse financial consequences for the firm. Here, the term *management* implies reducing the consequences of risk to the point where there is no significant negative impact on the firm's financial well-being. Although we have not used the term "risk management" in previous chapters, it should be obvious that this is one of the financial manager's most important functions. We now turn to the basics of risk management along with some common risk management techniques.

KEY CONCEPTS

> Risk can be classified in many ways and different classifications are commonly used in different industries.

Here's one list that provides an idea of the wide variety of risks to which a firm can be exposed: speculative risks, pure risks, demand risks, input risks, financial risks, property risks, personnel risks, environmental risks, liability risks, and insurable risks.

> Firms often use the following three-step approach to risk management: (1) identify the risks faced by the firm, (2) measure the potential impact of the risks identified, and (3) decide how each relevant risk should be minimized.

There are several techniques to help minimize risk exposure:

- *Transfer the risk to an insurance company.* Often, it is advantageous to insure against, and hence transfer, a risk. However, insurability does not necessarily mean that a risk should be covered by insurance. Thus, it might be better for the company to *self-insure*, which means bearing the risk directly rather than paying to have another party bear the risk.

- *Transfer the function that produces the risk to a third party.* In some situations, risks can be reduced most easily by passing them on to some other company that is not an insurance company.
- *Reduce the probability of occurrence of an adverse event.* In some instances, it is possible to take action to reduce the probability that an adverse event will occur.
- *Reduce the magnitude of the loss associated with an adverse event.*
- *Totally avoid the activity that gives rise to the risk.*

Risk management decisions, like all corporate decisions, should include a rigorous cost/benefit analysis for each feasible alternative. The same financial management techniques that are applied to other corporate decisions also can be applied to risk management decisions.

Insurance is one of the cornerstones of risk management. There are four basic characteristics of insurance: (1) pooling of losses, (2) payment for random losses only, (3) risk transfer, and (4) indemnification.

The *pooling,* or *sharing, of losses* is the heart of insurance. *Pooling* means that losses are spread over a large group of policyholders, so that each policyholder realizes the average loss of the pool rather than its own actual loss. Thus, it involves the grouping of a large number of homogeneous *exposure units* so that the law of large numbers can apply.

A *random loss* is a loss that is unexpected and occurs as a result of chance. Insurance is based on the premise that payments are made only for losses that are random.

Risk transfer means that the risk is transferred from the insured to the insurer, which, because of the law of large numbers, can reasonably forecast the losses expected and cover them with the premiums collected.

Indemnification for losses provides that the insured is reimbursed if a loss occurs.

The very presence of insurance reduces the incentives for the insured party to avoid the loss. This basic characteristic of insurance highlights the *moral hazard* problem.

Insurance companies try to modify the behavior of policyholders through their pricing structures and contractual provisions. For example, if the insurer can monitor a company's loss prevention efforts, it can structure the premium to reflect the degree of effort.

Often, insurance companies will require customers to take certain actions before a policy will be written.

The problem of moral hazard stems primarily from asymmetric information; the insurer cannot easily monitor all actions taken by companies to prevent losses.

From the policyholders' standpoint, the moral hazard problem is merely an application of rational financial behavior -- companies will consider the financial rewards of lower premiums when assessing the value of any costly loss prevention program.

The problem of *adverse selection* also stems from information asymmetries. Adverse selection means that those potential policyholders who are most likely to experience losses will purchase insurance, whereas those that are least likely to incur losses will self-insure.

Insurance companies attempt to deal with the adverse selection problem by underwriting provisions, which control the selection and classification of candidates for insurance.

At one extreme, insurance companies could offer the same premium for each company regardless of its own risk characteristics. This type of underwriting policy can exist only in situations where the insurance is provided under government controls, such as currently exists for flood insurance. At the other extreme, if no information asymmetries existed and hence perfect information were available, insurance companies could segregate policyholders into a large number of risk groups and charge a premium to the members of each group on the basis of that group's expected losses over the coming year.

Competition among insurers, as well as the availability of information on loss experience, helps reduce the adverse selection problem.

Risk identification and measurement involves systematically and continuously identifying the potential losses confronting the firm, and then measuring these potential losses by estimating their likelihoods of occurrence and loss potentials.

Most corporate risk managers use a prepared checklist to identify risks; smaller firms often rely on risk management services of insurance companies to identify and measure the risks that they face.

After the risks have been identified, it is necessary to measure the firm's degree of exposure to each risk. This involves estimating *loss frequency* (the probability of a loss) and *loss severity* (the dollar value of each loss).

- In general, loss exposure is more a function of the severity of losses than of their frequency. A risk with the potential of a catastrophic loss, even though its frequency is rare, is far more serious than a risk that is expected to produce frequent but small losses.
- Two approaches to measuring loss severity include (1) the maximum loss approach and (2) the average loss approach. The *maximum loss* is the dollar loss associated with the worst-case scenario, while the *average loss* is the average dollar loss associated with a particular peril.

Property loss exposures involve both real property (land and buildings) and personal property.

Physical, social, and economic perils are the three categories most commonly associated with property losses.

Direct losses to property occur when it is destroyed, damaged, or lost. *Indirect* losses stem from direct loss: for example, the loss of profits during the time when fire damage is being repaired.

To measure a firm's potential exposure to property losses, the risk manager must attach a value to the firm's property. Property appraisers utilize several standards of measurement for assigning property values:

- *Original cost* is the dollar cost at acquisition.
- *Book value* is the original cost less the accumulated depreciation.
- *Market value* is the current value of an asset as set by supply and demand conditions in the marketplace.
- *Tax appraisal value* is often set at less than true market value to reduce valuation appeals.
- *Economic value* is the present value of the cash flows that it is expected to produce.
- *Replacement value* is the cost to replace the property at the time of the appraisal.

In general, property loss exposures are managed either by retaining the risk or by passing it to an insurer.

Businesses also face *liability loss exposure.* The term liability involves the concept of a penalty that can be imposed when a responsibility is not met. Companies risk liability losses through five categories of exposure: *bailee exposure, ownership exposure, business operation exposure, employee actions exposure,* and *professional exposure.*

A business may enter into a transaction called a *bailment*, in which a business takes possession of another's property to perform some service, and then returns the property to the owner. Businesses that act as *bailees*, then, must be fully aware of the liability exposure that such arrangements create.

Ownership of real and personal property brings with it significant liability exposure. For example, injuries that occur on a firm's real property or as a result of its personal property may give rise to liability losses.

Liability exposure that arises from business operations is often the most critical exposure that firms face. It can include the following types:

- *Nuisance* exposure involves activities, such as environmental pollution, which can harm third parties.
- *Patent and copyright infringement* are violations of invention or creative work protection laws.
- *Unfair trade practices* also create the potential for large liability exposures.
- *Product liability* stems from defects in the firm's goods and services provided.

Improper actions of employees, such as sexual harassment, is another type of liability exposure.

Professional liability can impact firms that provide services requiring advance training and licensing. The cost and number of malpractice lawsuits have increased dramatically in recent years.

Diversification is one of the most effective risk management techniques. Diversifying a company's product line and planning and reacting quickly to global uncertainties are effective strategies to reducing risk exposure.

Firms are subject to numerous risk exposures due to price fluctuations in the financial markets. There are a number of ways to limit *financial loss exposure.*

Price risk and reinvestment rate risk exposure can subject firms to financial losses. *Price risk* is the risk that the price of a debt security will fall as a result of increases in interest rates, and *reinvestment rate risk* is the risk of earning a return less than expected when debt principal or interest payments are reinvested at rates less than the yield to maturity.

- If interest rates *fall*, and the portfolio is invested in relatively short-term bonds, then the reinvestment rate penalty exceeds the capital gains, so a net shortfall occurs.
- If interest rates *rise*, and the portfolio is invested in relatively short-term bonds, then gains from high reinvestment rates will more than offset capital losses, and the final portfolio value will exceed the required amount.

Zero coupon bonds and stripped Treasuries can be used to eliminate reinvestment rate risk.

Bond portfolios can be *immunized* against price and reinvestment rate risk. The immunization process involves selecting maturities for the bonds in a portfolio such that gains or losses from reinvestment exactly match gains or losses from price changes.

One of the most useful tools for reducing both *security and commodity price exposure* is to *hedge* in the futures markets.

- *Futures*, or *futures contracts*, call for the purchase or sale of a financial or real asset at some future date, but at a price which is fixed today.
- When futures contracts are purchased, the purchaser does not have to put up the full amount of the purchase price; rather, the purchaser is required to post an initial *margin*. However, investors are required to maintain a certain value in the margin account, called a maintenance margin.
- An *option* is similar to a futures contract, but it merely gives someone the right to buy (call) or sell (put) an asset, but the holder of the option does not have to complete the transaction.

Firms are exposed to price losses when securities are being issued and when securities are held as part of investment portfolios. In addition, firms are exposed to risk when floating rate debt is used to finance an investment that has a more-or-less fixed income stream. These types of risk can be reduced by using *derivatives*, which are securities whose values stem, or are derived, from the values of other assets. *Futures and swaps* are two types of derivatives used to manage security price exposure.

- *Futures markets* are used for both speculation and hedging: *Speculation* involves betting on future price movements; *hedging* is done by a firm or individual engaged in a business where a price change could negatively affect profits.

- The futures and options markets permit flexibility in the timing of financial transactions, because the firm can be protected partially against changes that occur between the present and the time when a particular transaction will be completed.
- Firms must weigh the benefit versus the cost of the commissions plus the opportunity cost of the margin money.

- A *swap* is another method for reducing financial risks. It is an exchange of cash payment obligations, in which each party to the swap prefers the payment type or pattern of the other party.
- Although the corporate use of derivatives to hedge risk is a relatively new phenomenon, it has caught on like wild fire. In fact, about 90 percent of the largest 200 companies in the U.S. currently use derivatives on a regular basis.
  - There is, however, a downside to derivatives: Problems can quickly arise when hedges are improperly constructed or when corporate managers, eager to boost profits, use derivatives for speculation rather than hedging.
  - While the use of derivatives to hedge risk is an important tool for risk managers, if used improperly, derivatives have the potential to create very large losses in very short periods.

DEFINITIONAL QUESTIONS

1. _________ _____________ generally involves the management of unpredictable events that have adverse financial consequences for the firm.

2. Firms often use a three-step approach to risk management: (1) _________ the risks faced by the firm, (2) __________ the potential impact of the risks identified, and (3) decide how each relevant risk should be ____________.

3. ________-_________ means bearing the risk directly rather than paying to have another party bear the risk.

4. Risk management decisions, like all corporate decisions, should include a rigorous _______/__________ analysis for each feasible alternative.

5. __________ is one of the cornerstones of risk management. It has four basic characteristics: (1) _________ of losses, (2) payment for _________ losses only, (3) _______ __________, and (4) ________________.

6. _______________ for losses provides that the insured is reimbursed if a loss occurs.

7. The very presence of insurance reduces the incentives for the insured party to avoid a loss. This is referred to as the __________ __________ problem.

8. ________ ________ means that those potential policyholders who are most likely to experience losses will purchase insurance, whereas those that are least likely to incur losses will self-insure.

9. After the risks have been identified, it is necessary to measure the firm's degree of exposure to each risk. This involves estimating loss __________ (the probability of a loss) and loss ___________ (the dollar value of each loss).

10. There are two approaches to measuring loss severity: (1) the __________ __________ approach and (2) the ___________ ___________ approach.

11. ___________ losses to property occur when it is destroyed, damaged, or lost.

12. ________ _________ represents the present value of the cash flows the property is expected to produce, while _________ __________ represents the current value of an asset as set by supply and demand conditions.

13. ____________ involves the concept of a penalty that can be imposed when a responsibility is not met. Companies risk this type of loss through five categories of exposure: _________ exposure, __________ exposure, business operation exposure, employee actions exposure, and _________ exposure.

14. ____________ is one of the most effective risk management techniques.

15. The _____________ process involves selecting maturities for the bonds in a portfolio such that gains or losses from reinvestment exactly match gains or losses from price changes.

16. Futures markets are used for both hedging and speculation: _________ involves betting on future price movements, while ___________ is done by a firm or individual engaged in a business where a price change could negatively affect profits.

17. ___________ are securities whose values stem, or are derived, from the values of other assets.

18. A(n) ____________ is an exchange of cash payment obligations, in which each party to the transaction prefers the payment type or pattern of the other party.

Conceptual Questions

19. Speculative risks are risks that offer the chance of a gain as well as a loss, while pure risks are those which can only lead to losses.

a. True **b.** False

20. If a large disaster occurs, and an insurance company is not well capitalized and diversified, there is some chance that the company will not be able to pay all valid claims against it. This risk to the policyholders is known as the adverse selection problem.

a. True **b.** False

21. Immunization is the process of eliminating, or at least minimizing, a bond portfolio's interest rate (price) risk and reinvestment rate risk. The process involves selecting securities such that the duration of each security in the portfolio matches the due date of some future cash outflow.

a. True **b.** False

22. The two basic types of hedges involving the futures market are long hedges and short hedges, where the words "long" and "short" refer to the maturity of the hedging instrument. For example, a long hedge might use stocks, while a short hedge might use 3-month T-bills.

a. True **b.** False

23. Which of the following statements about adverse selection is most correct?

a. Adverse selection means that those potential policyholders that are most likely to experience losses will purchase insurance, while those that are least like to experience losses will not purchase insurance.
b. Insurance companies can eliminate the adverse selection problem by charging all policyholders the same premium.
c. The underlying cause of adverse selection is information asymmetries between insurers and policyholders.
d. Insurance companies attempt to control the adverse selection problem by using underwriting provisions.
e. Statements a, c, and d are all correct.

24. Which of the following statements about liability loss exposure, if any, is incorrect?

a. The liability exposure that arises from business operations is often the most critical exposure that firms face.
b. Professional liability applies to doctors, lawyers, and other service providers that require advance training and licensing.
c. Liability exposures are typically handled by either self-insuring or passing the risk to an insurance company.
d. Bailment is the act of taking possession of personal property owned by another person or business and performing some service on that property.
e. Companies that do not produce consumer products have minimal liability exposure.

25. A swap is a method for reducing financial risk. Which of the following statements about swaps, if any, is incorrect?

a. A swap involves the exchange of cash payment obligations.
b. The earliest swaps were currency swaps, in which companies traded debt denominated in different currencies, say dollars and pounds.
c. Swaps are generally arranged by a financial intermediary, who may or may not take the position of one of the counterparties.
d. A problem with swaps is the lack of standardized contracts, which limits the development of a secondary market.
e. All of the above statements are correct.

26. Which of the following statements about interest rate and reinvestment rate risk is correct?

a. Variable, or floating rate, securities have a high degree of interest rate (price) risk.
b. Price risk occurs because fixed-rate debt securities lose value when interest rates rise, while reinvestment rate risk is the risk of earning less than expected when interest payments or debt principal are reinvested.
c. Reinvestment rate risk can be eliminated by purchasing zero coupon bonds.
d. Reinvestment rate risk can be eliminated by purchasing variable, or floating, rate bonds.
e. Statements b and c are both correct.

PROBLEMS

27. What is the duration of a 5-year zero coupon bond?

a. 0 years **b.** 5 years **c.** 10 years **d.** undefined **e.** infinity

28. What is the approximate duration of an 8 percent, 3-year, annual coupon bond selling at its $1,000 par value?

a. 2 years **b.** 2.2 years **c.** 2.5 years **d.** 2.8 years **e.** 3.0 years

ANSWERS

1. Risk management
2. identify; measure; minimized
3. Self-insure
4. cost/benefit
5. Insurance; pooling; random; risk transfer; indemnification
6. Indemnification
7. moral hazard
8. Adverse selection
9. frequency; severity
10. maximum loss; average loss
11. Direct
12. Economic value; market value
13. Liability; bailee; ownership; professional
14. Diversification
15. immunization
16. speculation; hedging
17. Derivatives
18. swap

19. a. This statement correctly defines speculative and pure risks.

20. b. The adverse selection problem means that those potential policyholders who are most likely to incur losses will purchase insurance, whereas those that are least likely to incur losses will self-insure.

21. a. This statement is correct.

22. b. Long hedges are futures contracts bought to guard against price increases, while short hedges are futures contracts sold to guard against price declines.

23. e.

24. e. Liability involves the concept of a penalty that can be imposed when a responsibility is not met. Thus, it has broad encompassing effects.

25. d.

26. e.

27. b. For a zero coupon bond, duration is the same as maturity.

28. d.

t	CF	PVCF	PVCF/V	t(PVCF/V)
1	$80.00	$74.07	0.0741	0.0741
2	80.00	68.59	0.0686	0.1372
3	1,080.00	857.34	0.8573	2.5720
			Duration =	2.7833 ≈ 2.8.

CHAPTER 26
BANKRUPTCY, REORGANIZATION, AND LIQUIDATION

OVERVIEW

The financial manager of a failing firm must know how to ward off his or her firm's total collapse and thereby reduce its losses. The ability to hang on during rough times often means the difference between the firm's forced liquidation versus its rehabilitation and eventual success. At the same time, an understanding of business failures and bankruptcies, their causes, and their possible remedies is also important to financial managers of successful firms, because they must know their firms' rights when their customers or suppliers go bankrupt.

KEY CONCEPTS

Financial distress experienced by firms can range from a vague uneasiness about future profitability to complete disintegration of the firm. Common definitions of financial distress include the following:

Economic failure signifies that a firm's revenues do not cover its total costs, including its cost of capital. These firms can keep on operating as long as investors are willing to provide additional capital and their owners are willing to accept below-market rates of return.

Business failure is a term used by Dun & Bradstreet to define a business that has terminated operations *with a resultant loss to creditors,* regardless of whether the firm has entered formal bankruptcy proceedings.

A firm is considered *technically insolvent* if it cannot meet its current obligations as they fall due. Technical insolvency may denote a temporary lack of liquidity.

A firm is *insolvent in bankruptcy* when its book value of total liabilities exceeds the true market value of its assets. This is a more serious condition than technical insolvency because it is a sign of economic failure, and it often leads to liquidation of the business.

Legal bankruptcy occurs when the firm has filed for bankruptcy under federal law.

> A number of factors combine to cause business failures. Case studies show that financial difficulties are usually the result of a series of errors, misjudgments, and interrelated weaknesses that can be attributed directly or indirectly to management, and signs of potential financial distress are generally evident before the firm actually fails.

Although bankruptcies are more common among smaller firms, it is clear that large firms are not immune.

Government and industry seek to avoid failure among larger firms for many reasons. For financial institutions the reason is to prevent an erosion of confidence and a consequent run on the banks. The fact that bankruptcy is a very expensive process gives private industry strong incentives to avoid outright bankruptcy.

> Financial distress begins when a debtor is unable to meet scheduled payments to creditors or when the firm's cash flow projections indicate that it will soon be unable to do so.

Several questions arise as to how a firm should proceed:

- Is the situation temporary or a permanent problem?
- If temporary, can an agreement with creditors be worked out? If permanent, who should bear the losses?
- Is the company "worth more dead than alive"?
- Should the firm file for bankruptcy or should it use informal procedures?
- Who should control the firm while it is being liquidated or rehabilitated?

Because of the high costs of formal bankruptcy, it is often desirable to reorganize or liquidate a firm outside formal bankruptcy through use of informal settlements.

Informal reorganization can be used in the case of an economically sound company in temporary distress. Voluntary plans, called *workouts,* usually require some type of *restructuring* of the firm's debt, because current cash flows are insufficient to service the current debt structure.

- A debt restructuring begins with a meeting between the failing firm's managers and creditors. An *adjustment bureau* run by the creditor managers' association often arranges the meeting. A great deal of negotiation is involved to reach a final debt restructuring agreement.
- Creditors often prefer an *extension* because it promises eventual payment in full. They may also agree to accept a lower interest rate on loans during the extension.
- In a *composition*, creditors agree to reduce their fixed claims on the debtor.
- Such voluntary settlements are not only informal and simple but also relatively inexpensive because legal and administrative expenses are held to a minimum. Creditors often recover more money, and sooner, than if the firm were to file for bankruptcy.
- Perhaps the biggest problem in informal reorganizations is in getting all the parties to agree to the voluntary plan. This problem is called the *holdout problem.*

Informal liquidation is the result of determining that a firm is more valuable dead than alive. *Assignment* is an informal procedure for liquidating a firm, and it usually yields creditors a larger amount than they would receive in a formal bankruptcy liquidation. In an assignment, the title to the debtor's assets is transferred to a third party, known as an assignee or trustee, who is instructed to liquidate the assets through a private sale or public auction, and then to distribute the proceeds among the creditors on a pro rata basis. Assignments are feasible only if the firm is small and its affairs are not too complex.

- An assignment does not automatically result in a full and legal discharge of all the debtor's liabilities, nor does it protect the creditors against fraud.

A firm is officially bankrupt when it files for bankruptcy with a federal court. Formal bankruptcy proceedings are designed to protect both the firm and its creditors. Chapter 11 of the 1978 Bankruptcy Reform Act deals with business reorganization.

If the problem is technical insolvency, then the firm may use bankruptcy proceedings to gain time to solve its cash flow problems without foreclosure by its creditors.

If the firm is bankrupt in the sense that liabilities exceed assets, the creditors can use bankruptcy procedures to attempt to ensure that the firm's owners do not siphon off assets which should go to creditors.

Bankruptcy law is flexible, and it provides much scope for negotiations between a company and its creditors and stockholders.

Two problems often arise to stymie informal reorganizations and thus force debtors into Chapter 11 bankruptcy.

The *common pool problem* occurs because individual creditors have an incentive to foreclose on the firm even though the firm is worth more collectively as an ongoing concern. A solution to the common pool problem is the Chapter 11 *automatic stay provision*, which limits the ability of creditors to foreclose unilaterally on the debtor to collect their individual claims.

The *holdout problem* can also make it difficult to reorganize a firm's debts. If all creditors agreed to a reorganization plan, it would benefit the creditors and the firm simultaneously. However, there is an advantage for a creditor to "hold out" since his or her claim would be higher than that of those who would agree to a lower settlement. Thus, it is likely that none of the creditors would accept the offer. Because of this problem, it is easier for a firm with few creditors to informally reorganize than it is for a firm with many creditors.

While bankruptcy gives the firm a chance to work out its problems without the threat of creditor foreclosure, it does not give the debtor free reign over the firm's assets. Fraudulent conveyance statutes protect creditors from unjustified transfers of property by a firm in financial distress.

In bankruptcy, it is much easier to gain acceptance of a reorganization plan, because the bankruptcy court will lump the creditors into classes.

A *cramdown* is a procedure in which the court mandates a reorganization plan in spite of dissent. The ability of the court to force acceptance of a reorganization plan greatly reduces the incentive for creditors to hold out.

Filing for bankruptcy under Chapter 11 has several benefits besides automatic stay and cramdown that are not inherent in informal restructurings.

Interest and principal payments may be delayed without penalty until a reorganization plan is approved.

The firm is permitted to issue *debtor in possession (DIP) financing* which enhances the ability of the firm to borrow funds for short-term liquidity purposes, because such loans are senior to all other unsecured debt, regardless of the provisions in those contracts.

The debtor firm's managers are given the exclusive right for 120 days after filing to submit a reorganization plan, plus another 60 days to obtain agreement on the plan from the parties affected.

The primary role of the bankruptcy court in a reorganization is to determine the *fairness* and the *feasibility* of proposed plans of reorganization.

The *fairness doctrine* states that claims must be recognized in the order of their legal and contractual priority.

The primary test of *feasibility* in a reorganization is whether the fixed charges after reorganization will be adequately covered by earnings.

Recently a new type of reorganization called *prepackaged bankruptcy* combines the advantages of both the informal workout and formal Chapter 11 reorganization. Here the debtor firm gets all, or most of, the creditors to agree to the reorganization plan prior to filing for bankruptcy. Then, a reorganization plan is filed along with the bankruptcy petition.

The three primary advantages of a prepackaged bankruptcy are (1) reduction of the holdout problem, (2) preserving creditors' claims, and (3) taxes.

If a company is "too far gone" to be reorganized, then it must be *liquidated.*

Liquidation should occur when the business is worth more dead than alive, or when the possibility of restoring the firm to financial health is so remote that the creditors run a higher risk of greater loss if operations are continued.

Chapter 7 of the Federal Bankruptcy Reform Act addresses three important problems during a liquidation:

- It provides safeguards against fraud by the debtor.
- It provides for an equitable distribution of the debtor's assets among the creditors.
- It allows insolvent debtors to discharge all their obligations and thus be able to start new businesses unhampered by the burden of prior debt.

The distribution of assets in a liquidation under Chapter 7 is governed by the following priority of claims: (1) Secured creditors, (2) trustee's costs, (3) expenses incurred after an involuntary case has begun but before a trustee is appointed, (4) wages due workers if earned within 3 months prior to filing the bankruptcy petition, (5) claims for unpaid contributions to employee pension plans, (6) unsecured claims for customer deposits, (7) taxes due, (8) unfunded pension plan liabilities, (9) general (unsecured) creditors, (10) preferred stockholders, and (11) common stockholders.

> Normally, bankruptcy proceedings originate after a company cannot meet its current obligations. However, bankruptcy law also permits a company to file for bankruptcy if its financial forecasts indicate that a continuation of current conditions would lead to insolvency.

> Many critics today claim that current bankruptcy laws are not doing what they were intended to do.

Before 1978, most bankruptcies ended quickly in liquidation. Then, Congress rewrote the laws giving companies more opportunity to stay alive, believing that this was best for managers, employees, creditors, and stockholders.

Critics believe that bankruptcy is good business for consultants, lawyers, and investment bankers, who reap hefty fees during bankruptcy proceedings, and for managers, who continue to collect their salaries and bonuses as long as the business is kept alive.

Bankruptcy cases can drag on in court for many years, depleting assets that could be sold to pay off creditors and shareholders. In effect, critics say, maintaining companies on life support does not serve the interests of the parties that bankruptcy laws were meant to protect.

> *Multiple Discriminant Analysis (MDA)* is a statistical tool which can predict the possibility of bankruptcy, thus allowing firms to take steps to avoid bankruptcy or at least reduce its impact. MDA uses a set of economic variables, such as the current ratio and debt ratio, to establish the possibility of failure.

In a classic paper, Edward Altman applied MDA to a sample of corporations, and he developed the following discriminant function:

$$Z = 0.012X_1 + 0.014X_2 + 0.033X_3 + 0.006X_4 + 0.999X_5.$$

- Here, X_1 = net working capital divided by total assets; X_2 = retained earnings divided by total assets; X_3 = EBIT divided by total assets; X_4 = market value of common and preferred stock divided by book value of debt; and X_5 = sales divided by total assets.
- Altman's *zone of ignorance* was from Z = 1.81 to Z = 2.99; and the higher the Z score, the lower the probability of bankruptcy.

DEFINITIONAL QUESTIONS

1. __________ __________ experienced by firms can range from a vague uneasiness about future profitability to complete disintegration of the firm.

2. ________ _________ signifies that a firm's revenues do not cover its total costs, including its cost of capital.

3. _________ ___________ is defined as any business that has terminated operations with a resultant loss to creditors, regardless of whether the firm has entered formal bankruptcy proceedings.

4. A firm is considered ________ ________ if it cannot meet its current obligations as they fall due.

5. ____________ ___________ can be used in the case of an economically sound company in temporary distress. Voluntary plans, called ________, usually require some type of restructuring of the firm's debt.

6. Creditors often prefer a(n) _____________ because it promises eventual payment in full.

7. In a(n) _____________, creditors agree to reduce their fixed claims on the debtor.

8. ______________ is an informal procedure for liquidating a firm, and it usually yields creditors a larger amount than they would receive in a formal bankruptcy liquidation.

9. Two problems often arise to stymie informal reorganizations and thus force debtors into formal Chapter 11 bankruptcy: the __________ __________ __________ and the ________ __________.

10. A(n) ____________ is a procedure in which the court mandates a reorganization plan in spite of dissent.

11. _________ ______ ____________ financing enhances the ability of the firm to borrow funds for short-term liquidity purposes, because such loans are senior to all other unsecured debt, regardless of the provisions in those contracts.

12. The __________ doctrine states that claims must be recognized in the order of their legal and contractual priority, while the primary test of __________ in a reorganization is whether the fixed charges after reorganization will be adequately covered by earnings.

13. ____________ _____________ __________ is a statistical tool which can predict the possibility of bankruptcy, thus allowing firms to take steps to avoid bankruptcy or at least reduce its impact.

CONCEPTUAL QUESTIONS

14. Economic failure is the term used by Dun & Bradstreet to define any business that has terminated operations with a resultant loss to creditors.

    a. True   b. False

15. A firm is insolvent in bankruptcy when its book value of total liabilities exceeds the true market value of its assets.

    a. True   b. False

16. Financial distress begins when a firm is unable to meet scheduled payments to creditors, not when the firm's cash flow projections indicate that it will soon be unable to do so.

    a. True   b. False

17. Bankruptcies are more common among larger firms than smaller firms.

a. True **b.** False

18. Informal reorganization can be used in the case of an economically sound company in temporary distress. One type of voluntary plan is called a workout.

a. True **b.** False

19. Which of the following statements is most *correct*?

a. In an extension, creditors voluntarily reduce their fixed claims on the debtor by accepting a lower principal amount, by reducing the interest rate on the debt, by accepting equity in place of debt, or by accepting some combination of these changes.
b. Technical insolvency occurs when a firm's book value of total liabilities exceeds the true market value of its assets.
c. Although many people use the term *bankruptcy* to refer to any firm that has "failed," a firm is not legally bankrupt unless it has filed for bankruptcy under federal law.
d. Both statements a and c are true.
e. All of the statements are false.

20. Which of the following statements is most *correct*?

a. The automatic stay provision provided for in Chapter 11 is only granted to certain debtors in bankruptcy. It limits the ability of creditors to foreclose unilaterally on the debtor to collect their individual claims and, as a result, it provides a solution to the holdout problem.
b. Fraudulent conveyance statutes, which are a part of debtor-creditor law in most states, protect creditors from unjustified transfers of property by a firm in financial distress.
c. In a cramdown, creditors postpone the dates of required interest or principal payments, or both.
d. The common pool problem occurs because individual creditors have an incentive to foreclose on the firm even though the firm is worth more collectively as an ongoing concern.
e. Both statements b and d are true.

21. Which of the following statements is most *correct*?

a. Chapter 11 of the Federal Bankruptcy Reform Act addresses liquidation, while Chapter 7 deals with business reorganization.
b. Preferred stockholders have priority over general, or unsecured, creditors in the distribution of claims in a liquidation.
c. In multiple discriminant analysis the higher the Z-score, the higher the probability of bankruptcy.
d. Multiple discriminant analysis is a statistical tool which can predict the possibility of bankruptcy, thus allowing firms to take steps to avoid bankruptcy or at least reduce its impact.
e. All of the above statements are true.

PROBLEMS

22. The Stanton Marble Company has the following balance sheet:

Current assets	$15,120	Accounts payable	$ 3,240
		Notes payable (to bank)	1,620
		Accrued taxes	540
		Accrued wages	540
		Total current liabilities	$ 5,940
Fixed assets	8,100	First mortgage bonds	2,700
		Second mortgage bonds	2,700
		Total mortgage bonds	$ 5,400
		Subordinated debentures	3,240
		Total long-term debt	$ 8,640
		Preferred stock	1,080
		Common stock	7,560
Total assets	$23,220	Total liabilities and equity	$23,220

The debentures are subordinated only to the notes payable. Suppose Stanton Marble goes bankrupt and is liquidated with $5,400 being received from the sale of the fixed assets, which were pledged as security for the first and second mortgage bonds, and $8,640 received from the sale of current assets. The trustee's costs total $1,440. How much will the holders of subordinated debentures receive?

a. $2,052 b. $2,448 c. $3,240 d. $2,709 e. $3,056

The following data apply to the next three problems.

The Lockwood Corporation's 1993 balance sheet and income statement are as follows (in millions of dollars). Lockwood and its creditors have agreed upon a voluntary reorganization plan. In this plan, each share of the $6 preferred will be exchanged for one share of $2.40 preferred with a par value of $37.50 plus one 8 percent subordinated income debenture with a par value of $75. The $10.50 preferred issue will be retired with cash.

Balance Sheet:

Current assets	$336	Current liabilities	$ 84
Net fixed assets	306	Advance payments	156
Goodwill	30	Reserves	12
		$6 preferred stock, $112.50 par value (2,400,000 shares)	270
		$10.50 preferred stock, no par, callable at $150 (120,000 shares)	18
		Common stock, $1.50 par value (12,000,000 shares)	18
		Retained earnings	114
Total assets	$672	Total claims	$672

Income Statement:

Net sales	$1,080.0
Operating expense	1,032.0
Net operating income	$ 48.0
Other income	6.0
EBT	$ 54.0
Taxes (50%)	27.0
Net income	$ 27.0
Dividends on $6 preferred	14.4
Dividends on $10.50 preferred	1.3
Income available to common stockholders	$ 11.3

23. What is the value (in millions of dollars) of total assets on the balance sheet?

a. $680 **b.** $620 **c.** $636 **d.** $654 **e.** $645

24. What is the value (in millions of dollars) of the new preferred stock?

a. $105 **b.** $90 **c.** $110 **d.** $80 **e.** $95

25. What is the net income available to common stockholders (in millions of dollars) after the proposed recapitalization takes place?

a. $17 b. $11 c. $14 d. $13 e. $16

The following data apply to the next six problems.

At the time it defaulted on its interest payments and filed for bankruptcy, the Southeastern Manufacturing Company (SMC) had the following balance sheet (in thousands of dollars). The court, after trying unsuccessfully to reorganize the firm, decided that the only recourse was liquidation under Chapter 7. Sale of the fixed assets, which were pledged as collateral to the mortgage bondholders, brought in $1,600,000, while the current assets were sold for another $800,000. Thus, the total proceeds from the liquidation sale were $2,400,000. Trustee's costs amounted to $200,000; no single worker was due more than $2,000 in wages; and there were no unfunded pension plan liabilities.

Current assets	$1,600	Accounts payable	$ 200
		Accrued taxes	160
		Accrued wages	120
		Notes payable	720
		Total current liabilities	$1,200
Net fixed assets	2,400	First mortgage bonds[a]	1,200
		Second mortgage bonds[a]	800
		Debentures	800
		Subordinated debentures[b]	400
		Common stock	200
		Retained earnings	(600)
Total assets	$4,000	Total claims	$4,000

[a]All fixed assets are pledged as collateral to the mortgage bonds.
[b]Subordinated to notes payable.

26. How much of the proceeds (in thousands of dollars) from the sale of assets remain to be distributed to general creditors after distribution to priority claimants?

a. $432 b. $500 c. $375 d. $300 e. $320

27. How much of the proceeds (in thousands of dollars) do the second mortgage holders receive after distribution to general creditors and subordination adjustments arc made?

a. $400 b. $451 c. $51 d. $375 e. $500

28. How much of the proceeds (in thousands of dollars) do the holders of the subordinated debentures receive after distribution to general creditors and subordination adjustments are made?

a. \$51 **b.** \$102 **c.** \$142 **d.** \$0 **e.** \$25

29. How much of the proceeds (in thousands of dollars) from the liquidation do the common stockholders receive?

a. \$0 **b.** \$51 **c.** \$25 **d.** \$102 **e.** \$142

30. SMC's EBIT was \$320,000 based on sales of \$4,800,000, and its common stock market value was \$800,000. What Z-score is obtained when using Altman's multiple discriminant function, $Z = 0.012X_1 + 0.014X_2 + 0.033X_3 + 0.006X_4 + 0.999X_5$.

a. 1.22 **b.** 1.72 **c.** 1.48 **d.** 1.33 **e.** 1.66

31. Assume that you used Altman's multiple discriminant function in Problem 30 and calculated a Z-score of 1.1. What does this score mean?

a. The Z-score falls in the zone of ignorance, which means that we are uncertain about how the firm should be classified.
b. Because the Z-score falls below 1.81, there is a likelihood that the firm will not go bankrupt: the lower the Z-score, the lower the probability of bankruptcy.
c. Because the Z-score falls below 1.81, there is a likelihood that the firm will go bankrupt: the higher the Z-score, the lower the probability of bankruptcy.
d. All the statements are false.

ANSWERS

1. Financial distress
2. Economic failure
3. Business failure
4. technically insolvent
5. Informal reorganization; workouts
6. extension
7. composition
8. Assignment
9. common pool problem; holdout problem
10. cramdown
11. Debtor in possession
12. fairness; feasibility
13. Multiple discriminant analysis

14. b. This is the definition for business failure, not economic failure.

15. a. This statement is correct.

16. b. Financial distress also begins when the firm's cash flow projections indicate that it will soon be unable to meet scheduled payments to creditors.

17. b. Just the reverse is true; however, large firms are not immune to bankruptcy.

18. a. This statement is correct.

19. c. Statement a is false; it describes a composition, not an extension. Statement b is false; a firm is considered technically insolvent if it cannot meet its current obligations as they fall due. Statement c is true. Thus, statements d and e are both incorrect.

20. e. Statement a is false; automatic stay is granted to all debtors in bankruptcy and it is a solution for the common pool problem. Statement b is true. Statement c describes an extension, not a cramdown. Statement d is true; thus, statement e is correct.

21. d. Statement a is false; the chapters have been reversed. Statement b is false; general, or unsecured, creditors have priority over preferred stockholders in the distribution of claims. Statement c is false; the higher the Z score, the lower the probability of bankruptcy. Statement d is true. Thus, statement e is false.

22. a.

Claimant	Claim Amount (1)	Priority Distribution and General Creditor (2)	Subordinate Adjustment (3)	Percent of Claim (4)
Accounts payable	$ 3,240	$ 2,448	$ 2,448	75.56%
Notes payable	1,620	1,224	1,620	100.00
Accrued taxes	540	540	540	100.00
Accrued wages	540	540	540	100.00
1st mortgage bonds	2,700	2,700	2,700	100.00
2nd mortgage bonds	2,700	2,700	2,700	100.00
Subordinated debentures	3,240	2,448	2,052	63.33
Preferred stock	1,080	0	0	0.00
Common stock	7,560	0	0	0.00
Trustee	1,440	1,440	1,440	100.00
Total	$24,660	$14,040	$14,040	56.93%

Explanation of the columns:

(1) Values are taken from the balance sheet.

(2) Since the firm's total debt obligations (including trustee costs) equals \$16,020 and only \$14,040 is received from the sale of assets, the preferred and common stockholders are wiped out. These stockholders receive nothing.

The \$5,400 from the sale of fixed assets is immediately allocated to the mortgage bonds. The holders of the first mortgage bonds are paid off first, so they receive \$2,700. The remaining \$2,700 from the sale of fixed assets is allocated to the second mortgage bonds, so these bondholders are also paid off.

By law, trustee expenses have first claim on the remaining available funds, wages have second priority, and taxes have third priority. Thus, these claims are paid in full.

We now have \$6,120 remaining and claims of \$8,100, so the general creditors will receive 75.56 cents on the dollar:

$$\frac{\text{Funds available}}{\text{Unsatisfied debt}} = \frac{\$14{,}040 - \$5{,}400 - \$1{,}080 - \$1{,}440}{\$3{,}240 + \$1{,}620 + \$3{,}240} = 0.7556.$$

General creditors are now initially allocated 75.56 percent of their original claims.

(3) This column reflects a transfer of funds from the subordinated debentures to the notes payable to the bank. Since subordinated debentures are subordinate to bank debt, notes payable to the bank must be paid in full before the debentures receive anything. The notes are paid in full by transferring the difference between their book value and initial allocation (\$1,620 − \$1,224 = \$396) from subordinated debentures to notes payable. This reduces the allocation to subordinated debentures and increases the allocation to notes payable by \$396.

23. d. The pro forma balance sheet follows (in millions of dollars):

Current assets[a]	\$318	Current liabilities	\$ 84
Net fixed assets	306	Advance payments	156
Goodwill	30	Reserves	12
		Subordinated debentures[b]	180
		\$2.40 preferred stock, \$37.50 par value (2,400,000 shares)[c]	90
		Common stock, \$1.50 par value (12,000,000 shares)	18
		Retained earnings	114
Total assets	\$654	Total claims	\$654

[a]\$336 million - \$18 million = \$318 million used to retire the \$10.50 preferred stock.
[b]2,400,000 shares × \$75 par value = \$180 million.
[c]2,400,000 shares × \$37.50 par value = \$90 million.

24. b. See the balance sheet shown in response to Problem 23.

25. c. The pro forma income statement (in millions of dollars) follows:

Net sales	$1,080.0
Operating expense	1,032.0
Net operating income	$ 48.0
Other income	6.0
EBIT	$ 54.0
Interest expense[a]	14.4
EBT	$ 39.6
Taxes (50%)	19.8
Net income	$ 19.8
Dividends on $2.40 preferred[b]	5.8
Income available to common stockholders	$ 14.0

[a]0.08($180 million par value) = $14.4 million.
[b]$2.40(2,400,000 shares) = $5.76 million ≈ $5.8 million.

26. e. Distribution to priority claimants (in thousands of dollars):

Proceeds from the sale of assets	$2,400
Less:	
1. First mortgage (paid from sale of fixed assets)	1,200
2. Second mortgage (paid from sale of fixed assets)	400
3. Fees and expenses of bankruptcy	200
4. Wages due to workers	120
5. Taxes due	160
Funds available for distribution to general creditors	$ 320

Distribution to general creditors (in thousands of dollars):

General Creditor Claims	Amount of Claim	Pro Rata Distribution[a]	Distrib. After Subord. Adj.[b]	% of Orig. Claim Received
Unsatisfied 2nd mortgage	$400	$ 51	$ 51	56[c]
Accounts payable	200	25	25	13
Notes payable	720	91	142	20
Debentures	800	102	102	13
Subord. debentures	400	51	0	0
Total	$2,520	$320	$320	

[a]Pro rata distribution: $320/$2,520 = 0.127 = 12.7%.
[b]Subordinated debentures are subordinated to notes payable. Unsatisfied portion of notes payable is greater than subordinated debenture distribution so subordinated debentures receive $0.

[c]Includes $400 from sale of fixed assets received in priority distribution.

27. b. See the distribution worksheet shown in response to Problem 26.

28. d. See the distribution worksheet shown in response to Problem 26.

29. a. Because the amount of funds available for distribution to general creditors is $320,000 and the total claims of these general creditors is $2,520,000, the common stockholders will receive nothing.

30. c. First, compute the five variables required in the Altman model (in thousands of dollars):

X_1 = Net working capital/Total assets = ($1,600 - $1,200)/$4,000 = 0.10 = 10%.

X_2 = Retained earnings/Total assets = -$600/$4,000 = -0.15 = -15%.

X_3 = EBIT/Total assets = $320/$4,000 = 0.08 = 8%.

X_4 = Market value of common and preferred stock/Book value of debt
= $800/$4,400 = 0.18 = 18%.

X_5 = Sales/Total assets = $4,800/$4,000 = 1.20.

Next, determine the Z-score:

$Z = 0.012(10) + 0.014(-15) + 0.033(8) + 0.006(18) + 0.999(1.2) = 1.48.$

31. c. Finally, compare the Z-score of 1.48 with Altman's standard:

Bankrupt	Zone of Ignorance	Nonbankrupt
1.81	2.99	

A Z-score of 1.48 indicates a likelihood of bankruptcy—the higher the Z-score, the lower the probability of bankruptcy.

CHAPTER 27
MULTINATIONAL FINANCIAL MANAGEMENT

OVERVIEW

As the world economy becomes more integrated, the role of multinational firms is increasing. Although the same basic principles of financial management apply to multinational corporations as well as to domestic ones, the financial managers of multinational firms face a much more complex task. The primary problem, from a financial standpoint, is the fact that the cash flows must cross national boundaries. These flows may be constrained in various ways, and, equally important, their values in dollars may rise or fall depending on exchange rate fluctuations. This means that the multinational financial manager must be constantly aware of the many complex interactions among national economies and their effects on international operations.

KEY CONCEPTS

A *multinational corporation* is one that operates in two or more countries. The growth of multinationals has greatly increased the degree of worldwide economic and political interdependence.

Companies, both U.S. and foreign, go "international" for six primary reasons:

- After a company has saturated its home market, growth opportunities are often better in foreign markets.
- Many of the present multinational firms began their international operations because raw materials were located abroad.
- Because no single nation holds a commanding advantage in all technologies, companies are scouring the globe for leading scientific and design ideas.
- Still other firms have moved their manufacturing facilities overseas to take advantage of cheaper production costs in low-cost countries.
- Firms can avoid political and regulatory hurdles by moving production to other countries.
- Finally, firms go international so that they can diversify and, consequently, cushion the impact of adverse economic trends in any single country.

The past decade has seen an increasing amount of investment in the U.S. by foreign corporations. This "reverse" investment has been growing at a higher rate than U.S. investment abroad. These developments suggest an increasing degree of mutual influence and interdependence among business enterprises and nations.

In theory, financial concepts and procedures are valid for both domestic and multinational operations. However, there are several factors which distinguish financial management as practiced by firms operating entirely within a single country from management by firms that operate in several different countries.

Cash flows will be denominated in different currencies, making exchange rate analysis necessary for all types of financial decisions.

Economic and legal differences among countries can cause significant problems when the corporation tries to coordinate and control worldwide operations of its subsidiaries.

The ability to communicate is critical in all business transactions. U.S. citizens are often at a disadvantage because they are generally fluent only in English.

Values and the role of business in society reflect the cultural differences that may vary dramatically from one country to the next.

Financial models based on the traditional assumption of a competitive marketplace must often be modified to include political (governmental) and other noneconomic facets of the decision.

Political risk, which is seldom negotiable and may be as extreme as *expropriation*, must be explicitly addressed in financial analysis.

An exchange rate specifies the number of units of a given currency that can be purchased for one unit of another currency.

An exchange rate listed as the number of U.S. dollars required to purchase one unit of foreign currency is called a *direct quotation*. The number of units of foreign currency that can be purchased for one U.S. dollar is called an *indirect quotation*. Normal practice in the U.S. is to use indirect quotations for all currencies *other than British pounds, for which direct quotations are given.*

Converting from one foreign currency to another foreign currency may require the use of *cross rates*. For example, if the direct quotation between pounds and dollars is \$1.7875 and the indirect quotation between francs and dollars is FF5.6344, the cross rate between pounds and francs can be calculated as follows:

$$\text{Cross rate} = \frac{\text{Dollars}}{\text{Pound}} \times \frac{\text{Francs}}{\text{Dollar}} = \frac{\text{Francs}}{\text{Pound}}$$
$$= 1.7875 \text{ dollars per pound} \times 5.6344 \text{ francs per dollar}$$
$$= 10.0715 \text{ francs per pound.}$$

The International Monetary Fund (IMF) was the center of a fixed exchange rate system that operated for 25 years after World War II.

Under this system, the U.S. dollar, which was linked to gold by a fixed price of $35 per ounce, was the base currency, and the relative values of all other currencies to the dollar were controlled within narrow limits, but then adjusted periodically.

- Currency fluctuations depend on supply and demand, capital movements, and the activities of international speculators. However, these fluctuations were kept within limits by the actions of the various central banks, which bought or sold currency to maintain specific prices.
- If a country *devalued* its currency, then fewer units of another currency would be required to buy one unit of the devalued currency. Its "price" would be reduced, making the country's goods cheaper and thus stimulating exports and discouraging imports. A country could devalue its currency only with the approval of the IMF.

In 1971, the *fixed exchange rate system* was replaced by a system under which the U.S. dollar was permitted to "float."

- A *floating exchange rate system* is one under which currency prices are allowed to reach their own levels without much governmental intervention.
- The present managed floating system permits currency rates to move without any specific limits, but central banks do buy and sell currencies to smooth out exchange rate fluctuations.

The inherent volatility of exchange rates under a floating system increases the uncertainty of the cash flows for a multinational corporation. This uncertainty is known as *exchange rate risk*, and it is a major factor differentiating the multinational corporation from a purely domestic one.

Not all currencies are *convertible*. A currency is convertible when the issuing nation allows it to be traded in the currency markets and is willing to redeem the currency at market rates. Lack of convertibility significantly inhibits the ability of a country to foster foreign investment.

The rate paid for delivery of currency no more than one day after the day of trade is called the *spot rate*.

Importers, exporters, and tourists, as well as governments, buy and sell currencies in the foreign exchange market, which consists of a network of brokers and banks based in New York, London, Tokyo, and other financial centers.

When currency is bought or sold and is to be delivered at some agreed-upon future date, usually 30, 90, or 180 days into the future, a *forward exchange rate* is used.

- If one can obtain more of the foreign currency for a dollar in the forward market than in the spot market, then the forward currency is less valuable than the spot currency, and the forward currency is said to be selling at a *discount.*
- If a dollar will buy fewer units of a currency in the forward market than in the spot market, then the forward currency is worth more dollars than the spot currency, and the forward currency is said to be selling at a *premium.*

Individuals and firms buy or sell forward currencies to *hedge* against unwanted changes in exchange rates by using *futures or forward contracts.*

Relative inflation rates have many implications for multinational financial decisions. Equally important, they have a dominant influence on relative interest rates as well as exchange rates.

A foreign currency on average will depreciate at a percentage rate approximately equal to the amount by which its country's inflation rate exceeds the U.S. inflation rate. Conversely, foreign currencies in countries with less inflation than the U.S. will, on average, appreciate relative to the U.S. dollar.

Countries experiencing higher rates of inflation tend to have higher interest rates.

Gains from borrowing in countries with low interest rates can be offset by losses from currency appreciation in those countries.

There exists a well-developed system of international capital markets.

Americans can invest in world markets by investing in the stock of U.S. multinational corporations or by buying the bonds and stocks of large corporations (or governments) headquartered outside the United States.

- Investment by U.S. firms in foreign operating assets is called *direct investment.*
- Investment in foreign stocks and bonds is called *portfolio investment.*

The *Eurodollar market* is essentially a short-term market for handling dollar-denominated loans and deposits made outside the United States.

- A *Eurodollar* is a U.S. dollar placed on deposit in a foreign (normally European) bank, including foreign branches of U.S. banks.

- The major difference between a dollar on deposit in Chicago and a dollar on deposit in London is the geographic location. The deposits do not involve different currencies, so exchange rate considerations do not apply. However, Eurodollars are outside the direct control of the U.S. monetary authorities, so U.S. banking regulations, such as fractional reserves and FDIC insurance premiums, do not apply.
- If interest rates in the United States are above Eurodollar rates, these funds will be sent back and invested in the United States, while if Eurodollar deposit rates are significantly above U.S. interest rates, more dollars will be sent out of the United States.
- Interest rates on Eurodollar deposits (and loans) are tied to a standard rate known as the *London Interbank Offered Rate (LIBOR)*, the rate of interest offered by the largest and strongest London banks on dollar deposits of significant size.

Two international bond markets have developed which trade in long-term funds.

- *Foreign bonds* are bonds sold by a foreign borrower but denominated in the currency of the country in which the issue is sold.
- *Eurobonds* are bonds sold in a country other than the one in whose currency the issue is denominated.

More and more, European financial transactions are being made in *European currency units*, or *ECUs*, units of account that are made up of the currencies of the twelve countries that belong to the European monetary system.

In addition to direct listing, U.S. investors can invest in foreign companies through *American depository receipts (ADRs)*, which are certificates representing ownership of foreign stock held in trust.

New issues of stock are sold in international markets for a variety of reasons.

- Firms are able to tap a much larger source of capital than their home countries.
- Firms want to create an equity market presence to accompany operations in foreign countries.
- Large multinational companies also occasionally issue new stock simultaneously in multiple countries.

There are several important differences in capital budgeting analysis of foreign versus domestic operations.

Cash flow analysis is much more complex for overseas investments.

- Usually a firm will organize a separate subsidiary in each foreign country in which it operates.

- Any dividends or royalties repatriated by the subsidiary must be converted to the currency of the parent company and thus are subject to exchange rate fluctuations.
- Dividends and royalties received are normally taxed by both foreign and domestic governments.
- Some governments place restrictions, or exchange controls, on the amount of cash that may be remitted to the parent company in order to encourage reinvestment of earnings in the foreign country.
- The only relevant cash flows for analysis of an international investment are the financial cash flows that the subsidiary can legally send back to the parent.

The cost of capital may be higher for foreign investments because they may be riskier than domestic investments.

- *Exchange risk* refers to the fact that exchange rates may fluctuate, increasing the uncertainty about cash flows to the parent company.
- *Political risk* refers to the possibility of *expropriation* and to restrictions on cash flows to the parent company.

Political risk premiums are not added to the cost of capital to adjust for this risk. If a company's management has a serious concern that a given country might expropriate foreign assets, it simply will not make significant investments in that country.

Companies can take steps to reduce the potential loss from expropriation in three major ways: (1) by financing the subsidiary with local capital, (2) by structuring operations so that the subsidiary has value only as a part of the integrated corporate system, and (3) by obtaining insurance against economic losses from expropriation.

Significant differences have been observed in the capital structures of U.S. corporations in comparison to their German and Japanese counterparts. An analysis of both bankruptcy and equity reporting costs leads to the conclusion that U.S. firms use more equity and less debt than firms in Japan and Germany.

The objectives of working capital management in the multinational corporation are similar to those in the domestic firm, but the task is more complex.

The objectives of cash management in the multinational corporation are to speed up collections and to slow disbursements, to shift cash rapidly from those parts of the business that do not need it to those parts that do, and to obtain the highest possible risk-adjusted rate of return on temporary cash balances. The same general procedures are used by multinational firms as those used by domestic firms, but because of longer distances and more serious mail delays, lockbox systems and electronic funds transfers are especially important.

Granting credit is more risky in an international context because, in addition to the normal risks of default, the multinational corporation must also worry about exchange rate changes between the time a sale is made and the time a receivable is collected. Credit policy is generally more important for a multinational firm than for a domestic firm.

- Much of the U.S.'s trade is with poorer, less-developed countries; thus, granting credit is generally a necessary condition for doing business.
- Nations whose economic health depends upon exports often help their manufacturing firms compete internationally by granting credit to foreign countries.

The physical location of inventories is a complex consideration for the multinational firm. The multinational firm must weigh a strategy of keeping inventory concentrated in a few areas from which they can be shipped, and thus minimize the total amount of inventory needed to operate the global business, with the possibility of delays in getting goods from central locations to user locations around the world. Exchange rates, import/export quotas, the threat of expropriation, and taxes all influence inventory policy.

DEFINITIONAL QUESTIONS

1. The ___________ ______ determines the number of units of one currency that can be exchanged for another.

2. International financial transactions were carried out under a(n) ______ _____________ _______ system from the end of World War II until 1971.

3. The organization which controlled the fixed exchange rate system was the _________ ___________ ______, which served as a world central bank.

4. Under the fixed rate system, the relative values of various currencies were based on the _____ _____ ______________, and were controlled within narrow limits, but then adjusted periodically.

5. Countries with export surpluses and a strong currency might have to ________ their currencies upward.

6. In 1971, the ___________ rate system was replaced by one that permitted the U.S. dollar to __________ against other currencies.

7. Evaluation of foreign investments involves the analysis of dividend and royalty cash flows that are _______________ to the parent company.

8. Some foreign governments restrict, or block, the amount of income that can be repatriated to encourage ______________ in the foreign country.

9. __________ risk refers to the possibility of restrictions on cash flows or the outright _________________ of property by a foreign government.

10. A dollar deposited in a non-U.S. bank is often called a(n) ___________.

11. Firms can hedge against exchange rate movements by buying or selling _________ or __________ contracts.

12. Investment by U.S. firms in foreign operations is called ___________ investment, while the purchase of foreign bonds and stock by U.S. citizens or firms is called ___________ investment.

13. __________ bonds are bonds sold by a foreign borrower but denominated in the currency of the country in which the issue is sold.

CONCEPTUAL QUESTIONS

14. Financial analysis is not able to take into account political risk.

a. True **b.** False

15. When a central bank of a country buys and sells its currency to smooth out fluctuations in the exchange rate, the system is referred to as a managed floating system.

a. True **b.** False

16. A foreign currency will, on average, appreciate at a percentage rate approximately equal to the amount by which its inflation rate exceeds the inflation rate in the United States.

a. True **b.** False

17. The cost of capital is generally lower for a foreign project than for an equivalent domestic project since the possibility of exchange gains exists.

a. True **b.** False

18. Which of the following statements concerning multinational cash flow analysis is *not* correct?

a. The relevant cash flows are the dividends and royalties repatriated to the parent company.
b. The cash flows must be converted to the currency of the parent company and, thus, are subject to future exchange rate changes.
c. Dividends and royalties received are normally taxed only by the government of the country in which the subsidiary is located.
d. Foreign governments may restrict the amount of the cash flows that may be repatriated.

PROBLEMS

19. The "spot rate" for Greek drachmas is 0.0313 U.S. dollars per drachma. What would the exchange rate be expressed in drachmas per dollar?

a. 0.0313 drachmas per dollar
b. 3.1300 drachmas per dollar
c. 31.9489 drachmas per dollar
d. 319.4890 drachmas per dollar
e. 400.0000 drachmas per dollar

20. The U.S. dollar can be exchanged for 942.1432 Italian lire today. The Italian currency is expected to appreciate by 10 percent tomorrow. What is the expected exchange rate tomorrow expressed in lire per dollar?

a. 836.1935 lire per dollar
b. 841.3167 lire per dollar
c. 847.9289 lire per dollar
d. 958.2334 lire per dollar
e. 965.9813 lire per dollar

21. You are considering the purchase of a block of stock in Galic Steel, a French steel producer. Galic just paid a dividend of 10 francs per share; that is, D_0 = 10 francs. You expect the dividend to grow indefinitely at a rate of 15 percent per year, but because of a higher expected rate of inflation in France than in the United States, you expect the franc to depreciate against the dollar at a rate of 5 percent per year. The exchange rate is currently 5 francs per U.S. dollar, but this ratio will change as the franc depreciates. For a stock with this degree of risk, including exchange rate risk, you feel that a 20 percent rate of return is required. What is the most, in dollars, that you should pay for the stock?

a. \$20.90 b. \$31.70 c. \$46.00 d. \$53.60 e. \$60.34

22. Refer to Problem 21. Now assume that the franc is expected to appreciate against the dollar at the rate of 1 percent per year. All other facts are unchanged. Under these conditions, what should you be willing to pay for the stock?

a. \$20.90 **b.** \$31.70 **c.** \$46.00 **d.** \$53.60 **e.** \$60.34

ANSWERS

1. exchange rate
2. fixed exchange rate
3. International Monetary Fund (IMF)
4. U.S. dollar
5. revalue
6. fixed; "float"
7. repatriated
8. reinvestment
9. Political; expropriation
10. Eurodollar
11. forward; futures
12. direct; portfolio
13. Foreign

14. b. Political risk must be explicitly addressed by international financial managers.

15. a. This statement is correct.

16. b. The foreign currency will depreciate if its inflation rate is higher than that of the United States.

17. b. The cost of capital is generally higher because of exchange risk and political risk.

18. c. Dividends and royalties received will generally also be taxed by the U.S. government, but the total taxes paid to both governments will not exceed that which would be paid had the earnings occurred in the United States.

19. c. The exchange rate for drachmas per dollar would be the reciprocal of the exchange rate of dollars per drachma: 1/(0.0313 dollars per drachma) = 31.9489 drachmas per dollar.

20. c. 942.1432(0.90)/\$1.00 = 847.9289 lire per dollar.

21. a. First, the valuation equation must be modified to convert the expected dividend stream to dollars:

$$D_t = D_0(1 + g)(ER),$$

where ER = exchange ratio. ER = 1/5 today, but if francs depreciate at a rate of 5 percent, it will take more francs to buy a dollar in the future. The value of ER at some future time (t) will be

$$ER_t = \frac{\text{Dollars}}{\text{Francs}} = \frac{1}{5(1.05)^t}.$$

Therefore, D_t in dollars may be calculated as follows:

$$\begin{aligned} D_t \text{ (in dollars)} &= (10 \text{ francs})(1 + g)^t(ER_t) \\ &= \frac{\$10(1.15)^t}{5(1.05)^t} \\ &= \frac{\$2(1.15)^t}{(1.05)^t} \\ &= \$2\left(\frac{1.15}{1.05}\right)^t \\ &= \$2(1.0952)^t. \end{aligned}$$

Thus, if the dividend in francs is expected to grow at a rate of 15 percent per year, but the franc is expected to depreciate at a rate of 5 percent per year against the dollar, then the growth rate, in dollars, of dividends received will be 9.52 percent. We can now calculate the value of the stock in dollars:

$$\hat{P}_0 = \frac{D_1}{k_s - g} = \frac{\$2(1.0952)}{0.20 - 0.0952} = \frac{\$2.1904}{0.1048} = \$20.90.$$

22. e. Solve the problem as above: $ER_t = 1(1.01)^t/5$.

$$\begin{aligned} D_t \text{ (in dollars)} &= (10 \text{ francs})(1 + g)^t\left(\frac{(1.01)^t}{5}\right) \\ &= (\$10/5)(1.15)^t(1.01)^t \\ &= \$2(1.1615)^t. \end{aligned}$$

Thus, the franc dividend is expected to increase at a rate of 15 percent per year, and the value of these francs is expected to rise at the rate of 1 percent per year, so the expected annual growth rate of the dollar dividend is 16.15 percent. We can now calculate the stock price:

$$\hat{P}_0 = \frac{D_1}{k_s - g} = \frac{\$2(1.1615)}{0.20 - 0.1615} = \frac{\$2.3230}{0.0385} = \$60.34.$$

CHAPTER 28
PENSION PLAN MANAGEMENT

OVERVIEW

Pension plans are an important component of the U.S. financial system for five reasons: (1) Pension funds, which have an aggregate market value of over $3 trillion, are important participants in the financial markets. (2) Pension plans provide employees with retirement income protection. (3) Pension plans play a vital role in governmental and corporate compensation plans and hence contribute to both labor productivity and economic stability. (4) The effectiveness of corporate pension plan management has an impact on stockholder wealth. (5) Many pension plans, through Employee Stock Ownership Plans (ESOPs), are important participants in corporate governance.

KEY CONCEPTS

Most companies, and practically all government units, have some type of employee pension plan.

The *chief financial officer (CFO)* typically administers the plan. He or she must decide on the general nature of the plan, determine the required annual payments into the plan, and manage the plan's assets.

The company does not have total control over these decisions. Employees and the federal government have a major say about the plan's structure and rules on certain aspects of the plan.

Under a typical plan, the company (or governmental unit) agrees to provide some type of retirement payments for employees. These promised payments constitute a liability, and the employer is required to establish a *pension fund* and place money in it each year, with the idea being to have sufficient assets to meet the pension payments as they come due.

Pension plan assets represent a very large pool of value for many firms.

Because pension fund administration requires so much specialized technical knowledge, companies typically hire specialists as consultants to help design, modify, and administer their plans.

The following concepts are used frequently in pension plan management.

A *defined contribution plan* is one in which a company agrees to make specific payments into a retirement fund and then retirees receive benefits from the plan that depend on the plan's investment success.

- The firm is obligated, in bad times as well as in good times, to make specified contributions on behalf of participating employees.
- Such plans are *portable* in that assets belong to the employee whenever he or she terminates employment.
- Because the sponsoring firm does not guarantee any specific dollar payments to participants upon retirement, participants in a defined contribution plan bear all of the investment risk associated with poor portfolio performance. However, participants can often choose among several investment alternatives so each individual can match his or her own risk preference.

Under a *defined benefit plan,* the employer agrees to give retirees a specifically defined benefit, such as $500 per month or 50 percent of the average salary over the five years preceding retirement.

- The sponsoring firm, not the participants, bears the risk of poor portfolio performance. Thus, the firm has a debt obligation to its retirees that must be met regardless of how well or poorly the pension plan assets are managed.
- Most defined benefit participants still bear purchasing power risk because inflation could eat away at the purchasing power of a fixed pension payment.

A *profit sharing plan* calls for the employer to make payments into the retirement fund, but with the payments varying with the level of corporate profits. These plans can be operated separately or in conjunction with defined benefit or defined contribution plans.

If employees have a right to receive pension benefits even if they leave the company prior to retirement, then their pension rights are said to be *vested*; if the employee loses pension rights if he or she leaves the company prior to retirement, the rights are said to be *nonvested.*

- Most defined benefit plans today have *deferred vesting,* where pension rights are nonvested for the first few years, but become fully vested if the employee remains with the company for a prescribed period.
- Companies with defined benefit plans are required to vest participants at least as fast as either the five-year rule (*cliff vesting*) or the 3-to-7-year rule (partial vesting).

A *portable* pension plan is one that an employee can carry from one firm to another. It is extremely important in occupations such as construction where workers move from one employer to another fairly frequently.

- Defined contribution plans are always portable, because the plan's assets are held in the employees' names. For a defined benefit plan to be portable, both the old employer and the new employer must be part of the same plan.

A plan is said to be *fully funded* if the present value of expected retirement benefits is equal to assets on hand. If assets exceed the present value of benefits, the plan is *overfunded*. Conversely, if the present value of benefits exceeds assets, the plan is *underfunded*, and an unfunded pension liability exists.

The discount rate used to determine the present value of future benefits under a defined benefit plan is called the *actuarial rate of return*. Higher actuarial rate assumptions lead to lower current contributions, and vice versa. Thus, the actuarial rate of return has a significant impact on the plan's annual contributions.

The *Employee Retirement Income Security Act of 1974 (ERISA)* is the basic federal law governing the structure and administration of corporate pension plans. ERISA requires, among other things, that companies fully fund their defined benefit pension plans, although it gives them up to 30 years to correct for underfunding of past service benefits.

- ERISA mandates that pension funds be managed according to the "prudent man" rule, which focuses on diversification as the cornerstone of portfolio management.
- ERISA sets the mandatory vesting requirements so situations where long-term employees are fired or laid off just before their benefits are vested are avoided.

The Pension Benefit Guarantee Corporation (PBGC) was established by ERISA to insure corporate defined benefit pension funds. The PBGC steps in and takes over payments to retirees of bankrupt companies with underfunded pension plans. However, a number of restrictions apply:

- PBGC does not cover company-promised health insurance for retirees.
- PBGC payments are capped at about $28,000 per year per plan, which for some highly paid hourly workers, is considerably less than their plan originally promised.
- PBGC does not guarantee pensions that are paid by annuities purchased by plans from insurance companies.

Both the Financial Accounting Standards Board (FASB) and the SEC have established rules that require firms operating pension plans to report specific information in its annual report. While the reporting of defined contribution plans is relatively straightforward, the reporting of defined benefit plans is much more complex.

The calculation of the present value of expected future benefits is of primary importance in defined benefit pension plans. This calculation determines both the required contribution to the fund for the year and the reported unfunded liability or surplus.

The assumed rate of return can make a substantial difference in the annual contribution. Assumptions about how long the worker will live, years before retirement, and, if the payment is based on salary, annual raises will have similarly large effects on the required annual contribution.

Different types of plans differ with regard to the certainty of cash contributions, investment earnings, and promised benefits at retirement.

In a *defined contribution plan,* the corporation, or plan sponsor, contributes a guaranteed amount which will be invested for eventual retirement payments to the beneficiaries of the plan. No guarantee is made about either the rate of return earned on the funds contributed or the final payments. Thus, the beneficiaries assume the risk of fluctuations in the rate of return on the invested money.

A *profit sharing plan* is similar, except that the sponsor's cash contributions are also uncertain, thus increasing the risk to the beneficiaries. Retirees' incomes could be quite large or quite small, depending on how profitable the corporation is and how well the plan's assets are managed.

In a *defined benefit plan,* the corporate sponsor assumes all risks of unexpected variations in rates of return on investment. The resulting annual contributions, however, could vary if the defined benefits are based on some average of the final years' salaries. Further, these contributions cannot be reduced if the corporation's profits fall, as they could be with a profit sharing plan.

Therefore, a defined benefit plan is by far the riskiest from the standpoint of the sponsoring corporation, but the least risky from the standpoint of the employees, although employees still bear purchasing power risk.

Risks to a corporation under a defined benefit plan can be divided into (1) uncertainty about the annual cash contribution and (2) uncertainty about the firm's obligations in the event it goes bankrupt.

- The *minimum annual cash contribution* is the sum of the amount needed to fund projected future benefit payments that were accrued during the current period, the amount that must be contributed to make up for not having funded all benefits for service that occurred prior to the current period, and an additional amount required to offset unexpected deviations from the plan's actuarial assumptions.

- There are three key types of actuarial assumptions which reflect real-world risks:
    - *decrement assumptions,* which allow the actuary to adjust annually for the probability that any employee will leave the company;
    - *future salary assumptions,* which take into account expected future average wage increases; and
    - *discount rate assumptions,* which explicitly forecast the portfolio's expected future rate of return.
- At the end of each year, the assumptions are examined and modified if necessary, and actuaries determine the present value of expected future benefits.
- Prior to the passage of ERISA, employees had no claim against a corporation's assets in the event of bankruptcy. By passing ERISA, Congress elevated the priority of unfunded vested pension liabilities in the event of bankruptcy.
- The value of a firm's stock is affected by the financial condition of its pension plan. However, devising a reasonable set of accounting procedures for reporting both the annual pension expense and the corporation's pension liabilities has proved to be quite difficult.

Not all risks associated with defined benefit pension plans are borne by the PBGC or corporate sponsor; its participants can also face uncertainties. For example, bankruptcy of a firm still imposes hardships on workers; it has been a major factor in unions' acceptance of reduced wages and benefits in situations where corporate bankruptcy with corresponding layoffs would otherwise have occurred.

As an employee, choosing between a defined benefit or a defined contribution plan is not an easy decision to make. It depends on both the specifics of the plans being offered and the unique situation of the individual making the decision.

The actual choice of a plan type is often dictated by competitive conditions in the labor market.

Unions generally seek defined benefit plans in order to cushion the beneficiaries from the investment risks that would exist under a defined contribution or a profit sharing plan.

A defined benefit plan provides tax-planning flexibility because firms can vary the fund contribution from year to year. Thus, in highly profitable years, firms can make large contributions, which decrease taxable income and hence reduce taxes. Defined contribution plans do not afford such flexibility because the specified contributions must be made each year regardless of the firm's profitability.

In recent years, small firms have tended to adopt defined contribution or profit sharing plans, while larger firms tend to adopt defined contribution plans. The regulatory burden of ERISA has in fact driven many firms to terminate their defined benefit plans.

Assuming that a firm had decided on a defined benefit plan, proper strategic planning requires integrating the plan's funding and investment policies into the company's general corporate policies.

- The *funding strategy* involves deciding how fast should any unfunded liability be reduced, and what rate of return should be assumed in the actuarial calculations.
- The *investment strategy* must determine how should a portfolio that minimizes the risk of not achieving an assumed actuarial rate of return be structured.

Pension fund investment tactics depend on three characteristics: (1) the dollar size of a fund's investable assets, (2) the mix of the funds' liabilities between those attributable to active workers and those attributable to retired beneficiaries, and (3) the tax situation facing the corporate sponsor.

A common investment tactic involves segregating pension fund assets into two parts: a "retiree portfolio" that provides income to current retirees and a "worker portfolio" that builds value for current workers. Then, as current workers retire, the assets of the fund are shifted from the worker portfolio to the retiree portfolio.

Pension fund sponsors need to evaluate the performance of their portfolio managers on a regular basis and then use this performance evaluation information as a basis for allocating the fund's assets among portfolio managers.

In general, a fund's assets are invested on either an *active* or a *passive* basis. Active managers select stocks with the idea of "beating the market," while passive management is based on the idea of achieving average returns while minimizing transactions costs and management fees.

There is an ongoing debate about whether excess assets in a defined benefit plan belong to the sponsoring company or to the employees. Legally, they belong to the company, but a number of union leaders have argued that they ought to belong to the workers.

Sixty-five percent of all companies, especially medium-size and small firms, have scrapped or cut back on their retiree health benefits, which are normally a part of the retirement package. Surging healthcare costs, an aging population, and new accounting rules have all put pressure on sponsoring firms to reduce or eliminate health benefits for its beneficiaries.

DEFINITIONAL QUESTIONS

1. The ________ __________ __________ typically administers the pension plan.

2. A(n) ________ __________ plan is one in which a company agrees to make specific payments into a retirement fund and then retirees receive benefits from the plan that depend on the plan's investment success.

3. Under a(n) _______ __________ plan the employer agrees to give retirees a specific amount, such as $500 per month or 50 percent of the individual's average salary over the five years preceding retirement.

4. A(n) ________ __________ plan calls for the employer to make payments into the retirement fund, but with the payments varying with the level of corporate profits.

5. If employees have a right to receive pension benefits even if they leave the company prior to retirement, then their pension rights are said to be _________; if the employee loses pension rights if he or she leaves the company prior to retirement, the rights are said to be ____________.

6. Most defined benefit plans today have _________ __________, where pension rights are nonvested for the first few years, but become fully vested if the employee remains with the company for a prescribed period.

7. A _________ pension plan is one that an employee can carry from one firm to another.

8. A plan is said to be _________ __________ if the present value of expected retirement benefits is equal to assets on hand.

9. If assets exceed the present value of benefits, the plan is ___________.

10. If the present value of benefits exceeds assets, the plan is ___________, and an _______ _________ ________ exists.

11. The ___________ ___________ __________ _____________ _________ of 1974 is the basic federal law governing the structure and administration of corporate pension plans.

12. The _________ _________ __________ ___________ was established to insure corporate defined benefit pension funds.

13. In a defined benefit plan, the ________ ________ assumes all risks of unexpected variations in rates of return on investment.

14. The ________ __________ __________ __________ is the sum of the amount needed to fund projected future benefit payments that were accrued during the current period, the amount that must be contributed to make up for not having funded all benefits for service that occurred prior to the current period, and an additional amount required to offset unexpected deviations from the plan's actuarial assumptions.

15. There are three key types of actuarial assumptions which reflect real-world risks: __________ assumptions, which allow the actuary to adjust annually for the probability that any employee will leave the company, __________ __________ assumptions, and ________ __________ assumptions.

16. In general, a fund's assets are invested on either a(n) __________ or a(n) __________ basis. ____________ managers select stocks with the idea of "beating the market," while _________ management is based on the idea of achieving average returns while minimizing transactions costs and management fees.

17. Pension fund investment tactics depend on three characteristics: (1) the ________ ________ of a fund's investable assets, (2) the ___________ of the fund's liabilities between those attributable to active workers and those attributable to retired beneficiaries, and (3) the ___________ situation facing the corporate sponsor.

CONCEPTUAL QUESTIONS

18. Under a defined benefit plan, employees agree to contribute some percentage of their salaries, up to 20 percent, to the firm's pension fund.

a. True **b.** False

19. If employees have a right to receive pension benefits even if they leave the company prior to retirement, their pension rights are said to be deferred.

a. True **b.** False

20. From a pure cost standpoint, a firm with a defined benefit plan would be more likely to hire older workers than a firm with a defined contribution plan.

a. True **b.** False

21. The performance measurement of stock portfolio managers must recognize the risk inherent in the investment portfolio. One way to incorporate risk into performance measurement is to examine the portfolio's z-score, which measures the vertical distance of the portfolio's return above or below the Security Market Line.

a. True **b.** False

22. Which of the following statements about pension plans, if any, is most *correct*?

a. A defined contribution plan is, in effect, a savings plan that is funded by employers, although many plans also permit additional contributions by employees.
b. Under a defined benefit plan, the employer agrees to give retirees a specifically defined benefit, such as $500 per month or 50 percent of the employees final salary.
c. A portable pension plan is one that an employee can carry from one employer to another.
d. An employer's obligation is satisfied under a defined benefit plan when it makes the required contributions to the plan. The risk of inadequate investment returns is borne by the employee.
e. Statements a, b, and c are all correct.

23. Which of the following statements about defined contribution plans, if any, is *incorrect*?

a. A defined contribution plan places the risk of poor pension portfolio performance on the employee.
b. In general, employees can choose the investment vehicle under a defined contribution plan. Thus, highly risk-averse employees can choose low-risk investments, while more risk-tolerant employees can choose high-risk investments.
c. In a defined contribution plan, the employer must make larger-than-average contributions to the pension plan when investment returns have been below expectations.
d. Large corporations tend to use defined benefit plans, while small corporations tend to use defined contribution plans.
e. All of the above statements are correct.

24. Which of the following statements about pension plan portfolio performance, if any, is *incorrect*?

a. Pension fund sponsors must evaluate the performance of their portfolio managers periodically as a basis for future asset allocations.
b. Alpha analysis, which relies on the Capital Asset Pricing Model, considers the risk of the portfolio when measuring performance.
c. Peer comparison examines the relative performance of portfolio managers with different investment objectives.
d. A portfolio annual return of 12 percent from one investment advisor is not necessarily better than a return of 10 percent from another advisor.

e. Index fund managers are evaluated against the index whose returns they attempt to match.

PROBLEMS

25. The Apex Company has just hired Mr. Smith, who is age 25 and is expected to retire at age 60. Mr. Smith's current salary is $30,000 per year, but his wages are expected to increase by 5 percent annually over the next 35 years. Apex has a defined benefit pension plan in which workers receive 1.5 percent of their final year's wages for each year of employment. Assume a world of certainty. Further, assume that all payments occur at year-end. What is Mr. Smith's approximate expected annual retirement benefit?

a. $35,000 b. $57,000 c. $87,000 d. $116,000 e. $132,000

26. Midwest Investment Consultants (MIC) operates several stock investment portfolios that are used by firms for investment of pension plan assets. Last year, one portfolio had a realized return of 12.6 percent and a beta coefficient of 1.25. The average T-bond rate was 7 percent and the realized rate of return on the S&P 500 was 12 percent. What was the portfolio's alpha?

a. -0.65% b. -0.25% c. 0% d. +0.25% e. +0.65%

27. The Ritz Company has a 40-year old employee that will retire at age 60 and live to age 75. The firm has promised a retirement income of $20,000 at the end of each year following retirement until death. The firm's pension fund is expected to earn 7 percent annually on its assets. What is Ritz's annual pension contribution for this employee? (Assume certainty and end-of-year cash flows.)

a. $2,756 b. $3,642 c. $4,443 d. $4,967 e. $5,491

ANSWERS

1. chief financial officer
2. defined contribution
3. defined benefit
4. profit sharing
5. vested; nonvested
6. deferred vesting
7. portable
8. fully funded
9. overfunded
10. underfunded; unfunded pension liability
11. Employee Retirement Income Security Act

12. Pension Benefit Guarantee Corporation
13. corporate sponsor
14. minimum annual cash contribution
15. decrement; future salary; discount rate
16. active; passive; Active; passive
17. dollar size; mix; tax

18. b. Under a defined benefit plan, the employer agrees to give retirees a specifically defined benefit.

19. b. The employee's pension rights are vested.

20. b. It is much more costly to a company to hire older workers if it operates under a defined benefit plan than if it operates under a defined contribution plan.

21. b. Alpha analysis adds substantially to a pension manager's knowledge about his or her equity portfolio's results. Alpha measures the vertical distance of a portfolio's return above or below the Security Market Line.

22. e. The risk of inadequate investment returns in a defined benefit plan are borne by the corporate sponsor.

23. c. In a defined contribution plan, the corporate sponsor agrees to make *specific* payments.

24. c. Peer comparison examines the relative performance of portfolio managers with similar investment objectives.

25. c. Final year's salary = $\$30,000(1.05)^{35} = \$165,480.46$.
Salary multiplier = 35(1.5%) = 52.5%.
Pension benefit = 0.525($165,480.46) = $86,877.24.

26. a. Portfolio's required rate of return

$$\begin{aligned} &= k_{RF} + (k_M - k_{RF})b \\ &= 7\% + (12\% - 7\%)1.25 \\ &= 7\% + (5\%)1.25 = 13.25\%. \end{aligned}$$

Alpha = 12.6% - 13.25% = -0.65%.

27. c. Find the PV (at retirement) of the 15-year pension payment:

$$\$20,000(PVIFA_{7\%,\ 15\ years}) = \$182,158.28.$$

Alternatively, using a financial calculator input the following: N = 15, I = 7, PMT = 20,000, FV = 0, and then solve for PV = $182,158.28.

Find the annual payment needed to accumulate the above amount over 20 years:

Annual payment = $\$182{,}158.28/FVIFA_{7\%,\ 20\ years}) = \$4{,}443.37$.

Alternatively, using a financial calculator input the following: N = 20, I = 7, PV = 0, FV = 182,158.28, and then solve for PMT = \$4,443.37.

CHAPTER 29
FINANCIAL MANAGEMENT IN NOT-FOR-PROFIT BUSINESSES

OVERVIEW

Financial management is important in not-for-profit organizations, which range from government agencies such as school districts and colleges to charities such as United Way and the American Heart Association. One type of not-for-profit organization is the not-for-profit business, which sells goods and/or services to the public but which has not-for-profit status. Indeed, the healthcare industry, which is one of the fastest growing sectors of the economy, includes thousands of not-for-profit businesses. Such firms require the same financial management functions as do investor-owned firms, but they do not have stockholders, and their goal is not shareholder wealth maximization.

KEY CONCEPTS

Not-for-profit businesses differ considerably from *for-profit,* or *investor-owned,* firms.

Unlike an investor-owned firm, a not-for-profit firm can qualify as a *tax-exempt* corporation if it fits the definition of a charitable organization and hence qualifies as a *501(c)(3) corporation.*

- In addition to being organized for a charitable purpose, a not-for-profit corporation must be administered so that it operates exclusively for the public, none of the profits is used for private inurement, no political activity is conducted, and, if liquidation occurs, the assets will continue to be used for a charitable purpose.
- Since not-for-profit businesses have no shareholders, no group of individuals has ownership rights to the firm's residual earnings. No outside group exercises control of the firm; rather, control is exercised by a board of trustees which is not constrained by outside oversight.
- Individual contributions to 501(c)(3) corporations can be deducted from taxable income by the donor, so not-for-profit businesses have access to tax-advantaged contribution capital.

There are almost an unlimited number of ways of organizing within the corporate structure.

- At the most basic level, a not-for-profit business can be a single entity with one operating unit where all financial management decisions are performed by a single set of managers who must raise the needed capital and decide how to allocate it within the organization.
- Alternatively, corporations can be set up with separate operating divisions or as holding companies, with wholly owned or partially owned subsidiaries. Holding companies are especially useful when a corporation is engaged in both for-profit and not-for-profit activities.

Since not-for-profit businesses do not have stockholders, shareholder wealth maximization cannot be the goal of such organizations. Rather, not-for-profit businesses serve and are served by a number of *stakeholders*, which include all parties that have an interest (financial or otherwise) in the organization.

Managers of not-for-profit businesses must try to please all the stakeholders because there is no single, well-defined group which exercises control.

Typically, the goal of a not-for-profit business is stated in terms of some mission, and financially weak organizations cannot continue to accomplish their stated missions over the long run.

Cost of capital estimation for not-for-profit businesses is similar to investor-owned businesses, but there are two major differences: (1) Since not-for-profit businesses pay no taxes, there are no tax effects associated with debt financing. (2) Not-for-profit businesses raise the equivalent of equity capital, called *fund capital.*

Fund capital is raised in three ways: (1) by earning profits, which by law must be retained within the business, (2) by receiving grants from governmental entities, and (3) by receiving contributions from individuals and companies.

Determining the opportunity cost of fund capital has been controversial. Historically, at least four positions have been taken with regard to the cost of fund capital:

- It has been argued that fund capital has zero cost, since contributors do not expect a monetary return and the firm's stakeholders do not require an explicit return on the capital retained by the firm.
- In addition to zero cost, it has been recognized that, when inflation exists, fund capital must earn a return to enable the organization to replace existing assets as they wear out.
- Another position is that fund capital has some cost but that it is not very high, probably roughly equal to the return available on short-term, low-risk securities such as T-bills.
- Others have argued that fund capital to not-for-profit businesses has about the same cost as the cost of retained earnings to similar investor-owned firms. This

"opportunity cost" can be defined as the return available from investing the fund capital in alternative investments *of similar risk.*

In general, the opportunity cost principle applies to all fund capital -- this capital has a cost which is equal to the cost of retained earnings to similar investor-owned firms.

When making capital structure decisions within not-for-profit businesses, managers must decide to what extent capital structure theory applies to their own not-for-profit businesses.

Although not-for-profit businesses do not pay taxes, many of these businesses have access to the tax-exempt debt market. Thus, not-for-profit businesses have about the same effective cost of debt as do investor-owned firms.

Not-for-profit businesses are subject to the same types of financial distress and agency costs that are borne by investor-owned firms. Therefore, we would expect the tradeoff theory to be applicable to not-for-profit businesses. Problems can arise, however, in practice: Not-for-profit firms do not have access to the equity markets -- their sole source of "equity" capital is through government grants, private contributions, and profits.

Managers of not-for-profit businesses do not have the same degree of flexibility in either capital investment or capital structure decisions as do their counterparts in for-profit firms.

The primary goal of a not-for-profit business is to provide some service to society, not to maximize shareholder wealth. Thus, capital budgeting decisions must consider many factors besides the project's profitability. Noneconomic factors such as the community's well-being must also be taken into account, and such factors may outweigh financial considerations.

In general, the same project analysis techniques that are applicable to investor-owned firms are also applicable to not-for-profit businesses. However, project analysis should consider *social value* along with financial, or cash flow, value.

Thus, total net present value (TNPV) can be expressed as

$$TNPV = NPV + NPSV,$$

where NPV is the standard net present value of the project's cash flow stream, and NPSV is the net present social value of the project. A project deemed to be acceptable has a TNPV greater than or equal to zero.

To ensure the financial viability of the firm, the sum of the NPVs of all projects initiated in a planning period, plus the value of the unrestricted contributions received, must equal or exceed zero.

In estimating a project's NPSV, it is necessary (1) to quantify the social value of the services provided by the project in each year and (2) to determine the discount rate that is to be applied to those services.

Not-for-profit businesses are often subject to capital rationing.

Risk analysis of not-for-profit firms differs in many ways from that of investor-owned firms.

Stand-alone risk would be relevant if a firm had only one project. However, most not-for-profit businesses offer a myriad of different products or services; thus, they can be thought of as having a large number of individual projects. Thus, the relevant risk of a new project is its corporate risk, which is the contribution of the project to the firm's overall risk as measured by the impact of the project on the variability of the firm's overall profitability.

As with investor-owned firms, in most situations is quite difficult to develop accurate quantitative assessments of projects' corporate risk. Thus, managers are often left with only an assessment of a project's stand-alone risk plus a subjective notion about how it fits into the firm's other operations.

Capital budgeting decisions in not-for-profit organizations require the blending of objective and subjective factors to reach a conclusion about a project's risk, social value, effects on debt capacity, profitability, and overall acceptability.

While not-for-profit businesses have access to many of the same types of capital as do investor-owned firms, there are two major differences: (1) not-for-profit firms can issue tax-exempt debt but (2) they cannot issue equity, although they can solicit contributions.

Not-for-profit businesses can issue tax-exempt, or municipal, bonds, generally called "munis."

- There are several types of munis: *General obligation bonds* are secured by the full faith and credit of a government unit whereas *special tax bonds* are secured by a specified tax. *Revenue bonds* are those bonds where the revenues derived from such projects as roads, bridges, and airports arc pledged as security for the bonds.
- Most municipal bonds are sold in serial form, which means that a portion of the issue comes due periodically, generally every six months or every year, over the life of the issue.

- In contrast to regular corporate bonds, municipal issues are not required to be registered with the SEC, and their issuers do not have to provide periodic reports to the SEC.
- About half of all munis outstanding are held by individual investors, in large part because of the munis' exemption from state and federal taxes.
- Unique to municipal bonds, *credit enhancement,* or *bond insurance,* is used for upgrading an issue's rating to AAA. A bond insurance company guarantees that bondholders will receive the promised interest and principal payments, regardless of the inherent credit rating of the issuer. Thus, bond insurance protects investors against default by the issuer. However, there is a premium charged for this insurance.

While not-for-profit businesses can retain earnings, they cannot sell stock to raise equity capital. They can, however, raise equity capital through *charitable contributions.*

DEFINITIONAL QUESTIONS

1. Unlike an investor-owned firm, a ______-______-_________ firm can qualify as a _______-__________ corporation if it fits the definition of a charitable organization and hence qualify as a 501(c)(3) corporation.

2. In addition to being organized for a __________ ___________, a not-for-profit corporation must be administered so that it operates exclusively for the ________, none of the profits is used for ___________ ___________, no political activity is conducted, and, if liquidation occurs, the assets will continue to be used for a ___________ ___________.

3. No outside group exercises control of the not-for-profit business; rather, control is exercised by a ______ _______ __________ which is not constrained by outside oversight.

4. Since not-for-profit businesses do not have stockholders, ________ ________ _________ cannot be the goal of such organizations. Rather, not-for-profit businesses serve and are served by a number of __________, which include all parties that have an interest in the organization.

5. Typically, the goal of a not-for-profit business is stated in terms of some ___________.

6. Cost of capital estimation for not-for-profit businesses is similar to investor-owned businesses, but there are two major differences: (1) Since not-for-profit businesses pay no taxes, there are no tax effects associated with _________ __________. (2) Not-for-profit businesses raise the equivalent of equity capital, called _________ ___________.

7. Fund capital is raised in three ways: (1) by __________ __________, which by law must be retained with the business, (2) by __________ __________ from governmental entities, and (3) by __________ __________ from individual and companies.

8. In general, the opportunity cost principle applies to all fund capital -- this capital has a cost which is equal to the cost of ________ __________ to similar ______-________ ________.

9. Although not-for-profit businesses do not pay taxes, many of these businesses have access to the ______-______ ________ market. Thus, not-for-profit businesses have about the same effective cost of debt as do __________-________ __________.

10. Capital budgeting decisions in the not-for-profit firm must consider many factors besides the project's profitability. __________ factors such as the community's well-being must also be taken into account, and such factors may outweigh ____________ considerations.

11. Project analysis within the not-for-profit firm should consider __________ __________ along with __________, or cash flow, value.

12. To ensure the financial viability of the firm, the sum of the __________ of all projects initiated in a planning period, plus the value of the __________ __________ received, must equal or exceed zero.

13. ________ ________ __________ are secured by the full faith and credit of a government unit, whereas __________ ________ ________ are secured by a specified tax.

14. Unique to municipal bonds, ________ ________, or __________ __________, is used for upgrading an issue's rating to AAA.

15. In contrast to regular corporate bonds, __________ __________ are not required to be registered with the SEC, and their issuers do not have to provide periodic reports to the SEC.

Conceptual Questions

16. The primary goal of investor-owned firms is shareholder wealth maximization, while the primary goal of not-for-profit firms is to maximize managers' utility.

    a. True **b.** False

17. Not-for-profit firms have fund capital in place of equity capital. Since fund capital does not have to provide a return to stockholders, its appropriate cost is the return available on short-term Treasury securities.

a. True **b.** False

18. Not-for-profit firms do not pay taxes, but they still receive tax benefits from debt financing because they can issue municipal (tax-exempt) debt.

a. True **b.** False

19. The net present social value model formally recognizes that not-for-profit firms must consider the social value along with the financial value of proposed new projects, but it does not recognize the time value of social value.

a. True **b.** False

20. Which of the following statements about project risk analysis in not-for-profit firms is *incorrect*?

a. The market risk of a project is not relevant to not-for-profit firms.
b. A project's corporate beta measures the contribution of the project to the overall corporate risk of the firm.
c. A project's corporate beta is found (at least conceptually) by regressing returns on the project against returns on the firm.
d. A project's corporate beta is defined as $(\sigma_P/\sigma_F)r_{PF}$, where σ_P is the standard deviation of the project's returns, σ_F is the standard deviation of the firm's returns, and r_{PF} is the correlation among the two sets of returns.
e. In practice, it is usually easy to directly measure a project's corporate risk, so stand-alone risk plays no role in project risk analysis.

21. Which of the following statements about municipal bond financing is most *correct*?

a. In contrast to corporate bonds, municipal bond issues are not required to be registered with the Securities and Exchange Commission.
b. Whereas the vast majority of Treasury and corporate bonds are held by institutions, about half of all municipal bonds are held by individual investors.
c. The primary attraction of municipal bonds to individual investors is their high before-tax yields.
d. Municipal bonds issued in one state are free from state taxes in all states.
e. Statements a and b are both correct.

22. Which of the following statements about a not-for-profit firm's ownership is most *correct*?

- **a.** Not-for-profit firms are governed by a board of trustees whose members are elected by the community at large.
- **b.** The residual earnings (profits) of not-for-profit firms can be distributed to the firm's top managers.
- **c.** Not-for-profit firms are exempt from federal, state, and local taxes, including property taxes.
- **d.** Upon liquidation of a not-for-profit firm, the proceeds from the sale of its assets are distributed, on a pro rata basis, to the firm's employees.
- **e.** Not-for-profit firms issue municipal debt directly to investors.

23. Which of the following statements about a not-for-profit firm's cost of capital estimate is most *correct*?

- **a.** Since a not-for-profit firm has no shareholders, its WACC estimate does not include a cost of equity (fund capital) estimate.
- **b.** The capital structure weights for a not-for-profit firm are set at 50/50, because such firms can raise $1 of debt financing for each dollar of retained earnings.
- **c.** The cost of tax-exempt debt issued by not-for-profit firms is increased ("grossed up") by 1 - T in the WACC estimate to reflect the fact that such firms do not pay taxes.
- **d.** Equity (fund) capital has a cost that is roughly equivalent to the cost of retained earnings to similar investor-owned companies.
- **e.** None of the above statements are correct.

24. Which of the following statements about a not-for-profit firm's fund capital is most *correct*?

- **a.** Fund capital is equivalent to equity capital in investor-owned firms.
- **b.** The sources of fund capital include the excess of revenues over expenses, contributions, and government grants.
- **c.** Fund capital, like equity capital, has an opportunity cost associated with it.
- **d.** Statements a and c are both correct.
- **e.** Statements a, b, and c are all correct.

25. Which of the following statements about a not-for-profit firm's sources of capital is most *correct*?

- **a.** Since not-for-profit firms are tax exempt, there is no tax advantage to debt capital.
- **b.** Fund capital is obtained by retaining earnings--if all earnings are paid out as dividends, no fund capital is created.
- **c.** Preferred stock is never used by not-for-profit firms.
- **d.** Statements a and b are both correct.
- **e.** Statements a, b, and c are all correct.

ANSWERS

1. not-for-profit; tax-exempt
2. charitable purpose; public; private inurement; charitable purpose
3. board of trustees
4. shareholder wealth maximization; stakeholders
5. mission
6. debt financing; fund capital
7. earning profits; receiving grants; receiving contributions
8. retained earnings; investor-owned firms
9. tax-exempt debt; investor-owned firms
10. Noneconomic; financial
11. social value; financial
12. NPVs; unrestricted contributions
13. General obligation bonds; special tax bonds
14. credit enhancement; bond insurance
15. municipal issues

16. b. Typically, the goal of a not-for-profit business is stated in terms of some mission.

17. b. In general, the opportunity cost principle applies to all fund capital -- this capital has a cost which is equal to the cost of retained earnings to similar investor-owned firms.

18. a. This statement is correct.

19. b. The total net present value of a project can be expressed as the net present value of the project's cash flow stream and the net present social value of the project.

20. e. In most situations, it is very difficult, if not impossible, to develop accurate quantitative assessments of projects' corporate risk.

21. e. The primary attraction of most municipal bonds is their exemption from federal and state (in the state of issue) taxes.

22. c. Not-for-profit firms are controlled by a board of trustees but not elected by the community; residual earnings must be retained in the firm; and if the firm is liquidated, the assets must continue to be used for a charitable purpose.

23. d. In general, the opportunity cost principle applies to all fund capital.

24. e. Statements a, b, and c are all correct.

25. c. Since individuals cannot benefit from not-for-profit corporations' profits, such organizations cannot pay dividends; therefore, no common or preferred stock is sold.